Programmers at Work

1st Series

INTERVIEWS

By Susan Lammers

VisiCalc
DAN BRICKLIN

Framework
BOB CARR

VisiCalc
BOB FRANKSTON

BASIC
BILL GATES

Lucasfilm SoundDroid
MICHAEL HAWLEY

ac Operating System
NDY HERTZFELD

Programmers at Work

1st Series

MICROSOFT PRESS

INTERVIEWS

Pac Man
TORU IWATANI

CP/M
GARY KILDALL

Inversions
SCOTT KIM

Alto PC
TLER LAMPSON

VPL
JARON LANIER

Symphony
RAY OZZIE

PFS:FILE
JOHN PAGE

dBASE
C. WAYNE RATLIFF

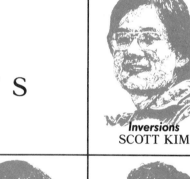

e Macintosh Project
JEF RASKIN

T/Maker
PETER ROIZEN

Lotus 1-2-3
JONATHAN SACHS

Multiplan, Bravo
CHARLES SIMONYI

PostScript
JOHN WARNOCK

PUBLISHED BY
Microsoft Press
A Division of Microsoft Corporation
16011 N.E. 36th, Box 97017, Redmond, Washington 98073-9717

Library of Congress Cataloging in Publication Data
1. Electronic digital computer—Programming.
2. Computer programmers.   I. Beley, Jim.
QA76.6.P751345   1986   005   86-5175
ISBN 0-914845-71-3

Printed and bound in the United States of America.

1 2 3 4 5 6 7 8 9 FGFG 8 9 0 9 8 7 6 5

Distributed to the book trade in the United States by
Harper and Row.

Distributed to the book trade in Canada by General Publishing
Company, Ltd.

Distributed to the book trade outside the United States and Canada by
Penguin Books Ltd.

Penguin Books Ltd., Harmondsworth, Middlesex, England
Penguin Books Australia Ltd., Ringwood, Victoria, Australia
Penguin Books N.Z. Ltd., 182-190 Wairau Road, Auckland 10, New Zealand

British Cataloging in Publication Data available

TABLE OF CONTENTS

INTRODUCTION

The idea for this series of interviews with notable programmers of our time originated with Min S. Yee, the publisher of Microsoft Press. As a man familiar with the struggle and triumph of the creative process, having authored several books of his own, it is not surprising that while working at Microsoft (primarily a software company, but also a publishing house), he noticed parallels between the work of the writer and that of the programmer. His conversations with program designers at Microsoft revealed a multitude of nuances in the art, craft, and science of programming. When Yee looked in bookstores, he discovered innumerable "how to" books about programming, but a dearth of information that presented the experiences, approaches, and philosophies of software designers in a personal, in-depth manner. So Microsoft Press decided to look into the minds and personalities behind the software. The best way to do this, we decided, was to let the individuals speak for themselves in published interviews.

The purpose of each interview was not to interrogate the programmer about secret projects or gather opinions about day-to-day developments within the software industry. Instead, we aimed to discuss timeless matters that often get overlooked in this hectic, fast-paced industry. We wanted to uncover the magic and mystery that goes into developing an operating system such as the Macintosh's, an application program such as Lotus 1-2-3, or a computer game such as Pac Man. We asked questions: Where did the idea come from? How difficult was it to bring the idea into reality? What does it feel like to develop a major program? Is it an art or a science? A craft or a skill? Can you do it again?

As the interviewer, my goal was not to dominate, or trick, or manipulate. I did not try to put words in people's mouths. My goal was to stay in the background as much as possible, to give the programmer the freedom to ruminate, to look inside himself and then verbalize his views on his own method of programming.

In the interviews, I tried to ask all the programmers a common set of questions to provide a framework by which the interviews could later be read and compared. We felt the open-ended, general questions would help highlight the similarities and differences in approaches to programming, and allow the personality and special interests of each programmer to come to the fore. And indeed, they did. Some individuals, such as Gary Kildall and Butler Lampson, gave sage words of advice on the theory and practice of programming. Others, such as Dan Bricklin and Bob Carr, concentrated on tracing the development of a particular program, while still others, such as Bob Frankston and Jaron Lanier, speculated about the future of software and the microcomputer. The result of these revealing, varied discussions is the beginning of a detailed composite portrait of today's programmer.

In some cases, the programmers and I met two or three times for several hours—musing, talking, exploring. But once the interviews were done, that was not the end of the process. We transcribed the interviews from tape, edited and refined them, and then we returned them to the programmers so they could read what had been said. We gave them the opportunity to rework the interview, so that it expressed exactly what they meant.

In addition, we asked each programmer to provide us with samples of his work—either a piece of code, a program, some sketches or doodles of program designs to provide our readers with a glimpse of the programmer's style when he puts his thoughts down on paper. We received a wide range of material. Some of it has great historical value. From Dan Bricklin, for example, we received his sketches of the early design of VisiCalc. What Andy Hertzfeld sent stands on its own: We received from him a complete program, over 30 pages long, called "IconBounce" for the Macintosh. The result of all this is a revealing, in-depth look into the minds and work of these individuals.

There are a great number of fine programmers in this world. You will not find all of them in this book. That is why this is the first book in a continuing series of discussions with outstanding programmers of our time.

Each day, in this ever-changing industry, a new breakthrough is made, an innovative piece of software is introduced, a new company is formed. Stars in the industry rise and fall almost overnight. It would have been foolhardy for us to attempt to identify the twenty or so best programmers in the world. Instead, we include a cross section of specialties and experiences, primarily focusing on programmers of microcomputers, though some programmers included here have also had a good deal of experience on minicomputers and mainframes.

The title of this book was somewhat problematical because of various meanings associated with the word "programmer." In the software industry, "programmer" is commonly used to describe a person who writes and develops the software that makes a computer perform. As the software industry becomes increasingly sophisticated and complex, more and more often a distinction is made between a software designer and a programmer. For the purposes of this book, the word programmer is defined as a developer of software or a designer of software, often but not always involved in the actual writing of source code. Some individuals included in this book, Butler Lampson, Toru Iwatani, and Jef Raskin among them, admitted they do not actually write the source code of their programs and they do not consider themselves programmers per se, but rather software designers. They may have conceived of the idea for the program, developed the algorithms, written the specs, and designed the features, but they may not have typed in the lines and lines of code that constitute the program. It is always difficult to categorize individuals as varied and multi-talented as these.

This book strives to be a sampling of a very large pool of talented programmers. Some of the people in this book have had their photos on the covers of magazines, while others are more obscure. We have included a range of ages and experiences from the older, well-established programmers in their forties who first set off the microcomputer revolution, to the younger, energetic, less traditional thinkers who are intent upon taking the computer revolution far beyond the boundaries we know today. There are those who work for corporations, such as C. Wayne Ratliff and Charles Simonyi, and there are the more steadfastly independent, such as Jonathan Sachs and Peter Roizen, as well as the intense entrepreneurs such as Ray Ozzie, Gary Kildall, and Bill Gates. Some we found to be inspired, others were disillusioned; some have met with great success, others less so. Yet there is no doubt that the programmers featured in this book are exceptional and offer intriguing insights into the creative process of programming and the variety of personalities and experiences within the computer industry.

While the intent of the interviews was to discuss the programmer at work, what has come along with the interviews is an informal history of the software industry, as told by some of the major participants involved. The order of the book roughly reflects the history of the industry, though many of the people have gone on to pursue other products and specialties beyond their original software contributions.

We start with Charles Simonyi, who was the first person interviewed for the book. His involvement with computers reaches back to Hungary in the sixties, when he worked on the Russian-made Ural II computer. Then we move on to Butler Lampson, who was Charles Simonyi's professor at U.C. Berkeley and an associate at Xerox PARC. Lampson was involved with the development of the Alto personal computer, and participated in many of the other fundamental discoveries that prompted the microcomputer revolution. John Warnock, another Xerox PARC researcher and a developer of PostScript, came to the West Coast from the University of Utah, where he participated in the heyday of research in computer graphics under the leadership of Evans and Sutherland.

Next we have Gary Kildall, who developed the first operating system, called CP/M, for the personal computer. Bill Gates follows, because of his work with BASIC, one of the most widely used computer languages. John Page, the designer of the PFS line of software, created one of the first programs tailored for newcomers to personal computers in business. C. Wayne Ratliff developed dBASE, a program that has maintained its reputation since the very early days of the microcomputer revolution as one of the most sophisticated database programs. Then we turn to the East Coast portion of the software industry, where we find Dan Bricklin and Bob Frankston, originators of VisiCalc, one of the first spreadsheet programs for the personal computer. Jonathan Sachs, programmer of Lotus 1-2-3, follows, and then we talk with Ray Ozzie, who before developing Symphony for Lotus worked for Jonathan Sachs at Data General, and Dan Bricklin and Bob Frankston at Software Arts. Next is Peter Roizen, who developed T/Maker, another spreadsheet program that came out six months after VisiCalc, followed by Bob Carr, who developed Framework, a competitor to Symphony. Then we turn our attention to the Macintosh, presenting the interviews of Jef Raskin, who was originally in charge of the Macintosh project, and Andy Hertzfeld, who is credited with developing the Mac operating system.

The last group of programmers featured in this book includes the more offbeat, experimental, and artistic programmers. We found the designer of the phenomenally successful game Pac Man, Toru Iwatani, in Tokyo, Japan, and talked with him about the philosophy behind his work. Scott Kim, a graphic designer and musician as well as a programmer, discussed fourth-party software and radical new user-interface design ideas. Jaron Lanier, who is also a musician and former game programmer, is involved with visual programming languages, which he believes will add a new dimension to our computer experience and revolutionize programming. And finally, we conclude our interviews with Michael Hawley from Lucasfilm. At 24, he is the youngest programmer (and musician) featured in the book. His work involves developing software for the Sound Droid, a new computer that will be used to edit and compose the audio component of films.

We hope this book will serve as a learning tool for aspiring young programmers, as well as professionals who wish to learn the secrets of success in the software industry from the experts. But even aside from its instructional value, this book is a good read; it brings the software industry to life for those who are curious about what goes on behind the scenes, and it details the myriad of ideas, methods, and personalities that go into developing innovative software products.

Susan Lammers

```
5200    22 7200 4    5240    16 5006 4        5220    16 5006 4    5260    16 5005 0
   1    00 0001 0       1    22 6570 4           1    02 0000 4       1    25 2267 0
   2    13 5214 0       2    22 5376 0           2    22 5332 0       2    22 5074 0
   3    22 5311 0       3    22 5306 0           3    11 0001 0       3    22 5015 4
   4    22 5171 4       4    02 7542 0           4    21 5415 4       4    22 5015 4
   5    22 5341 0       5    14 5515 0           5    25 2304 0       5    22 5134 4
   6    22 6631 4       6    21 5123 0           6    22 5074 0       6    02 5011 0
   7    11 0014 0       7    02 5121 0           7    22 7342 4       7    11 0001 0

5210    21 5345 4    5250    16 5012 0        5230    00 0002 0    5270    22 5157 4
   1    25 2302 0       1    22 5373 0           1    14 5514 0       1    22 5522 0
   2    22 5074 0       2    22 5171 4           2    21 5415 0       2    22 5435 4
   3    11 0002 0       3    00 0000 0           3    25 2300 0       3    22 6512 0
   4    21 5355 4       4    11 0016 0           4    22 5074 0       4    22 5435 4
   5    22 7000 4       5    21 5415 4           5    02 6077 0       5    22 5022 0
   6    56 0000 4       6    22 6570 4           6    16 5012 0       6    22 7342 4
   7    02 5002 4       7    22 5036 0           7    02 5002 4       7    00 0002 0
```

```
Oct  8 11:59 1985  example1 Page 1


        vfli.dypAfter = 0;
        if (vfli.cpMac == caPara.cpLim)
                {
                int dyp = vpapFetch.cyaAfter / dyaPoint;
                vfli.dypLine += dyp;
                vfli.dypBase += dyp;
                vfli.cypAfter = dyp;
                }
/* First, need to scan thru grpchr, till we find a chr whose ich is >= ichMac
(this can happen because we add a chr and then decide to do the line break
before the character indexed by chr.ich) or until we reach &(**vhgrpchr)[vbchrMac]
*/
        for (pchr = pchrBeg = &(**vhgrpchr)[0],
                (char *) pchrMac = (char *) pchr + vbchrMac;
                pchr < pchrMac;
                (char *) pchr += pchr->chrm)
                if (pchr->ich >= vfli.ichMac)
                        break;
/* Now, enter chrmEnd in grpchr. Note: no need to check for sufficient space*/
        vbchrMac = (char *) pchr - (char *) pchrBeg;
        pchr->chrm = chrmEnd;
        pchr->ich = vfli.ichMac;

        Scribble(5,' ');
        CkFli();
        return;
}
```

Top: code written in 1965 on the Russian-made Ural II computer. All changes had to be patched using goto's (instructions beginning with "22").
Bottom: "Hungarian" code from Microsoft Word. The name vbchrMac, for example, shows that the variable is: global (v), current maximum pointing one beyond the last element (Mac) based pointer to a group (b) of chr structures. The name chr has further meaning: character run, which is specific to Word. See the Appendix (page 383) for a sample of Simonyi's "early Hungarian style."

Charles Simonyi

BORN ON *September 10, 1948 in Budapest, Hungary, Charles Simonyi was introduced to computers and programming while attending high school, when his father arranged for him to assist an engineer who was working on one of the few computers in Hungary at the time.*

By 1966 Charles had not only completed high school but also his first compiler. With the experience gained from writing the compiler, he was able to obtain employment at A/S Regnecentralen in Copenhagen, Denmark. In 1968 Charles left Denmark to study in the United States at the University of California at Berkeley, where he received his bachelor of science degree in 1972, and his doctorate degree from Stanford University in 1977.

Simonyi has worked at the UC Berkeley Computer Center, the Berkeley Computer Corporation, the ILLIAC 4 Project, Xerox PARC, and, since 1981, Microsoft Corporation. While at Xerox, Charles created the Bravo and Bravo X programs for the Alto personal computer. At Microsoft, Charles organized the Application Software Group, which has produced Multiplan, Microsoft Word, Microsoft Excel, and other popular application products.

Almost everywhere in the microcomputer world, Charles Simonyi has made his mark, either by something he has accomplished or by influencing someone with whom he has worked. He's a modest but spirited fellow, quick to smile and able to comment on just about any topic, computer related or not.

During the two times we met with Charles, once over lunch and the other time in his office, the conversations ranged from the attributes of Microsoft Excel, to flying helicopters, to certain facets of modern poetry. His speech is distinguished by a Hungarian accent which has become Charles' trademark both in speaking and programming. Clad almost daily in a uniform of weathered jeans jacket, shirt, and worn jeans, he retains the appearance of a Berkeley student during the sixties, but his breadth of knowledge, manner, and accomplishments exhibit a wealth of wisdom and experience.

INTERVIEWER: Your first computer program was done before you graduated from high school in Hungary, correct?

SIMONYI: Yes. There is my first program and then my first *professional* program. The first program I ever wrote filled in a magic square, where all the columns and rows added up to the same sum. I programmed it into an ancient tube computer. I spent the whole afternoon pushing buttons just to enter it into the machine. That evening, I arrived home with an incredible headache and giant rolls of paper with printouts of 80-by-80 magic squares. That was in 1964.

INTERVIEWER: What was the first computer you worked on?

SIMONYI: It was a Russian-made computer, a Ural II. It had only 4K of memory, a 40-bit floating point, and 20-bit operations. The computer was programmed totally in octal absolute [no assembler]. I wrote thousands of lines of code in octal absolute.

All the action in this computer was directed through the console; it was truly a hands-on, one-on-one experience. Programmers didn't have to stand around waiting for a computer operator to run a batch of cards. The Ural II was exactly like a personal computer because it was just you and the machine and no one else. With 4K of memory and the slow speed, it was very similar to the Altair, which was introduced in 1974. The excitement I experienced with the Ural II in 1964 was the same kind of excitement that Bill Gates experienced with the Altair in 1974.

Obviously, the Ural II differed from a personal computer in *some* respects. The Ural II was the size of a very, very large room and the method for input and output was incredibly primitive—primarily through console switches. The console looked like an old-fashioned cash register. There were six full columns of switches and an enter key on the right. Each column had keys numbered from zero to seven. You entered numbers just like you would on a cash register. So to enter 2275, you pushed the keys for two, two, seven, and five. If you made a mistake, you could correct it before pushing the enter key on the right. All this was exhilarating because there was a lot of noise associated with it. Every time I hit the switch, it clicked very firmly. Whenever I cleared it—it was all done mechanically—all the keys released at once with a great "thunk."

INTERVIEWER: What was your first professional program?

SIMONYI: The first professional program that I wrote was a compiler for a very simple, FORTRAN-like, high-level language. I sold it to a state organization as an innovation and made a fair amount of money, none of which I ever spent, since I left Hungary soon after.

It was during this time that I met some Danish computer people at a trade fair in Budapest. I approached them and got a lot of information about their new machine. At the next trade fair, I came prepared with a small demonstration program I had written. It provided feedback on exactly which part of a lengthy expression the machine was analyzing at any point in time. I asked one of the guys to take the program back to Denmark and show it to somebody in charge. They must have liked it because they gave me a job. That's how I got out of Hungary.

I worked for a year and a half at the programming job in Denmark and saved enough money to go to the University of California at Berkeley. I became a programmer at the computer center there. I made just enough money to pay for the tuition.

While I was at Berkeley I wrote a very nice SNOBOL compiler. One of the computer science professors, Butler Lampson, liked the compiler very much and had his computer science students use it in class. When he and a bunch of other professors started Berkeley Computer Corporation, I was offered a job there. When BCC went under, the core group was picked up by Xerox PARC.

INTERVIEWER: Who influenced your style of programming?

SIMONYI: I had two influences—an engineer in Hungary and the computer I worked on in Denmark. My mentor in Hungary was an engineer who worked on the Ural II computer. I was kind of a groupie, just being underfoot and offering free services in exchange for being tolerated in a place where I wasn't supposed to be. This was not a place for kids. It was one of maybe five computers in all of Hungary and was considered a great asset.

INTERVIEWER: *How did you manage to get underfoot?*

SIMONYI: My father was a professor of electrical engineering and this engineer was a student of my father's. I think my father asked him to let me in once as a favor. I made myself useful. First I brought him lunch, then I held the probes, and finally I offered to be a night watchman.

"What is programming? Some people call it a science, some call it an art, some call it a skill..."

They always turned the computer off at night and turned it back on in the morning. When you turn tubes off and on, the filaments tend to break when they are cooled and heated. In a machine with two thousand tubes, one will break every time you turn the machine on. So they had to spend the first hour of every workday finding the one that broke. When I was there at night, they could leave the computer on and save all that work. So while I was watching it at night, I also managed to use it.

Anyway, the engineer and I became good friends. He was a mathematical genius. He taught me many of the early tricks about how to think arithmetically, about symbolic problems.

The Danish computer also had an incredible influence on me. At that time, it had probably the world's best Algol compiler, called Gier Algol. Before I went to Denmark, I had complete listings of the compiler, which I had studied inside and out. It was all written in machine language, so it was both a lesson in machine-language programming and an aesthetically beautiful way of thinking about a compilation process. It was designed by Peter Naur. He is the letter N in BNF, the Backus-Naur Form of syntax equations. I knew that program inside and out and I still know it.

The SNOBOL compiler I wrote at Berkeley, for example, was just a variation on the same theme. I think the Gier Algol program is still in my mind and influences my programming today. I always ask myself, "If this were part of the Algol compiler, how would they do it?" It's a very, very clever program.

One notion that sticks in my mind is how they scanned the source text backwards. It turns out that in some cases, if you do things backwards, problems that previously appeared complex suddenly become very simple. For instance, resolving forward references can be difficult. If you scan backwards, they become backward references, which are easy to resolve. Just by looking at a program in a new way, what formerly might have been rather difficult to solve becomes easy to solve. The Algol compiler was absolutely full of wonderful tricks.

INTERVIEWER: *How did you arrive at Microsoft?*

SIMONYI: Once I made a decision to leave Xerox, I put out some feelers. I had lunch with Bob Metcalfe, the Ethernet guy and chairman and founder of 3Com, who left Xerox a couple of years before me. He made up a list of people I should see. Number one on the list was Bill Gates. I don't remember who number two was because I never got that far.

INTERVIEWER: *Is programming a technique or a skill?*

SIMONYI: What is programming? People argue about it all the time. Some people call it a *science*, some people call it an *art*, some people call it a *skill* or *trade*. I think it has aspects of all three. We like to pretend that it has a lot of art in it, but we know it has a lot of science.

Kids learn mathematics in school, and when they finish high school they think of mathematics as addition and multiplication, and maybe even algebra and calculus. But there is an incredible supporting science behind arithmetic, even for a simple operation like addition.

There is also a tremendous amount of supporting science behind computer programming. For example, the mathematical proof for Gödel's Theorem is very long and complex, but if you use some of Turing's theorems from computer science, the proof is trivial. Information theory and the other aspects of computer science have a great effect on mathematics, and vice versa.

There is a lot of science in programming, and at the same time it is somewhat of a trade. In fact, for many people, programming is a complex skill, very much like toolmaking, that requires a lot of care. I think if you take a healthy dose of all three [science, art, and skill], you can get some very exciting results.

INTERVIEWER: *What is the part of programming that you consider to be art? Is it designing the user interface?*

SIMONYI: I think that there is certainly an aesthetic aspect to programs, not only in the design, but even in the *appearance*, of the user interface. The artistic limitations of programmers come to light when you look at some ugly screens. Otherwise, computer programming is an art just as high-energy physics is an art.

INTERVIEWER: Is the aesthetic aspect related only to how the user perceives the program, or would it also be apparent to another programmer who looks at the program and sees how it is written?

SIMONYI: Absolutely, absolutely. I think the aesthetics of the listings and of the computers themselves have always fascinated me.

The Russian machine, for example, looked like a science-fiction computer because each flip-flop [the on-off device that stores one bit of information] in the machine had a little orange, old-fashioned gas discharge light. Hundreds of orange lights flickered behind glass doors and cabinets. The whole life of the machine pulsed right in front of your eyes.

The Danish computer was a beautiful piece of furniture. It was about the size of an antique wardrobe closet. The front of the computer had three teak doors. I once saw an American executive look at it in disbelief because it was paneled in teak. It even had a Danish-modern console. The whole machine had the intriguing smell of teak.

The Berkeley computer was quite large, about 20 feet long, 6 feet high, and 2 feet deep. It was hidden in a concrete vault that was painted completely black. The computer was a little like the monolith in the film *2001* because of the way it was placed inside the vault with spotlights shining on it.

INTERVIEWER: What do you perceive as aesthetically beautiful or pleasing in either the listing or the structure of the algorithms when you look at a particular program?

SIMONYI: I think the listing gives the same sort of pleasure that you get from a clean home. You can just tell with a glance if things are messy—if garbage and unwashed dishes are lying about—or if things are really clean. It may not mean much. Just because a house is clean, it might still be a den of iniquity! But it is an important first impression and it does say something about the program. I'll bet you that from ten feet away I can tell if a program is bad. I might not guarantee that it is *good*, but if it looks bad from ten feet, I can guarantee you that it wasn't written with care. And if it wasn't written with care, it's probably not beautiful in the logical sense.

But suppose it looks good. You then pick deeper. To understand the structure of a program is much, much harder. Some people have different opinions about what makes the structure beautiful. There are purists who think only structured programming with certain very simple constructions, used in a very strict mathematical fashion, is beautiful. That was a very reasonable reaction to the situation before the sixties when programmers were unaware of the notion of structuring.

But to me, programs can be beautiful even if they do not follow those concepts, if they have other redeeming features. It's like comparing modern poetry with classical poetry. I think classical poetry is great and you can appreciate it. But you can't limit your appreciation to just classical poetry. It also doesn't mean that if you put random words on paper and call it poetry, there will be beauty. But if a code has some redeeming qualities, I don't think it needs to be structured in a mathematical sense to be beautiful.

> *"Programming is an art just as high-energy physics is an art."*

INTERVIEWER: *Is it possible that someone could read some of your source code and say, "Charles Simonyi wrote this code"?*

SIMONYI: Oh yes, no doubt. Whether I wrote it myself or not might be fairly difficult to tell, but one thing is for sure: You could look at it and know if it was written in my organization or under my influence. This is because all the code that I have written since about 1972 has been written with certain naming conventions that are popularly called "Hungarian." You can immediately recognize all the code that has been written under my influence, including Microsoft Word and Multiplan, Bravo, and many others written with those conventions.

INTERVIEWER: *What do you mean by "Hungarian" naming conventions?*

SIMONYI: It's called "Hungarian" as a joke. You know they say, "That's Greek to me," meaning they don't understand it, so it might as well be written in Greek. "Hungarian" is a twist on that phrase because these naming conventions are actually supposed to make the code more readable. The joke is that the program looks so unreadable, it might as well be written in Hungarian. But it's a set of conventions that controls the naming of all quantities in the program.

If you were to break up a program, put it into a grinder, and then sort the pieces, you would find that the bulk of the program is in names. If you just write, "apples + oranges," the name "apples" is six characters, the operation "+" is one character, the name "oranges" is seven characters, for a total of fourteen characters. Only one character, the plus sign, had to do with the operation. So to me it seemed logical that to make an impact or improve things, I would try to improve the greatest bulk—and that was the names. "Hungarian" is a way of almost automatically creating a name from the properties of the named quantity. Very similar to the idea of calling people Taylor if they were tailors and Smyth if they were blacksmiths.

So if you have a structure with certain properties, instead of giving it some arbitrary name and then having everybody learn the association between the name and the properties, you use the properties themselves as the name. This method has a lot of advantages. First, it's very easy to create a name—as you think of the properties, you write them down and immediately have the name. Second, it is very understandable, because as you read something you learn a lot about the properties from the name. As these properties get more and more numerous, it becomes difficult to describe them concisely. So "Hungarian" introduces some abbreviated notation to encode the properties in a short space. Of course this is a complete jumble to the uninitiated, and that's the joke.

Some people think if they can read each of the words in a code, then the program is readable. In fact, readability is in that sense unimportant. Nobody takes a listing, goes up to a podium, and reads a program out loud. It's comprehension that counts. The fact that you can just read the words and pronounce them is useless. When people see a listing in "Hungarian," they find these words difficult to pronounce, so they might think it isn't readable. But in fact, it's easier to comprehend and easier to communicate because of the association between the name and the properties. People who use Hungarian to program usually continue to use it even after they leave my organization. I have a lot of splinter organizations at Apple Computer, 3Com, and many other companies.

INTERVIEWER: *Let's talk about the process you go through in creating programs. Is there a process you can apply to all programs?*

SIMONYI: Sure. If we're talking strictly about programming, then let's assume I already know what I want to do. If I don't, then there is some aspect of the process that is common to all problem solving: What am I trying to do? What is the goal?

For example, I want a text editor to be menu driven, fast, have a spelling checker, and so on. I need to know the end product before true programming begins. Sometimes the choice of the goal depends on what I already have in my bag of tricks. In the case of Bravo, the program was guided by the algorithms. Butler Lampson described a couple of interesting algorithms, so we attempted to write the editor around those algorithms to exploit them. Also, J Moore—he is the Moore of the Boyer-Moore string search algorithm—had some very interesting algorithms for editing documents. Again, we said, "Hey, let's do an editor that includes the Moore editing algorithm, the Lampson screen-update algorithms, and a couple of caches." Once I have a good feel about the goals, then the real programming begins. I shift gears and sit down, close the door, and say, "Now I want to program."

INTERVIEWER: *When you shift gears and actually start programming, what do you do first?*

SIMONYI: The first step in programming is imagining. Just making it crystal clear in my mind what is going to happen. In this initial stage, I use paper and pencil. I just doodle, I don't write code. I might draw a few boxes or a few arrows, but it's just mostly doodles, because the real picture is in my mind. I like to imagine the structures that are being maintained, the structures that represent the reality I want to code.

Once I have the structure fairly firm and clear in my mind, then I write the code. I sit down at my terminal—or with a piece of paper in the old days—and write it. It's fairly easy. I just write the different transformations and I know what the results should be. The code for the most part writes itself, but it's the data structures I maintain that are the key. They come first and I keep them in my mind throughout the entire process.

INTERVIEWER: *Is that the biggest step?*

SIMONYI: Absolutely, that is the biggest step: The knowledge of the best algorithms is the science, and the imagining of the structure is the art. The details of algorithms, writing efficient lines of code to implement transformations on those structures, is the trade aspect of programming. Technically, this is called maintaining the invariances in the structures. Writing the code to maintain invariances is a relatively simple progression of craftsmanship, but it requires a lot of care and discipline.

INTERVIEWER: *Do you ever get tired of programming?*

SIMONYI: Yes.

INTERVIEWER: When you write a program, is it a painful process or a pleasurable process?

SIMONYI: It's a mixture. I think it's foolish to pretend that every minute is a pleasure. Like the athletes say, "If it doesn't hurt, you're not working hard enough." After twenty years, I don't get the feeling of novelty that I did after I had been programming for one or two years. I still get it sometimes, but not as often, no way.

INTERVIEWER: Do you have a routine? Do you program every day or do you walk away from the problem for a while and then stay up for a week to work on it?

> *"Really good programs live forever. . . at least as long as the hardware exists, maybe even longer."*

SIMONYI: I don't have a chance to program every day. I don't have to walk away from a problem, because people interrupt me. My routine is that I program at night and I am interrupted during the day.

INTERVIEWER: Do you come to the office to work at night or do you work at home?

SIMONYI: I work here at the office. I live very nearby, so it's easy. It's like going to a different room in your home. Instead of going to the den to program, I come to the office. It's just two minutes away.

INTERVIEWER: How do you supervise the programmers who work for you? Do you find that you are doing more supervising now than programming?

SIMONYI: I do both, and right now I'm doing more programming. In the Bravo days, the supervision of the programmers was very, very direct. Once I actually wrote an incredibly detailed work order, which was called a metaprogram. It was almost like a program, except written in a very, very high-level language. We hired two bushy-tailed guys from Stanford as "experimental subjects." They wrote the program exactly the way I wanted it to be written and we accomplished two things. First, it was easier for me to work in this incredibly high-level language, essentially programming these people. Second, they really learned the program much better than if I had finished it and given them the listing and said, "Study this program." They learned it because they wrote it. See, everybody could claim that they wrote the program. I wrote the program and they wrote the program. That was really great.

I think the best way to supervise is by personal example and by frequent code reviews. We try to do code reviews all the time.

INTERVIEWER: If you have more than one programmer working on a program, does it develop more quickly?

SIMONYI: Not necessarily. The actual amount of code produced per person is smaller, the more people there are writing the program. Consequently, the total code produced is greater for a while, and then it may actually decrease. With two people, you might get 50 percent more code per unit of time.

By the way, the efficiency of the code also decreases with an increase in the number of people working on the program. The most efficient programs are written by a single person. The only problem is, it might take forever to write, and that is unacceptable. So you have two or three, five or ten, or hundreds of people working on a project.

INTERVIEWER: Can you predict how long it will take to write a program?

SIMONYI: We have great difficulty in predicting the time it will take to write a program. There are valid reasons why this is so. It doesn't mean we shouldn't try our best to predict, because there are reasons why a prediction might be useful, just like when a weather prediction has economic as well as other benefits.

Really good programs will live forever and take forever to write, at least as long as the hardware exists, and maybe even longer. Certainly, Bravo lived for as long as the Alto existed. The people who wrote it were just there for the summer. At the end of the summer, one of them left and the other stayed. So the first release took about three months. There were about fourteen releases over about a five-year period.

The same thing is going to be true for Multiplan. When you consider that Multiplan lives in Microsoft Excel, then Multiplan is going to be a continuing story. And Microsoft Excel on the Macintosh is not going to be the last application in the chain either. It's going to continue on Windows.

INTERVIEWER: When you wrote Bravo, did you think that the Xerox Alto was a machine that everyone was going to use?

SIMONYI: I did, because I was naive. But I was right insofar as the successors of Alto are becoming something everybody can use. In a way, the Macintosh computer and the Windows program are successors of ... [Simonyi stops to answer the telephone and talks briefly, then continues]. That was Tom Malloy, one of the summer students I just mentioned—the one who stayed. I haven't talked to him in a year. He went to Apple and did the editor program for the Lisa.

INTERVIEWER: *Why do you write programs? Do you see it as a job, or a profession, or a way of making money? Is it something you are born with?*

SIMONYI: I think it is all of those. I had some aptitude when I was young. Even when I didn't know programming, I knew things that related a lot to programming. It was easy for me to remember complex things. As you get older, it gets harder. The images get less clear.

INTERVIEWER: *Why do the images become less clear?*

SIMONYI: It's probably just that aging changes your mode of thinking. Right now, I have to really concentrate and I might even get a headache just trying to imagine something clearly and distinctly with twenty or thirty components. When I was young, I could imagine a castle with twenty rooms with each room having ten different objects in it. I would have no problem. I can't do that anymore. Now I think more in terms of earlier experiences. I see a network of inchoate clouds, instead of the picture-postcard clearness. But I do write better programs.

INTERVIEWER: *Are there any formulas to follow in order to be a good programmer?*

SIMONYI: I doubt it.

> *"I do programming because it's a business. Not just because I love it, but because I love the business."*

INTERVIEWER: *Is it inherited talent or education?*

SIMONYI: There are a lot of formulas for making a good candidate into a good programmer. We hire talented people. I don't know how they got their talent and I don't care. But they are talented. From then on, there is a hell of a lot the environment can do.

Programmers get a couple of books on their first day here. One of them, called *How to Solve It,* is by George Polya, the mathematician. [Simonyi takes the book from a bookcase next to his desk and opens it to a certain page.] These two pages are important. The rest of the book just elaborates on these two pages. This is like a checklist for problem solving. This is the preflight, the takeoff, and the landing checklist. It doesn't mean this will tell you how to fly, but it does mean if you don't do this, then you can crash even if you already know how to fly.

We follow these four steps of problem solving: first, understanding the problem, then devising a plan, carrying out the plan, and, finally, looking back. We have about four books like this and I think we make the programmers better than when they arrive.

INTERVIEWER: *How do you see the role of the programmer in the future?*

SIMONYI: If you are asking if we are going to be as bigheaded as the physicists were, who knows? When any particular science has a string of great successes, there seems to be a tendency for those involved to say, "We *knew* we were really bright." Then they want to solve problems in other areas.

What comes to mind is the physicists after 1945. They said, "We really did it! Now let's look around." And they looked at biology and cybernetics and they said, "These guys studying brains don't know anything. They don't even know how memory is stored. No wonder, because they are turkeys. Let *us* look at it. *We'll* fix it. We'll apply Heisenberg's equations, or quantum mechanics, or whatever worked before, and we'll apply it to brain research and something great will come out of it."

Sometimes it works and sometimes it doesn't work. Who knows? Maybe computer science will help decode DNA, and not just by supplying tools. Disassembling DNA could be a hacker's ultimate dream.

INTERVIEWER: *Do you see any great change in the way programs will be written in the future?*

SIMONYI: I think computers will be quite a bit more effective than they are now, but I don't think there will be any great differences. I don't know that the sixth or the thirty-second generation will do something really drastically different or that great. I am wary of new methods promising wonderful new benefits. I can see incredible possibilities for improvement within the confines of our current methods. I have much more faith in the current methods, not because I am conservative, but because I know that I am not going to lose any of the current benefits either.

I have always worried that when these claimed incredible new benefits come, we will lose all the old ones. Then it becomes a kind of trade-off situation where you have to see if you are better off. I like clear wins. I would bet on improving what we have while maintaining all the benefits and eliminating the drawbacks, rather than introducing new games where there are new benefits and new drawbacks. But I might be wrong, and I'll be the first to jump on the bandwagon. I have no doubt things will change drastically for the better, but it's going to take some time.

INTERVIEWER: *Why is it taking so much more time?*

SIMONYI: Because a lot of dumb ideas have to die first. That's why progress takes time. First, new ideas have to evolve, then the bad ideas that stop progress have to die. That's always been the case. Even with relativity and quantum mechanics, the good ideas had to crystallize. And then people with vested interest in the old physics had to die out.

INTERVIEWER: *Can you give an example?*

SIMONYI: If I mentioned something that is universally abhorred like punched cards I would not be contributing much. So I will have to take a potshot at something that most people believe in. I think that the "cult of simplicity," the idea that simplicity is a desirable end in itself, is highly suspect. For many years this has been a heuristic enabling us to focus on the problems with the quickest payoffs. But it is just a means. I think that computer science, together with all the other symbolic sciences (mathematics, physics, and modern molecular biology) will be revamped by the understanding of very complex phenomena. Mathematics is leading the way with the discovery of very complex fundamental objects. The traditional name for a class of these objects, "simple groups," ironically reflects the old belief that "fundamental" is equal to "simple." Well, maybe it isn't. In computers we may not get anywhere with real artificial intelligence, user interfaces, languages, and so on by harping on simplicity.

INTERVIEWER: *What do you do when you aren't programming? Do you have any other interests?*

SIMONYI: There are some other interesting things that I wouldn't mind spending some time with. I have dabbled just a bit in Egyptian hieroglyphics. Learning other languages, traveling, and seeing the world are great activities, and I wouldn't mind doing them. I also have a private rotorcraft (helicopter) pilot's license.

I don't think programming is that much more important than anything else. But if you look at the business side, then it becomes a different story. It's really the business that keeps me occupied more than just programming. In the course of business, I program more than I want to.

INTERVIEWER: *Do you think your time might be better spent on the business side of programming?*

SIMONYI: No. I'm just saying I do programming because it's a business. Not just because I love programming, but because I love the business. It's not because with every line I write I say, "Hey, I get great pleasure from writing one more line, so let's write because I'm getting more pleasure." No way. I probably wrote this line ten times already. It can get pretty tiring just typing the bloody thing until my fingers hurt. So when I'm doing that, I'm doing it because it's part of the business, and I want to do the business.

The key difference between programming in the abstract and programming as a business is that there is a solid purpose in business. Otherwise, it is just an abstract activity, like playing a game of chess. When you are at the end of the game, you jumble the pieces. The game is gone. When the program is done, some people use it, and I see they enjoy it, and I derive enjoyment from that. Some of them even pay for it, and some of that money finds its way into my pockets, which I then spend on visiting Egypt, or flying a helicopter for half an hour, which is, by the way, a lot like programming projects: The launch and landing are spectacular, the ride can get very tiring, and the whole thing can come apart at any time.

INTERVIEWER: How do you regard other programmers of your time?

SIMONYI: I have a great regard for the men who influenced me in the past. I regard them very highly. But I also have a great regard for the people I work with now.

INTERVIEWER: Do you associate with any other programmers who have developed major programs? Do you trade ideas with them?

SIMONYI: I have great regard for the competition. I've had the pleasure of meeting Bob Frankston and Dan Bricklin [the founders of Software Arts and writers of VisiCalc] at a couple of trade shows. I once met Jonathan Sachs [a founder of Lotus Development Corporation]. But unfortunately we don't move around much and not many of these programmers have a reason to come to Seattle. Bruce Artwick [who wrote and designed Flight Simulator] sometimes visits, and the guys at Apple, like Bill Atkinson [one of the Lisa programmers who later developed the MacPaint program for the Apple Macintosh computer]—I think Atkinson is the greatest—and Bill Budge [who programmed Pinball Construction Set for Electronic Arts]. These guys are all great.

We don't have much to talk about. We feel good vibes and exchange three or four words. I know that if one of these guys opens his mouth, he knows what he is talking about. So when he does open his mouth and he does know what he is talking about, it's not a great shock. And since I tend to know what I am talking about, too, I would probably say the same thing, so why bother talking, really? It's like the joke tellers' convention where people sit around and they don't even have to tell a joke. They just say the joke number and everybody laughs.

It would be great to be able to work with all these guys, but we are business competitors. I think we could do incredible stuff together. Maybe the Martians will invade and we will have to do a Manhattan project in computers. We would all be shipped to New Mexico. Who knows?

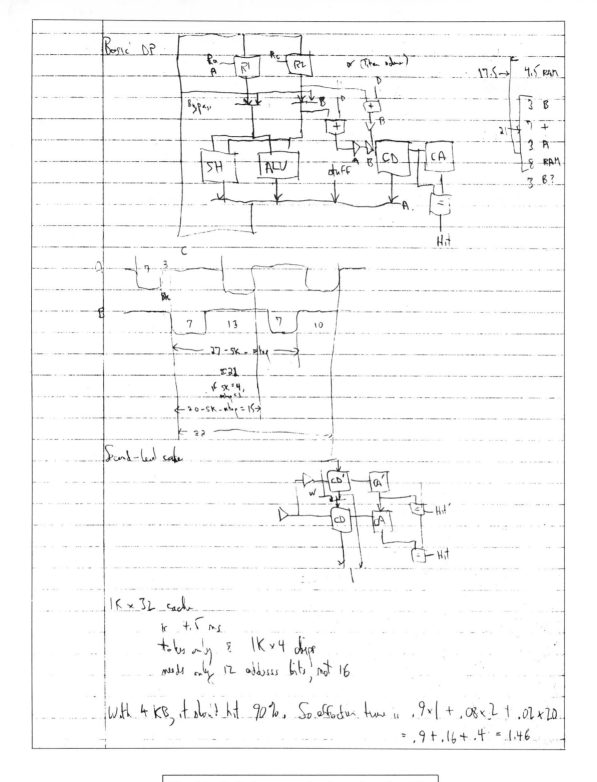

Sketch by Butler Lampson of a design for a fast CPU with a two-level cache. See the Appendix (pages 373-382) for additional specifications for this CPU and other programs.

Butler Lampson

CURRENTLY a senior engineer at the Systems Research Center of Digital Equipment Corporation in Palo Alto, California, Butler Lampson was an associate professor of computer science at the University of California, Berkeley, a founder of the Berkeley Computer Corporation, and a senior research fellow at Xerox PARC's Computer Science Laboratory.

Lampson's many accomplishments in so many areas of computer design and research make him one of the most highly regarded professionals in the field. He has worked on hardware systems, such as the Ethernet local network and Alto and the Dorado personal computers; operating systems, such as the SDS 940 and Alto; programming languages, such as LISP and Mesa; application programs, such as the Bravo editor and the Star office system; and network servers, such as the Dover printer and the Grapevine mail system.

I met Butler Lampson in Palo Alto at the offices of Digital Equipment Corporation where he works one week out of a six-week cycle; the other five weeks he works in Philadelphia. He is what he calls a "tele-commuter," doing much of his work via telecommunication lines.

Unlike so many others in this fast-paced, quickly growing industry, Butler Lampson doesn't exhibit many entrepreneurial interests. His focus is singular: He is concerned with the successful design of a computer system, whether it be hardware, software applications, languages, or networks. Lampson writes very little source code today; he is a system designer, the person with the vision and expertise who lays the groundwork for a complex system. And he is undoubtedly one of the best.

INTERVIEWER: *What attracts you to computers?*

LAMPSON: I think the computer is the world's greatest toy. You can invent wonderful things and actually make them happen.

INTERVIEWER: *But you can do that in other fields too. . . .*

LAMPSON: It's much, much harder to make things happen in other fields. If you're a physicist, you have to live with what nature has provided. But with computer science, you invent whatever you want. It's like mathematics, except what you invent is tangible.

INTERVIEWER: *Is your background in math and physics?*

LAMPSON: I studied physics at Harvard. Toward the end of my studies I did quite a bit of programming for a physics professor who wanted to analyze spark-chamber photographs on a PDP-1. When I went to Berkeley to continue studying physics, a very interesting computer research project was going on, but it was well concealed. I found out about it from a friend at a computer conference I attended in San Francisco. He asked me how this project was doing. When I said I'd never heard of it, he told me which unmarked door to go through to find it.

INTERVIEWER: *And what lurked behind this door?*

LAMPSON: It was the development of one of the first commercial time-sharing systems, the SDS 940.

INTERVIEWER: *Did you get involved with the project?*

LAMPSON: Deeply. I eventually gave up physics, because I found computer work a lot more interesting. That was fortunate because, if I had stayed in physics, I would have gotten my Ph.D. right around the time of the great crash for physics Ph.D.s.

INTERVIEWER: So you walked through an unmarked door into a concealed computer project and changed from physicist to computer scientist? Apart from programming on the PDP-1, did you have any earlier contact with computers?

LAMPSON: Yes, a friend and I did some hacking on an IBM 650 while I was still in high school. The 650, which was the first business computer, was nearing the end of its useful life, so there wasn't much demand for time on it.

INTERVIEWER: You've studied a range of sciences. Do you see an overlap between physics, mathematics, and computer science?

LAMPSON: Only in the sense that physics and mathematics, like other respectable disciplines, require that you think clearly to succeed in them. That's why many successful computer people come from these fields. It's harder to do what people do nowadays—start in computer science and stay in it—because it's a very shallow discipline. It doesn't really force you to exercise your intellectual capabilities enough.

INTERVIEWER: Do you think the field is shallow because it's so primitive and young?

LAMPSON: That's the main reason. There seems to be some evidence of it becoming less shallow, but it's a slow process.

INTERVIEWER: Do you consider computer science to be on the same level as physics and mathematics?

> *"I think the computer is the world's greatest toy. You can invent wonderful things and actually make them happen."*

LAMPSON: I used to think that undergraduate computer-science education was bad, and that it should be outlawed. Recently I realized that position isn't reasonable. An undergraduate degree in computer science is a perfectly respectable professional degree, just like electrical engineering or business administration. But I do think it's a serious mistake to take an undergraduate degree in computer science if you intend to study it in graduate school.

INTERVIEWER: Why?

LAMPSON: Because most of what you learn won't have any long-term significance. You won't learn new ways of using your mind, which does you more good than learning the details of how to write a compiler, which is what you're likely to get from undergraduate computer science. I think the world would be much better off if all the graduate computer-science departments would get together and agree not to accept anybody with a bachelor's degree in computer science. Those people should be required to take a remedial year to learn something respectable like mathematics or history, before going on to graduate-level computer science. However, I don't see that happening.

INTERVIEWER: *What kind of training or type of thought leads to the greatest productivity in the computer field?*

"To hell with computer literacy. It's absolutely ridiculous. Study mathematics. Learn to think. Read. Write."

LAMPSON: From mathematics, you learn logical reasoning. You also learn what it means to prove something, as well as how to handle abstract essentials. From an experimental science such as physics, or from the humanities, you learn how to make connections in the real world by applying these abstractions.

INTERVIEWER: *Like many influential programmers, in the early seventies you spent time at the Xerox PARC think tank, surrounded by great minds. Was that an inspiring time for you?*

LAMPSON: It was great. We felt as though we were conquering the world.

INTERVIEWER: *Did any of your colleagues from that time influence your thinking?*

LAMPSON: We all influenced each other. There was a lot of give and take. Bob Taylor's influence was very important. It was a combination of how he ran the laboratory and his consistent view of the ways in which computers are important.

INTERVIEWER: *Even though Xerox created a think tank of computer experts, they failed to implement and bring to market many of the ideas. Did that disappoint you; did you think the world wasn't ready for those products?*

LAMPSON: It's always hard to know what people are ready for. Were we aware of the outside world? Yes, we knew that it existed. Did we understand the whole situation perfectly? Probably not. Were we surprised when Xerox was unable to sell Stars? No, not really.

My view of the whole enterprise at Xerox PARC was that we couldn't expect something like that to last forever. It lasted almost 15 years, so that was pretty good.

The purpose of PARC was to learn. You owe something to the company that's paying you to learn, and we felt we should do what we could, within reasonable bounds, to benefit Xerox. But it wasn't critical that Xerox develop those ideas. Their failure was not really surprising, because they were trying to get into a new business that nobody knew much about. There were many ways for things to go wrong. Some things went wrong in marketing—the quality of the technical people was high, but they never got the quality of marketing people the company needed.

For example, Bob Sproull and I spent a lot of time designing this project called Interpress, which was a printing standard. I put a lot of energy into that, and I would have really liked Xerox to take it and make everybody adopt it. Instead, they completely screwed it up. As a result, some of the people who worked on it went off and started Adobe Systems, and invented a similar product called PostScript, which is clearly a standard everyone will now adopt. That sort of thing is annoying, but the main product of a research laboratory is ideas.

INTERVIEWER: Are there any research labs devoted to ideas today?

LAMPSON: I have my own biases on that. The best research places are Digital Equipment Company, where I am now, and Bell Labs.

INTERVIEWER: Do you feel that research has a practical limit?

LAMPSON: I think it is unlikely that expert systems are going to work. In the early seventies, it was clear that the projects we were involved in then could be made to work. At least, I couldn't see any fundamental reasons why they should not work, whereas now I can see a lot of fundamental reasons why artificial-intelligence systems are unlikely to work. It seems that some people have taken a very small number of experiments, which often have very ambiguous outcomes, and have made generalizations about those results in a totally crazy way.

INTERVIEWER: Why do you think people are so fascinated by the idea of artificial intelligence?

LAMPSON: Well, I'm not sure. Part of it is the basic computer fallacy that states the computer is a universal engine that can do anything. If there is no obvious way to show that something is impossible, then some people assume it must be possible. A lot of people don't understand what the consequences of complexity are, and without that understanding they are likely to get burned. If they are not willing to take the word of someone who has gotten burned, then the only way they are going to find out is to try it and get burned themselves. Very few of the people who are excited about artificial intelligence have tried it.

I see really extreme versions of this. For instance, the Defense Advanced Research Projects Agency is funding a program that is supposed to use all of these wonderful expert systems and AI techniques, as well as parallel computing, to produce truly wonderful military devices, such as robot tanks. They published a ten-year plan that included a foldout showing lines of development and milestones when breakthroughs would be made. It's all nonsense because no one knows how to do these things. Some of the problems may be solved within the next ten years—but to have a schedule! The world doesn't work that way. If you don't know the answers to the problems, you can't schedule when you're going to finish the project.

INTERVIEWER: You seem to scorn complexity. When you design a system, do you strive for simplicity?

LAMPSON: Right. Everything should be made as simple as possible. But to do that you have to master complexity.

INTERVIEWER: In practical terms, how do you achieve that?

LAMPSON: There are some basic techniques to control complexity. Fundamentally, I divide and conquer, break things down, and try to write reasonably precise descriptions of what each piece is supposed to do. That becomes a sketch of how to proceed. When you can't figure out how to write a spec, it's because you don't understand what's going on. Then you have two choices: Either back off to some other problem you do understand, or think harder.

Also, the description of the system shouldn't be too big. You may have to think about a big system in smaller pieces. It's somewhat like solving problems in mathematics: You can write books that are full of useful hints, but you can't give an *algorithm*.

INTERVIEWER: I know your experience with computers is broad. You've developed computers, operating systems, and applications. Does each of these require a different discipline?

LAMPSON: Obviously, if you want to develop applications, you need a fair amount of sensitivity about user interface, which is not as important in developing a piece of hardware. When you design hardware, typically you're much more concerned with the arbitrary constraints imposed by the particular technology that you are working with. Nobody knows how to build really complicated hardware systems, so designing hardware tends to be simpler. Software is much more complicated.

INTERVIEWER: *Do you still program?*

LAMPSON: Only in an abstract sense. I no longer have the time to write actual programs. But I've spent the first half of this year writing a twenty-five page abstract program for a name server. To give you a sense of the relationship between an abstract program and a real program, the abstract has been translated into about seven thousand lines of Modula-2 code. So I cheat. I haven't done full-time programming for about six or seven years. I did a lot of it before that.

INTERVIEWER: *What are some of the more important programs that you wrote?*

LAMPSON: I wrote sizeable chunks of the 940 operating system and I wrote two or three compilers for an interactive language for scientific and engineering calculations. I wrote a SNOBOL compiler. In addition, Peter Deutsch and I designed a programming language that was one of the predecessors to C and wrote a compiler for it. I've written design-automation programs, and another operating system that I did in the early seventies at Xerox.

INTERVIEWER: *Is it easier for you to develop programs now than it was ten or fifteen years ago?*

LAMPSON: Designing programs is probably harder now because the aspiration level is so much greater. But the actual programming is a lot easier now than it used to be. The machines have much more memory so you don't have to squeeze as hard. You can concentrate more on getting the job done and not worry about getting the most out of limited resources. That helps a lot. Also, the programming tools are somewhat better now. But, since I don't write code anymore, development is *much* easier for me.

INTERVIEWER: *What sort of processes do you go through when you design or develop a program?*

LAMPSON: Most of the time, a new program is a refinement, extension, generalization, or improvement of an existing program. It's really unusual to do something that's completely new. Usually I put into a new program an extension or improvement on something that's already a model in an existing

> *"Everything should be made as simple as possible. But to do that you have to master complexity."*

31

program or user interface. For example, Bravo was the result of two ideas I had. One was about how to represent the text that was being edited inside the computer model and the other was how to efficiently update the screen. But the basic idea for Bravo came from a system called NLS that was done in the late sixties by Doug Englebart at SRI. NLS provided a mouse-oriented, full-screen display of structured text. The confluence of those ideas led to the development of Bravo.

In the old days, I would scribble notes down on a piece of paper and start hacking, or get somebody else enthralled and start them hacking. Nowadays, I try to write the crucial parts of the idea in fairly precise, but abstract, language. Typically, there's a lot of iteration at that stage.

For example, I worked on a name-server project with Andrew Birtell and Mike Schroeder. At Xerox, they had built a system called Grapevine, which was a distributed name server. Grapevine could handle a few thousand names, and it started to break down as it grew toward the few-thousand limit. After we did that project, we had some idea of how a name server should hang together, but we wanted to handle a few billion names, which posed some significant design problems. I decided that its basic elements should be local databases, and each one would essentially implement a fairly standard tree-structured name scheme. And all of these databases would fit together in a loosely coupled way.

The operations were defined and programs were written on a fairly high level, without too much concern for detail. We ended up with a twenty-five or thirty-page combination of program and specifications. This served as a detailed design from which a summer student turned out the seven thousand lines of prototype implementation.

That's usually the process I follow. How long it takes depends on how difficult the problem is. Sometimes it takes years.

INTERVIEWER: Did the languages you developed take as much work?

LAMPSON: Sometimes it's quick: Peter Deutsch and I had the first version of one language going in about two months. On the other hand, I've been working with Rod Burstall on a kernel programming language that we work on two or three times a year. That project's been going on for about five years now and we still don't have an implementation. We keep changing our minds.

INTERVIEWER: Do you think there are certain techniques that lead to a good program or a good system?

LAMPSON: Yes. The most important goal is to define as precisely as possible the interfaces between the system and the rest of the world, as well as the interfaces between the major parts of the system itself. The biggest change in my design style over the years has been to put more and more emphasis on the problem to be solved and on finding techniques to define the interfaces precisely. That pays off tremendously, both in a better understanding of what the program really does, and in identification of the crucial parts. It also helps people understand how the system is put together. That's really the most important aspect of designing a program.

Designing a program is completely different from inventing algorithms. With algorithms, the game is to get the whole plan in your head and then shuffle all the pieces around until you settle on the best way to accomplish it. The trick here is to sufficiently define the algorithm so that you can get it completely in your head.

INTERVIEWER: *When you design a system or a program, what makes you certain that it can be implemented?*

LAMPSON: One possibility is to carry the design down to a level of programming where two things are true. First, I already know about the primitives I write the programming in — they have been implemented many times before, so I have a high degree of confidence that the program will work. Second, I understand the primitives well enough to estimate within a factor of two or three how much memory they are going to cost. I can then design my program in a sensible way. So I can be fairly confident that it's possible to implement a function, and I can roughly estimate its performance. Of course, it's possible to do that and overlook something very important. There's no way around that.

The other possibility is to very carefully and formally write down what properties the program should have and then convince yourself that it has them. You always do that in an informal way, but as you do it more formally, it gets to be a lot more work, and the chance of missing something important gets smaller. At some point, the formal analysis becomes counterproductive. But if you do too little of it, the risk of missing something important increases. If you don't find out about the missing element until the program's all coded, then a tremendous amount of work has been thrown away.

Of course, what usually happens is that you don't throw that work away; you try to patch it up. That has very bad consequences. First of all, you don't solve the problem. You just convert it into another problem, which isn't the one you should really be solving. And then you patch the program until it solves the other problem. That approach is very unsatisfactory.

Sometimes I think that the goals people are trying to reach are just too much to ask for. Programmers often lose sight of the fact that the problems in building software systems arise because what they are trying to do is just too hard. They believe the computer is a universal engine that can do anything. It's very easy to be seduced into the proposition that a group of one or five or ten or fifty or a thousand programmers can make the computer do anything. That's clearly not right.

> "...few people who are excited about AI have tried it."

INTERVIEWER: What qualities does a programmer need to write a successful program?

LAMPSON: The most important quality is the ability to organize the solution to the problem into a manageable structure, with each component specified in a simple way. Sometimes successful programmers can do that but can't explain what they did, because they can't see the structure. Some people are good programmers because they can handle many more details than most people. But there are a lot of disadvantages in selecting programmers for that reason—it can result in programs that no one else can maintain. That doesn't seem to happen so much anymore, because now it's more fashionable to have one person or group design the programs and then hire someone else to write all the code.

INTERVIEWER: Do you see a hazard in that approach?

LAMPSON: The hazard is that eventually the designer can lose touch with reality, and that leads to designs that can't be implemented.

INTERVIEWER: And have you ever designed programs that could not be implemented?

LAMPSON: No, I don't think so. The closest I've come to that was in the mid-seventies, at Xerox PARC. With several other people, I designed a file system that provided *transactions*. That's the ability to make several changes to stored data as an *atomic* operation: Either all the changes get made or none of them do. An example of a transaction is the transfer of money from an account at one bank to an account at a different bank. You don't want to leave the system in a state where the money was removed from one account but not added to the other. I worked a lot on an early design of that system, and it was built. It did work, but was generally judged to be quite unsatisfactory.

INTERVIEWER: Can you describe a beautiful program?

LAMPSON: I don't know if it's possible to answer that question. I can't tell you what a beautiful painting is, or a beautiful piece of music. Perhaps it's easier to describe a program because it is composed of diverse qualities; it is an engineering object as well as art.

A beautiful program is like a beautiful theorem: It does the job elegantly. It has a simple and perspicuous structure; people say, "Oh, yes. I see that's the way to do it."

INTERVIEWER: If you could draw a parallel between programming and another art, such as painting, writing, composing music, or sculpture, which one would it be?

LAMPSON: It would be better to choose architecture, which encompasses major engineering considerations. Very few programs can be regarded as pure art. A program is expected to do something and art is part of it. But when I say programming is an art, it's in the same way that mathematics is: People don't normally classify mathematics as an art.

INTERVIEWER: In what sense is computer science a science?

LAMPSON: The easiest answer is that it's a science to the same extent that mathematics is a science. A computer program can be viewed as a mathematical object. One way to understand such an object is to make abstract statements about it that you can prove. The only other way of understanding the object is trial and error, which doesn't work very well. If it is the least bit complicated, you can try for a long time and never find out what an object's properties are.

INTERVIEWER: Do you think the way that systems are designed and developed will radically change?

LAMPSON: Well, yes and no. What really makes design better is the development of higher levels of abstractions to work with. For instance, you can program a VisiCalc spreadsheet more easily than you can write a BASIC program to solve a certain type of problem.

On the other hand, our aspirations are constantly increasing, so the development of better abstractions doesn't make the task of programming much easier: It means we can do more elaborate things. We can do more because the primitives that we are using are much more powerful.

INTERVIEWER: Do you think the microcomputer and personal computer are part of a phase that will pass into something else?

LAMPSON: Of course not! I give a talk to general audiences titled *The Computer Revolution Hasn't Happened Yet*. Its basic theme is that major changes in the world take a long time. Look at the industrial revolution. It was at least sixty years or more from the time it started until it had a major impact on people's lives. That was true for the second industrial revolution as well. Telephones and electric lights were invented around 1880 but it wasn't until the twenties that their use became widespread.

I think this is true for the computer revolution. People like to think that we're moving much faster because we go from idea to finished product in six months. That's nonsense. Computing is just beginning to become a significant part of the economy and just starting to affect people's lives. Technical trends are going to increase at a furious rate, and the natural form for those trends is the so-called personal computer.

You can look at the trends in the base technology and see where it's going. It takes silicon, a rotating magnetic medium, a keyboard, and a display to make a computer. Each of those components is evolving so you can get more and more of what you want in a small box at a modest price. There's no indication any of that is going to change. I'm not saying there won't be any big computers, but there is an overwhelming trend toward personal computers.

INTERVIEWER: Where do you see the industry in five to ten years?

LAMPSON: The computer industry will increase at a good clip for at least another twenty years. There are innumerable other things that computers eventually will do that they're not doing currently because they're not quite cheap enough, fast enough, or people simply do not understand a problem well enough.

INTERVIEWER: Do you think the status of computer science or the computer industry in our society will change? Will computer scientists become like the physicists in the early twentieth century, making great breakthroughs that significantly change society?

LAMPSON: No. It will be nothing like the status of physicists in the early twentieth century. Most people didn't even know physicists existed until 1945, when they became well known because of the atom bomb. I don't think computers are dramatic enough to compare with that. But the saying, "The computer revolution hasn't yet begun," means that in twenty years there will be a computer on every fingernail. They will be pervasive in ways we can foresee, and in many ways which we can't. This will result in a tremendous change in the way the world works, just as the automobile resulted in a tremendous change. But it will also take a long time, just as the automobile took a long time to change society. In 1920 when the automobile was first introduced, it was very hard to predict the consequences. Some were obvious, but not all of them. This will be even more true with the computer because the changes it creates will be much more profound.

INTERVIEWER: *Do you see any problems with a computer on every finger-nail in twenty years?*

LAMPSON: I don't see anything wrong with that. Certainly on every wrist. Computers are there to help and I hope they will do that in a positive way.

I recently read an interesting article about how encryption techniques could give individuals more control over how their personal data is disseminated. It is always hard to predict how these things will actually come out because a lot of political issues are involved as well as technical ones, but that article is an interesting illustration of how computer technology can give individuals more control over their lives. Even in situations where big organizations like banks are intimately and unavoidably involved in our lives, we can still find ways to give individuals far more control by using machines cleverly. Ten years ago nobody could have imagined that computers would give us more individual control. In fact, everybody thought the exact opposite would happen.

> *"I can see a lot of fundamental reasons why artificial intelligence systems are unlikely to work."*

INTERVIEWER: *What do you see as problem areas for the personal computers that exist today?*

LAMPSON: Personal computers are fairly junky. I don't define that as a problem. They're new and people are learning about them, and they're getting better rapidly. Alan Kay made a great comment about the Mac—it was the first computer good enough to criticize. It makes sense for people who are building the next generation of computers or programs to think about what's wrong with the current ones, in order to make the next ones better.

That's why I think the idea of computer literacy is such a rotten one. By computer literacy I mean learning to use the current generation of BASIC and word-processing programs. That has nothing to do with reality. It's true that a lot of jobs now require BASIC programming, but the notion that BASIC is going to be fundamental to your ability to function in the information-processing society of the twenty-first century is complete balderdash. There probably won't be any BASIC in the twenty-first century.

INTERVIEWER: *So how should we prepare ourselves for the future?*

LAMPSON: To hell with computer literacy. It's absolutely ridiculous. Study mathematics. Learn to think. Read. Write. These things are of more enduring value. Learn how to prove theorems: A lot of evidence has accumulated over the centuries that suggests this skill is transferable to many other things. To study only BASIC programming is absurd.

INTERVIEWER: *Is the industry being overrun by BASIC programmers?*

LAMPSON: No, and I don't think there's anything particularly harmful about programming in BASIC. What is bad is that people get very worried and feel that their children won't have a future if they don't learn to program in BASIC. There's no reason for them to worry.

INTERVIEWER: *But nobody knows for certain what skills will be required.*

LAMPSON: Well, there's some truth to that, but we have some idea of the direction in which computer science is evolving. You can look at the systems that are built in research laboratories and get a feeling for it. You could have visited Xerox in 1975 and gotten a very good sense of what the high end of the personal computer world was going to be like in 1985.

INTERVIEWER: *Do you think we'll see the day when everyone will write their own programs?*

LAMPSON: There are different degrees of programming. When the SmallTalk system was built, Alan Kay said one of his visions was that children would be able to use it and write interesting programs. But it didn't work that way. He said SmallTalk was like providing children with a lot of bricks: Children can build certain kinds of structures from bricks, but it's a very rare child that will be able to invent the arch.

If programmming just means giving the computer instructions, I think everybody will do that at some level. Most business people operate a spreadsheet and that's programming in some sense. I think you'll see more of that. Creative programming is another matter.

INTERVIEWER: *As a programmer, did you find that your work became an all-consuming part of your life?*

LAMPSON: I went through that stage earlier in life, but not anymore. I'm too old for that.

Making Grey scale encoded characters from high resolution bit maps.

The strategy presented here allows one to make grey scale encoded characters from high resolution bit maps.

Given a bit map of $m \times n$ bits sampled a p bits/inch

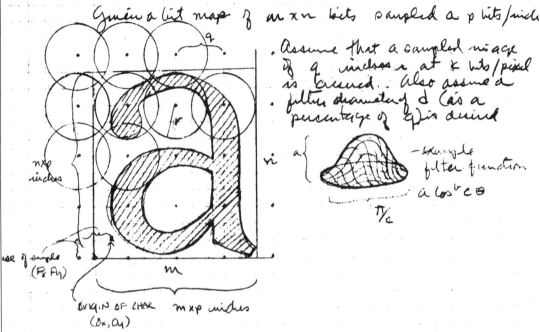

- Assume that a sampled image of q inches at k bits/pixel is desired. Also assume a filter diameter d (as a percentage of q) is desired.

— example filter function

$a \cos^b c \theta$

$\pi/2$

ORIGIN OF CHAR
(O_x, O_y) $m \times p$ inches

The strategy is to convert all numbers to bit map space so that convolution can be done with indexing.

1.) In bits $q' = q \times p$ represents the spacing between sample points.

2.) $2\sqrt{q'}$ is the array dimension of the filter.

3.) The filter domain (the sample points where the filter has a non-zero intersection with the bit map) is:

$$\text{INT}(-kq' - F_x), \quad \text{INT}(-kq' + F_y)$$

Notebook page showing how to make gray-scale characters from high-resolution bit maps.

John Warnock

BORN IN 1940 and raised in
Utah, John Warnock was educated at the University of Utah, where he received both a bachelor's and master's degree in mathematics, and a Ph.D. in
computer science. He switched to computer science at the time Dave Evans
established the famed research and development group to study interactive design and computer graphics at the University of Utah. After completing his
studies, Warnock tried his hand at being an entrepreneur with a company in
Vancouver, British Columbia, for a short time, then he joined Computer Sciences of Canada and worked in Toronto. After that he traveled to Washington,
D.C., where he was employed at the Goddard Space Flight Center.

In 1972, Warnock moved to California to work with Dave Evans and Ivan
Sutherland on the Illiac IV Project, the NASA space flight shuttle simulator,
and airplane simulators. In 1978, Warnock went to Xerox PARC where he
spent four years working in the Computer Sciences Laboratory. While at Xerox
PARC, Warnock worked on improving the typographic quality of computer
gray-scale displays.

In 1982, Drs. John E. Warnock and Charles M. Geshchke formed Adobe
Systems to develop software that integrates text and graphics, and is also output device independent. Their effort resulted in PostScript, Adobe System's
first product.

One can't help but notice the sign for Adobe Systems as you enter the company's office building, located in Palo Alto off of the Embarcadero, a road dotted with high-tech companies. The sign is rather large and it shines like gold. It is indicative of the success Warnock's company has recently experienced. Like so many others, Warnock took his ideas out of Xerox PARC into the real world, where he turned them into a language, PostScript, and a company, Adobe Systems.

John Warnock has a professorial look, with a full beard and tousled brown hair. He has an unassuming air and a casual manner. He wore a tweed jacket, a white shirt with an open collar, and wool slacks. His corner office is impressive, with clean lines and a contemporary look. I got the impression my visit was one of many Warnock has received since his company has met with such success. We swapped gripes about being on the road for so long. These days, the time Warnock spends programming is restricted to doing routines with PostScript, but he remains one of the programming wonders of our time.

INTERVIEWER: *What was it like at the University of Utah computer center while you were there in the mid-sixties?*

WARNOCK: It was quite interesting because Dave Evans, who had been at Berkeley, got a huge ARPA research and development grant for about five million dollars a year to develop interactive design and computer graphics. He was able to attract Ivan Sutherland, Tom Stockham, and some other great professors to work with him.

The computer-science department went from mediocre to really, really good, practically overnight. At that point, I switched my studies from mathematics to computer science.

While still in the mathematics department, I had been doing some work for the computer center, a service center for the rest of the University, creating a student-registration system. One day at work, a student of Dave Evans came along and said, "Gee, I'm trying to solve this hidden-surface problem, can you give me any insight into this?" and I said, "Well, it seems to me the problem needs to be organized this way," and I proceeded to get really interested in it and coded up the solution that I had in mind. My solution reduced by a large order of magnitude the amount of processing that had to go on. All of a sudden the computer-science department dragged me in and I became part of their group instantly, giving talks all across the country about my work on this hidden-surface problem and the coding solution I came up with.

Sutherland, who did Sketchpad in 1963, brought a lot of synergy and fresh ideas to this new group at Utah. This very talented group did an enormous amount of work in a very short amount of time. Ed Catmull, who later became head of Lucasfilm Ltd., and Jim Blinn, who does all the incredible Jupiter fly-bys, came out of Utah. Martin Newell, who later worked for Xerox PARC and is now at CAD Link, was there. Alan Kay, his mentor Bob Barton, and Patrick Boudelier, who did a lot of the research work at PARC, also came out of Utah. Bob Taylor was at Utah for a while, and Henry Fuchs. Most of those people were students of Dave Evans. In fact, it's quite remarkable when you look back and realize that the work done by this small group of people at Utah made possible the use of computer graphics in films produced by Lucasfilm Ltd. at Digital Productions and in much of television advertising today.

"Never make an assumption that you know something somebody else doesn't."

INTERVIEWER: *A lot of Dave Evans' students went on to become systems designers. What do you think makes a good systems designer?*

WARNOCK: There are very few really talented designers. Some people are very good at one particular thing or another, but systems design takes real balance, taking a list of options here and a list of options there, and combining them so they really work well together. A lot of people design an algorithm and then design the system around that algorithm.

Good systems design is much more of an engineering activity; it's a set of trade-offs and balances among various systems' components. I think the most difficult part of systems design is knowing how to make those trade-offs and balances among the various components.

INTERVIEWER: *When did you come up with the original idea for the PostScript language?*

WARNOCK: PostScript started in the Evans and Sutherland days when we were doing a harbor simulator for the Maritime Academy. We had to build a digital model of New York harbor, with 1,500 buildings and tank farms, and all the bridges and buoys and everything—all the landscape. The simulator was going to project the view of the harbor as seen from the bridge of the ship. We needed to write a huge, three-dimensional database and a lot of real-time software to make the simulator work the way they wanted it to.

We had a year to complete this massive undertaking. It was a full-color model with all three dimensions. We decided the most stupid thing we could do was to design this database in a form that would be used directly by the simulator. In other words, to bind it up too tightly. We decided to create a text file and then write a compiler to compile the text file into the form that the simulator would need (whenever we decided what that would be). We still didn't know what the simulator was going to look like.

So we started building this huge database in text form. In digitizing the database and in building this big three-dimensional model, it became very obvious that rather than having a static data structure in the text file, it was much more reasonable to have a language. It needed to be a very simple, easily parsed, and extensible language. So that's where the basic ideas of PostScript got started, in developing a language for this three-dimensional graphic database.

INTERVIEWER: After working with Evans and Sutherland, you went to Xerox PARC, correct? What was your experience like at Xerox PARC?

WARNOCK: Going to PARC was very interesting. I went there in 1978, and stayed about four years. There were several political factions within PARC. One was the Mesa group that previously had done BCPL. The Mesa group used traditional languages. And then there was the AI group, which used LISP.

I worked for Taylor's lab, which was the Computer Sciences Laboratory. I prefer the LISP-style languages, because they're more interactive and they're interpreters; I like the interpretive environment. But it would have been political suicide to use LISP when I belonged to this group because my work would simply have been ignored.

Martin Newell and I decided to reimplement the E&S design system in Mesa. We called it JaM. Reimplementing the design system took about three months. It became an interpretive language that we could use as an experimental workbench to try out all kinds of new ideas.

After a couple of years, when the Imaging Sciences Laboratory broke away from the Computer Sciences Laboratory, JaM was used as a primary development tool. We started hooking in all the graphics procedures to drive the displays and printers. Then that basic language structure evolved into Interpress, which is Xerox's printing protocol. This same language structure has again been implemented a third time as PostScript. They're essentially all the same language. It's really a ten- or eleven-year-old language that's had a lot of proving and a lot of reimplementation ideas in the process.

INTERVIEWER: What made you focus on the PostScript text printing aspect of the language structure?

WARNOCK: Well, first of all, the language property you want for printing is a straightforward syntax. PostScript is like FORTH because the syntax is so simple to parse. This means that if I want to communicate to another processor, all I have to do is send the serial stuff across the wire and it can be consumed by the processor on the other side in a straightforward way.

Another nice benefit of simple syntax is that other computer programs can generate new programs easier. The straightforward, simple syntax made this language structure a natural candidate for a printing protocol; if you want your printing protocol to be procedurally based, and to be a programming language as opposed to a static data structure.

Bob Sproull and William Newman at PARC developed a format, called Press Format, that consisted of static data structures. But they found that it wasn't the most flexible way to handle printing. To add a feature, you had to essentially rebuild the system with more features in it.

We felt it was really important for the printing protocol to be extensible. So if you need more features, you can use the machinery of the language itself to build the features, as opposed to designing them from the beginning. You can't predict what features you'll want in the future.

So Interpress was a good candidate for a printing protocol. Chuck and I tried to get Xerox to do something reasonable with Interpress for two years, but it became clear that in the process of getting it out to consumers, they were going to destroy it. They were going to add some features and take away other features that would make it not only difficult to implement but difficult to maintain, and difficult to educate people about. We felt that if we were on our own, we could create a product in a much more straightforward and reasonable way.

Essentially, we took the original, clean design and extended it in a number of ways to make it a practical language; then we went after printing. We chose printing because all the computer companies were trying to do printer products at that time and were dumping a lot of money into research and development to get laser printers to work. But they weren't having a great deal of success. Most of the products didn't adapt easily.

We felt that we could effectively market PostScript to the computer companies because it was device-independent. It avoided dependencies to a specific machine, so the computer companies had the flexibility to take on new technology without having to change software. We believed this would be perceived as a great value and easy to sell, and it has been. Whereas in the screen business you're competing against everybody else's screen package and you have operating-systems considerations; this was a nice, clean, separate piece of business without a lot of the hassle.

> *"My saving grace in life is that I was not introduced to computers at an early age."*

INTERVIEWER: *In what direction is the PostScript language still evolving?*

WARNOCK: Well, for the printing application, it probably has slowed down to a crawl. Now I think it makes sense to go into the screen world and give work stations the model that the printer has. There we must adapt it considerably, because of the different requirements of the screen. The requirements are very high-speed activity for certain kinds of garbage-collecting operations, and the memory-management tasks aren't necessarily part of the printer world. We're writing that code and it's evolving in that direction.

INTERVIEWER: *Do you still write code?*

WARNOCK: Oh, absolutely, almost every day. It has a great intellectual value; it's fun.

INTERVIEWER: *What kind of code do you write now?*

WARNOCK: Mostly PostScript code; just making a more elaborate page than the last time, or some little utility function. I don't do any of the serious system code around here.

I get involved a lot in the design aspects and things like that, and the general philosophy and direction, and how things should be done, but I don't actually sit down and put pen to paper. We have people who are a lot better at it than I am; it's much easier to get their brains to work together with mine.

INTERVIEWER: *Is it easier for you to write good code today than it was back ten or twenty years ago?*

WARNOCK: The tools are better. The programming environments are better. The languages are more expressive. Computers are much more powerful now than ten or twenty years ago. But there are more options available, which also means more options for many more mistakes.

INTERVIEWER: *But doesn't all of your experience make it a lot easier?*

WARNOCK: Oh yes. It's a trade-off—all of the experience for the vitality I had when I was younger. As I get older, perhaps I don't take as many false steps, but I don't have the strength to get up and run as hard as I used to.

INTERVIEWER: *Do you approach writing code differently today? Do you have a different method? Do you plan everything out beforehand?*

WARNOCK: I think a lot before I do anything, and once I do something, I'm not afraid to throw it away. It's very important that a programmer be able to look at a piece of code like a bad chapter of a book and scrap it without looking back. Never get too enamored with one idea, never hang onto anything tenaciously without being able to throw it away when necessary; that should be the programmer's attitude.

Also, never make an assumption that you know something somebody else doesn't know. There will always be some smart guy who will come along and figure out a better algorithm, or figure out an easier way of performing some task. One of the tricks of the trade is to recognize this early, adopt it quickly, and exploit it without having a "not-invented-here" hangup about doing it your way.

INTERVIEWER: *What makes for a good program?*

WARNOCK: When you run a performance check on a good program, the performance looks flat. This tells you there are no bottlenecks in the code. The balance of the program makes it good. It's not one particular clever trick.

I've been in the business since 1963, so I've been writing programs for more than twenty years. With lots of experience you collect hundreds of algorithms over the years; you remember tricks you've learned, you remember bugs you've had, and blind alleys you've gone down. You remember all the things you've done wrong and all the things that have worked out well. It's a matter of picking and choosing from that smorgasbord to make a good menu, so to speak, to do a given task. You can have a great dish here and a great dish there, but together they may taste like dog food. Putting a meal together in a very delicate and sophisticated way is what makes a good cook. Putting the pieces of a program together in the same way is what makes a good computer programmer.

INTERVIEWER: *How do you discern a good programmer from an ordinary programmer?*

WARNOCK: It's hard. The interview process normally doesn't distinguish the good programmers from the bad ones. It's like hiring a writer. You can't tell how well someone writes simply from an interview. But if the person has written a number of prize-winning novels, you have a much better understanding of their talent. So we hire most of our people through the grapevine. When you've been in the business a long time, you get to know a lot of the people. You can pretty much find who you're looking for by their reputation in the industry.

INTERVIEWER: *There aren't any set rules?*

WARNOCK: I have never figured out any. The range of personalities and different kinds of talent in this business are just enormous. Some people are really good at certain kinds of programming and some people are good at other kinds. It's like writing comedy versus writing a serious dramatic novel.

INTERVIEWER: *When did you get interested in computers and computer programming?*

WARNOCK: I had planned on becoming a college professor and teaching mathematics. In 1963, near the end of my graduate studies, I was looking for a summer job. It was late to be looking and the only summer job I could find was recapping tires for Firestone. Working there was hot, dirty, and incredibly noisy. After just three weeks, I said, "I have a master's degree in mathematics; I don't need this."

I went to the local IBM office and applied for a job. They put me through all of their tests and then made me an offer for more money than I had ever heard of. IBM sent me to Seattle and Los Angeles for training to become a systems engineer. Then IBM gave me the two largest accounts in the Salt Lake district.

After a while I decided to leave IBM and go back to school at the University of Utah to get my doctorate in mathematics. Then I got married and needed a real job to support myself, so I worked at the computer center at the university. And that's what led me into the computer-science field.

INTERVIEWER: *If you had your education to do over again, would you concentrate in mathematics or computer science?*

WARNOCK: Oh, I've always liked mathematics; problem solving has always been fun. My saving grace in life is that I was not introduced to computers at an early age.

INTERVIEWER: *Why wouldn't it help to learn about computers earlier?*

WARNOCK: I went through the university, all the way to the master's level, so I got a good, solid liberal education. I believe it's really important to have a very solid foundation in mathematics, English, and the basic sciences. Then, when you become a graduate student, it's okay to learn as much as you can about computers.

If you really want to be successful, being acculturated to the rest of the society and then going into computers is a much more reasonable way to approach the problem. I like computers because they let you realize things that you can only put on paper in mathematics. You get a tangible result. And debugging programs, actually getting them to work, is fascinating. You can finally give the machine a set of parameters and have it come out with the correct answers.

It's just great fun; it's very satisfying, sort of like mountain climbing. It's like a lot of activities in life: When you're successful at it and you finally get it to work right, it feels good and you get a big kick out of it.

INTERVIEWER: *When you were working at PARC, did you ever think you would have a business like the one you have today?*

WARNOCK: No. Starting the business was interesting. When we first thought about it, we thought about what the world could probably use and we concluded that we ought go into the service business. We could build electronic printers that personal computers could dial up to do the printing. Then we went to Hambrecht and Quist for venture capital, but they said the service business was no good. The service business is something venture capital people won't talk to you about. It's very specialized financially, and the only way you make money is through franchising it. That's really hard unless you're gifted at franchising, and we weren't.

"Society is totally dependent upon technology today, and I don't see any reason why that will ever change."

We decided we needed a more traditional business plan. We came up with creating a work station with document-preparation software, hooking laser printers and typesetters to that, and selling documentation systems. This is the same sort of business plan as ViewTech, Interleaf, XYVision and Texet—the whole list. It's the same business plan that they've all had.

After three months of work and after talking with a couple of major

49

computer companies, we decided it was a silly business plan. We would have to build a marketing distribution channel and a light-manufacturing facility. Essentially we would have to build the whole business. And we obviously had no particular expertise in that domain.

We did have expertise at building a specialized piece of software in demand by computer companies. So we switched our business plan and became an OEM supplier of software. We wouldn't have to be in manufacturing, marketing, or distribution. And we could service the generalized computer community. It has turned out very well.

> *"As with most projects, the last two percent takes fifty percent of the time."*

INTERVIEWER: *In the future, do you see computers basically the same as they are today? Or do you see radical changes?*

WARNOCK: Considering the level of change over the past four or five years, I think it's enormously difficult to predict. Technological growth has been spectacular in this period. For instance, five years ago 64K chips were about all you had. And now we're talking about megabit chips, and CD ROMs. I don't see anything to indicate that the growth is going to slow down. Today no one can say what the next innovation is going to be. The information age is just a giant feedback loop; every new tool you get helps you build another tool that's much better. So if anything, the growth will probably be more explosive.

INTERVIEWER: *What role do you think computers will play in society in the future?*

WARNOCK: Computer literacy will have to become essential. People deal with computers every day and don't realize it. There will have to be a corresponding improvement in user interfaces, so that people can deal more effectively with machines; those go hand in hand. Society is totally dependent upon technology today, and I don't see any reason why that will ever change.

INTERVIEWER: *What do you think is going to happen to the publishing industry?*

WARNOCK: The publishing industry is adopting technological innovations much more rapidly than I expected. I thought this whole process would take years to mature, that it would come through a slow evolution into the use of electronic-publishing techniques. But it's happening at an unbelievable rate.

The heavy-duty publishers are accepting the technology immediately. The Knight-Ridder chain has many laser printers and Macintosh computers. The Gannett newspaper chain has purchased a lot of laser printers. The Hearst paper chain has bought some, and recently we heard that the Associated Press is sending PostScript programs across the wire. That's incredibly gratifying because it's been just a few months since the laser printers entered the market. I thought that kind of acceptance would take many more years as opposed to a few months.

Many businesses are now doing their own newsletters on Macintosh computers and LaserWriter printers instead of going to traditional typesetters. People are seeing the benefit of the new technology. The office market, the traditional word-processing market, is going to move fairly quickly to the laser printers for better quality.

INTERVIEWER: How long do you think it will be before the quality of output from laser printers will be comparable to typesetters?

WARNOCK: It will be a while. Certain physical properties of toner particles and other problems make it difficult to get very high resolution. Typesetters are inherently precise devices that expose very clean edges, and it's very hard to reproduce that.

Xerography has a basic toner particle-size problem to deal with. It works with little spots of charge, so it's a matter of how small the charge units can be and still attract toner. The quality is good now, but if you compare pages done with typesetting and xerography under a magnifying glass, you can see that xerography can't compare yet. Maybe some of the thermal technologies and ink-jet technologies will succeed before xerography.

Typesetters will get cheaper, and the quality of xerography will get better. Xerography will also get cheaper. You will see laser printers in the $2,000 range in a couple of years. I think typewriters using fixed-pitch fonts will be replaced by high-quality typefaces—at least that's what I hope.

INTERVIEWER: What's the secret of success in this industry?

WARNOCK: To be successful, you want to surround yourself with very talented folks whose skills blend very well. That's the secret of success.

INTERVIEWER: What is your approach to programming?

WARNOCK: I don't know if there's a single set of things. I've touched on some. Don't bind early; don't ever make decisions earlier than you have to. Stay an order of magnitude more general than you think you need, because you will end up needing it in the long term. Get something working very quickly and then be able to throw it away.

Learn from small experiments rather than large ones. Don't go into a two-year development with nothing coming out in the middle. Have something come out every two months, so you can evaluate, regroup, and restart.

Often programmers overdefine their approach from the beginning. They may start out with a central idea and begin coding on day one. Then they find that they have a concentric-ring approach where everything starts to grow because of the dependency on so many other factors. But if you keep the process fairly loose and free and move quickly at the end, you get a much better product in the long term.

INTERVIEWER: *Why do you think you're in software instead of hardware?*

WARNOCK: It's probably the mathematician in me; I prefer the abstract. I would rather play with ideas and combinations of ideas than combinations of objects. I was never very mechanical.

INTERVIEWER: *What do you like about writing software?*

WARNOCK: It's always challenging. I look at software writing like authorship, like normal writing. You're trying to combine ideas and concepts in a way that will make other people think, that will be new and exciting. The software business is like the publishing business. You're trading ideas; that's your commodity. I like it because I'm moderately good at it and I've had success in thinking of some new ideas along the line. That's a great kick.

INTERVIEWER: *What would you pinpoint as the new ideas you've thought of for software?*

WARNOCK: The most obvious is the original hidden-line work I did at Utah. It was fairly original at the time, and a lot of programs have been built on top of it. I really get a kick out of solving something that looks hard, and making it look easy. That was Ivan Sutherland's great claim to fame. He could dissect any problem, pull it apart, and make it look easy. He was very good at that kind of work.

I also enjoy having people use the things I create. I was very frustrated at Xerox because I'd see great products coming out in the marketplace and I knew that I could do the same thing. Now, to pick up a magazine and leaf through it and see pictures and advertisements done on a LaserWriter is a great kick. I really enjoy seeing other people use the fruits of my labor. That's the ultimate satisfaction.

INTERVIEWER: What's your work routine? Do you work mostly at your office or home?

WARNOCK: I do work at home, but I also work at the office and travel a lot. I talk to customers and I speak at conferences. Right now my function is a combination of doing some inside work and a lot of outside work.

INTERVIEWER: Has owning your own business changed your life in a significant way?

WARNOCK: Yes. In the first year and a half I worked almost totally on development, getting everything to work. Now the project has gone into a marketing, public relations, and customer-support phase. Most of my daily activity is meeting people and dealing with corporations, talking to VPs within corporations and signing contracts. But it's all fun. It's a little different this year than it was last year, and last year was a little different from the year before. That's what life's all about.

INTERVIEWER: How many people were working on PostScript during the development period?

WARNOCK: PostScript probably took twenty man-years to develop. It's a fairly substantial piece of code when you consider all the fonts. In the Laser-Writer, we blew half a megabyte of ROM, and none of it could be wrong. It's all cast in concrete, going out with every machine. I think that's one of the larger single pieces of code ever put into ROM. Getting the testing done was a shaky period around here.

INTERVIEWER: What was the biggest problem faced in the development of PostScript?

WARNOCK: As with most projects, the last 2 percent takes 50 percent of the time. Getting the code to completely hold together took a while. Then you have to be sure you can exercise it by all the communication protocols, that you can have all the interrupts and everything, and that it doesn't break.

INTERVIEWER: Do you prefer any language in general?

WARNOCK: People around here are experienced enough so they don't necessarily prefer one thing over another. We use whatever has the most reasonable environment and set of compilers; those are the considerations. Computer languages are computer languages. Once you've learned a half dozen, the next half dozen aren't very hard to learn.

INTERVIEWER: Why do you think there are so few languages being used by designers today?

53

WARNOCK: There's no motivation to have a great variety. Some people take certain design lines, as Mesa took a particular design line. But they felt that the problem was getting thirty or forty programmers to write a huge system together, so it was designed to aid in that process. If you believe good software is written that way, that might be a language you would design. But I believe good software is written by small teams of two, three, or four people interacting with each other at a very high, dense level. The best pieces of code come out of those kinds of effort. I would try to make the system so it would be impossible to get twenty people involved.

INTERVIEWER: Is that because there are too many different ideas? Or too many ways of approaching a design?

WARNOCK: There are too many styles and interfaces. I once heard that any programs you write reflect the organization in which you work. At PARC, the Computer Sciences Laboratory was an incredibly flat structure with Bob Taylor at the top. But they had to have a common tool for this diverse group, because there were about thirty people designing this one, huge, programming system. So Mesa and its programming environment modeled the way PARC worked.

Adobe was started as a very small company with about a half dozen people. The code was written by a half dozen people and the structure shows it. Certain parts belong to person X and certain parts belong to person Y, and they all have their own character and their own interfaces. On the other hand, IBM is a huge organization and their code is convoluted, with self feedbacks and different strategies that reflect separate divisions of the company. A fairly standard rule is that if you want to keep something simple, then the organization that develops it has to be simple.

INTERVIEWER: What happens when little companies grow up into huge corporations?

WARNOCK: The trick is to learn from the Hewlett-Packard approach: Keep it as twenty different, small companies. Keep breaking it up and never let it become a huge organization, except at some level that nobody cares about. In terms of working relationships, keep the number of people small and their focus localized, project-oriented, so they can work at their best. That would be my goal.

INTERVIEWER: Before computers, what did mathematicians do?

WARNOCK: A lot of mathematics! Actually, I really don't know whether mathematics is as good as it was ten years ago. There probably has been a huge drain on the number of mathematicians in the world. It seems that some of the early theory, the best theoretical work on computers, was done in the fifties. The best mathematics of computation was done before the advent of computers. Mathematicians laid much of the groundwork of what could and couldn't be done in computers. I don't know if there is any good theoretical work in computing being done now. I guess there is, but there are none of the huge, major breakthroughs that occurred earlier.

INTERVIEWER: *Do you consider computer science a science?*

WARNOCK: No, not really. It's more of an engineering discipline; a very good, fruitful engineering discipline. To me, science is postulating hypotheses and doing experiments to create models in the world. Computers have nothing to do with that. They are self-fulfilling prophecies about a model of the world. They're great information tools; they're great artifacts of the society for manipulating and controlling information. But I don't know what truth computer science is trying to learn.

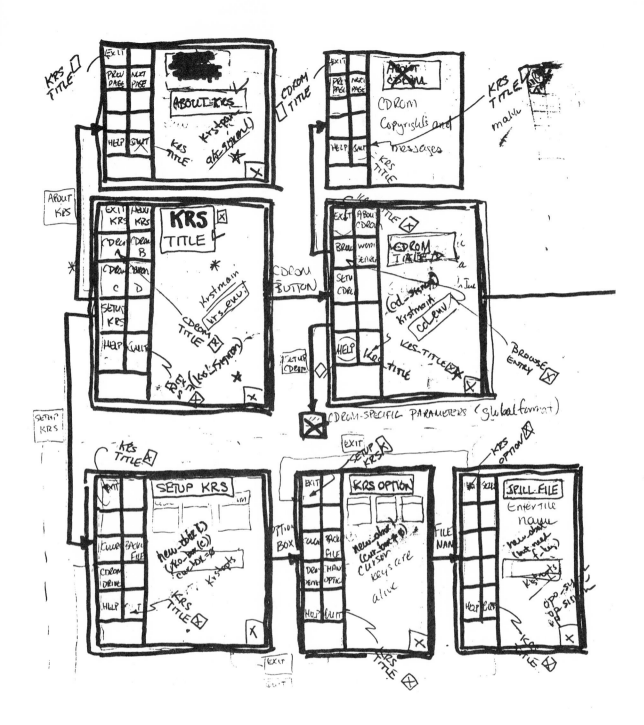

Gary Kildall made this sketch during development of the Knowledge Retrieval System to provide a graphic picture of the menu tree design. The Appendix (pages 370-371) shows more details of this menu.

Gary Kildall

AS THE *founder and chairman of the board of Digital Research, Gary A. Kildall developed the first operating system for a microcomputer during 1972 and 1973. He called it the CP/M (Control Program/Monitor) operating system and it became his company's first product. In addition, he designed the DR Logo programming language for the IBM PC and he developed PL/1, one of the first high-level languages for microcomputers.*

A native of Seattle, Kildall was born on May 19, 1942. He received his Ph.D. in computer science from the University of Washington in 1972. He then joined the Navy and taught computer science at the Naval Postgraduate School in Monterey, California, where he continued to teach after his discharge from the Navy.

In 1984 Kildall formed a new company called Activenture Corporation (recently renamed KnowledgeSet Corporation) to explore the potential of optical-disc publishing. In 1985, Activenture announced they would publish Grolier's Encyclopedia in a CD ROM format. Kildall retains the position of chairman of the board at Digital Research along with his position as president of KnowledgeSet Corporation.

We went to Digital Research on a Monday morning via Highway 1 along the California coastline. The scenery is some of the most spectacular in the country and the coastline is dotted with more resorts than computer-related businesses. Digital Research and KnowledgeSet, both started by Gary Kildall, are two of the few high-tech companies in the area. I couldn't help but wonder how one could coop oneself up in the characteristic dingy, dimly lit office to write source code, knowing that such stunning beauty was right outside the door. But Gary Kildall seems to have no difficulty devoting attention to his work, and appreciating the surroundings during his leisure time. Kildall likes to work and play equally hard. His "toys" include a new Lamborghini Countach, a Pitts aerobatic biplane, and a Rolls Royce.

Gary came to meet with us in a conference room around noon. He is tall, with red hair and a trim beard, and he was wearing crisp new western-style blue jeans, a white cowboy snap shirt, and boots. Having just come from a weekend in Tahoe where, he confessed, he ate too much, he ordered a Diet Pepsi while the rest of us called for sandwiches. And with that, Gary, in his reserved and calculated manner, discussed programming with great seriousness and passion. In fact, we had pulled him away from writing source code for his latest CD ROM encyclopedia project in order to do the interview. One reason he had started KnowledgeSet was so that he could get back to the nuts and bolts of programming, away from the management demands of his first company, Digital Research, which has grown so large. Gary often turned to the white board to draw diagrams or illustrate important points as he explained the meticulous, creative process he goes through to write code that makes computers perform.

INTERVIEWER: You taught at the Naval Postgraduate School. If you were to go back and teach again, would you teach any differently?

KILDALL: Probably not, because I don't program any differently now than when I was teaching. I would teach the course I enjoyed most, the data-structures course. It goes back to the fundamentals of programming: simplifying the problem. Part of the programming process is general problem solving. How do you solve a problem that's complex, whether it's designing a computer program or constructing a building? You start at the point where you think it's too hard to solve, and then you break it down into smaller pieces. That's what I try to teach.

INTERVIEWER: *It's difficult to teach problem-solving principles. How did you go about it?*

KILDALL: On the first day in a particular data-structures class, I said, "We're going to have a little test. Put your books on the floor and get a piece of paper. I want you to write a program that will symbolically solve differential equations. Given a polynomial, the program should differentiate the polynomial and produce the symbolic, not numeric, result." So the students started writing away, thinking, and scratching their heads. This went on for about ten minutes, then I told everyone to stop. I asked them to think about how they approached solving that problem. What tools were they using? Were they starting to write a program? Were they thinking about mathematics? Were they starting to write little examples down? That whole quarter we worked with the techniques and tools of problem solving. Then, in the final exam, I gave them the same problem I had given them to solve on the very first day.

> *"It's fun sitting at a terminal and letting the code flow."*

INTERVIEWER: *What were the most important principles your students had learned when they completed your classes?*

KILDALL: I taught two things that are important for students to learn: problem solving and how to study. Knowing how to study takes care of getting through tests and leads to other school-survival skills. And if you learn how to solve problems, you can go through life and do pretty well.

INTERVIEWER: *How would you characterize your own particular style of writing programs?*

KILDALL: I follow very definite procedures which work for me, though they may not work for other people. I start with drawing the data structures, and I spend a lot of time thinking about them. I also think about what the program has to go through before I start writing code.

Programs are like mechanical devices; the way one piece of code works with another is very similar to the way one gear meshes with another gear. Building code is a little like building a transmission. The PL/1 compiler I wrote a few years back is a good example. People said it was impossible to write a compiler on a microcomputer, but after a couple years of work, it was considered one of the best optimizing compilers around.

Once the data structures are developed, I start writing small chunks of code that I improve and monitor along the way. Checking them as I go assures me that the changes I make are localized; and if I have problems, I discover them immediately. This whole process of iterative improvement requires speed, so for me at least, it's very important to have fast edit, execute, and debug cycles. This method doesn't work as well on a mainframe or a card-batch system because you can't make small changes and check them out.

INTERVIEWER: Do you prefer to work in an interpretive environment?

KILDALL: No, I don't like existing interpreters very much. I'd like to have one for a systems language like C that would parallel an existing compiler, but it's still questionable how well that would work, because most systems programs are performance-oriented or timing-dependent. If I had a very effective interpreter—something like I used when I developed PL/M, or now maybe C—an interpreter might be worthwhile using.

INTERVIEWER: How did you get interested in programming?

KILDALL: I originally planned to be a high school math teacher, and started taking math courses at the University of Washington. But a friend of mine had this FORTRAN statement card, showed it to me, and told me it was going to be a really big thing. I became so intrigued I had to get into it. So I took an assembly-language programming course and FORTRAN right after that, and I was hooked. I found I liked programming for the same reasons I liked to build models, cars, and things of that sort. I found constructing a program to be a similar experience.

INTERVIEWER: Do you remember the first program you wrote?

KILDALL: Yes. It calculated the number of seconds between any two times of the day and any two calendar dates. That program is still around; every time I clean my desk I find it, like old clothes I find in my closet.

INTERVIEWER: What about the first professional program you wrote?

KILDALL: I wrote it at the navigation school my father owned. We used to prepare tide tables by hand for one of the local publishing companies in Seattle. I wrote a FORTRAN program that calculated the tides. It was the first program I made money on—$500 or so.

INTERVIEWER: So how did you happen to begin working on the CP/M operating system?

KILDALL: The operating system was actually just a little fragment of a very large project. I was working with XPL, a language for mainframe computers, written by Bill McKeeman at Stanford. I developed a similar language called PL/M, a programming language for microcomputers. I was trying to get PL/M to run resident on the 8080 microprocessor, and I had to write an interface to communicate with a disk drive. It turned out that the operating system, which was called CP/M for Control Program for Micros, was useful too, fortunately.

INTERVIEWER: So when you were developing CP/M you had no idea it would be so successful?

KILDALL: No, I didn't know CP/M would be such a hit, but it was very clear to me that floppy disks would be. I had been working with paper tapes for a year and a half. A floppy-disk drive was $500 and a paper-tape reader with a fancy punch was over $2,000. Just by looking at the cost comparision of the two drives, I realized the floppy disk would be a commercial success.

INTERVIEWER: Some programmers throw out code and start over when they run into extremely serious problems with their code. Do you ever do that?

KILDALL: No, because my problems never get serious enough to start over. I never would have been coding if I didn't think I had the right data structure. Whenever I tear code apart, it is usually because the underlying data structures weren't any good, not because of the algorithms I applied.

INTERVIEWER: Do you use comments when you write code?

KILDALL: Rarely, except at the beginning of procedures, and then I only comment on the data structure. I don't comment on the code itself because I feel that properly written code is very much self-documented. Once I get the algorithms down, I start writing code directly on the machine. I don't even write it on a piece of paper before it goes into the computer; it just doesn't seem necessary. The actual coding process has always been a little scary for me because I don't know if I'm writing the right code, nor do I know what I'll write next. It just seems to come out. Sometimes I realize the code's not exactly right, but I also realize intuitively that it will relate to something else—it will factor out and become right even if I don't know exactly how at the time I'm writing it.

The magical part is that, at some point, all at once the whole thing comes together. It's like taking a logical Boolean expression that simplifies and simplifies until, bam, you've got it. When I reach the point where the code coalesces, I'm certain the program will work, and I also have no doubt I did it about the best way it could be done. I don't completely understand the process, but it sure seems to work for me, even when I make fairly massive changes to data structures and algorithms.

INTERVIEWER: *Is writing code always an unknown and difficult process?*

KILDALL: No. When I code without pressure to meet a deadline, it's very relaxing. Sometimes when I'm scheduled for a long plane ride, I'll take a little portable along and code just for fun. In fact, even when there's a deadline, it's fun to sit at a terminal and let the code flow. It sounds strange, but it just comes out of my brain; once I'm started, I don't have to think about it.

INTERVIEWER: *Have you ever been unable to get the code to work just the way you envision?*

> *"The only time I don't want to come back is when the code explodes."*

KILDALL: There are very few cases where someone has gone into my code and said, "We could have done it a lot better," but there are times when it just doesn't come together. The editor in the DR Logo interpreter is a good example. I had some pieces of code I knew were not quite right—it worked fine but hadn't factored out correctly and just wasn't right. The engineers who took over the code zeroed in on that piece of programming, but we didn't have time to make changes because we had to get the product out. That's the kind of thing you hope never happens, but it does sometimes, so you go back and fix it, and learn something about your style.

INTERVIEWER: *Do you think programming is something you can practice as you would practice the piano?*

KILDALL: Well, you can practice in a sense. Seymour Papert has this notion that kids learn to be inventive by tinkering with gears and other mechanical gadgets. The skills you learn and practice with this kind of play carry over into other areas. Papert is certainly talking about my childhood experience. My father was a great craftsman. I used to stay and watch him by the hour, and then I would go outside and try to imitate him with my own hammer and nails.

Data structures, which are the foundations of programs, are mechanical by nature, like the things I played with as a kid. So, in that sense, I practiced programming. The big difference is that building something out of wood or steel takes hours of labor; if you don't do it right, you have to go back and rebuild. Programs can be altered instantly.

INTERVIEWER: *How else can you build your repertoire as a programmer?*

KILDALL: You need to study other people's work. Their approaches to problem solving and the tools they use give you a fresh way to look at your own work. You need to learn only a small set of procedures before you can write a program. For example, when you're writing compilers, the first thing you write is a scanner, which is a little tool you use a lot. Once you learn those tools, it becomes a matter of putting pieces together. You grab pieces from here and there and stick them all together. Looking at programs others have written gives you new ideas for constructing coherent code. That's why, as a teacher, I spent a lot of time with students showing them clean algorithms I had picked up.

INTERVIEWER: *You've talked about how you taught others. Has anyone or anything influenced your style of programming?*

KILDALL: I'm very pragmatic. I like to build programs that are fast and small, and use clear, concise algorithms. I learned that style from the early Burroughs 5500, a very advanced machine for the day, which was based upon the ALGOL philosophy of block-structured languages. The ALGOL compiler was probably one of the nicest pieces of code to come out at that time. I spent hours trying to fix and change the compiler. Working with it so closely affected the way I think about programming and had a profound influence on my style. Fortunately, the ALGOL philosophy became the basis for design of popular languages like Pascal and C, so the style works for me.

INTERVIEWER: *One hears stories about the crazy hours programmers keep. How about you? Do you have a certain routine?*

KILDALL: My pace varies during the development of the program. At some points, the code gets explosive and I have everything inside my brain at one time: all the variable names and how they relate to one another, where the pointers start and where they end, disk access, et cetera. All sorts of things go on in my brain that I can't put on paper simply because I'm always changing them. I'd spend more time writing than I would coding, and I'd never get the project done in a reasonable amount of time.

When the data structures are so new, they require intense concentration to keep them organized in your head. So at this point in the process, I'll usually start at 3:00 a.m. and work until maybe 6:00 p.m. Then I'll have dinner, go to bed early, get up again pretty early in the morning, and keep banging on it until things are calmer.

During the calm times, when my pace is more relaxed, I come up with solutions for the next phase. When I'm trying to solve a problem that has a series of steps, I take them in order, one at a time—step A, step B, then step C.

I've tried, but I just can't work on C until B has been Completed.

I take short vacations during the lulls because I like to enjoy life, too. That's the time I go out and fly airplanes just to get away. It's good for my work, because I always come back with some fresh ideas.

INTERVIEWER: Does your flying airplanes have any other impact on your programming?

KILDALL: I certainly hope my program planning is better than my flying. I've heard that quite a few programmers are also fliers. I know Charles Simonyi flies a helicopter. And both Fred Gibbons and Vern Rayburn were very interested in flying.

Programmers like flying a plane because it is a mechanical process just like programming. Also, people who like computers like gadgets, and airplanes are just loaded with gadgets. They've got all the dials and wheels and knobs you could ever want to play with. You get to play a little dangerously because it's the real thing, not just a video game. Computers are very abstract, but airplanes are real.

INTERVIEWER: Do you ever get tired of programming?

KILDALL: I don't think of my work as tedious, if that's what you mean. When I go on vacation I look forward to returning to work. The only time I don't want to come back is when the code explodes. Then it becomes tough because I'm working under pressure to get the code back together. When you've got the code all ripped apart, it's like a car that's all disassembled. You've got all the parts lying all over your garage and you have to replace the broken part or the car will never run. It's not fun until the code gets back to the baseline again.

INTERVIEWER: Do you find anything aesthetically pleasing in your work?

KILDALL: Oh, absolutely. When a program is clean and neat, nicely structured, and consistent, it can be beautiful. I guess I wouldn't compare a program with the Mona Lisa, but it does have a simplicity and elegance that's quite handsome. Stylistic distinctions of different programs are intriguing, very much like the differences art critics might see between Leonardo's Mona Lisa and a Van Gogh. I like the LISP programming language so much because it's so pleasing. There's a concise form of LISP called the M expressions. When you write an algorithm using M expressions, it's so beautiful you almost feel it could be framed and hung on a wall.

When I was working on my Ph.D. thesis, I was trying to solve a difficult global flow analysis problem. I knew there had to be a solution, but I just couldn't crack it. Finally, when I got a clean mathematical model, I coded the algorithms in LISP. The program took only two hours to write, and it was beautiful; it did exactly what I wanted it to do. At that point, I had no direct proof the program worked, but every example I ran through LISP was functioning the way I expected. I wrote the same program in XPL, which is a systems language for running compilers. Later, when I got proof that the program was correct, I found it was based on the concepts of the very pretty LISP program, not the concepts developed in the relatively ugly XPL program.

INTERVIEWER: Do you consider programming to be an art or a science?

KILDALL: There certainly is some art in it. But a lot of programming is invention and engineering. It's much like a carpenter who has a mental picture of a cabinet he's trying to build. He has to wrestle with the design and construction to get it into a physical form. That's very much what I do in programming.

> *"When you've got the code all ripped apart, it's like a car that's all disassembled."*

Programming has some science as well, though not a lot. Experimental science means you hypothesize, try things, and compare results, and in that way programming is science. You may have a concept of how a retrieval system should work, but it's not until you run it with sufficient data that you can see the mechanism operating and get some statistics.

But remember, I'm in one special area of programming: compilers, operating systems, retrieval, and other system software. A programmer who specializes in graphics, for example, may have an entirely different view of the programming world. Because graphics programmers are dealing more with the physical world—talking about the way light sources affect objects, for instance—there may be a lot more mathematics and science involved in their work. You know, I also think programming is very much a religious experience for a lot of people.

INTERVIEWER: What do you mean when you say programming is a religious experience for a lot of people?

KILDALL: Well, if you talk about programming to a group of programmers who use the same language, they can become almost evangelistic about the language. They form a tight-knit community, hold to certain beliefs, and follow certain rules in their programming. It's like a church with a programming language for a Bible.

FORTH is a good example; it's a programming language that is probably close to being a religious experience for many people. When FORTH first came out, its disciples claimed any algorithm could be done ten times faster. That was a typical claim. If you argued that point or any other, you found yourself talking to a brick wall and you definitely weren't allowed in the church. Now I don't mean to be derogatory about the people who use that language. It's a very supportive group and a very effective language, but the discussions were not based on reason. They were based on belief. By saying this, I'll probably get about a thousand letters about FORTH and the religious experience people are having over it. But I'm not putting myself in a special category either; I can preach about the wonders of LISP all day.

INTERVIEWER: *What do you think will be the future role of computers?*

KILDALL: Basically, our technology tends to simplify mechanical processes. That's why computers have been so successful: We take things normally done with cogs, wheels, and relays, and do them with vacuum tubes and then with semiconductors. Look at automobiles, for example. More and more of the processes in the automobile, like in the 1984 Corvette, are being turned over to the semiconductor or its equivalent. When semiconductors take the place of speedometer cables and tachometers, they turn the car into a less expensive and more reliable product that is easier to produce. Computer systems are going through identical changes right now; the hard disk drive is a mechanical device. Because it is mechanical, we know it will eventually go away. We don't know how it will go away, but we know it's a prime target.

Some gadgets and processes will continue to function mechanically, such as wheel bearings on cars, because it's pretty hard to make those from a semiconductor. But many other things in our daily lives will go through the transition from mechanical to electronic. The print industry is a good example; CD ROMs and optical storage are becoming important there now. Computers help to get away from the mechanical processes of printing: running printing presses, laying out and pasting up by hand, setting up the cameras. The semiconductor will take over the mechanical process. But computers won't stop there. Right now they control the production of print but not the actual display of information.

Right now, a very big bottleneck—one of the reasons why the personal computer industry is in the doldrums—is that we have a difficult time thinking about what to do with computers once we get past spreadsheets and word processing. We don't know what the next step is. We're stuck.

It goes back to what I was saying about the dependence of programming on beliefs rather than reason. Ultimately the problem is that we, as a society, took the big computers that we understood and applied their underlying architecture, languages, and concepts to the development of microcomputers. As we move toward using computers as controllers, we will find that communication between processors will become more important than the processes they are carrying out. Then we will be forced to change the way we code. That will be a very slow evolutionary process.

INTERVIEWER: *So the future really depends on our ability to free ourselves from old patterns of thinking?*

KILDALL: I felt strongly in the early days of microprocessors that they should be used primarily as embedded processors, talking to one another and coordinating the transition from mechanical to electronic processes. That's where I felt the computer industry was going. I saw them as replacements for random logic, with engineers being the primary users of these small machines. In fact, someone from Lawrence Livermore Labs suggested I develop a BASIC for the microcomputer—that was probably in 1974. I told him that was the most stupid idea I had ever heard. Who would want to do a BASIC for microprocessors when they were being put into such tools as inventory-control systems, cathode-ray tube displays, and word processors? Obviously, I was wrong about that. It turns out that one of my thesis students, Gordon Eubanks, did very well with C BASIC, as did Paul Allen and Bill Gates.

Somehow we have to break loose from the ways we think about microcomputers if we want to stimulate advances in computers. People at home don't want to buy another computer system. They bought one and there was no real use for it. They don't want to be ripped off again. And we're talking about 95 percent, not 5 percent, of computer users. There are 16 million television sets sold every year; there's no reason why we shouldn't sell 16 million gizmos with embedded microprocessors.

INTERVIEWER: *You mentioned CD ROM a minute ago, and its potential impact on the printing industry. Will it have any other role in the evolution of computers?*

KILDALL: Optical storage will clearly pull the computer industry in a new direction. When we worked with floppy disks, we were just making little machines out of big machines. And we haven't yet gone a whole lot farther than that today.

Optical storage is completely different. We're not talking about computing anymore; we're talking about putting information into people's hands. People now might buy personal computers because somebody else told them they should, but with optical storage, people will buy computers because they want the information. Computers will be competing more with publishing.

> *"I also think programming is very much a religious experience for a lot of people."*

INTERVIEWER: *So information could take the form of an electronic encyclopedia, like the one you're putting on CD ROM? How do you envision the design—both the retrieval system and the enhancements?*

KILDALL: I take the concept for the initial product, get an overall idea of what I want to do, and start coding right from the nucleus, letting it expand in the direction it flows. As long as I don't limit the fundamental data structures, features can be added. We did a videodisc called the Knowledge Disc, which carried over nicely into CD ROM retrieval systems. All text was done with bit-mapped fonts at the pixel level. A very nice side effect of working with pixels is that pictures go into the whole thing very cleanly and nicely. So we don't have to go back and do total redesigns of anything to add images to text that already exists on the CD ROM.

It's a problem if the design doesn't let you add features at a later date. If you have to redo a program, the hours you spend can cause you to lose your competitive edge. A flexible program demonstrates the difference between a good designer and someone who is just getting a piece of code out.

Right now, we're going full speed ahead just to blast as many people out of the water as we possibly can. We're hoping to be ready by the first part of 1986. Economically, we have no choice but to go fast and to use this technology. It's the best. Then we make sure that we license the rights to it.

INTERVIEWER: *Are knowledge systems part of where you see the home market going?*

KILDALL: Yes. People don't usually go home to work. Some tasks people do at home are related to work, like keeping track of taxes or running a little home business. But mostly they go home to relax. I think games and entertainment are valuable. We have a lot of trouble figuring out how to entertain people at home. And TV does a good job right now; competing with "Dynasty" is extremely difficult.

One possible computer application is something to help kids study. My fourteen-year-old daughter is taking some hard courses and she needs help studying. Computer applications like that would give me a direct benefit: My child does better and that helps her in the future. That's clearly an important area for development.

Another area for development is providing general information about selected subjects, such as medicine. People go to doctors for many reasons. Some are psychological. But sometimes they only want medical information. It costs a lot to go to the doctor, and if people had less expensive ways to access that data, they would. Here's another example: When I want a car, I try and shop L.A., San Francisco, and San Jose to get the best prices. But it's virtually impossible to get the facts about car dealers because people who don't want you to be able to shop like that are protecting the information. I'd be a candidate for that information because it could save me thousands of dollars, not to mention a lot of time. I'd pay a reasonable amount to get it.

We want to develop applications that will give people a definite economic advantage if they buy them. That's why we went for an encyclopedia as the first CD ROM application. Everyone knows encyclopedias usually cost about $1,000. Someone can rationalize buying a computer that has the encyclopedia, if it's in the same price range as the printed encyclopedia.

INTERVIEWER: *How friendly will this machine be?*

KILDALL: Well, I don't think it's a matter of friendliness, because ultimately if the program is going to accomplish anything of value, it will probably be relatively complex.

Some people suggest that machines would be friendlier if input could be in a natural language. But natural language is probably the worst kind of input because it can be quite ambiguous. The process of retrieving information from the computer would be so time-consuming that you would be better off spending that time getting the information directly from an expert.

Expert systems will be the ultimate in user friendliness. But we're a long way from having the expert in the box. The doctor-in-a-box, although a phenomenal product, is incredibly complex. It would have to be perfect. Someday, we'll have programs like that. I just don't know how far off they are, and there are lots of problems to solve along the way, but that's the fun part.

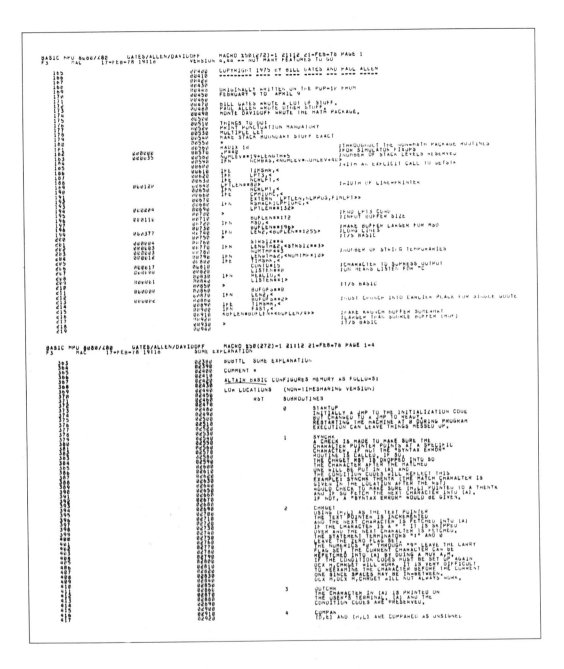

Excerpts from a listing of the source code for BASIC 8080, the first high-level language written for a microcomputer. Note writing credits in lines 172 to 174 and the reference to the MITS Altair computer in line 367. Refer to the Appendix (pages 348-356) for more excerpts from this program and other Altair programs.

Bill Gates

AS CHIEF executive officer of *Microsoft, William H. (Bill) Gates is considered one of the driving forces behind today's personal computing and office automation industry. Gates started his career in computer software at a young age. Both Gates and Microsoft co-founder, Paul Allen, worked as programming consultants while attending high school in Seattle, Washington. In 1974, Gates, then an undergraduate at Harvard University, worked with Allen to develop a BASIC programming language for the first commercial microcomputer, the MITS Altair. After the successful completion of this project, the two formed Microsoft to develop and market software for the emerging microcomputer marketplace.*

Microsoft has set standards for the software industry in languages, operating systems, and application software. Gates has provided the vision for the company's new product ideas and technologies. He also provides hands-on guidance to the technology groups that develop new products, devoting his time to reviewing and refining the software that Microsoft sells.

Gates is a native of the Seattle, Washington area and resides there today. He was born in 1955.

INTERVIEWER: *You obviously have a lot of responsibilities as chief executive officer of Microsoft. Do you still program?*

GATES: No, I don't. I still help design algorithms and basic approaches, and sometimes I look at code. But since I worked on the IBM PC BASIC and the Model 100, I haven't had a chance to actually create a program myself.

INTERVIEWER: *What kind of role do you play in the development of programs at Microsoft?*

GATES: I do two key things. One is to choose features to put into programs. To do that, you have to have a reasonable understanding of what's easy and what's not easy to do. You also have to understand what sort of product "family" strategy you're pursuing, and what's happening with the hardware.

I also work on the best way to implement that new feature, so that it will be small and fast. For example, I wrote a memo about how to design and implement a feature we used on Excel to make the program recalculate the formulas every time the screen changes.

In the first four years of the company, there was no Microsoft program that I wasn't involved in actually writing and designing. In all those initial products, whether it was BASIC, FORTRAN, BASIC 6800, or BASIC 6502, not a line of code went out that I didn't look over. But now we have about 160 programmers, so I mostly do reviews of products and algorithms.

INTERVIEWER: *What do you consider your greatest achievement ever in programming?*

GATES: I'd have to say BASIC for the 8080, because of the effect it's had, and because of how appropriate it was at the time, and because we managed to get it so small. It was the original program we wrote when we decided to start Microsoft.

Three of us knew that original program by heart. We got a chance to completely rewrite it one summer down in Albuquerque, and I thought we could save a few bytes and tighten things up. We just tuned the program very, very carefully, and ended up with a 4K BASIC interpreter.

When you know a program that well, you feel that nobody can look at the code and say, "There's a better way to do this." That feeling's really nice, and the fact that the program was used on a lot of machines makes it an exciting program to have written.

I also feel really good about the software on the Model 100, especially about how we squeezed in a very useful small editor. I worked with Jey Suzuki, a Japanese programmer, to put that together. We had very limited time to finish the project. When you do software that gets burned into ROM, you don't get an opportunity to make mistakes.

INTERVIEWER: What do you consider the most difficult part of computer programming?

GATES: The hardest part is deciding what the algorithms are, and then simplifying them as much as you can. It's difficult to get things down to their simplest forms. You have to simulate in your mind how the program's going to work, and you have to have a complete grasp of how the various pieces of the program work together. The finest pieces of software are those where one individual has a complete sense of exactly how the program works. To have that, you have to really love the program and concentrate on keeping it simple, to an incredible degree.

"The fact that people are getting exposed to computers at such young ages will change the thinking in the field."

INTERVIEWER: With computers increasing so much in power and memory, are programs becoming more complex, or just sloppier? How is that affecting the way people write programs?

GATES: We're no longer in the days where every program is super well crafted. But at the heart of the programs that make it to the top, you'll find that the key internal code was done by a few people who really knew what they were doing.

It's not quite as important now to squeeze things down into a 4K memory area. You're seeing a lot more cases where people can afford to use C, instead of using assembly language. Unfortunately, many programs are so big that there is no one individual who really knows all the pieces, and so the amount of code sharing you get isn't as great. Also, the opportunity to go back and really rewrite something isn't quite as great, because there's always a new set of features that you're adding on to the same program.

The worst programs are the ones where the programmers doing the original work don't lay a solid foundation, and then they're not involved in the program in the future. Working with those programs gets to the point that I call "experimental programming." The programmers understand so little about those programs that they can't understand how changes might affect speed, for instance. They might use code that already exists, or they might not understand what dependencies will break if they change something. So they add new code, and then they run it and they say, "Oh look, it doesn't work that way." That's a very, very inefficient way to deal with a program, but a lot of projects end up exactly like that.

INTERVIEWER: In a company like Microsoft, where you have 160 programmers, how do you go about creating an environment where you can develop successful programs?

GATES: One way is to have small project teams, typically four or five people, and one of those people has to have the proven ability to really absorb a program. And when that lead person is uncertain about something, he or she should be able discuss it with even more experienced programmers.

Part of our strategy is getting the programmers to think everything through before they go to the coding phase. Writing the design documents is crucial, because a lot of simplification comes when you see problems expressed as algorithms. They're kind of in the smallest form then, where you can see what the overlap is.

Another important element is code review, making sure that you look through the code and see if senior people can provide hints about how to do something better. And you have to review similar projects that have gone super, super well; programmers can look at how those other people performed previously, and get ideas from the other project about how to improve their own program.

INTERVIEWER: Where do the ideas for programs come from?

GATES: Well, there's no formal process, that's for sure. At Microsoft, there's usually a brainstorming session at night or on the weekends. Everybody has a general idea, like, we want to do the world's best word processor. And we want it to allow a technical publications department to do everything they want to do. We'll sit and talk. Well, how could we make it really fast? Could we put a drawing capability in, or could we do kerning without making the program super slow? A variety of problems will get talked through and some neat ideas will come up.

INTERVIEWER: Basically it's a group effort?

GATES: In terms of deciding what programs are going to do, a fairly large group makes suggestions. Then there's a filtering process. Eventually I'll decide which of the ideas makes sense, and I'll make sure we have champions who are personally involved in making that product succeed. We decide to do very, very few projects because it takes incredible focusing on a lot of resources to get a product out there and set a new world-class standard.

INTERVIEWER: *There's a lot of talk about how large software companies find it difficult to attract talented people who can produce great software, because these mavericks are so independent that they want to work on their own. How do you attract and keep good people at Microsoft?*

GATES: Great programmers are critical to create software products. But we don't believe in a prima donna approach, where just because somebody's good we let him not comment his code, or not communicate with other people, or impose his beliefs on everyone else.

We want people who really respect each other. I think most great programmers like to be around other great programmers. When they think up an incredible algorithm, they like having peers who can appreciate the cleverness that went into it, because when you're creating something like that and you have that model in your mind, it's a lonely thing. If you thought a process had to be complicated, and then you figure out a way to make it simpler, that makes you feel great. But you want to get some feedback from other people. Once you get a few great people, then others come.

The old rule used to be that a manager of a programmer was always a better programmer, and there were no what we called "technical inversions," where a programmer works for somebody who doesn't know how to program. We still follow that philosophy: At certain levels we've got business managers, but we don't have non-programmers really managing programming projects.

INTERVIEWER: *Do you think there are any particular rules for creating a good program?*

GATES: Some people just jump in and start coding, and others think it all through before they sit down, but I think you'd find that the programmers who sit down and code at the beginning are only using that as a scratch pad. It's what's going on in their heads that's most important.

You've got to have somebody who's super smart. A great programmer thinks about the program on a constant basis, whether driving or eating. That method takes an incredible amount of mental energy.

INTERVIEWER: How would you describe your style of programming?

GATES: I like to think the whole program through at a design level before I sit down and write any of the code. And once I write the code, I like to go back and rewrite it entirely one time.

The most important part of writing a program is designing the data structures. The second most important part is breaking the various code pieces down. Until you really get in there and write it out, you don't have the keenest sense of what the common subroutines should be.

> *"Within the next five years we'll have tools that will be able to do as good a job as a human programmer."*

The really great programs I've written have all been ones that I have thought about for a huge amount of time before I ever wrote them. I wrote a BASIC interpreter for a minicomputer in high school. I made massive mistakes in that program, and then I got to look at some other BASIC interpreters. So by the time I sat down to do Microsoft BASIC in 1975, it wasn't a question of whether I could write the program, but rather a question of whether I could squeeze it into 4K and make it super fast. I was on edge the whole time thinking, "Will this thing be fast enough? Will somebody come along and do it faster?"

I have an image in my head of this person named Norton that I met at TRW. He always showed me when I wasn't doing super well. So if I'm sloppy or lazy, I always imagine that he's going to walk up, look at the program, and tell me, "Look, here's a better way to do that." Little inefficiencies can slip into the program along the way, and if you want to really feel good about it, you've got to maintain the thought that you're not going to let that stuff creep in. That's why it's kind of painful sometimes if you have somebody else working on the project. They never code stuff exactly the way you like to see it coded. I remember when we were working on BASIC, I'd go back and recode other people's sections of code, without making any dramatic improvement. That bothers people when you go in and do that, but sometimes you just feel like you have to do it.

INTERVIEWER: When you were working with a group, were you always the design lead?

GATES: Yeah, on all the programs I've been directly involved with, I was the design lead. On the original BASIC, I scribbled out the design on pieces of paper. Paul Allen, who is a co-author, designed an implemented all the development tools.

Before I sit down to code something, most of the instructions have already run through my head. It's not all laid out perfectly, and I do find myself making changes, but all the good ideas have occurred to me before I actually write the program. And if there is a bug in the thing, I feel pretty bad, because if there's one bug, it says your mental simulation is imperfect. And once your mental simulation is imperfect, there might be thousands of bugs in the program. I really hate it when I watch some people program and I don't see them thinking.

One of the most fun programming experiences I ever had was when we were doing BASIC. I had done the 8080 BASIC, and then I had about two weeks allocated to work with Mark Chamberlain on the 6809 version of BASIC. I read the instruction set at the start of those two weeks, and I wrote about three or four programs. And I looked at some other programs to see how people used the instruction set. It was great fun to take a problem I understood and map it onto this new instruction set, and see how tightly we could put the thing together.

Programs today get very fat; the enhancements tend to slow the program down because people put in special checks. When they want to add some feature, they'll just stick in these checks without thinking about how they might slow the thing down. You have to have a programmer who knows the program inside out to guard against that. In the case of our BASIC, after I and the other original people moved away from it, we went through a period of about three years when we didn't do anything innovative. It's only in the last year and a half that we've gotten people in who feel total ownership and total understanding of our BASIC and can say, "Oh, yeah, putting subroutines in and getting rid of line numbers is easy." We've always had those goals, but until you've got that person who knows how to go into the middle of the parts or the statement analyzer and not just tack things on, you don't feel comfortable fiddling with it.

It's true that we're going to allow programs to be a little fatter than they have been. But in terms of speed, it's just laziness not to allow something to be as fast as possible, because users, even though they might not be able to say so explicitly, notice programs that are really, really fast. In the most successful programs, the speed of execution is just wonderful.

INTERVIEWER: How do you decide on the trade-offs between speed and performance?

GATES: Sometimes it's a trade-off between adding features and executing really fast, but there are ways of having lots and lots of features and still making things fast. Basically you want to decide what the common cases are in a program, and make sure that they go straight through, that they don't get bogged down with all these special case checks. If your main interactive loop has all sorts of checks in it, then your program is going to be slower than somebody else's.

INTERVIEWER: When you come up with an idea to do the greatest word processor in the world, what do you do? How do you design it? Do you look at all the other word processors that are out there?

GATES: Yeah, feature-wise, you look at all the other word processors out there and you say, "Does anybody do kerning on the screen, or do they show you exactly what the printed page is going to look like? How fast do they do it?" Usually, at the top of the product line, there's somebody who took very, very expensive hardware and used brute force to solve a problem. We can't do that; the computer we're working with has very finite speed. A lot of things we do have been done on more powerful computers; we're just trying to make it reasonable to do them on the machine that there are millions of.

You can do an amazing number of tricks inside of a product. You build up your feature list at the same time you're trying to answer the question, "Why will our algorithms be better than anybody else's?" Features are kind of crummy in a way, because the more features you have, the bigger the manual is. And features are only beneficial if people take the time to use them, whereas speed—if you can print the pages faster, or show it on the screen faster, or recalc it faster—that's worth an incredible amount. If you can give the users a few simple commands and make the program efficient enough to do what they want with those few commands, then you're much better off One sign of very good programs is that even internally they follow that philosophy of simplicity. If they want to do something complex, they call the code with simple operations internally, rather than doing the complex operation from scratch.

INTERVIEWER: How important is the end user? How do you know what the database manager out there really needs or wants in his database or in his spreadsheet?

GATES: Well, some programmers don't pretend to have any intuition for exactly what end users want, and they're still world-class programmers. But that knowledge of the market is important, especially in the applications group, so we have full-time people who just show customers the code, or look at other specifications, and things of that nature. When Microsoft first started, we did only systems programs. We knew what programmers wanted, because we're programmers. So we wrote BASIC.

INTERVIEWER: What was the most innovative aspect of BASIC?

GATES: The way we allowed the person to get at the full power of the machine. We put in PEEK and POKE, where you can read and write the machine status. We put in tracing routines called TRON and TROFF. We still let the users, even though they were up in this high-level language, get at all the crazy little things they might want to add onto the machine. And they can understand how memory is used without BASIC. We let them feel like they are in control of their machines.

> *"If you ever talk to a great programmer, you'll find he knows his tools like an artist knows his paintbrushes."*

To fit BASIC into 4K, we used a scheme called a single-representation interpreter. It was a very good choice. I'd never seen an interpreter done that way before. It was kind of risky to do it that way, but I felt incredible confidence in the scheme. I'd run it through in my head and felt good about it.

INTERVIEWER: When you were writing it, did you have any idea it would be as successful as it was?

GATES: No, no way. Paul Allen had brought me the magazine with the Altair on it, and we thought, "Geez, we'd better get going, because we know these machines are going to be popular." And that's when I stopped going to classes and we just worked around the clock. The initial program was written in about three and a half weeks. We ended up spending about eight weeks before I had it fully polished the way that I really liked it. And then I later went back and rewrote it.

No great programmer is sitting there saying, "I'm going to make a bunch of money," or, "I'm going to sell a hundred thousand copies." Because that kind of thought gives you no guidance about the problems. A great programmer is thinking: Should I rewrite this whole subroutine so that four people, instead of three, could call it? Should I make this program 10 percent faster? Should I really think through what the common case in here is so I know how to order this check? If you're a great programmer, you make all the routines depend on each other, so little mistakes can really hurt you. That's why you have to have such fine judgment, and be willing to back up and change things.

INTERVIEWER: *When more than one person works on a program, how can you make sure all the different elements are working together properly?*

GATES: Well, first of all, the programming team has got to be made up of people who respect each other, because the work is really intimate; it's like being in the same play together. So much judgment and creativity goes into a programming project. Some of the great programmers can't work on teams; they just like to work on their own. But I think there's an element of greatness that comes in learning how to work with other people and teach them. I really get satisfaction from somebody else on the team becoming a great programmer. Not quite as much as I do from writing the program myself, but that is really a positive event. The way I make someone else a great programmer is to sit and talk with him a lot, and I show him my code. In a team project, you make the code everybody's code.

INTERVIEWER: *Did this kind of process just evolve here or was it through deliberate implementation?*

GATES: Before Paul and I started the company, we had been involved in some large-scale software projects that were real disasters. They just kept pouring people in, and nobody really knew how they were going to stabilize the project. We swore to ourselves that we would do better. So the idea of spending a lot of time on structuring groups has always been very important.

The best ideas are the obvious ones: Keep the group small, make sure everybody in the group is super smart, give them great tools, and have a common terminology so everybody can communicate very effectively. And outside the small groups, have some very experienced senior people around who can give advice on problems. There is an amazing commonality in the types of difficulties you run into. In design reviews, I really enjoy being able to provide advice, based on programs that I have done.

INTERVIEWER: *Do you think there will ever be a radical change in the way people go about programming, or in the way computers operate?*

GATES: Software tools are getting so much better. It is possible that we will eventually be able to take just specifications and a description of what the machine is efficient at, and then have some super high-level compiler do a lot of the work that programmers do now.

People still get great satisfaction out of the fact that a compiler, like the C compiler, still can't write code as well as a human being. But we may mechanize some parts of the process quite a bit over the next three or four years. People will still design algorithms, but a lot of the implementation could be done by machines. I think that within the next five years we'll have tools that will be able to do as good a job as a human programmer.

INTERVIEWER: You mentioned mathematics earlier. What's the relationship between computer science and mathematics?

GATES: Math really affects computer science. Most great programmers have some mathematical background, because it helps to have studied the purity of proving theorems, where you don't make soft statements, you only make precise statements. In mathematics, you develop complete characterizations, and you have to combine theorems in very non-obvious ways. You often try to prove that a problem can be solved in less time. Math relates very directly to programming, maybe more so in my mind than in other people's minds, because that's the angle that I came from. I think there's a very natural relationship between the two.

INTERVIEWER: Is computer science really a science?

GATES: It will be. See, it's such a new thing. People used to get Ph.D. theses for doing work that we now expect programmers to do as part of their jobs. Computer science is developing very quickly, but unlike math, where they've had 300 years of geniuses developing mathematical theory, we just have our 20 or so years of the people who decided to get involved. Really brilliant people are getting involved and contributing; programming is much more of a mainstream activity now. The fact that people are getting exposed to computers at such young ages now will help change the thinking in the field. A lot of great programmers programmed when they were in their teens, when the way you think about things is perhaps more flexible.

In the past, it wasn't considered enough just to be a wonderful programmer; you had to manage people or go do other things. Fortunately, that's changing. Now people realize that it's a science that is worth sticking to and teaching other people.

INTERVIEWER: Does accumulating experience through the years necessarily make programming easier?

GATES: No. I think after the first three or four years, it's pretty cast in concrete whether you're a good programmer or not. After a few years, you may know more about managing large projects and personalities, but after three or four years, it's clear what you're going to be. There's no one at Microsoft who was just kind of mediocre for a couple of years, and then just out of the blue started optimizing everything in sight. I can talk to somebody about a program that he's written and know right away whether he's really a good programmer. If he's really good, he'll have everything at the tip of his tongue.

"We're going to create the software that puts a computer on every desk and in every home."

It's like people who play chess. When you're really into playing chess, it's easy to memorize every move in ten chess games, because you're involved in it. Other people look at that recall in chess players, or in programmers, and they think it's like some freak show. But it's completely natural. To this day, I can go to the blackboard and write out huge slabs of source code from the Microsoft BASIC that I wrote ten years ago.

INTERVIEWER: *What does it feel like when you are programming?*

GATES: When I compile something and it starts computing the right results, I really feel great. I'm not kidding, there is some emotion in all great things, and this is no exception. It's tempting to just start typing the code in, but there's nothing worse than typing in a routine just to get the results, and then realizing that all the hard stuff still has to be written. Because if that's true, you're going to have to change what you've already done. I like to wait and really build the foundation before I let myself have the enjoyment of coding it and seeing it run. It's like saving the best thing on my plate for last.

INTERVIEWER: *Do you see a difference between the way young programmers go about programming and the way older programmers do?*

GATES: Programmers just starting out today never had to squeeze, so it's a little harder for them to get the right religion because they always think of resources as being immediately available. Ten years ago every programmer ran into resource limitations, so the older programmers are always thinking about those things.

Programming takes an incredible amount of energy, so most programmers are fairly young. And that can be a problem, because programming requires so much discipline. When you're young, your goals aren't as stable; you may get distracted by one thing or another. Young programmers should stick with it, though, and they'll get better. I think I improved dramatically as a programmer between 1975 and 1980. In '75, I would have said, "Hey, watch out, I can do anything." I really thought I could, because I had read so much code, and I never found a piece of code that I couldn't read very quickly. I still think that one of the finest tests of programming ability is to hand the programmer about 30 pages of code and see how quickly he can read through and understand it.

INTERVIEWER: *Do you think that's a talent?*

GATES: It's a talent, you bet. It's kind of like pure I.Q. You have to just concentrate on the code and relate back to programs you've written. A lot of people would say, "I want days and days to read this." A really good programmer would say, "Let me take that home with me. I'll just spend an hour tonight and go through the whole thing." The difference of ability there is vast.

INTERVIEWER: *Is studying computer science the best way to prepare to be a programmer?*

GATES: No, the best way to prepare is to write programs, and to study great programs that other people have written. In my case, I went to the garbage cans at the Computer Science Center and I fished out listings of their operating system.

You've got to be willing to read other people's code, then write your own, then have other people review your code. You've got to want to be in this incredible feedback loop where you get the world-class people to tell you what you're doing wrong. You can't let little idiosyncrasies get in the way of getting that feedback. Some of the world-class people will harp on some purely idiosyncratic detail, like how you comment the program. You have to cut through all that stuff, because in a way, they're trying to create programmers in their own image; they're trying to get you to do arbitrary things the same way they do. And it may not relate to pure quality issues.

If you ever talk to a great programmer, you'll find he knows his tools like an artist knows his paintbrushes. It's amazing to see how much great programmers have in common in the way they developed—how they got their feedback, and how they developed such a refined sense of discipline about what's sloppy and what's not sloppy. When you get those people to look at a certain piece of code, you get a very, very common reaction.

INTERVIEWER: Has anyone in particular influenced you in the way you write code?

GATES: Everybody who wrote the PDP operating system influenced me. And John Norton from TRW, who wrote memos about people's code—I'd never seen anything like that before. I started trying to do that with other people's code myself.

There's been a mixing of ideas between Paul Allen and me, because so much of the programming we've done, we've done together. It is nice to have somebody who's up to speed to talk to when you're debugging code or you aren't sure about some particular trade-off. In a sense, it's a way of taking a break, relieving the intensity without having to switch topics, just going in and discussing it with somebody. In the creative process, it's good to have the pressure off a little bit and yet still have your attention focused. Paul and I learned how to work together in an effective way. You don't find too many partnerships like that. He's had a huge influence on me. And then, in the Microsoft period, Charles Simonyi and some of the other people here have influenced me, too.

INTERVIEWER: What do you think is in store for software? Are we just going to keep doing another great word processor or another great spreadsheet? Or will computers branch out into areas we don't even dream of today?

GATES: We're just moving down the spectrum of more and more thinking on the part of the computer. I've coined the term "softer software." That refers to a program that molds itself to the user's needs and the user's interests over time. There are going to be more great word processors and spreadsheets, and we'll use networking and graphics and new architectures. And there'll be massive storage with compact disks (CDs), where you can store encyclopedias.

What's going to really be different is rule-based programming. It's different, because instead of just writing the program and saying: "If this happens, do this and if this happens, do this," which is the way programs work now, you'll write rules, and then you have this little reasoning engine that looks at the current set of facts and the rules. Then it tries to derive new facts and act appropriately. For example, the program might have rules about gravity, and if something falls off the table, the program knows that if it's glass, it might break. So the program generates results in a very non-obvious fashion, compared to normal-type programming.

This is the technique on which so-called expert systems are built. Rule-based programming is the idea of having the derivations done through a proving machine, not just laid out explicitly in the program. Perhaps these techniques won't have an impact for four or five more years. A young programmer who wants to make his mark might be smart to focus on this new type of programming.

INTERVIEWER: Can rule-based programming handle disparate information more effectively than traditional programming?

GATES: Well, it's somewhat hard to explain. Let's say you have a program that figures out how to build bridges. It's got all this stuff about stress and bending and the properties of metal. Embedded into that program is knowledge about engineering and materials and things of that nature. If you come along and say, "We want to build bridges out of plastic," to that program, that's as massive a change as to say, "I want to build bridges on Mars."

In rule-based programming at its extreme, all the physical principles embodied in how much stress metal can take, and how gravity works, would be stated explic-

> *"CD ROM is the technology we're going to use to get personal computers into the home."*

itly as rules. And all the deductions would come from examining those rules and working them through. Today we don't have good enough rule-proving engines; it is unbelievably inefficient to try to do things this way. But this is one of the techniques we are making progress in, and it is on the horizon as something that might change programming. That, and another idea: that we might have hundreds of computers all running in parallel at the same time. In fact, that might help us to run this rule-based stuff efficiently. That sort of major architectural change might influence how people program or how they think about programming.

The scariest thing to programmers is that compilers will get so good or computers will get so fast that programmers won't count any more. I used to always have the fear that when I chose to specialize in something, its importance might diminish over time.

INTERVIEWER: Microsoft is a broadly based company and the industry as a whole is changing rapidly. How do you keep up with everything?

GATES: Well, I don't keep up with everything. I'm working with the top people at IBM, at Apple, at DEC, and in Japan. I have to know what's going to happen; I can't waste a lot of time guessing. When I fly somewhere with somebody from Microsoft, we talk about what's happening. And the E-Mail system at Microsoft is an efficient vehicle that helps me keep up.

One way to keep up is to use personal computers, and to make sure that I've read the manuals and used the top ten software products. Those products don't change so often that I can't be very familiar with each of them. If you really give a darn about personal computing, you will have used every one, and know something about them and think about how you could do better than those packages.

In a sense, personal computers have become simpler. Now we have just the two architectures: the PC and the Mac. Back in the good old days we had thirty or forty different machines that were totally incompatible, and there were a whole bunch of languages that people were messing around with. Because we've brought millions and millions of people in, we've had to make it more homogeneous, more standardized, so that they can get some sense of what's going on. A lot of what goes on in the industry doesn't really advance the state of the art. I like to concentrate on networking or graphics, because what we're going to do there might have something to do with the state of the art, instead of concentrating on did this retail chain go bankrupt, did this guy bribe that guy, or did this company give this guy enough stock? Who cares? The really smart people here are focused on their areas; they bring me anything they think is of significance, any project that's going to have real impact.

INTERVIEWER: *Where do you see Microsoft in ten years?*

GATES: Our goals are very simple. We're going to create the software that puts a computer on every desk and in every home. I don't know if that'll take ten years—that's not my expertise, guessing those exact time frames. Microsoft also wants to participate in helping to make sure those machines are good machines, building the system software into them, and then doing a lot of the important applications they'll use.

And even though there'll be more and more machines, our present thinking is that we won't have to increase the size of our development groups, because we'll simply be making programs that sell in larger quantities. We can get a very large amount of software revenue and still keep the company not dramatically larger than what we have today. That means we can know everybody and talk and share tools and maintain a high level of quality.

One of the new areas we're focusing on at Microsoft is compact-disk applications. CD ROM is the technology we're going to use to get personal computers into the home.

INTERVIEWER: *Why do you think it will succeed in the home when other things haven't?*

GATES: Today, if you buy a computer, and then go buy an educational program, you'll find the process is not very educational. The number of responses, the variety, and the way that the program simulates real life is just nothing. With the massive storage of the CD, we can create a situation you can directly relate to, where the amount of information, the variety of responses, the involvement you feel in it, will be just so dramatic.

It's a competitive world. With educational software, we're competing with newspapers, books, and TV. The software programs we put out today just aren't competitive. Unless you're just trying to save your kid from being dumb or something, then there's no real reason to buy the machine; it doesn't engage you. It doesn't engage a non-computer person.

INTERVIEWER: *Do you think the new CD ROM applications will compete with television?*

GATES: Television is passive entertainment. We're betting that people want to interact, choose different paths, and get feedback from the machine about what they've really learned. They can look up something specific that they're interested in. It's the interactive nature of the device that differentiates CD ROM from just turning on a TV and watching something.

INTERVIEWER: *Will you apply a lot of the same principles that go into designing your applications to CD ROM software products?*

GATES: CD ROM is totally different. We hope with CD ROM you'll be able to look at a map of the United States, point somewhere, click, zoom in and say, "Hey, what hotels are around here?" And the program will tell you. And if you're in the encyclopedia and you point to one of Beethoven's symphonies, the computer will play the song. It's a new interface; it's got nothing to do with productivity tools like word processors or spreadsheets. CD ROM programs will solve totally different problems. Like any new media, it'll be incredibly competitive. How can we use programming skills to make a better CD ROM application than somebody else? That requires some very profound thinking. It's not another market for programs we have already done. It's a market where we hope our intelligence will allow us to create something new and appropriate.

INTERVIEWER: *So it's not so simple as taking a bunch of newspapers and putting them on a CD ROM and writing a retrieval program?*

GATES: Well, some people will do that, but we won't; that's not exciting. We really believe we're going to have CD ROM machines in every car and in every house. And when you go to a new area of the country, you're going to stick that little disk in there and pan around and have it show you routes, and have it tell you about points of interest.

Take an area like sports. You'll have a sports disk that you push in and you'll get records and pictures of the guys. You'll be able to look at the old games, and you'll be able to look up rules. Every single disk will have lessons to teach you an area you want to learn about. Every single disk will have quizzes, like, "Hey, you think you're so smart about baseball. Well, who was this guy, or what did he do?"

"If a kid is addicted to a personal computer, I think that's far better than watching TV..."

Every disk will have interactive games on it; on the sports disk that's pretty obvious. On the music disk, the game will be "Name That Tune," and you'll be able to look at scores, look up people who wrote music, and hear how different instruments sound. You'll sit there and type in your own little scores. And if you're a pilot, you'll probably be interested in pictures of airports and planes, and stuff like that; we'll have it on a disk for you.

INTERVIEWER: *Will these CD ROM applications be sold in bookstores?*

GATES: Eventually. In the bootstrap period, we are trying to decide which channels we appeal to. Specifically, is there a role for the specialty computer retail store? I personally don't think so, but it's hard to say.

Some CD applications sound like a fantasy. But how often is a new media invented? Almost never. Videotape's not a new media, it's just delayed broadcast to TV; there's nothing different about videotapes. Interactive video disk had a chance to be a new media, but it didn't reach critical mass. It didn't get enough material, low-cost players, convenience; it didn't get absorbed into the culture. Compact disks are a superset of interactive video, but we'll have to do even better.

The changes that CDs cause will be great. I just don't see parts catalogs being issued in print form ever again. For anything that's reference oriented, where you don't want to just turn pages, but want to look up the information and manipulate it and see it in different ways, this electronic form is just far, far superior to most other forms. Our toughest competition is clearly books. We're not going to really hurt the book market, but CDs will substitute for catalogs and certain types of reference materials.

INTERVIEWER: Do you think a culture is going to grow out of this, like the television culture?

GATES: I don't know what a culture is, but CDs are more interactive than television. The CD isn't just specific to programming like personal computing is today. And yet it has the same sort of addictive, involved-type attributes. You're going to be involved, you're going to be quizzed, you're going to say, "I'm a superstar, let me try this out." We'll do the quiz so you can have multiple people involved in picking a question for the other person to answer. If a kid is addicted to a personal computer, I think that's far better than watching TV, because at least his mind is making choices. I'm not one of these people who hates TV, but I don't think it exercises your mind much. I don't happen to own one.

INTERVIEWER: Do you think that the development of CD ROM could be crippled if different standards are used?

GATES: There is massive political maneuvering on the part of Microsoft and companies hundreds of times our size, to establish standards in this area. There is the potential for two, or even three, incompatible viewers. And given the cost to create the software for this stuff, that would be unfortunate. So that's where a lot of our focus and attention goes. We're trying to make sure that *our* standard is *the* standard. That's going to be hard; it's going to be a challenge. We have to move very, very quickly to get all the activity focused around one standard, and we have to make sure it's a decent standard.

A viewer like this couldn't be done if it wasn't for the semiconductor industry. It's the unbelievable low cost of memory and high-speed processors, video chips and audio chips, that allows us to make computers a multi-media thing. The semiconductor industry is performing the miracle. It's only over the last two years that all the components have been purchased in incredibly high volume for other uses, and therefore have been driven to an attractive lower price.

INTERVIEWER: Do you see CD ROMs merging with expert systems?

GATES: No, the two don't rely on each other. Eventually you may distribute the data for expert systems on a CD, because you can put quite a large database on it. But neither one requires the other. They both have their own difficult challenges to face.

The mix of skills required to do the world's best CD is pretty intimidating, because it's video, it's audio, it's programming, and it's interactive. It's hard, just like any new media. When people were first on TV, they felt they were so much better than people on radio, but they'd just stand there. It took a long time to invent the colorful peacock, all the action, the three-dimensional padding, and the special effects that you see on TV today. Just like TV, CDs will get better as we get more experienced with the media. I can sit here and tell you all the mistakes we won't make, and five years from now, I could sit here and tell you all the mistakes that we did make. As creative as we are, we won't be able to exploit the media to its absolute fullest right away.

INTERVIEWER: Do you ever wish you were back programming on your own again?

GATES: Oh, sure, absolutely. Then you control everything. There's no compromise. Every line is yours and you feel good about every line. It's kind of selfish, but it's like being allowed to do pure mathematics, and yet you have the feedback of making something really work. I sometimes envy my colleagues who get to focus just on the program they're writing.

John Page

*BORN IN London, England on
September 21, 1944, John Page began working with computers as a teenager
in London, and has continued to work in the computer field for over twenty
years, his entire professional career.*

*In 1970, Page joined Hewlett-Packard. He provided technical support for
HP for four years in London, Geneva, and other parts of Europe. In 1974 he
moved to Cupertino, California, the headquarters of Hewlett-Packard, to manage worldwide technical support for the HP 3000 computer. Later, he moved
into research and development in software, where he developed the Image
Database Management System. While with Hewlett-Packard, Page studied artificial intelligence at Stanford University and did his postgraduate work in
computer science.*

*In 1980, Page left Hewlett-Packard and teamed up with Fred Gibbons and
Janelle Bedke to start Software Publishing Corporation. Page, working out of
his garage, developed Software Publishing's first product, which later became
PFS: FILE. The PFS series now includes over six programs on all facets of information management. John Page is vice president of corporate research and
development for the Software Publishing Corporation.*

John Page is a trim, fit, slightly boyish-looking man with kind eyes, a warm smile, and a slight English accent. He wore a blue shirt with the collar buttons undone, and gray slacks. Page escorted me through the comfortable California-style, redwood-beamed offices of Software Publishing into a large, vacant conference room. There Page relaxed into a state of reflection and analysis on his approach to programming and running a software business.

When I asked John Page to share with us a sample of his source code to reproduce in the book, he refused, saying the request seemed to him "a crazy idea. Architects would publish examples of the churches and museums they've built, not blueprint fragments." He thought a code sample would be relatively meaningless to the reader. Instead he suggested we list his many achievements and contributions to the computer world. It was this remark, more than any other, that exemplified Page's approach to programming. He has the ordinary user in the forefront of his thoughts as he goes about the task of developing software. It is the end result, not so much the means used in getting there, which fascinates and motivates Page.

INTERVIEWER: *What led you to develop the PFS: FILE program and the PFS line of software?*

PAGE: When I was transferred to the Hewlett-Packard factory in California that makes the HP3000, I got heavily involved in software. There I began my work with Image, a database-management program that runs on the HP 3000. It is the most widely installed database-management system on mainframes and minicomputers.

After I'd spent a lot of time at Hewlett-Packard on database-management systems, I was struck by how much they were tailored to programmers rather than end users. That was all right at the time because companies wanted a development tool more than a product for users. But as I watched the development of personal computers, I saw that it would be feasible to create a database-management system that was genuinely usable by ordinary people. Then I began toying with the idea of such a project.

Hewlett-Packard wasn't interested in personal computers at the time, much less software for them. I met up with Janelle Bedke and Fred Gibbons, with whom I later began the company. We discussed the project and decided to look for a software publisher. We couldn't find one. But once we realized the software business was booming, we knew there was an opportunity to start a company, so we founded SPC. We developed a business plan that told us the amount of growth and market penetration we could expect. Once we finally made a decision to go ahead with the company, I had a vehicle to develop software ideas that had been in my head for about a year, the PFS series of programs.

INTERVIEWER: How did you want to make PFS different from other programs on the market at the time?

PAGE: What I thought was missing was an application ordinary people could use, much like a telephone or car. The goal was to design a program that would be as easy to learn as an appliance. It was an interesting design trade-off because it meant I should pursue maximum understandability rather than maximum performance and functionality. It's a bit like the phone system, which isn't very sophisticated on the outside. You dial the number, the phone rings, and you talk to people. That's all it does. That's not much, right? But to make that happen, a great

> *"Complicated programs are far easier to write than straightforward programs."*

deal of complex technology has to be marshalled behind the scenes. Designing PFS worked in the same way as the phone system: simple on the outside, backed by sophisticated technology.

In designing PFS, I stumbled over an odd software design principle: Complicated programs are far easier to write than straightforward programs—the exact opposite of what you'd expect. It's easy to write complicated programs because you reflect the complexity back onto the user; you force the user to make all the hard decisions. For example, suppose the user wants to know how many blocks there are in the file. You set it up so he can find out himself. What he does with the information, God knows. With a very simple program, however, the designer has to figure out the answers himself. It was fascinating to move from developing very complex software primarily for programmers to developing programs for Joe Everyman.

INTERVIEWER: Why was PFS written in Pascal?

PAGE: Don't forget the PFS program is the most long-lived program on the market now that VisiCalc is gone. Back then, five years ago, there was no C, so it was a choice between BASIC, Assembler, or Pascal. BASIC was just not it. I didn't want to hack the whole thing out in Assembler—it would take too long. So I needed a high-level language that had some muscle to it. Pascal was the only choice. Remember, too, this was before the invention of the IBM PC, so the only machine on the market worth considering was the Apple II, and Pascal was the only program language that met my needs on that machine.

We're switching to C as we develop new versions because it is a better development language than Pascal. But Pascal hasn't been bad to us, certainly not as bad as the program nerds believe. I think you can only be 5 or 10 per cent more productive in C than in Pascal.

> *"... know your customer, know the machine, and design the very best product for that customer and that machine."*

INTERVIEWER: *You said PFS was extremely difficult to develop. How long did it take to design and write?*

PAGE: It took me about eighteen months to design and write FILE and Report. I did it primarily on my own, although I had some help at the end.

INTERVIEWER: *What presented the biggest problem in developing the program?*

PAGE: Back then the biggest problem was shoehorning the whole thing into a 48K Apple and making it run at a reasonable speed. The Pascal was interpreted, which meant its performance left a whole lot to be desired. And once the program was finished, it was extremely slow, so I isolated all of the areas where the performance bottlenecks occurred and recoded those in Assembly language. That fixed the problems and I got the program to perform on target, but recoding something in Assembler with no debugging tools was just a horrible experience.

The other problem was a strategic business problem. Just at the time we came out with PFS, a 48K Apple was regarded as a very large configuration: In fact, it was the top-of-the-line, while a 32K machine was typical. There was a 64K Apple but the extra 16K board cost $550. Remember that back then computers really were personal; people spent their own money on these machines, and a $500 to $600 board was a significant purchase. We had to make a decision.

There was no way we could get the programs to run on 32K. We had already put FILE and Report into two programs because they wouldn't fit together in the 48K Apple II. It's still two programs although not for much longer. Would we be successful in requiring a 48K machine? More memory was risky because it cut down the market size. I lay awake many nights wondering if we would get away with it.

INTERVIEWER: *Were other database programs coming out then?*

PAGE: At the time, we were quite worried that Stoneware DB Master would give us a run for our money. But we got around the problem by segmenting the market—causing DB Master to be perceived as a high-end product, too complicated for people to use. It's funny how our fortunes have differed over the years.

INTERVIEWER: *Did you have any idea PFS would be the big success it turned out to be?*

PAGE: I had no idea. What I tend to do in life is work out my goals, and once they're set, I never re-examine them, or think about how hard it is, or whether it's still worth doing, or whether it will be successful. I just go about my tasks with tunnel vision. I did that with FILE. When it began to sell, I was shocked. I thought, "My God, it worked. Look at that."

INTERVIEWER: *Do you still program?*

PAGE: It's still fun, but I don't program as much as I'd like to. For the morale of the company, you can't get too involved in the projects or in the programming. In a bigger company, people require leaders who know everything but not so much that the people who work for them feel inadequate and unneeded. Company employees need to feel ownership of what they're doing and have psychological ownership of the ideas they're implementing, otherwise they're not motivated.

I often wonder what it must be like at Microsoft, because somebody at the head of the company is technically very dominant and well known. I wonder whether he has a negative effect on the morale of the software people in the company. I also wonder if having someone keep control puts a cap on a company's growth potential. When the company ultimately gets to the size where the founder can't do it all, others must be ready to take ownership and lead it the way he would have. At SPC, we are trying to get out of the limelight to set the stage for more growth later.

INTERVIEWER: *Did you find it difficult to make the transition from being a computer programmer to running a huge company?*

PAGE: The transition was very gradual because I've managed people for about twenty years. If you want to know the truth, the hard part was going from being the manager back to being a programmer. Before we started the company, I was accustomed to being in charge of a lot of people at Hewlett-Packard. When I went back to programming, I was forced to rely purely on myself. That was a shocker. It was kind of frightening—I wondered if I could still write programs. But it's like riding a bike—you don't ever forget; you just pedal off into the sunset.

INTERVIEWER: *Since now you don't do the programming yourself, how do you go about hiring good programmers?*

PAGE: Companies need people who are true architects—people who can see beyond the basic tools to understand what should be built, who understand which technical things to take advantage of and how. For instance, a clever engineer who knows that memories will get incredibly large will sit down and ask what it means in terms of the design. What assumptions have I been making because I thought memory was scarce? How do I challenge the old ideas and sweep them away? How do I develop a different design that reflects a different way of looking at things? A company must have those people working for it.

Companies also need people who can write lumps of code for the grand architecture—people who are just good mechanics. What needs to be done is very well specified and can be given to anyone straight out of school with a bachelor's degree in computer science. They'll probably do alright. The question then becomes how to get the right balance of these two kinds of people.

INTERVIEWER: *What is the difference between writing a program by yourself and writing it with a team of people?*

PAGE: If the product requires four or five people, then you go about it differently than if you write it by yourself. I believe very strongly that one person, certainly no more than two, should do the design and high-level structure. You get a consistency and elegance when it springs from one mind. You can be misled by trying to make it fun for everybody and have a committee design the thing. That is absolutely fatal.

So I have a very small team working at the definition stage and then I expand it to implement the design, if necessary. The bigger the team that is required to implement the design of a program, the more disciplined you have to be about breaking the structure into manageable pieces and defining the interfaces. You don't have to do many structured-program reports, documenting every step, unless the program is so big that it has to be done by more than two or three people.

Some systems, like designing a program to control the space shuttle, require a hundred programmers. Then you must have the discipline to break the structure into pieces so it all works. It's possible to overstructure a small program and understructure a big one—you have to match the techniques to the size of the problem. That's the way I do it.

INTERVIEWER: What about the programmers who didn't have a hand in the design; how do you get them to work on a project?

PAGE: They may be disappointed. But you tell them at the beginning they must accept the absence of design input as a condition of working on the project. Fortunately, you find programmers who are fairly new to the game and want to be apprenticed to a good, high-level designer. It gives them a way into the industry and a path to follow to meet their own goal of designing something themselves.

INTERVIEWER: How do you manage a team working on a program?

PAGE: When a team is first assigned a project in our company, they have a lot to learn when doing things the SPC way—we think about a problem in a way that makes our product distinctive from others. I coach them on those principles from the beginning. I don't tell them how to design, but rather try to teach the process I'd use to design. In other words, I try to educate them. I try to impart skills that will be useful to them forever. At times they'll come up with things I don't like, but then sometimes they don't like the way I do things, either. We find the first programs a team builds have a few stumbles in them. But we deliberately go through that pain because I want to have people in the company who can carry the future stages of growth so we don't get ulcers. It's working out very well. We've got teams in the company working on their third product and they're very, very good. They do a better job than I would. I find myself learning things from them; I get a real kick out of that.

> *"I think the real challenge is to design software that is simple on the outside but complex on the inside."*

INTERVIEWER: What is distinctive about the way SPC thinks about problems? Are there certain techniques or rules that programmers must follow?

PAGE: There are no basic principles except that you must know your customer, know the machine, and design the very best product for that customer and that machine.

You must understand the customers and what they want. Then you can design the correct product for them. The program may range from one that appears very simple, like PFS: FILE, to one that appears extremely complex, like a compiler. The first you design for an ordinary user, the other for a programmer or engineer. I don't tolerate software engineers who only want to work on the more complicated programs. First, I regard that attitude as immature. A good architect takes as much pleasure in designing a small gazebo as designing a museum; each has its own challenge. Second, I think the real challenge is to design software that is simple on the outside but complex on the inside. People who don't want to take that challenge puzzle me because to me it's a very fascinating challenge.

"Each generation of the PC is more complicated and harder to use . . . and the elegance is being washed out."

INTERVIEWER: *In the years you've worked in the computer field, you must have developed some impressions about how computers have changed over time.*

PAGE: Computers are stuck in a rut because nothing new has happened in quite a while. The market has sucked us into overly complicated systems and the fault is mostly IBM's. All the "new" features being installed are borrowed from minicomputers and mainframes. Each successive generation of the IBM PC is more complicated and harder to use than the last. The PC is fast regressing to being a minicomputer and IBM may even be successful in turning it back into a mainframe. The old complexities are coming back and the elegance is being washed out. Even the poor old Macintosh is being battered because it doesn't have all the things that managers of management-information systems love. Macintosh designers will probably be forced to put all those complexities into the Mac, too. It's sad that such things will probably happen sooner or later.

The net result is that personal computers are becoming more popular with people in large corporations who used to use mainframes. They're beginning to embrace the personal computer but still trying to treat it as if it were a minicomputer. It's not; it's a giant personal calculator and we've lost sight of that.

INTERVIEWER: *Do you think this trend toward complexity will continue?*

PAGE: I hope not. I've got a feeling the personal computer will develop in two directions. There will be personal desktop business computers, which use all the same tools the mainframe required, like COBOL and all that horrible stuff. MIS managers are still programming in COBOL, just the way they did twenty years ago. If you try to give them anything at all innovative, they just say, "No. Make life simple. I want my dear old COBOL language."

I'm also optimistic that the industry will return to making proper personal computers that people will be able to use, like the original Apple. They will be lower in price, have more power, and be easier to use. We're derailed right now. Developing that true personal computer will breathe some life into the whole industry.

INTERVIEWER: How do you develop programs to keep pace with the changing consumer?

PAGE: You can take two directions to adjust a product to a changing market. One kind of growth is driven by the computer and its technology. You find new applications for the computer even when they diverge from the applications you began with. That kind of growth produces quite different needs from the ones you started out with. For instance, if you diversify into typesetting, you suddenly realize personal computers are great for typesetting. It will require software that's grossly different from what you had originally developed, and you must make it tremendously functional to make it sell.

The other kind of growth is driven by the changes in your customers' experience. As they become more aware of what the computer can do for them, their demands increase but their desire for complexity doesn't. They want the new programs to do more but to stay simple. Our challenge is to satisfy that need because that's the kind of growth we've chosen. I also think you must satisfy consumer needs to advance the state of the art; for example, making a program more functional without increasing its complexity. It costs us intellectual effort, but that's when we make genuine advances. Unfortunately, the industry is infatuated with complexity and wants that complexity to show for some perverse reason.

INTERVIEWER: So you think the industry as a whole is technology driven rather than market driven?

PAGE: Right. They want the technology almost for show. It's a bit like those expensive stereos—the more you pay, the more lights and knobs it has. It's lunacy if you talk to a real user like the wife of the guy who buys it. You will find those gadgets just confuse the hell out of her. I bet if you could fingerprint the controls to see which ones are actually touched, you'd find that only three of the ninety are ever used. Nobody knows what the others do and no one touches them because the stereo works without them.

People are that way about programs, too. They'll buy a gross, poorly designed word-processing program because they want to write letters or reports. But it's full of controls nobody ever touches or wants. The trick is to get around that infatuation with technology. Unfortunately, because SPC deliberately hides the technology from the user, we are often regarded as a company not dedicated to sound technology. It's annoying, too, to have worked so hard to hide the complexity and then get dinged by the trade because the program does not appear complex.

INTERVIEWER: *How can you go about hiding the complexity?*

PAGE: I'll give you an example. In PFS Report, when you want a nice, calm report, you simply point to the four items you want in your report: the company's name, address, total sales, and salesman's name. The program searches through the database to find the width for the biggest column. Then it applies a heuristic routine which calculates the width ratio of intercolumn space to margins. The heuristic routine in the program is a complicated devil. It tries different things until it comes out with a "pleasingness" quotient on each one, ranks them, and chooses. This makes the report look aesthetically balanced, with the same margins on both sides and not too narrow, and the columns not too far apart.

The program uses a vertical-tabulation scheme to ensure the report is centered vertically on the page. The ratio strikes a balance between looking nice and fitting the data. We try to wriggle the data around in different layouts until it looks right on the page. These reports look just great 99 percent of the time and even the 1 percent are perfectly usable. The net result is that most people get nice looking reports just by specifying the items without having to think about layout.

Less sophisticated report writers require the user to specify the width of each column and where to put it on the paper. They force the user to think out how wide the name column is. The user may make a big guess—he can't imagine a name longer than, say, twenty-five characters. Sure enough, there is one and it gets chopped off. The user expends a great deal of energy on making a decision about where to put things on the paper, and the result is horrible because they don't quite visualize that it will look lopsided.

But here is the real "grabber." The programs that are more difficult to use make a selling point out of that difficulty. They turn it into a feature: The user of a complex system can specify exactly where the columns go, whereas PFS puts them where it wants. The truth of the matter is that almost anybody who uses the more complex program changes the report five times before it looks just right. Or else they put up with a rotten-looking report. I question if that's productive. The design problem becomes an issue of control versus productivity. You can have either high productivity or a great deal of control. That's the trade-off programmers and users find themselves making all the time.

INTERVIEWER: It sounds as though it takes so much more time to develop a program that's easy to use. How can you afford to do it?

PAGE: We do it because it benefits the user. That separates us from our competition. We build programs with automatic transmissions, which are harder to design than programs with manual transmissions. But it's what our customer wants. We've got over two million programs out there, so we believe in making that extra investment because it also benefits us.

"The prediction that computers will permeate every aspect of society will absolutely come true."

INTERVIEWER: How do you keep coming up with new ideas for programs?

PAGE: I wonder about that myself sometimes, but the real answer is staying in touch with the customers. I want the raw data and I want to interpret it myself. So periodically, at a quiet point in the day, I go through our owner-registration cards and call people at random. I ask them why they bought our product and what they're using it for. People are incredibly shocked by the personal attention, but they will usually tell you quite a lot about what they're doing with the product.

We watch the competition closely but we're not seduced by industry group-think. We go to a number of conventions and meetings where our compatriots aren't present. We like conferences that aren't strictly centered around the computer industry but where computers are likely to be discussed. Investment conferences usually involve people from multiple disciplines—the semiconductor industry, hardware, software, and distribution. We try to visit dealers through our adopt-a-dealer plan. Everyone's point of view goes into forming the mosaic of the industry.

Luck also plays a role. The name Software Publishing Company is very misleading because we don't publish software. But almost anybody who's got a program they want marketed sends it to us. So we see hundreds of new ideas from all over the country.

The biggest source of ideas comes from within the company. We use our own products—in fact we require our employees to use our products as much as possible because we want the feedback on their successes and failures. With 200 employees using our programs, we get a lot of data. And of course, people in the lab come up with their own ideas too.

INTERVIEWER: *Do you interact with other programmers much?*

PAGE: We try to spend time with software people because there are people out there who come up with good ideas. But surprisingly, we don't interact much. There are some very clever people out there. But what's odd about most programmers is that often they know the skills but haven't figured out what to do with them. They tend to get together at conventions and talk until the early hours of the morning about listings or things like that. My response is total boredom. I think, "Well, great, that's interesting but that's not the meaning of life."

There aren't very many places where you can go to meet the people who are concerned with solving problems in the way I am. I find it stifling that I keep meeting builders and never architects. I wish there were a way to meet people who are designers in disciplines other than computers—aerospace, building construction, or engineering. I know lots of parallels can be drawn, though I don't know what they are. It would be fun to pull together a meeting like that some day.

INTERVIEWER: *What role do you think computers will play in the future?*

PAGE: They will always play an absolutely central role in everything. Information is a fundamental fabric of the universe. Information about things is almost as valuable as the things themselves, and computers process information. I was reading a very interesting article in *Business Week* about the power of information. People are beginning to realize how important having good information is. One man who has billions of dollars invested said he honestly believed the information about his investments was more valuable in real dollars than the investments themselves.

Think about it—that means that information is a resource or a raw material as valuable as gold. Think about how careful you would be in using it, processing it, and protecting it. That is just what computers do so well. The prediction that computers will permeate every aspect of society will absolutely come true.

INTERVIEWER: In what particular fields will computers develop?

PAGE: I see two significant areas that are still ripe for development in the next ten to fifteen years. One will be to get personal computers back on track and make them genuinely personal—the size of a book and $300. That will happen within two years.

The second area is communications. Right now, the way information is moved about is crude—slow, cumbersome, and expensive. Better ways are beginning to happen because of the competition and new technology. The breakup of AT&T is interesting from this point of view.

INTERVIEWER: What impact will computers have on communications?

PAGE: Communications will be faster and cheaper. Information is only useful if you can get it, and right now you can't. I don't think people realize how poorly informed they are. Once they realize the many possibilities, they won't believe they ever lived without complete information.

Access to information will make a profound difference in our lives. For example, you will be able to communicate by digitized voice. Remember the messages you left for me the first time you called? You got my answering machine, which is a computer. Your voice was digitized and stored on disk in a computer that serves the entire building. I can forward your message to somebody else, and I can alter those messages and forward them from my home. I just dial into the system using the push-button phones. Without computers, that would not be possible. Soon we'll have a home version that will cost about $300—answering machines will actually be able to talk to each other. That's the scary part.

INTERVIEWER: What kind of information do you think we'll have access to in the future?

PAGE: Let me give you an example of what could be available. Let's say you want to go some place in Europe for your vacation. You want good drinking water, a nice hotel on the beach with a lap pool, and hang gliding nearby. How on earth would you find out all those things? You might find the good hotel near a beach in travel brochures, but they probably don't mention the things that interest you most, like hang gliding and a lap pool. Unless you happen to see a photo, you have virtually no information on which to base your vacation decision. So you end up going back to the same vacation spot each year because you can't find a new place that's any better. There are many other examples and tons of information we don't have about almost every aspect of our lives.

INTERVIEWER: *Do some of these information resources exist today?*

PAGE: Yes. For example, I'm a flier. My ability to fly has been enhanced 20 to 30 percent because I can log onto the weather service and get briefings off my computer. The other way to get the weather is much less efficient. I call the weather service and I may be put on hold for half an hour. If I do get through, I may not hear the weather correctly or I may make a mistake copying it down. I just type in my request on my computer and there it is—fast and accurate. And funny thing—I have better information than the controllers do. It's actually better because I tap straight into the National Weather Service in Boulder, Colorado, whereas they get their weather information through some antiquated system the federal government can't afford to update. I still have to phone in my flight plans, but that will change soon so I can file them on line.

INTERVIEWER: *Why do you think so many programmers are into flying airplanes for recreation?*

PAGE: One reason is that programmers who are fairly successful have the financial resources to fly. Second, flying is an engineer's discipline because it involves manipulating complexity, which is something engineers love to do. Programmers also love to tame complexity and flying is extremely complicated, so it's a fun thing to master. Finally, flying is like programming. A good pilot gives the passenger a flawless, boring ride, while a good programmer gives the customer a flawless, boring experience on their computer.

INTERVIEWER: *Do you have other interests or pursuits?*

PAGE: I'm building a house, I play guitar, and I like swimming, not for its own sake, but for the exercise.

INTERVIEWER: *It doesn't sound like you're a workaholic.*

PAGE: No, the only time I get to be one is when I'm doing something very specific and I get that tunnel vision I mentioned earlier—I haven't done that in a while. In my role as a leader, I find I can't work long hours. Leadership is an interpersonal activity that's done during normal working hours. It is also incredibly draining. It takes a lot out of you without giving anything back. You see results indirectly in the growth of the people around you, the projects coming out of the company, and the company's success as a whole. It's fun to watch, but there's no direct joy of accomplishment as there is in programming. As a result, I find I can't stay at work too long. I have to find some time for me so I can stay balanced and not go crazy.

INTERVIEWER: As a programmer with that tunnel vision, is there a possibility of losing your balance?

PAGE: You have to say to all your relatives, "Look, I'm going to be gone from six to nine months. I'll be here physically, but I might as well not be. I'm going to be working on this thing and I'll be absent-minded. I want you to understand and tolerate that and I promise I'll make it up to you when I get to the other end." If you have loved ones it's important to come through on that promise. Working so hard can be devastating to your marriage and to other relationships.

Some people get such a high from completing the project, they roll straight to another one. Doing that will literally burn you out. Each time you go straight to a new project, you get worse at it.

Also, while you're working hard on a complicated program, it's important to exercise. The lack of physical exercise does most programmers in. It causes a loss of mental acuity. It also leads to physical weakness that can heighten the feeling of disillusionment that often comes after the second or third straight programming effort. You look in the mirror and say, "God, look at me, why did I do this?"

INTERVIEWER: Why are programmers so obsessive?

PAGE: You constantly try to hold the state of the entire system you're working on in your head. If you lose the mental image, it takes a long time to get back into that state. It's like being an air-traffic controller who has nine planes in his mind and knows exactly where they're all going. Distract him by asking him when his shift is over and he loses those planes—the model he had in his head. In programming, a big complicated model is very efficient once you're in the groove. If you get out of it, you've got to work on it quite a while to get back in.

INTERVIEWER: Do you have a programming routine?

PAGE: Personally, I do my best work in the morning. I like to get up very early, when it's quiet, and program. In fact, I try to do whatever requires concentration in the morning. I try to schedule meetings for the afternoons when my mental activity is not what it should be. I can talk alright, but I'm too tired to do creative problem solving at night. I'm useless from 6:00 p.m. until the next morning.

INTERVIEWER: *What process do you go through when you program?*

PAGE: I sit down and work out what I want the program to do. Then I mentally map out the components. I tend to zoom in first on the pieces where I think I've got problems and try to understand them. This looks hard, that looks hard and these other pieces are just normal files and old hash tables. Once I've dealt with the hard parts in isolation—maybe by writing a little program just to prove out some theory—I have a level of confidence about the whole program. I have pieces that are either a piece of cake or very difficult, but I know how I'm going to handle them all. Then I can go about structuring the program before I start implementing it.

I have to believe that what I want to do is achievable, otherwise I can be very distracted. I've seen some immature programmers who are so frightened about reaching the end goal, they just zoom in on some piece of the program and just start writing. They back into the program from a relatively minor position.

Once I've sketched the structure, I work on each piece in turn and define the interfaces between them. I don't like to have a nagging feeling that I'm designing something but don't know if a crucial component can be built. It gives me the willies, stops me from having the confidence level to proceed vigorously on the project.

INTERVIEWER: *If a certain part of it doesn't work, do you ever scrap the whole thing and start over?*

PAGE: I get excited when I've worked hard and begin to see why nobody's built that piece before I worked on it. If I can solve it, I can do something everyone thought was impossible. That gets my adrenaline going and my heart rate up. I just love it. I get like a dog with a bone—I will not put it down. I think about it driving around, swimming up and down, and in the shower. I just tease this problem to death until I find a way to solve it using some technique that maybe nobody's thought of. Eventually, of course, if it turns out to be totally intractable, I will give up. But often, if I think about it long and hard enough, I'll find a way around the problem. It may not be an elegant solution and it might not conform to all the rules of computer science, but to heck with that if it works.

I've always said computer science isn't really a science because you're not actually discovering anything about the physical universe—but that is only half true. Sometimes the solution to a problem just clicks into place like it had always been there and I uncovered it. I examine it and find it to be perfect. It's weird.

Take the design of PFS: FILE. I remember sitting down and producing about 4 or 5 designs radically different from each other. Some of them used a relational approach. Some used a natural-language approach. I reminded myself of the criteria I was looking for. I was looking for a way to design a program that could be extended to be a family of programs—report writers, word processors, and graphics programs. They needed to have a strong family resemblance and they couldn't surprise anyone about the way they worked. At the same time, the program had to be functionally complete. It had to do everything I wanted it to do, and be simple and easy. I synthesized ideas and tried different approaches to the design. Some worked in some areas quite well and in other areas they didn't. Each design met all the different criteria to a different degree. Then suddenly, it's as if I stumbled across the one that met all the objectives.

Sometimes, after I create a very good program, I feel as if I discovered it. After I'm done, I look at it and think I had to do it that way. It's almost as if I had no control—the solution happens to me. There was no other way. Those feelings are a sign I'm onto something. Yes, discovery is the way to do it, but it doesn't happen very often.

```
/*===================================================================*/
/*

strdcpy - copy string until a specified character is found (or entire
       string is copied)

    returns a pointer to 'chr' in from string (or terminator)
*/

char    *strdcpy(from, to, chr)
char    *from;
char    *to;
char    chr;
{
    char    c;

    while (c = *to = *from) {
        if (c == chr) {
            *to = '\0';
            return (from);
            }
        to++;
        from++;
        }
    return (from);
    }
/*===================================================================*/
/*

strtrim - trim off blank characters (and CR, LF) from right side of line

*/

strtrim(line)
char *line;
{
    int     i;
    char    *p;

    i = strlen(line);
    p = line + i - 1;                  /* RHE of line */
    while (i--) {
        if (*p == ' ' || *p == '\t' || *p == '\n' || *p == '\r')
            *p = '\0';
        else
            break;
        p--;
        }
    return;
    }
```

Two of Ratliff's subroutines written in C that illustrate
the same programming style he used in dBASE III.

C. Wayne Ratliff

FROM 1969 *to 1982*, C. Wayne Ratliff worked for the Martin Marietta Corporation in a progression of engineering and managerial positions. He was a member of the NASA Viking Flight Team when the Viking spacecraft landed on Mars in 1976, and wrote the data-management system, MFILE, for the Viking lander support software.

In 1978, he began writing the Vulcan program, which he marketed by himself from 1979 to 1980. In late 1980 he entered into a marketing agreement with Ashton-Tate and renamed the Vulcan product dBASE II. In mid-1983, Ashton-Tate purchased the dBASE II technology and copyright from Ratliff and he joined Ashton-Tate as vice president of new technology. Ratliff was the project manager for dBASE III, as well as designer and lead programmer.

Ratliff was born in 1946 in Trenton, Ohio and raised in various cities and towns in Ohio and Germany. He now resides in the Los Angeles area.

I went to an Ashton-Tate research center in Glendale to talk with C. Wayne Ratliff, the creator of dBASE. He welcomed me into his large office, where we sat down at a round table and talked at length about his accomplishments and insights about programming. Ratliff is a tall westerner who has an air of independence and a comfortable manner. After more than fifteen years in the computer industry, he still abounds in fresh enthusiasm. Unlike many programmers who tire of the actual writing of source code, Ratliff still thrives on working at all phases of program development every day.

INTERVIEWER: *What led you to become a programmer?*

RATLIFF: When I was in college, I was designing a little two-seater, rear-engine car. That was in the sixties when cars were big and fast. So, I started using a CDC 6400 computer to help design the car, because I wanted to get into car design from a real engineering standpoint, instead of simply guessing how big an engine I could fit into my design. I wrote a number of small programs to help design suspensions, figure out the center of gravity, and that sort of thing. It didn't take long until I started looking for other programs to write, because I was enjoying the programming more than I was enjoying building the car.

INTERVIEWER: *So programming swept you away from car design?*

RATLIFF: Computers themselves got me away from car design. Before I completed my degree, I got a job with Martin Marietta in Denver. I *was* a computer. My job title was computer. Other people have programmed computers, but I have been one.

INTERVIEWER: *You'd better explain that.*

RATLIFF: Well, it was a throwback to the earlier days of aerospace engineering. When people had, for instance, a differential equation to solve, they had an army of people with Monroe calculators, and each person would work on a separate segment of the equation. One person would do a certain group of adds, then hand their paper to the next person to do the multiplies, and so on. They called those people computers. Computers then were more like administrative assistants, except that they did engineering-related jobs instead of administrative jobs. Since I could program, that's how they used me. Then I got drafted during the heat of the Vietnam war in 1969.

INTERVIEWER: *Did you go to Vietnam?*

RATLIFF: No. As a result of the Martin Marietta job, I had a civilian-acquired skill, so I programmed. For two years I worked on a logistics war game called LOGEX, programming in COBOL. Most of my work was related to ordering equipment and supplies. It was like doing an inventory for an extremely large company, except there are unusual military policies you have to deal with—like nuclear weapons requiring presidential authorization.

INTERVIEWER: What experiences led you to your Vulcan program?

RATLIFF: After the army, I was a Martin Marietta employee and a contractor at Jet Propulsion Laboratory. I was with the Viking project, and wrote the data-management program for the Viking lander, called MFILE. That was in 1976, around the time that I became interested in designing and experimenting with natural language, so I bought an IMSAI 8080 8-bit computer kit and put it together. It took a year to put the thing together, mostly waiting for parts. I had to solder more than 2,200 joints. Of course, if I could have bought it assembled for the same price, or even close, I would have.

"My job title was computer. Other people have programmed computers, but I have been one."

Once I had put it together, all I had was a computer. Nothing was included except 1K of memory. You had to keep buying things, such as a keyboard. I had already spent $1,000 for the kit, then I had to spend another $159 for a keyboard. Eventually I ended up spending about $6,000. Now you can buy an AT, with a hard disk, complete and ready to roll for $6,000.

INTERVIEWER: Were your experiments with natural language the foundation for dBASE?

RATLIFF: dBASE started, oddly enough, from football games. I was in a football pool where you picked the winner and then a point spread. I've never known that much about football. It was the motivation to win, rather than the game itself, that interested me. I thought that if I devoutly applied myself to the mathematical process, I could win.

The way to do that was to look at all the statistics. Every Monday morning the newspaper publishes all the statistics for the weekend games—it takes up at least a double page. About four or five weeks into the season, I had an entire room completely layered with newspaper! I was trying to figure out how to pick a winner by going from paper to paper, a horrible process, and I decided it was too much to handle without a computer. Well, one thing led to another, and within a week, I'd totally forgotten about football. I had decided that the world needed a natural-language database manager. Obviously, the computer was the solution, and that's the reason why I originally bought the IMSAI 8080.

I went out and bought lots of books on natural language and artificial intelligence. I kept getting drawn from one place to another, and I did lots of experiments. I hadn't researched the database as much as I did the natural-language aspect.

I decided to use the database manager as a foundation for natural language to work on. Natural language by itself is a big "so what?" You need something for it to act on. I started thinking about the data-management program I had written for Viking, and I was essentially going to duplicate that on the 8-bit machine, the IMSAI. By accident, I ran across a description of a program called JPLDIS, or JPL Display and Information Systems. It was easy to understand, and very simple, very clean. I immediately thought it would be easy to implement on a microcomputer.

I believe JPLDIS was actually, in current terms, a clone or rip-off of an IBM product called Retrieve, which ran on some time-sharing systems. So there's a sort of progression from Retrieve to JPLDIS to my program, which I called Vulcan. I was going to take care of the database part first, and then do the natural-language approach, but I put off the natural language and still haven't developed that yet.

INTERVIEWER: What shape did this early version of the dBASE program, or Vulcan, take on?

RATLIFF: I took the JPLDIS concept, cut back on the specs, and wrote Vulcan. JPLDIS would handle two hundred fields, but I thought sixteen was plenty. I got it working and a little over a year after I started, I did my taxes on it. So, I figured Vulcan had some commercial potential, and I began to polish it up and get it to a sellable stage. In October 1979, I went to market and put my first ad for Vulcan in *BYTE* magazine, and I ran a quarter-page ad for four or five months thereafter. I got much more response than I could handle.

INTERVIEWER: So your response was immediately positive. Who were your competitors at that time?

RATLIFF: FMS 80, and later Condor and Selector. During the year and nine months that I was writing the code for Vulcan, my floppy disk drive broke down twice. Each time, it took three months to get it up and running again, so I lost six months. I kept thinking, if I had come out six months earlier, I would have been the very first.

INTERVIEWER: *So, suddenly you had a product that was penetrating the market. Did this success take you by surprise?*

RATLIFF: I got completely overstressed. I did everything myself. When an order came in, I typed out the order, filled out the invoice, packaged the program, made a fresh copy of the disk—the whole nine yards. I placed all the ads myself, and also I kept working on the program. I'd come home from my job, work again until midnight, go to sleep exhausted, get up the next day, and repeat the process. Vulcan was at the point where I needed to make a lot of advances to it. Over the months I really ran out of steam.

In the summer of 1980, I decided to quit advertising Vulcan and let it drop off to nothing. I would continue to support all the people who had purchased it, but I wasn't going to aggressively go out to find any new buyers.

INTERVIEWER: *Why didn't you try to sell it to a bigger company, or hire some help?*

RATLIFF: It didn't occur to me. There weren't any big companies then. As far as I knew, everybody was a real small outfit. A professor at the University of Washington and his wife were considering taking over marketing when George Tate and Hal Lashlee called. They came over and looked at a demo; even though something always goes wrong during a demo, they were understanding, they knew about demos. I was very impressed by that fact. When most people view a demo, after the first thing goes wrong they lose interest. George and Hal already had a business called Discount Software. They had one employee—they made it sound like they had a whole host of employees, but they really had only one. Also, they were close by, about ten or fifteen miles away. It seemed like a natural to me. They made an offer for exclusive marketing rights, and I accepted. We continued under that arrangement for about two or three years.

INTERVIEWER: *When you wrote Vulcan, did you have any notion that it would be so successful?*

RATLIFF: I went through various stages. Before I started marketing it myself, I had a delusion that if ten percent of the people who read *BYTE* bought it, I could quit my job and retire. That idea didn't last long. When the first deluge of orders did *not* come in, I revised my expectations. Even after I made the agreement with Ashton-Tate, I noted in my journal that I expected to net $100,000 on the deal. Total. I think that was an indication of how conservative my aspirations had become.

INTERVIEWER: Let's talk about the transition from Vulcan to dBASE. What kinds of advances did you make in Vulcan that led to the present product?

RATLIFF: Some advances were made in the user interface, and a few improvements in performance, but the big change was to draw it away from a teletype orientation to full-screen orientation. After I saw DataStar, I recognized that the two-dimensional screen was where everybody wanted to be.

"If I had followed my heart instead of advice, dBASE would be much closer to perfection today."

The new commands I added were almost exclusively in the user interface. I don't think I ever caught up on all the advancements it needed. My understanding of today's perception of dBASE is that the program is not very user-friendly. I think, in retrospect, if I had followed my heart instead of advice, dBASE would be much closer to perfection today.

INTERVIEWER: But it's a very successful, highly rated product. Is that just the perfectionist in you talking?

RATLIFF: I got advice on different things: Make it bigger, make it faster, make it smaller, go to 16-bit, make it multi-user, go to multiple languages, French, English, Dutch, German.... There was such a plethora of different directions that I tried to satisfy all of them a little bit. Ultimately, I think that was my mistake.

My intention was to make the program more powerful and more user-friendly. If I had stayed with that, the program would be better today, but I'm not sure it would be more successful. Maybe the advice I got was right. In many respects, it's hard for me to think of any way the program could have been more successful in terms of gross sales.

INTERVIEWER: Why do you think dBASE is so successful?

RATLIFF: There was a tremendous amount of luck. But dBASE was also the right program in the right place at the right time, and that's not totally luck, that's design. The fact that it is a language, as well as a database manager, has turned out to be enormously important.

dBASE caught people's imaginations because it's very open-ended. The way I've programmed all my life is as a toolmaker. When I compare myself, even ten years ago, with other programmers, I see that I was trying to generalize to a large extent; they were trying to write programs that would solve a specific need. Their programs would frequently be delivered much sooner than mine would be, but mine would have longer lifetimes. Once the specific need went away, their programs were dead, they had to be rewritten each time the needs changed. I always wrote in such a way that the program could solve a family of problems, rather than just a single one.

dBASE was different from programs like BASIC, C, FORTRAN, and COBOL in that a lot of the dirty work had already been done. The data manipulation is done by dBASE instead of by the user, so the user can concentrate on what he is doing, rather than having to mess with the dirty details of opening, reading, and closing files, and managing space allocation.

INTERVIEWER: *So from the very first, you had the user in mind during the design of dBASE?*

RATLIFF: Oh, absolutely. People frequently ask me questions such as, "Should we do it this way, or should we do it that way?" Intuitively, I go back and think, "What do users want? How are they going to use this? What good is it to them?" A lot of programmers think only about how something can be programmed. They've never sold, they've never marketed. They're very good programmers, but they're not thinking of the real market.

INTERVIEWER: *In that respect, would you advise programmers to be less technology-driven and more considerate of users and the market?*

RATLIFF: Yes. Do you think hacker is a good word or a bad word? If you think it's a good word, then they're hackers. They're good people, but they're thinking of *their* job rather than the user, and you have to go a little beyond that. That's how dBASE got started. I was thinking of how I wanted to use it.

INTERVIEWER: *You've seen major transformations come over the industry since you entered it. In what way have your programming techniques changed with the times?*

RATLIFF: The changes are not from what I have learned, but from the changes in computers. When I started working in computers, I always punched the programs up on cards, and ran in batch. I'd take my card deck to the operator and plead with him, turn my job in, and then I'd go back and check the window every half hour to see if it had run and had printed. In general, I'd write an entire program on paper, do a lot of erasing and editing, then give it to a keypunch operator to punch up the deck. That was the big bang approach: You'd write the whole program out and try to make it good on paper. Running it on a computer was just getting it to work. There was no gradual improvement.

Today, with CRTs, you can type in the program yourself. With personal computers, you have almost instant turnaround, but they aren't as powerful as the big machines, so it may take a long time to compile and execute. So I tend to write a few lines at a time and try it out, get it to work, then write a few more lines. I try to do the least amount of work per iteration to make some real substantive change. So now, programming is much more evolutionary, where before it was sort of a big bang.

INTERVIEWER: *Does the end product usually differ a lot from your beginning plan?*

RATLIFF: In some respects. I always get ideas and suggestions as I go along. When I plan a project now, it ends up doing virtually everything that I had initially planned, plus a lot more. Or, when I start playing with it, I see an opportunity for improvement. I'm always on the lookout for an opportunity in any form.

INTERVIEWER: *Do you still program today?*

RATLIFF: Not as much as I'd like to. I get too involved in the business.

INTERVIEWER: *Yes, it seems that a lot of programmers who have successful programs are swept away from their original roots, and transplanted into management....*

RATLIFF: That's happened a lot to me, but my involvement in management is going to decline, disappear even. I hope it does, because management siphons away an awful lot of time. When I come to the office, I don't do any programming at all. I talk, either on the phone, face-to-face, or in meetings. I do virtually all my programming at home.

INTERVIEWER: *How do you balance your home life with the business and the bouts of intense, late-night programming?*

RATLIFF: I generally work on programming projects when my wife, Carolyn, lets me. Before I was married, between marriages actually, I worked until around midnight. I like working at night because there are no distractions. The phone doesn't ring, the mailman and the gardener don't come. It's quiet, so there's time to concentrate.

INTERVIEWER: *Have you settled on a particular style of work you regard as genuinely productive for your own purposes?*

RATLIFF: I work well either alone or with extremely small groups of people. Once a group gets beyond six, it's totally out of control. Ted Glasser, who has a number of patents and is a very senior person in the computing industry, and is in *Who's Who*, once told people that the biggest team he could manage was one that could drive out to get pizza in a Volkswagen. Since then he's changed his tune—it's now a regular-size American car. I wholeheartedly agree with that.

As for multiple projects, I generally only do one thing to the exclusion of all else. If I switch, it's a total switch. I may have to put something aside, and it may stay on the sidelines, not worked on for months at a time, and then I go back to it. That's the only way I multiprocess. Once I start a project, I really like to finish. I may not get it to the final, complete state, but I get it to some acceptable state. There has to be some good reason for me to set something aside. Something bigger, like guilt. Guilt works well. If I feel that I'm violating a commitment I made to someone, then I'll put aside something that I really favor.

> *"With computers, if I need something at midnight that I don't have, I can make it, no matter what it is."*

I'm the kind of programmer who likes to do some planning, but I don't plan everything out in infinite detail. I have an idea of what the goal is, but the real job is to find out what the next step is to get toward that goal. I try to do the minimum that will get me one step further. Within a goal, within a step, I take the minimum subset. I don't go for the most difficult part first, nor the easiest. It's not mathematically defined. It's emotionally and intuitively defined.

INTERVIEWER: *Then you wouldn't consider yourself detail-oriented?*

RATLIFF: No, I do the details because I know they need to be done. It's not something I enjoy doing. I mean, trimming off nanoseconds is, I feel, totally unimportant. If the program runs at half the speed you think it really ought to, you know that a year from now, with the new machinery, it'll run right on.

INTERVIEWER: *What is it about programming that satisfies you?*

RATLIFF: Well, the custom-made sports car I worked on was a satisfying project because I could make something and have it appear in front of my eyes. The worst problem with that project was I needed parts that didn't exist.

With computers, if I need something at midnight that I don't have, I can make it, no matter what it is. The worst that can possibly happen is that it takes a long time to make.

Of course, that's not all I like about programming. I like the high-tech thing, I like being able to do something and have it appear on the screen. If you write a program well, it's very elegant; it sings, it's well built. I enjoy it from an engineering point of view, just like a well-built car, a well-built bridge, or a well-built building. Everything about it seems in balance, tuned.

INTERVIEWER: Can you elaborate on this feeling for balance and elegance?

RATLIFF: Balance takes many forms. The code should be crisp and concise. You should be able to explain any module in one sentence, and things should be in alphabetical order, if possible. Just from a visual view of indentation, it shouldn't go off the edge of the paper at any point. It shouldn't have one "if" that's huge and an "else" that's small. Everything should be balanced everywhere. Balance is the key word.

INTERVIEWER: When you write code, does it come out balanced the first time or does it need a lot of changes?

RATLIFF: I do a lot of changing. I like to make an analogy between writing code and sculpting a clay figure. You start with a lump of clay and then you scrape away, add more clay, then scrape away again. And every now and then you decide that a leg doesn't look right, so you tear it off and put a new one on. There's a lot of interaction.

The ideal module should be a page long. If it grows beyond a page, I have to decide, now what is it I'm doing here? How many separate things am I working on? Should they be broken down into separate modules? Part of the elegance, and the balance, is that at a certain level, in this layer-cake hierarchy of a program, all the modules should be about the same weight, same size, same duty, and same functionality.

INTERVIEWER: How does balance help a program?

RATLIFF: The program becomes maintainable. When you have a good balance, it's as though you've discovered some basic physical underlying principle and implemented it. When things get really out of balance, you know something is wrong. There's probably some inherent fault that makes it out of balance. Generally, when I get this feeling that something's out of whack when one module is just too big, I think about what I'm doing, and I reorient or rejuggle the pieces.

INTERVIEWER: Has anyone in particular influenced your programming?

RATLIFF: I was really impressed by a book by Gary Meyer, called *Software Reliability*. Other books have also influenced me in very simple ways. Putting things in alphabetical order is a trick I learned from programming style books. It makes things simple, it makes the program clean, and it's one step toward elegance. That's absolute simplicity: I can't imagine why I didn't think of it on my own.

Another influence was one of my bosses at Martin Marietta, Phil Carney. I used to write FORTRAN programs back then, and when I needed a new statement number, I'd pick the next one sequentially. You don't think of those things in order as the program goes, so I'd choose them arbitrarily. When he saw me do that, he got irritated and said, "Put these things in order, starting with one hundred, and increase them by ten each time." I thought that made a lot of sense. Those are small things, but small things really help.

INTERVIEWER: Do you ever tire of programming?

RATLIFF: When I find myself doing the same thing over and over and over again, I get bored. I remember having this vague feeling at JPL that I was writing the same loop over and over. Everything was a little bit different each time I did it, but the loop was basically the same. Then one day I was thumbing through the *Structured Programming* book, and I just happened to see this flowchart of structured-programming design, and I thought, that's what I need. And it was.

INTERVIEWER: Do you write a lot of comments in your programs?

RATLIFF: Actually, no. I have been criticized in this company for not writing very many comments. I figure there are two types of comments: one is explaining the obvious, and those are worse than worthless, the other kind is when you explain really involved, convoluted code. Well, I always try to avoid convoluted code. I try to program really strong, clear, clean code, even if it takes an extra five lines. I am almost of the opinion that the more comments you need, the worse your program is and something is wrong with it. A good program should not require a lot of comments. The program itself should be the commentary.

Modules should be relatively small. Once a module gets beyond a page of code, there's something wrong. You definitely need one line of comment at the top of each module, which explains what the module does in one sentence. If you can't explain it in one sentence, there's something wrong.

INTERVIEWER: *What qualities distinguish an outstanding programmer?*

RATLIFF: There's a spectrum of programming. At one end is a programmer who's working 100 percent for the user; at the other end is a programmer who's working on some mathematical problem and couldn't care less about the user. Curiously enough, game writers are most in tune with the user. The mathematics of the game are probably an irritant to that programmer, whereas, on the other end of the scale, the programmer writing a better square root algorithm finds deciding whether it's going to be at the top or the bottom of the screen an irritant. I would like to place myself about three-quarters of the way toward the game writer, toward the user-interface side.

"Programming is a little bit like the army. Now that I'm out, it's neat to have had the experience."

You can't compare across the spectrum, but you can compare up and down within the spectrum. Theodore Sturgeon said 90 percent of everything is garbage. That's not too far off. That might be a little bit pessimistic—maybe 60, 70, or 80 percent. There's very clear evidence that 3 percent of the population, in any identifiable subset, do 10 percent of the work, and then on the other side, 50 percent of the people only do 30 percent of the total work. That goes for football quarterbacks, programmers, newspaper reporters, and everybody else. There's always a few people who do six times as much work as that 50 percent. So there are good and bad programmers, just as there are good and bad employees in all areas.

INTERVIEWER: *When you're developing a program, is it a painful or pleasurable process?*

RATLIFF: It's a little of both. Programming is a little bit like the army. When I was in the army, I hated it passionately. I dreaded every minute of it. I looked forward to getting out. But now that I'm out, it's neat to have had the experience. When I'm programming, I enjoy figuring out little things along the way, and when I'm done, it's nice to have gone through it, but still I would rather accomplish more per unit of time. So, there's also a very small amount of agony all the time.

The moment of programming I enjoy the very most is when I get something almost complete. I try it for the first time, it fails miserably, and it continues to fail until about the one hundredth time, when it does pretty good. There's a peak experience there, because then I know I've got it. I just have to apply a little more elbow grease to weed out the rest of the bugs.

INTERVIEWER: Is a programmer's work so individual that someone could look at your code and say, "C. Wayne Ratliff wrote this"?

RATLIFF: Well, Gary Balleisen, who wrote SuperCalc and who used the source code from the early stages of dBASE, claims he can tell who wrote what by some style signature. I know some things I do, such as the way I terminate blocks, are at odds with everyone else here. And I'm convinced my way is by far the best.

For example, when I first saw C, I didn't like those curly braces that stick so far out to the left side in the listing. It was confusing. But by accident, I ran across a technique in some documentation from Digital Research that said to put those terminators at the same level as the indented code. Well, that's another one of these tiny little changes that make a big difference. And I've been trying to convince everyone else that's the right way to do it. I've been only moderately successful. I even modified one program, a C-beautifier program, to do it automatically. I can take someone else's code and run it through this program, and it will be indented the way I indent.

INTERVIEWER: Have you ever explored the field of artificial intelligence?

RATLIFF: I was really involved in AI at the start of this business. A little over a year ago, I turned to AI, because I thought that was the future. But I've grown away from it.

AI has a future, but it's not very immediate. First of all, there's the problem of natural language. If you have a natural-language system, you buy it and bring it home and put it on your computer. Then you have to go through a weeks-long, maybe months-long process to teach it what your particular words mean. The same word has different meanings in different contexts. Even what would appear to be a straightforward word, like "profit," can have a variety of meanings. It needs to be very explicitly defined, based on which business you're in and how your books are set up, and that sort of thing. So this long process necessary for training the machine kills AI, as far as it being a turnkey product.

But the other side, which is very interesting, is expert systems. My prediction is that within the next two or three years, expert systems will no longer be associated with artificial intelligence. That's been the history of AI: when something starts to become fairly well known, it splits off. Pattern recognition used to be considered AI, but now it is a separate field. That's the immediate destiny of expert systems. I think expert systems are going to be very important in our industry, analogous to vertical applications.

INTERVIEWER: Do you think there's going to be any major changes in what we think of as programs, in terms of the way we work and deal with them? Perhaps a new language so simple, so user-friendly that everyone can program?

RATLIFF: There'll be some evolution. Some of the arcane features will slowly disappear. A language like dBASE has some really bad things about it, but over time those will disappear through a gradual evolutionary process. And we can always cross our fingers and hope that there will be some breakthrough, like the spreadsheet was when it first appeared. I hope there will be something that neat again in the future, but it's totally unpredictable.

I'm really enamored with a UNIX program called yacc that builds you a parser. You give it specifications for your language in Backus-Naur form, which is widely accepted in the computer-science industry. It will crank out a C module that parses a language that fits the specs. I'd love to be able to do that for a higher-level program. Ideally, you'd write down your program just as specs, then you'd compile it, and the result would be the program. You could probably write something the size of dBASE in a month.

INTERVIEWER: Do you ever think of retiring from programming?

RATLIFF: No. I have every expectation of programming for years to come. My wife occasionally has dreams that we'll get rid of all the computers and spend all our time with our horses, and I say, "wait a minute, that's not what I want." I would like to get rid of the stress, but I don't want to get rid of programming.

INTERVIEWER: When a project as intense as dBASE is completed, is there a feeling of anticlimax when it's over?

RATLIFF: That's when you have to think of some new project. A program is a lot of fun at the very beginning, when you first have ideas about what it can do. Those ideas grow very rapidly. You have some little spark, and then you keep tacking other capabilities onto it. When that euphoria fades and you have to start coding, it gets tough.

I used to think that everybody was a designer in this business. I would go over to George Tate's house, and drink beer and eat pizza, and a lot of times Hal and George and I would meet for a half hour before the beer drinking got started, and in about a half hour, I could get a year's worth of work planned. Everybody wants to do the design work. The implementation, the year of work, and all the rest of it is left to someone else.

INTERVIEWER: But you don't do that at all. You write it as well as design it.

RATLIFF: Yes, but a lot of design is an ongoing process, it's not a flash of insight, and then an immediate implementation. One of the problems this company's struggling with is finding the best way to do software.

For whatever reason, they don't fel they can trust individuals, or at least a small number of individuals. The procedure now is that Marketing figures out what the program is supposed to do; then Marketing tells Development what they think that is; then Development spends several months and writes down a very detailed spec of what they think they heard; then many people in the company review that spec and negotiate exactly what it's supposed to do. Then the hard work's over. From then on, it's just coded.

This process may be appropriate if you're building bridges, because you know exactly what the bridge is supposed to do. It's supposed to go from one side of the river to the other, and you can specify exactly how much maximum weight it's going to carry, and all the other details ahead of time. In fact, with a bridge, I would imagine you can specify everything on one sheet of paper. That's about as much spec as I think a computer program should go through, too: one sheet of paper.

There's a general agreement in the company that the current process doesn't work, or it's so painful that it's not worth it. It's better to find somebody who has an idea, slip them money under the door, let them work for a long time unhindered, and when they think they're finished with it, you let other people work with the program and make their suggestions about how to improve it.

It's also important to try out the program on users to make sure it solves real users' needs. And that's where this company is going astray; it's ignoring users. They've gotten caught up in marketing, and what they're really fighting are other marketers. All the ads are done by marketers, they're not done by users saying this is what we need. It's one marketer, trying to pit his or her skills against another marketer, so they're fighting the battle of the specs. And I think that's wrong. You may look great in the ads, but so what? What has sold dBASE has not been its ads, although the first ads I think, in hindsight, were extremely good.

INTERVIEWER: What was the first advertising campaign?

RATLIFF: That was the dBASE versus the bilge-pump ad by Hal Pawluk.

It was sort of an inflammatory advertisement at the time it was written.

INTERVIEWER: *Why?*

RATLIFF: The first line of the ad said, "We all know that bilge pumps suck." The company that manufactures that particular bilge pump wrote a letter to George Tate, saying they didn't like having their bilge pump shown in a pejorative sense. George said, "okay, we'll put a little note down at the bottom of the ad that says this particular bilge pump doesn't suck." For some reason, they didn't like that ad either.

> ## "I'm an entrepreneur. I like to start from nothing and make something."

INTERVIEWER: *That's a pretty good ad. I guess back then business wasn't quite as rigid as it is now. Do you miss that sort of thing?*

RATLIFF: Oh, yeah. As a matter of fact, I'm not dealing well with the company right now. We have a lot of problems. I'm an entrepreneur, and as such, I like to start from nothing and make something. Some people like to take something small through the growth phase and make it something big, and some people like to take something big and nurture it into something even bigger, the mature phase. There are three phases. I think any two of the adjacent phases are fairly compatible, but I feel like I'm in phase one trying to be compatible with phase three. That's causing a lot of friction.

INTERVIEWER: *That's a good analysis. It seems that's happening in the industry, too. It's reaching the stage of bigness, companies have just shot up, and now people are having to deal with it, and they're just frustrated . . . .*

RATLIFF: But software hasn't changed. It's the companies that have changed. There is some evidence that the companies' attitudes are wrong. Certainly, it takes a businessman to run the company, but to some extent, people coming into the industry at this late date don't empathize with what software really is. They're in the *business* business, not in the software business.

INTERVIEWER: *What is software, in the context of that remark?*

RATLIFF: Ideally, it's a way of making a computer do something beneficial that ultimately helps people. I'm not so altruistic, that's not my goal. My goal is to write neat software, programs that are challenging. It's not my mission to solve social needs, but that can be another nice outcome of software.

INTERVIEWER: *Do you consider computer programming an art, a science, a skill, a trade . . . ?*

126

RATLIFF: I think there's some science and some art. The more human-ized it becomes the more art it is. Game writers are dealing mostly with an art form on the screen, and they're using a high-tech product to embody and convey that art. You'd be pretty much in the same boat if you really had to un-derstand the chemical makeup of clay to be a modeling sculptor. You can learn enough to sculpt clay in a few minutes, but to become adequate with a computer takes time, and more than time, it takes desire.

INTERVIEWER: *What's next after dBASE?*

RATLIFF: Opportunities are changing in scope. With the three classic productivity tools, databases, word processors, and spreadsheets, there's not much room for another new entry, though there are contenders all the time. Look at Paradox: They're trying to become the leading database, or at least get market share. And there's Javelin; it's supposed to destroy 1-2-3. I'm not sure who can be destroyed right now. None of the word processors have the dominant market share, but there are several of them that have a pretty good chunk. Between Microsoft Word, Multimate, WordStar, Word Perfect, Samna, and five hundred others, there's not much opportunity for coming up with a new successful word processor.

There's a lot of opportunity, but not in those areas. I think there's a lot of opportunity for people to be successful marketing expert systems; not just the shells, but the knowledge bases as well, that deal with a fairly large class of problems. With that kind of expert system, you could approach dozens of ver-tical markets.

INTERVIEWER: *Do you think it's possible to design a system that can ac-commodate a dozen or so of those vertical markets?*

RATLIFF: Possibly. At least you can attack one at a time. Even if there are a thousand vertical markets, each of those has several thousand potential buyers. And even if you just address one at a time, then theoretically, if you write a good product, with a small vertical market, you could get near sat-uration level because they are kind of cliquish.

INTERVIEWER: *Do you think IBM will continue to dominate?*

RATLIFF: I think so. It seems to me that Apple missed its bid, all across the board. They really missed it on the business side, and I think that proba-bly hurt them on the home side. I think there's a little bit of disillusionment about the Macintosh potential. AT&T doesn't seem to be going anywhere, and none of the other companies seems to be making a very strong bid. What keeps IBM on top, I suppose, are all the clones.

Actually, I like the way the market sits right now; the competition forces IBM to make advances, and the competitors know if they don't make advances on IBM, they're going to get hurt. If that can be perpetuated, it would be good. Where the other companies stay compatible with IBM, and in many regards have a superior product, they're kept in line by the fact that there is IBM. I'd like to see that they all live happily ever after. Back when IBM was much stronger in the mainframe business, I really disliked IBM computers.

> *"It's not my mission to solve social needs, but that can be a nice outcome of software."*

The 360s, 370s, 3030x's, and the 4340 series; I didn't like them at all. I was really glad to see the signing of the agreement between Microsoft and IBM. My fear was that IBM was going to develop their own operating system, and I've seen IBM-developed operating systems.

INTERVIEWER: *Do you ever reflect on the past and feel amazement at what has happened?*

RATLIFF: Oh, yeah. There are a lot of things that could have turned out differently. I remember very specifically the fear and anxiety I would have every time a new product came out. Back in the Vulcan days, I was working late one night, and some guy called me and said, "Have you heard about DataStar?" I said I hadn't heard about it.

"A full-page ad," he said, "a MicroPro product." I'd sold thirty or forty Vulcans at that time. I thought, it was fine while it lasted, but it's all over now, because I can't match their resources. I got really downhearted, but after a while, it went away. Then InfoStar was next. MicroPro fixed their problems with DataStar; a big advertising campaign, a big this, a big that, and I thought, oh, well. The same thing with Knowlege Man. When Knowledge Man came out I was so close to achieving some goals I had set out for myself. I was 60 or 70 percent of the way there, and then I thought some new thing was going to come out and kill me.

I started getting less worried each time. I didn't get very concerned about R:base. And I've gotten even less concerned about ANZA. It doesn't do any good to get worried, what happens, happens.

INTERVIEWER: *Have you seen Paradox yet?*

RATLIFF: No, I haven't looked at any of the competing products. I was talking to Eric Kim and Dave Hull in Marketing at a party last week, and they asked me what I thought of Paradox, and I said I hadn't seen it. "What, you haven't seen that?" they asked. I said, "I've never looked at any of these products—I haven't even seen R:base 4000." "You haven't seen R:base 4000?," they said. We went back through history and all the other ones I hadn't seen. They just couldn't believe that I hadn't seen them, hadn't played with them and gotten ideas from them.

INTERVIEWER: *What are you currently working on?*

RATLIFF: Recently, I've been working on a public-domain package that I have transcribed from Pascal to C. It's a design and documentation language, sort of a clone, or a superset of PDL, Program Design Language, proposed by Caine, Farber, and Gordon in Pasadena. It's neat because it feels like writing a program, but it doesn't actually execute on the computer. It's a way of doing specifications and design.

INTERVIEWER: *What's your advice to young programmers today?*

RATLIFF: If somebody *wants* to program, it will be easy for them. If they don't want to, no matter how hard they try, at best it will be difficult. More than likely, they'll become disillusioned. So my advice is, do what you want to do.

I've seen people who were not originally involved in programming or computers, and they got into it and liked it. And they just got drawn right in, and got to the heart of it all really fast. I've seen other people who tried to make themselves get involved in it, and they couldn't do it.

INTERVIEWER: *What is the magic? What do you think draws somebody into the heart of it?*

RATLIFF: Well, it's some combination. I used to play a mental game and ask myself, what would I be if I'd been born a hundred years earlier? I don't know, but one possibility is a detective, because there's a lot of detective work in programming, particularly in debugging. You work with hints, clues. One of the good things about programming is that you are dealing in hard reality, whereas in real detective work, you can't get an answer a lot of times. In programming, all it takes is hard work. You can always get the answer if you work at it hard enough. I see myself as a generalist, and I think for what I have done, that was important. There are better programers than me, there are better debuggers and designers, and better everything. I can't repeat in polite company exactly what a drill sergeant once said to me, but it was in essence that "I'm a jack of all trades and master of none."

← →   - Moves the cursor.

space   - Changes the direction indicator.

>   - Absolute move. Requests coordinates of where you want to move;
            you end coordinates with ↓.

!   - Recalculates all values (to force an extra recalculation).

label   - Start with a letter (A-Z), or ", and end with ←, →, or ↓.
entry   Use ESC to erase last thing typed.

value   - Start with a number (0-9), +, or -; end with ↓ or, if appropriate,
entry   ← or →. Entry references may be used wherever numbers are allowed;
            type coordinates or point with cursor. Evaluation is left to
            right with <u>no</u> precedence. ESC erases last thing typed.

/N   - Sets entry to N/A/ value.

/B   - Blanks out entry; erases what was there.

/OO   - Sets order of recalculation to C (down columns) or R (across rows).
/OR   - Sets recalculation to be auto (A) or manual (M)   characters
/OC   - Sets size of columns on the screen (must be >0). End with ↓.
            If screen is split, only affects part of screen with cursor.

/R   - Replicates entry. Needs range (such as A2-D2) specifying where
            to place copies (followed by ↓). If replicating an expression,
            it will ask for each entry reference whether it should not be
            modified (N), or should always refer to entry in same relative
            position (R).

/S   - Screen control, sets split screen (H for horizontal, or V for
            vertical) at cursor position, undoes split and makes it one
            screen (1), sets label areas at cursor position (L), or undoes
            label areas and returns screen to normal (N). └ prompts for Horizontal (H)

;   - If screen is split, moves cursor from one half to another.   " Vertical (V
                                                                          " normal (N)

©1978, 1986 Daniel S. Bricklin

Bricklin's reference card for an early version of Visi-
Calc (called Calculedger or CL at the time), which he
wrote and typed on a rented IBM Selectric typewriter
to use in a demonstration at Apple. The Appendix
(pages 332-333) contains additional mementos from
the early days of VisiCalc.

Dan Bricklin

PHILADELPHIA native
Dan Bricklin was born on July 16, 1951. He graduated from MIT in 1973 with a bachelor's degree in electrical engineering and computer science, then worked as a programmer for Digital Equipment Corporation and Fas Fax Corporation before entering graduate school in business at Harvard University. While at Harvard, he designed an electronic spreadsheet program, drawing upon the expertise and advice of his classmates and professors.

In 1978, while still at Harvard, he teamed up with Bob Frankston, an old classmate from MIT, to develop a workable version of the program. This became VisiCalc. They formed a company called Software Arts, which they incorporated in January of 1979, and in April of the same year they signed a contract with Personal Software, the company that was to market the VisiCalc program. (Personal Software eventually became VisiCorp.) The news of VisiCalc spread rapidly. By May 1981, VisiCalc sales had exceeded 100,000 units. In 1983, cumulative sales topped 500,000 units. The success of Software Arts continued until 1984 when it entered into an extended legal battle with VisiCorp over the rights to VisiCalc.

In May 1985, Dan Bricklin left Software Arts to be a consultant at Lotus for a short time. Bricklin has since founded Software Garden, his newest venture, which was officially incorporated in November 1985. His first product is named "Dan Bricklin's Demo Program."

I met with Dan Bricklin at his suburban Boston home. He works out of an extra bedroom, which serves as the office for his new, one-person company, Software Garden. With a new philosophy stemming from his experience with the rise and fall of Software Arts, Dan Bricklin is starting over. This time it is not with the innocence, unleashed enthusiasm, and incredible energy of his first venture, but rather with a certain degree of caution, insight, and control. As Bricklin says, his intent is not to run a ranch or tend a farm, but to cultivate a garden of software, just like a garden in the backyard; one that is sufficient to meet his needs and from which he can gain pleasure and satisfaction.

It is evident that Bricklin's past experience with VisiCalc has weighed heavily upon him. He is a soft-spoken, easygoing, intelligent man. In a careful, reflective manner, Bricklin discussed his experience developing the VisiCalc spreadsheet program and running Software Arts, and shared his ideas of what he looks forward to achieving with his new program and his new company.

INTERVIEWER: *During the time you were studying at MIT, how were you involved with computers?*

BRICKLIN: In early 1970 I went off to MIT, and did computer-oriented work. I got a job at Project MAC, which is now known as the Laboratory for Computer Science. There I met Bob Frankston, David Reed, and other programmers who went on to do lots of good stuff.

I programmed there for a long time, all the way through undergraduate school. My first project was a calculator. It surprised me that the time-sharing system at MIT, Multics, did not have a command-line calculator where you could say, "Calc 2 plus 2," and it says, "4," or sine of X, or whatever, so I worked on one. An AI group upstairs was working on LISP. There was a wide variety of people at MIT, like Richard Stallman, the famous hacker. Also, MIT exposed me to some real, experienced professionals in many fields.

INTERVIEWER: *What other projects did you work on at MIT?*

BRICKLIN: I did a wide variety of things. I was a member of the team implementing APL, and by 1973 I was running the project that implemented APL. I was also involved in the LISP project.

In the fall of 1973 I took a job at Digital Equipment Corporation in Typeset-10, their computerized typesetting group. I had originally been offered a job in their languages group; my training was in languages. But during my interview at Digital, I ran into a person I had worked with at MIT, Michael Spier, who suggested I look at the typesetting group. My father was a printer and his father was a printer before him, so I found the typesetting group more intriguing than languages. Typesetting was more of a real-world application. We had video screens and computerized typesetters.

INTERVIEWER: What did you do for the Typeset-10 group?

BRICKLIN: The first thing I did was wire-service translation programs. The wires coming in would be translated into a language the computer could understand for its typesetting. I learned a lot about real-world systems on this job. If the program had a bug and caused printing to be late, the newspaper would be late, costing them a lot of money, and I'd hear about it. We were working to deadlines, under a lot of pressure.

The people at the newspaper just wanted to do their jobs. They were not interested in the technology. As long as the technology worked, they were satisfied and they didn't think about it. So I learned about how non-technical people perceive technology.

I remember when one newspaper advertised on the radio that they were going to have the transcripts of the Watergate tapes available, and the Watergate tapes were coming over the wire in a certain format that the program didn't know how to handle. To get it out in time, we had to modify the program on the fly. At the same time, we were reading the tapes coming off the wire for the very first time. I remember that very well. I was actually flying to another newspaper when that occurred and I was called back because of the problem. It was real exciting. All I had was a toothbrush in my pocket when I returned, because all my luggage had gone off to Canada.

The newspaper was a real-world system, with immense pressures, compared to being in a compiler development group or back at MIT, where people are very tolerant of problems and say, "We'll fix it next month."

Something else that made an impression on me was the realization that real users work differently than programmers. Whenever something would slow down, the people at the newspaper would arbitrarily give it a higher priority on the schedule, which would screw up the whole scheduling algorithm on the computer. And they wondered why things were "funny."

For example, they used a Model 33 teletype for the system console, and once a little bit of paper got stuck in the optical-character reader that was reading the typed copy. So, because of this little piece of paper, there were just a few more errors per page that the typesetting program would find and it would say "bad format." But all those messages were on the operator console, and the operator console got behind because it was a cheap, slow 33 teletype. The whole system was waiting for that machine to catch up.

> "To me, the most important part of a program is laying out the data structures."

So there they were, with this million-dollar computer system, and the entire newspaper ran late just because of this one little piece of paper, and because they had a slow 33 teletype. Then they went off and got themselves a thirty-character-per-second terminal a day or two later, and everything was fine.

INTERVIEWER: *What came after the Typeset-10 project was finished?*

BRICKLIN: The next thing I did was to get involved in the first word-processing effort at DEC. I had already done a typesetting terminal program for DEC, and then I went into word processing after having done some software work on another typesetting terminal. I got to microcode at a very low level, and I actually wrote the first pass of the microcode for a machine that had 512 bytes of memory. It was going to be burnt into ROM. Then I went into PDP-8s and word processing.

INTERVIEWER: *What kind of features did this word processor have?*

BRICKLIN: We had very strong limitations on our hardware. Basically, we had to use standard Digital hardware. We were able to get a minor modification to one of the Digital terminals to allow it to scroll down as well as up, but that was about it. We couldn't use any special hardware for word processing like most other companies ended up doing. I was the project leader for a group that designed a word-processing system. It was a PDP-8 that had 16K, 12-bit words. Our product was very competitive with today's WordStar in terms of features.

We had a good mailmerge, along with list processing and background printing. We could edit a document as large as a floppy because it was not an in-memory editor. We all designed it, and I wrote the actual specification for the word processor, as well as the code for the file system, the command system, and the background printer.

That experience taught me a lot about bringing a product to market. Designing computerized typesetters taught me about the great importance of using the screen effectively and minimizing the number of keystrokes, since many typesetters are paid by the keystroke. That knowledge later was important to me in designing word processors, and it was also valuable in my work with VisiCalc.

INTERVIEWER: *Was the workplace at DEC as high-pressure for you as that at Typeset-10?*

BRICKLIN: At Digital I was working usually from 11:00 in the morning until 1:00 at night. I wore torn blue jeans, beard out to here, and hair way down my back.

Digital moved up to New Hampshire and I didn't feel like moving with them, so I started looking around and talking to headhunters. It became obvious to me that I should get an MBA so I would be more marketable. I was also conscious of the people I saw who were in dead-end jobs as programmers, where they were competing against the young whippersnappers like myself, who had good training, would take lower salaries, and work longer hours. I could see it was going to be very hard to stay on top. I saw programmers in their fifties having problems getting jobs. Plus, I had always wanted to go into business for myself, so I thought business school would give me the proper training.

I applied to business school at Harvard and MIT and was accepted at both schools. Initially I wanted to go to MIT because it was a shorter program and I thought I should just get in and out quickly, but in the end I chose Harvard because I felt there was so much to learn I had better spend two years. While waiting to go to business school, I took another job that proved to be quite interesting.

The job was head of programming in a very small company, which made electronic cash registers based on micros. It used Motorola 6800s. They were able to put 64K on one of their boards. It used a coax cable, of sorts, which ran between each of the cash registers. It was programmed in some variant of FORTH. I did a lot of work on the existing system, maintaining it, adding some new features, and upgrading it to the new hardware.

The user base consisted of teenagers working in fast food stores. If something broke, it would take a day for a service technician to show up, and you don't want to stop a fast food place. It was a real sophisticated system. The home office would poll all their stores every night by computer and dump the information out electronically. They knew how many pickle slices were left on the shelf. When you said you wanted a Big Mac, it knew the recipe.

I watched a real small company actually exist selling against NCR and

> *"Maybe technology will pass me by, maybe not."*

places like that. It was a big change after Digital, which just had hit about a billion dollars in sales and had made the Fortune 500. I was primed for business school.

INTERVIEWER: *Did you come up with the idea for VisiCalc in business school? What prompted it specifically?*

BRICKLIN: In business school I used the DEC system when I needed to write a little BASIC program to help me with my homework. But it wasn't fast enough. Even if it only took me 15 or 20 minutes to throw together a little program to do the analysis we wanted for a group project, that wasn't fast enough, and the program usually had bugs.

That's when I came up with the idea for VisiCalc, putting together the immediacy of word processing and the fluidity of the screen.

INTERVIEWER: *How did you initially envision the design of VisiCalc?*

BRICKLIN: The original design was futuristic. I would have my hand on my calculator and the calculator would have a ball on the bottom of it, like a mouse, so you could move it around to position the cursor on the screen. It had the number key pad right there so you wouldn't even have to take your hand off in order to do a calculation. I wanted to implement a head-up display, as with a fighter plane where you see the numbers in front of you. I proto-typed it in BASIC in the spring of 1978.

INTERVIEWER: *When you got the idea, did you imagine it was destined to become as successful as it did?*

BRICKLIN: The program went through a lot of evolution before it be-came VisiCalc. I described it to a friend of mine at Harvard, John Reese, and he was very encouraging. The next thing I thought of was to use a Z80-based machine or something like it, and a TV screen. I thought it would still be nice if it had a mouse. But when I started to prototype it on the Harvard machine, which had no mouse, I had to figure out how to address things. I was faced with the problem of "how do you take these and do that, or take these and add it to that," because there wasn't a mouse on the Harvard machine. So I came up with the row-and-column way of doing it.

Then I told my production professor. He was very encouraging. He said: "You know, the type of stuff you're talking about, people do on blackboards now when they do production planning. And sometimes they have blackboards that stretch the length of two rooms. And they'll sit there and do the week-to-week planning of this many sold, this many manufactured, this many left. Your program sounds neat." I talked to another professor in accounting, Jim Cash, who encouraged me by saying, "Good human interface is what is really needed in commerical products. It's a big problem in many system designs." And I thought, this guy really knows what he's talking about.

Then I went to see my finance professor, who was discouraging. He looked up from his printouts and he said: "Well, there already are financial forecasting systems and people won't buy micros, for example, to do real estate. Go ask this guy, Fylstra. He's one of my students. He just did a survey to see why they won't buy it." So I called Fylstra to see what he was doing and he said, "Hey, my fiancé and I are making software and selling it out of my apartment here. We're going to be selling chess programs. If you've got anything of interest, why don't you show it to me." I didn't talk to him again until fall.

That summer I made the decision, while riding along on a bicycle on Martha's Vineyard, that when I graduated I was going to go into my own business and try to make this product work. If I had to, I'd sell it door-to-door. In the fall, I finally went over to see what Fylstra had in machine resources. He had an Apple II and a Radio Shack. He offered me the use of the Apple II if I wanted to use it to develop something.

So I spent a weekend writing a BASIC program that would do one screen's worth of a spreadsheet, and came up with the row-column, A-B-C, 1-2-3 coordinates way of doing things. I still wanted to use a mouse, but I made it work from cursor-moving paddles instead. But the game paddles only worked one direction, horizontal or vertical. So you would hit the fire button to get it to switch between horizontal and vertical. It turned out that the paddles were too slow in BASIC, so I went to the arrow keys. And since the Apple II only has two arrow keys, I used the space bar instead of the firing button to switch it from horizontal to vertical. I don't like shift keys. I like to minimize shifting. That's why I use slash to start commands, because it's un-shifted and on the home keyboard, minimizing keystrokes.

So I had this demo that would move the cursor on the screen; you could type numbers and formulas in. You could even point within the formula and say: "1 plus 7 and 1 plus A1," by pointing to A1, just like today's spreadsheets. It was just not able to scroll around, and would only do one screen's worth.It took about 20 seconds to recalculate, and it would make a sound on every cell so you could hear it calculating. It turned out half of the time went into making the sounds. But that demo gave a feel of what you could do.

> "We're making the users do more and more of the programming, but they don't know it."

I showed it to some classmates, like John Reese, who pointed out that when you're making a reference to another cell, you shouldn't have to instruct it to use that cell. I was thinking about parsing it; if you say "1 plus" and then hit an arrow key, you must mean one plus that cell. So I went through that to try to get the minimum number of keystrokes to do everything. This became the interface that we know today as the standard, simple-spreadsheet, VisiCalc type of interface.

I showed it to another professor, Barbara Jackson. Her comment was: "Look, if you want to get a chairman of the board of a company to do something, it's got to be really simple. This is getting close, but it's not there yet." So that encouraged me to make it simpler and simpler.

A year or two later when the product was on the market, I brought her in to see it and told her, "Since you're on the Calculator Committee at Harvard Business School, you've got to realize this program is important because you have students who are using it now. You've got to prepare for this." And in fact, that year the business professors used it to write answer sheets for their exams, freaking out all the other professors because they could do their work so fast. Of course, now Harvard requires you to buy a PC before you can go to their business school.

Once we got that human interface done, it was time to actually program it. I had been thinking of the data structure and doing a lot of figuring on how to make it as small and compact as possible, because we wanted it to run on a small machine. Most Apple IIs were 16K in those days, and floppy disks were not common.

INTERVIEWER: Was this when Frankston, you, and Fylstra decided to become partners?

BRICKLIN: Basically, yes. We shook hands over it. Frankston and I would make the program, Fylstra and his company (Personal Software) would sell it. We'd do it for the Apple first because Fylstra happened to have an Apple free to do development on and felt it was the best machine to start with. We also had tools available to work on the Apple.

INTERVIEWER: How did you actually go about designing VisiCalc?

BRICKLIN: I had designed the internals and much of the data structure and layout. To me, the most important part of a program is laying out the data structure. You also have to know what the human interface is going to be like. So I had a data structure that was compact enough to get a good amount of data, and it would be fast to access.

We also had to decide where we were going to base our operation. I was still in business school and Bob was consulting at Interactive Data Corporation. We finally decided to rent time from a large time-sharing system. Luckily they didn't bill for months at a time so we could live off the float.

Bob would write the code at night when time sharing was cheap. He'd get up around 3:00 in the afternoon, when I would come back from school. We'd go over what he did to the program; I'd test the program, figure out how to do new features, interview accountants, and do other startup procedures. Then I would be there sometimes as late as 11:00 at night. The rates would go down at 6:00 p.m. and again at 11:00 p.m., and the machine would become fast by 1:00 a.m. or 2:00 a.m. He'd work until morning, when he'd go to sleep. That's how we got the product written.

INTERVIEWER: Were you afraid another company would come up with a similar idea? What was your motivation for working so hard?

BRICKLIN: Once you get an idea that's so obvious, you want to get it done. We were real afraid that Texas Instruments would find out about it and put it in their new computer. Apple and Atari had been shown the product under nondisclosure. Atari was very excited to get a product, but they didn't have a machine yet. We got an early prototype which looked like a Cromemco machine, but they had pulled the board and put in an Atari board instead. It was a real prototype.

Apple was not that encouraging about the product. I was not there for the meeting; Fylstra, our publisher, took them a copy of what was to become

VisiCalc. As programmers, we thought we'd be done in four weeks. After about two or three weeks, Bob had enough of it going that it would scroll around and would add and subtract and recalculate. So Fylstra took that out for them to see. I kept on enhancing my BASIC prototype and trying out new things. Many ideas had to be dropped because we only had 16K of memory.

We got good response from the West Coast. I brought in some other professors. Another production professor, who was very encouraging, said, "Boy, you know, it's really neat to do all those calculations in almost no time. That would have taken hours to do it by hand. I'll have to update the examples in my book."

> "Even if it only took 15 or 20 minutes to throw together a program ... that wasn't fast enough."

So I wrote an early manual and Bob would try to implement what I wrote. We were a good team because whenever Bob would slack off, I would say "Bob, you've got to make this thing faster, it doesn't feel right," or I'd say, "you've got to put this feature in." And whenever I'd say, "Well, I think we should cut a corner here," he'd say, "No, no, no, let's put it in."

He ended up using a variation on my design for the cell storage. I did a lot of the design work, but the internal program structure was all his. And that's how we ended up with the VisiCalc program.

INTERVIEWER: *What was the initial reaction to the finished project?*

BRICKLIN: It got good reviews from a few people. Most of the magazines ignored it. It wasn't written up in some of the magazines for about a year. *BYTE* magazine had a little editorial about it and that was all. The guy who wrote the editorial was best man at Fylstra's wedding, Carl Helmer, and he already knew about it. And even that piece was written for engineers and talked about sine and cosine, which we hadn't implemented, but because it mentioned that, we had to implement it. I wasted my summer implementing sine and cosine, and other features like that.

We bought our own time-sharing system on borrowed money. I sold a house and used the money towards the down payment. Bob used his savings and borrowed from his family. We made the down payment on a minicomputer and moved into commercial quarters.

INTERVIEWER: *How did you decide to market VisiCalc?*

BRICKLIN: We had no idea how well the product would sell. We knew it was very good and everybody should have it, but it was unclear at that time whether everybody would jump on the bandwagon for electronic spreadsheets, since they had to buy this funny machine, and word processors had failed to take off.

INTERVIEWER: So once you set up your business, what did you have to do? Did you go around the country demonstrating it?

BRICKLIN: Our publisher, Personal Software, did a lot of that. We demonstrated it at the National Computer Conference, which is where it was publicly announced. We also demonstrated it at the West Coast Computer Fair and various shows.

Then we went back to do more work to put it on more and more machines. We put it on the TRS-80, which was a very important machine; it was the number two computer from our viewpoint. The programmer who did that was Seth Steinberg, who joined us. Steve Lawrence was our first employee. He did some of the programming to finish up VisiCalc, in the numeric area and some other functions. Then he set out to do the Atari and the Commodore PET versions.

For the Z80 version, Seth decided to do a literal line-by-line translation of the 6502 code into the Z80 code. And since we had a nice time-sharing system, he could invent all the tools he wanted. So he wrote a printing program that would list side by side the 6502 code and the Z80 code. We found out years later that bugs in the 6502 code were also in the Z80 code and vice versa. It was that good a translation. That code lasted for a long time. It became the IBM version, with some mechanical translation and some minor hand translation.

We were able to get on the IBM PC quickly. When IBM announced their PC, they announced it with VisiCalc. And they would not announce it unless VisiCalc was running to a certain percentage, enough to ship; they're very fussy. In order to do that, we couldn't use the standard conversion programs because we had our own assembler. One of our programmers, David Levin, modified the assembler to do the translation from the Z80 code into 8086 code, or 8088 code, and flagged the problems. It had to be pretty smart about doing the conversion; it was a lot smarter than most of the other converters around. Because of that, we were able to get up on the IBM quickly; shipping a few weeks after IBM shipped their PC, so we sold an awful lot of copies of the new product.

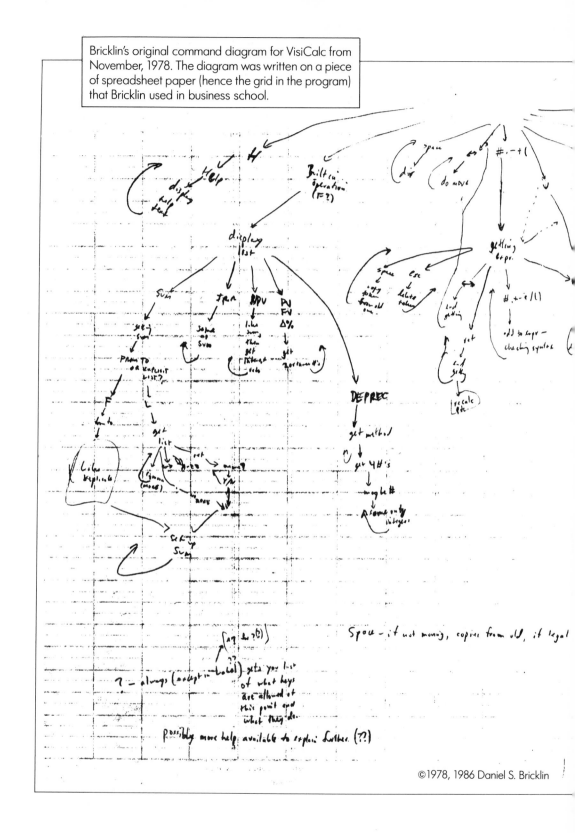

Bricklin's original command diagram for VisiCalc from November, 1978. The diagram was written on a piece of spreadsheet paper (hence the grid in the program) that Bricklin used in business school.

©1978, 1986 Daniel S. Bricklin

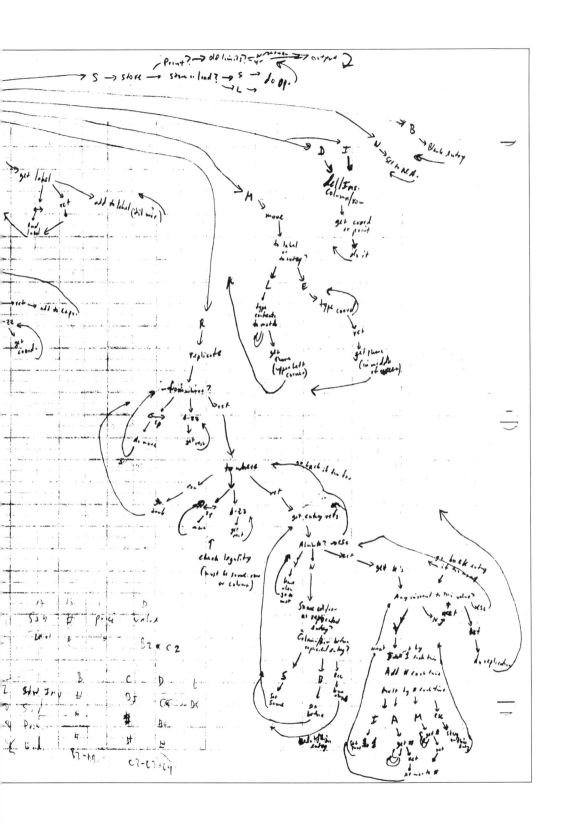

INTERVIEWER: How did you get the arrangement with IBM?

BRICKLIN: IBM came to us first because the copyright was ours. Our contract was that they should deal with Personal Software, so we sent them off to Personal Software. We actually had a three-way arrangement with IBM. When IBM called, we met with them the next day. We told them about our contract, showed them the parts of our contract that we were allowed to show them, and let them see how they would have to deal with us. We were very up-front about that.

Now remember, we had been dealing with a lot of different manufacturers, but we tried real hard with some who became successful and some who didn't. You never know which ones are going to make it.

INTERVIEWER: Did you sense at that point that IBM was going to make it?

BRICKLIN: It took a while before we knew what the machine was. It was obvious that the IBM machine was a great design. But the general idea of using an 8088, making it with a full keyboard, an 80 x 25 screen, and all that stuff, was something a lot of other people were doing at that time, including the best hardware designers around. It was clear it was a good design; that's why we felt we were going to make it.

We had a lot of contractual problems with Personal Software. For example, we had to put VisiCalc on whatever machines they wanted. They wanted to get out of our contract, but didn't want to pay enough to get out of it. And so we had to be able to put our product on as many machines as possible.

INTERVIEWER: Let me ask you about the rise and fall of Software Arts. Did you ever think you could go all the way down?

BRICKLIN: Even though I was all the way up, I lived in the same type of house I would have lived in if I worked at Digital, or anywhere else. I always kept myself down there in terms of spending so that I could afford to do what I'm doing now. I never wanted to depend on the company.

That's why we were trying to sell the company at our peak, but we ended up with a lawsuit at that point, and with a lawsuit, you can't sell a company very well. We had a company that was valued very highly. On paper, Bob and I were pretty rich, but unable to do anything about it, though we tried. By having visibility in our industry, I gained some "equity" that I took away with me. It made it possible for me to be an entrepreneur again.

The experience with the company was worthwhile. I've turned down some pretty good job offers at various companies over the last year. So I know if I want to I can go to work somewhere else, but I'm an entrepreneur.

I'm very happy looking back. It would have been nice if we had stayed at our peak and become very rich, but we didn't. I did better than if I had stayed at Digital—let's put it that way.

I liked working at Software Arts. I was very happy there, except during the period of business problems. But even that was a learning experience. I learned a lot about the life cycle of a business. I'm also more confident starting a business again after having gone through the whole cycle. By getting to the point of actually auctioning our chairs, our terminals, our pictures off the wall, my desk, and the T-shirt right off my back, I now know that you can go all the way up and all the way down, but you still survive.

INTERVIEWER: Looking back on Software Arts, would there be anything you'd do differently today?

BRICKLIN: Well, I would have liked to have not been sued; that would have made things different.

INTERVIEWER: How did that come about?

BRICKLIN: We got a notice in the mail saying, "You're sued." We had been having disagreements with our publisher, VisiCorp (Personal Software), for years, but we had been negotiating settlements for over a year or two at that point. For some reason, they decided that they wanted to bring it to a head as a lawsuit. Maybe they decided that they had a strong enough case and would get the money from their product, VisionCalc. But they didn't check to see if VisiOn was going to sell well first. They burned their bridges before they crossed them. We didn't expect them to actually sue us.

There are things that I could have done differently if I knew what I know now. Some things could have been done differently if the market had been different. Would some large publisher, like McGraw-Hill or somebody, have been willing to go into the business? Could we have convinced Apple to carry it? Who knows? But the outcome wasn't that bad, so why would I want to do it differently? I wouldn't have gone through all the experiences I had otherwise. I'm still healthy and I'm not poor and I have the respect of my colleagues. Other than in terms of becoming rich and having an unblemished history for my company, I've succeeded in just about every measure. And most people have their ups and their downs: Look at what happened with Apple.

INTERVIEWER: If the opportunity presented itself, would you go ahead and do the same?

BRICKLIN: Only if I thought it was correct. I like doing what I'm doing now. I've managed a big software business; I know what it's like. At this point, I can do what I want to do just as well with a small business. It'll get too cumbersome at some point, but it's a challenge. There are always different challenges; one was to build a big company. Now the challenge is to be successful in a very small company.

INTERVIEWER: *Do you see Software Garden growing out of your experience with Software Arts?*

BRICKLIN: Yes and no. At Software Arts, we got to try a lot of ideas: big company, great environment, an R&D organization. I decided that you either need a lot of money coming in from your product, or you've got to have very low overhead. And what I like to do is try different kinds of products. I've created a variety of products; I intend to do more in different areas. I intend to have a little garden here, not a farm where I'm going to emphasize one area, unless it turns out that one product is particularly lucrative.

I'm selling my products through the mail and through distributors who buy from me. I've already signed up one distributor and I'm working on a few more, selling the product inexpensively for $74.95, trying to get some publicity started.

INTERVIEWER: *What's the name of your new product?*

BRICKLIN: Dan Bricklin's Demo Program. Nice simple name, right? I decided I was going to call it Dan Bricklin something, because I know that's necessary to help sell it; enough people have told me that. The name is descriptive of what it is; it's for making demonstrations.

The packaging is real simple. See this Tyvek envelope? And the documentation will be typewritten, but nice. I decided to run the business out of my house, and for now, that's the way it is. The disk comes stuck on a piece of cardboard, and in this envelope. That's it.

I know how to do the real slick packaging, but what would I, as a user, do with my slick packaging? It takes up space on my shelf. The program sits in the computer. So I decided to go with simplicity. Why try to act like somebody I don't have to be?

INTERVIEWER: *Who do you see buying this program?*

BRICKLIN: Any person who is involved in designing programs, anybody who is involved in the development process. Documentation people will use it to write demos and tutorials. Once you try this program a couple times, it will pay for itself in terms of time saved.

I'm also trying to look at the viability of different businesses today. If you have the lowest possible overhead, a good product, good public visibility, and you have low prices, how many units can you sell? Some people have done very well in that area. I'd like to see what's there, because it will make a difference for what other things come out of the Garden.

INTERVIEWER: Do you think you'll always be programming software?

BRICKLIN: I guess so; I seem to have a knack for it. I don't know what it's going to be like when the technology changes. Maybe my skills are more appropriate in character-based screens where I've had most of my experience, as opposed to graphics, where I don't have as much experience. Maybe technology will pass me by, maybe not.

INTERVIEWER: Do you think there will continue to be these small types of software operations? Or will the software industry be dominated by a handful of huge companies?

BRICKLIN: No. People are writing their own programs. Anybody who uses a spreadsheet is writing their own programs; it's just that the language is different now.

Bob Frankston likes to tell a story about the telephone company. Back in the twenties they said that telephones were growing so fast that by 1950 everybody in the country would have to be an operator. By 1950 people said, "Ha, they were wrong." Well, it turned out they were right, because everybody was an operator; they just had dial telephones. The technology had made it easy enough to be an operator.

Well, that's the same thing with programming. We're just making the users do more and more of the programming themselves, but they don't know it. Using different style sheets with Microsoft Word is doing programming; using spreadsheets is doing programming.

There is an inherent cottage-industry component to programming. We constantly improve the tools that are available, the operating systems, environments, languages, and all. Consequently, an individual can always do a lot more than he used to.

It's like writing. An encyclopedia requires a large staff; an individual can't do it all. Some operating systems nowadays are encyclopedic. But there's also always the short story, the novel, and the poem. Those are useful in their own way, though they may seem simple and trivial to do.

Any large company could have a million programmers working on some idea to produce a better one, but they don't because it doesn't work that way. The economics aren't there. Sometimes the idea behind a program is one small creative effort. Just like in a short story, one little twist in the plot is the whole idea behind it. The same thing is true of the programs.

In terms of marketing, you do need a large marketing organization. But there's a variety of ways to do that, just like with books. You can self-publish or you can go to a publisher. With movies, you have the distribution company that takes care of it.

> *" . . . real users work differently than programmers."*

If you look at the biggest sellers in the software industry, in general they were written by very few people. 1-2-3 was in essence written and designed by two people, one programmer and one partial programmer; VisiCalc, the same way. dBASE, I think, was originally written by pretty much one person. Paradox was written by two people. That's the way things are done.

INTERVIEWER: *Do you think software will break into entirely new areas, or do you think it will remain in the same areas, such as spreadsheets, word processors, and so on?*

BRICKLIN: All sorts of products are developing now. People are saying, "What about networking, why can't we connect this stuff together?" What about the publication systems, like the inexpensive ones available on the Mac? And the really great ones that are available on the bigger machines, like Apollo and Sun? A few years ago, no one thought that in-house publishing was going to be a major use of computers.

People want things to move too fast. How long did it take for the mouse to be in commercial use? Was it fifteen years, or more? Englebart came up with it back in the sixties or early seventies. And compilers—FORTRAN was developed back in the fifties. We take those things for granted, but they were done in spans of five and ten years. Software has major advances every half decade or decade. Well, why should that change too much?

Once you have certain hardware, you have certain capabilities that you didn't have before. And frequently it turns out that you can do something without specific hardware. For example, certain systems on the IBM are done because the Macintosh had them and people want them. The new hardware, like the Mac, helped make it clear the systems are useful. Consequently, it is worth the effort to figure out how to do it on the old hardware.

The Apple II is another great example of that. When it started out, people thought they had pushed it as far as they could. But they are constantly finding more things the Apple II can do. It's like a test pilot pushing a new plane beyond its expected capabilities. A lot of people crash and burn; they did on the Macintosh.

INTERVIEWER: *What do you see as the failures of that machine?*

BRICKLIN: The Macintosh has sirens that work against you, calling you to the rocks, such as using fonts. To put in different fonts slows down a word processor quite a bit. You end up with an unzippy word processor, which is not what you want. People like something fast. Once you put in different size fonts, that'll make this slower and that slower, although the end result will be pretty. But you end up with a product that doesn't feel right because you listened to the sirens. Eventually you learn not to do that.

INTERVIEWER: *How important are speed, user friendliness, or other similar considerations?*

BRICKLIN: For some products, that's the whole product. That's what makes it what it is.

Suppose you had Microsoft Word running on a Hercules card. That would be really slow for certain things, slower than it could have been if they hadn't put so many enhancements into it. Then Word would be unusable to some people. Even though functionally it would be the same, the number of people who might want to use it would drop.

I think the feel of the product is very important. Lotus showed that. There was a product called Context MBA that was just as capable and had a lot of features, but it was so slow that many people never even considered using it, so it never caught on at all. What Lotus went after was speed.

On VisiCalc we got the same speed as the original Apple II. I said, "Bob, that's not fast enough, we want it faster. It's got to scroll as fast as the repeat key on your machine." I didn't know different machines repeated at different rates. Ours was about a medium rate. We tried to get that same feel in the IBM and it turned out to have a nice, crisp feel.

INTERVIEWER: *Do you consider programming a skill or a science?*

BRICKLIN: Well, parts of it are science and parts of it are skill. There are certain things described in a science that can be useful, like in power design and things like that. There is a craft component in which apprenticeship is the way to go. You learn skills by apprenticeship. And with some things, practice just makes perfect. So it's more like a lot of the arts or crafts. It's not like being an actuary; it's more of a standard type of craft.

You can see that in the feel of certain programs of developers; it shows up when you look at their code. People who have formal training often have an advantage over people who don't. Knowing what people have worked out academically is often very helpful. You know, some people have green thumbs and some people don't, but it helps if you learn a bit about the area first.

INTERVIEWER: *When you program, do you basically use the same method or approach every time?*

BRICKLIN: No. It depends on what I'm doing. I mean, I try to be professional; you don't have to be. But if you're producing products for commercial use and you want to get things out, you can't be very religious about your work, such as, "I only program in high-level languages," or "real programmers use only assemblers." You simply do whatever is appropriate for the particular situation.

INTERVIEWER: *What role do you see software or computers playing five or ten years from now?*

BRICKLIN: I think we'll see more forms of computers than we do now. One form is a box that sits on a desk, the personal computer of today.

I think the personal computer of tomorrow is going to be different than the desk computer, which now is like a telephone that sits on your desk. Desk computers didn't catch on in the home because the PC, as we know it today, is to the home as the mainframe is to a business—you have to go to the shrine, or connect up to it. A lot of people don't want to connect to the mainframe, send cards in, and stuff like that. People aren't going to want to go into the computer room in the den to check their recipe file. That's ridiculous.

The personal computer of the future should be more like a notebook. I carry my notebook around and why shouldn't it be a computer? Well, that's different than the PC as we know it. Computer technology is going to be used for all sorts of new areas like that.

Let's say years from now voice recognition has been worked out pretty well. You have a little tape recorder over there that understands commands, so why push a button? You just say, "Play me the last five minutes of the tape." It's not going to be connected to a PC on your desk to make it do that. It's going to be built in.

The computer you have on the desk is going to constantly improve. The price is a big factor. Take a copy machine; you can get new ones for about the same price as you used to pay for the old ones, but the capabilities have gone up. I think we are going to see personal computers that are going to have quite a few different embodiments.

Portia Isaacson used to say that she thought robots were going to be important because your computer should follow you around. One way to have a computer follow you around is to miniaturize it. Why go to all the trouble to put legs on it if we can miniaturize it to the point that we can carry it on our bodies. We're getting to the point soon where we can get a lot of computing power in a very small space.

Pages from a "gift catalog" created by a Software Arts employee for an auction the company held when it closed its doors.

Bob Frankston

*THIRTY-SIX-*year-old Bob
Frankston has been programming for more than twenty years. He grew up in Brooklyn, New York. As a preteen he developed a keen interest in electronics and computers. He went on to concentrate in these areas at MIT, where he earned two bachelor's degrees in 1970, one in mathematics, and one in electrical engineering and computer science (EECS). In 1974, he received two more degrees from MIT: an engineer's degree and a master's degree in EECS. As a student at MIT, Frankston met Dan Bricklin, and they became friends.

When Bricklin got the idea for an electronic spreadsheet while at Harvard Business School, he depended on Frankston to create a workable version of the program. Frankston worked out of his attic at odd hours of the night and day, and developed a version of the program from Bricklin's prototype design. The two incorporated Software Arts, and worked together until they completed their product, VisiCalc, in 1979. In spring 1985, when Software Arts dissolved after a prolonged legal battle with VisiCorp (formerly Personal Software, later Paladin), Frankston joined Lotus Development Corporation as chief scientist of the information services division.

The new Lotus office building is on Cambridge Street in Cambridge, right across the Charles river from Boston. On the day I was there, it was pouring rain, and the recently installed glass roof covering the three-story, open lobby was leaking in several places.

A short man with longish brown hair, dark-rimmed glasses, and carrying an umbrella entered the lobby doors. It was Frankston. Out of breath and soaking wet, he came up to me and we shook hands. We took the elevator up to his new office, which he had yet to move into. We walked through a large open room sectioned into cubicles. I noticed there were many vacant offices and wondered if it was because there were more offices than people or if most of the people just hadn't moved in yet.

Frankston's large office was situated in a corner of the building along a wall that faces out over the river. It was furnished with two large wooden desks and one round table but no chairs, so Frankston grabbed two chairs from a nearby conference room. Then he dashed out again and came back with two hot cups of coffee. He sat down, and pulled a wilted white paper bag out of his pocket. From this a fresh corn muffin appeared, which he shared with me as we began our discussion.

From the way Frankston talked and moved about, I gathered he is a man in a constantly busy state. A quick, sharp talker, he spoke rapidly, his thoughts flowing in jerks and starts. Though tight-lipped, quick-witted, and lively, there was a seriousness of purpose about Bob Frankston. He considers himself a creator in the engineering sense but he also struck me as a teacher, always trying to explain things in relation to the listener. As we talked, it seemed he threw as many questions at me as I could throw at him.

INTERVIEWER: *How did you get into the computer-software business?*

FRANKSTON: In 1963, I was a junior high student, but I sat in on a college course in New York to learn how to use an IBM 1620. I found the experience to be a nice creative output. I felt I could make a difference and I liked the malleability of programming.

INTERVIEWER: *Is programming an art, a science, a tool, or a trade?*

FRANKSTON: All those things. When we formed the company to develop VisiCalc, we named it Software *Arts*. A better question would be, "What is art versus engineering?"

INTERVIEWER: How would you describe the difference?

FRANKSTON: They're not that different. In engineering, it's easy to see when you're wrong, because something collapses. But good engineering is no different from good art. How understandable is it? How maintainable is it? Is it simple? Is it unnecessarily complicated? How do you perceive it? In that sense, art and engineering are similar. In pure art, there is less operational testing, so it's easier to get away with things. Engineering is more practical, in that you have something that has to "work." But does it work only once and then fall apart? Does fixing bugs in it generate even more bugs? The better the engineer, the more aesthetic and art-like the machine is, and the better the chances of it working.

INTERVIEWER: What do you find to be most aesthetically pleasing about a computer program?

FRANKSTON: I don't have just one test; it's a combination of elements. Is the program understandable? Is it elegant? Does it show a basic understanding and an elaboration of an ideal, rather than being just disparate pieces piled together? Is it easy to modify, easy to develop, easy to change?

INTERVIEWER: VisiCalc and Software Arts were your first success. How did the program and the company come about?

FRANKSTON: Dan Bricklin and I were writing VisiCalc and felt that it was better to protect the trademark by incorporating rather than using a partnership. I remember that we were in a restaurant, which I jokingly called "Kentucky Fried Fish," when we thought of the name Software Arts. The office of Software Arts was in the attic of my apartment. Dan was in school full time, so I did the programming, and he did a lot of the design and critique.

INTERVIEWER: Why did you and Dan Bricklin decide to gamble on VisiCalc? Nobody had done anything like that before.

FRANKSTON: Well, we had a lot of the necessary background. Dan had worked at Digital Equipment Corporation; he did the DEC word processor, which they still sell as the DecMate II, so he was used to screen interfaces. The original idea incorporated a TV screen and a hand-held calculator to remotely point to things on the screen.

INTERVIEWER: How long did the process take to evolve from the TV idea to the final product?

FRANKSTON: Several months. The programming took about four weeks from the time I started programming to when we did the first demo, then another ten months until we shipped the product. But we didn't spend all that time programming. We also were starting the company.

INTERVIEWER: *Were you surprised at the reaction the VisiCalc program got in the press?*

FRANKSTON: Well, success didn't come that fast, it took two years. We thought that people were disappointingly slow in understanding what Visi-Calc was. A lot of people still don't. They don't see it as a programming language, for example; they don't understand that aspect.

INTERVIEWER: *When you were developing VisiCalc, did you realize it was going to be a major success?*

> *"Ideas don't disappear. They change form ... merge with other ideas."*

FRANKSTON: No. We thought it was a nice program that would be useful, and it was better than having a salaried job. But mainly it was fun to create something that people would use, like creating a new machine. Once we got people to use the product, there was an interest not just in the programming, but in the aesthetics and usability as well. It was a proselytizing exercise based on the assumption that computers are useful, so let's try to make use of them.

INTERVIEWER: *Do you think there will always be variations on spreadsheets, word processors, and other working programs?*

FRANKSTON: Definitely. There will be variations of everything forever. People are still doing hieroglyphics. Ideas don't disappear. They change form, they merge with other ideas.

INTERVIEWER: *Do you still see Dan Bricklin?*

FRANKSTON: Yes. He doesn't live all that far from me. I still see a lot of the old people. Dan decided it was more fun to sit in a room by himself and program with very low overhead. I tend to want to build things that need more resources.

INTERVIEWER: *Do you think computers will continue to be used in the same way they are used today?*

FRANKSTON: No. Basically, I think they will disappear. Computers will become intelligence agents or appliances. Personal computers are going to fade into the woodwork. There's going to be a gradual change. For a while there'll be a lot of computing dedicated to a person with a PC, but that is by no means the ultimate evolution. People can't tell where the computing gets done now anyway, and who wants this huge box in the middle of your desk?

INTERVIEWER: So what's going to happen to software when computers become easier to use as a result of this change?

FRANKSTON: You will always need more and more software, but what you've got to do is make programs easier to write, which will make most programmers obsolete. Non-programmers are already programming. VisiCalc, as a programming language, is an example of that. Anybody who can master a telephone can certainly program.

INTERVIEWER: But even so, most of the programming done today is done by a relatively small group of individuals. What does it take to become a great programmer, as opposed to one of the many users?

FRANKSTON: What does it take to be a good anything? What does it take to be a good writer? Someone who's good is a combination of two factors: an accidental mental correspondence to the needs of the disciplines, combined with an ability to not be stupid. That's a rare combination, but it's not at all mystical.

A lot of good programming can be taught. A good programmer must enjoy programming and be interested in it, so he will try to learn more. A good programmer also needs an aesthetic sense, combined with a guilt complex, and a keen awareness of when to violate that aesthetic sense. The guilt complex forces him to work harder to improve the program and to bring it more in line with the aesthetic sense.

INTERVIEWER: If you would compare programming to an art form, would you compare it to writing, sculpting, painting, or composing music?

FRANKSTON: In music, and in various forms of art, we are trying to operate within rules, but we also go beyond them in a few respects. There are a lot of rules in music and you have to know when to break the rules and when to follow the rules, just as in programming.

You can teach writers to work from an outline, if that helps to organize them. In programming there are a lot of organizational techniques that can be taught. If you're a sculptor, you'd better know about the center of gravity or at least have a gratuitous sense of it, otherwise you might kill somebody when your art topples over!

In art, you also ask yourself how people will perceive your work. You are trying to establish a certain perceptual impression. I think a lot of artists look at subjects very differently, as do a lot of programmers. When you communicate, whether it be in writing or programming, what you say has to be understood by your recipients. If you cannot explain a program to yourself, the chance of the computer getting it right is pretty small.

INTERVIEWER: *Just how much of a science is computer science?*

FRANKSTON: The term computer science is overused; I'd rather refer to software engineering or computational engineering or information engineering. I tend to view things more as engineering simply because engineering is less pure. But there are definitely scientific aspects to programming.

I view computing as a more narrow term. A lot of the science is understanding the complexity of the interactions. But when I view the programming itself, it tends to be more of an engineering discipline.

INTERVIEWER: *What work strategies do you use in your programming?*

FRANKSTON: It's important to have a general sense of where I'm going on a project. Working from that, I tend to mull over the ideas for a while, and develop a framework from which to proceed. Then I build a working skeleton, which provides me with instant gratification, and also is a means whereby I can test out approaches and rework them if I need to. You could say the program's organic; I grow it. Finally, the project enters a phase when all the principles have been laid out, and then I've got to make sure that all the details are taken care of so we can ship it.

INTERVIEWER: *Is it easier for you to program today than it was when you began twenty years ago?*

FRANKSTON: I think it's easier but I'm also trying to do more complex projects. With modern computers, there's more opportunity to get oneself in over one's head than there used to be. I view myself as a B student in school. It doesn't matter what the course is. If I'm interested, I'll get an A; if I'm not, I'll get a B, and that's my measure, not the difficulty of the course. In the same sense, in programming I'll try to do as much as I can with the tools I have.

INTERVIEWER: *When you're programming, at a certain stage do you carry around a whole program in your head?*

FRANKSTON: I generally carry a sense of it. At various points, I have more of a context or less of a context. There are more periods in which I'm elaborating on it, adding little things here and there.

INTERVIEWER: *Do you write a lot of comments in your programs?*

FRANKSTON: It varies on how obvious I think a piece of code is. The higher the level of language, the fewer comments I write. I try to make and write readable code. I only use idioms that make sense in a language, and I will add comments if I think whatever I'm doing is not obvious.

I've had people say that it's easier to pick up my code, and I really do write it so people can pick it up. Also, I write so I can pick up the code and make local changes without worrying too much about the effect. The comments are mainly to warn about surprises.

INTERVIEWER: *Where do you get your ideas for programs?*

FRANKSTON: From projects I want to do. These needs tend to correlate with what other people find useful; I have to speak to other people. I'm not operating in a vacuum. I tend to work with people to create tools that are useful. I use the computer to express ideas of how I think things should be done.

"If you cannot explain a program to yourself, the chance of the computer getting it right is pretty small."

INTERVIEWER: *What are the projects you're currently working on?*

FRANKSTON: Well, a combination of tools and products. I'm working in new directions. It's more than just programming and trying to create products in the old problem areas.

INTERVIEWER: *What is the hardest part of programming for you?*

FRANKSTON: There are lots of different measures of that. In general, I'm trying to find the right perspective or sense of direction, but that's not just in programming. It's like in writing, what's the right level of explanation? What's the wrong position? Am I elaborating too much? The hardest part of programming is getting the product ready to ship, getting it to work, and meeting the constraints.

INTERVIEWER: *Is there a big difference when you start bringing a lot of programmers in on a project? What are the dynamics?*

FRANKSTON: Have you ever tried to write an article with ten writers? It's just the normal dynamics of any project. The problem is that to do large projects, you need to be able to work with a lot of other people, and you cannot be too ad hoc about the designs and issues. You've got to think about the end result and give people goals and rules, and not come in and say, "That was a bad idea, let's do it this way instead." You discover most people do not respond well to that if you do it too many times.

INTERVIEWER: *What would be your advice to young programmers?*

FRANKSTON: Basically, don't assume you know all that much, and try to learn and question the assumptions. Have a lot of confidence, but stay modest and assume you're doing something wrong. Get just enough guilt—not too much or you'll be afraid to do anything—but enough to develop an aesthetic sense. Try to develop a deeper understanding. Don't assume that just because you can get something to work once, there's nothing more to understand.

I think one of the problems right now with computers is you can get something to work in BASIC, and then you assume you understand when, in fact, you have just started. In programming, I find a lot of understanding comes from psychology, and from how people do things in dealing with the world. Ultimately, what you're doing is trying to understand how processes work in general. The program is only one small piece. But you need to have some curiosity. You can program with a lot less than that, but ideally you need to be curious and try to learn new ways of understanding.

> *"Anybody who can master a telephone can certainly program."*

INTERVIEWER: *What do you think about artificial intelligence?*

FRANKSTON: The problem is that the expression "AI" is being hyped a lot these days. Anytime you understand what's going on, you tend to be reluctant to use the word intelligence. Many commercial expert systems are simply decision tables that are too large to easily solve. There is nothing mystical about it. I tend to view AI as more interesting for understanding cognition and thinking in general systems.

I'm enthusiastic about AI as it applies to trying to understand how to address complicated problems. We can learn a lot from human intelligence, which manages to perform impressive feats with what may be a mediocre computing engine. In our attempts to understand this intelligence, we're developing principles for dealing with complexity. It's fair to say that much of what's done today in computing is derived from the quest for AI.

INTERVIEWER: *What do you think about the IBM PC?*

FRANKSTON: It's cute. There are a lot of them out there. Maybe I'm getting on in years, but I'd rather program on something that there are a lot of, that I can get leverage on. The current IBM has a lot of severe restrictions. The question is: How clever are we going to be about getting around them and expanding beyond them? I think the excitement is in really pushing yourself to accomplish goals in a larger domain. The programming is not an end in itself.

```
/*
Cubic spline fitting - Ellis-McLain Method
Jonathan Sachs
22-Oct-85

This method generates a single-valued function from an ordered set of x,y data.
It produces the best results when used on smooth functions since it reduces
discontinuities in the second derivative.

The findgrad procedure is called first to determine slopes at each data
point.  This step may be omitted if slopes are already given for each data
point.   Next the coeff procedure is called for each interval to generate the
coefficients of the cubic polynomial that fits the data in that interval.

Reference:

Ellis, T.M.R. and McLain, D.H. (1977) "Algorithm 514 - A new method of cubic
curve fitting using local data".  ACM Transactions on Mathematical Software,
Volume 3, pages 175-178.
*/

/*   find gradient at each data point

     findgrad(x,y,grad,n)

     x        n-vector of x coordinates of data points
              values must be in increasing order with no two equal

     y        n-vector of y coordinates of data points

     grad returned n-vector

     n        number of data points (must be at least 4)

*/

findgrad(x,y,grad,n)
double x[];
double y[];
double grad[];
int n;
{
    int i,iless2,iless1,iplus1,iplus2;
    double x0,x1,x2,x3,x4,y2;
    double prod1,prod2,num,denom,g;
    double coeff2,xdiff,xprod,weight;
```

Sachs wrote this short program that generates a sin-
gle-valued function from an ordered set of x,y data.
See the Appendix for a complete program listing.

Jonathan Sachs

BORN IN 1947, Jonathan Sachs grew up on the east coast, in New England. He earned his bachelor's degree in mathematics at MIT. Sachs spent a total of fourteen years both studying and working at MIT. His experiences there as a programmer were wide ranging: He worked for the Center for Space Research, the Cognitive Information Processing group, and the Biomedical Engineering Center. Sachs developed the STOIC programming language while he was working for the Biomedical Engineering Center.

In the mid-seventies, Sachs left MIT to work at Data General, where he supervised the development of an operating system. Next, he co-founded Concentric Data Systems, a company that is known for its database products. Jonathan Sachs is credited with writing the phenomenally successful Lotus 1-2-3 spreadsheet program. In 1981, Sachs teamed up with Mitch Kapor to develop and promote Sachs' spreadsheet program, and in April 1982, Lotus Development Corporation was formed, with eight employees. On January 26, 1983, Lotus began shipment of 1-2-3 for the IBM PC. By April 26 of the same year, 1-2-3 topped the Softsel best-seller list for the first time, and it has remained at the top ever since. It was the first program to displace VisiCalc. In 1984, Sachs left Lotus to form his own company.

Through the pouring autumn rain I made my way to the western edge of Cambridge where Jonathan Sachs had told me we were to meet. After some searching through the designated office complex, I found myself in front of a door with a simple plaque that read "Jonathan Sachs and Associates." I had expected something more grand.

I knocked and entered a large one-room office. Jazz music played in the background. On the clean white walls hung several prints by Ansel Adams. A tall, slightly greying, bearded man dressed in a wool sweater and corduroy jeans got up from his computer terminal to greet me in a soft-spoken voice. This was Sachs, the man who developed Lotus 1-2-3. I took a seat in a leather lounge chair as Jonathan turned off his IBM AT and swiveled his chair around to talk.

INTERVIEWER: *Did you start programming when you were in college?*

SACHS: Yes, I took an introductory programming course in 1964 when I was a freshman at MIT. Later, I had several summer jobs writing programs—I worked at Woods Hole one summer and at the Jet Propulsion Lab another. I also worked as a programmer when I dropped out of school in the middle of my senior year to earn some money. Programming was my one marketable skill, but I wasn't crazy about it in the beginning.

INTERVIEWER: *Why not?*

SACHS: For one thing, I was originally doing batch programming in FORTRAN. I don't have anything against FORTRAN, but getting only a couple tries per day to run your program is pretty frustrating. When I dropped out during my senior year, I analyzed satellite data at the MIT Center for Space Research. Later, I went to San Francisco, but I couldn't find a job there after looking for three months, so I came back to finish my degree. I got an interesting part-time job at MIT the first day I got back, working for the Cognitive Information Processing group. There they were developing a reading machine for the blind. I worked on a PDP-9 minicomputer, and helped to develop the character recognition part, where a scanner reads the page.

That was when I really got interested in programming. It was my first programming job where I was able to sit down and actually have a conversation with the computer. To have a computer respond the way you expect it to is exciting. There was a certain kind of electricity about that experience. I remember it very clearly.

INTERVIEWER: *Why did you decide to go back to MIT and get a degree?*

SACHS: For starters, it was very hard to get a job without one. And MIT was a secure place to be, since I had been there before.

After I got my degree, I went back to the Center for Space Research. They were planning to put up an X-ray satellite and wanted someone to set up a minicomputer to analyze part of the data that would come in over the telephone lines. I was in charge of the computer and did all the systems programming. Several graduate students wrote some of the analysis programs, and I wrote some of the others.

After the satellite was launched (a big success), I could no longer get computer time there, so I left to work at the MIT Biomedical Engineering Center. They were trying to develop medical instruments built around the 8080 chip. They needed someone to develop a programming language for them. So I wrote a language called STOIC, which is a variant of FORTH.

INTERVIEWER: *Why did you call it STOIC?*

SACHS: STOIC stands for Stack-Oriented Interactive Complier. I came up with it by filling a blackboard with all the possible first letters and trying to find the best ac-

"The development of 1-2-3 was ten months of nothing but eating, sleeping, and working."

ronym. STOIC is still around. It's in the public domain and every once in awhile I see a reference to it. In fact, I think Epson used STOIC to develop some software.

Anyway, after a total of about fourteen years at MIT, I decided it was time to leave. I wanted to get into management, so I took a job at Data General supervising the development of an operating system. I was there for about two and a half years. That job taught me that I didn't really like management, and that I never, ever, want to develop an operating system again. Now, I have a lot more sympathy for the people I used to complain about.

INTERVIEWER: *Were you developing the operating system on your own or were you managing a team of programmers?*

SACHS: Eight people were on the team at one point. Some time after I left Data General, the man I worked for, John Henderson, also left, and later the two of us formed a small consulting company called Concentric Data Systems. We did some contract programming, and we also wrote a spreadsheet to run on Data General hardware. But it soon became clear that we weren't going to make any money on the spreadsheet, although it seemed to be a good idea when we wrote it.

That experience destabilized my relationship with Henderson—he was doing contract work that was bringing in the money and I was doing product work that wasn't bringing in any money. One of our problems was that two technical people shouldn't try to run a company. We argued over technical issues when we should have been marketing. So we parted ways, and I took the rights to develop another spreadsheet based on the old one.

"The rate of innovation is rather slow. There are only a few really new ideas every decade."

I took the spreadsheet to Mitch Kapor, who had demonstrated some marketing success. He had sold Visi-Plot and VisiTrend personal software and was getting royalties. He knew what needed to be done and I knew how to do it. Our business relationship worked out fairly well.

INTERVIEWER: *At that point did you have just the idea or was the program already done?*

SACHS: The spreadsheet was already done, and within a month, I had converted it over to C. Then it started evolving from that point on, a little at a time. In fact, the original idea was very different from what ended up as the final version of 1-2-3.

INTERVIEWER: *What was your original idea for the program?*

SACHS: To build more of a programming language into it. But it soon became clear to us that there wasn't nearly as big a market for that as there was for a straight spreadsheet. Later we tacked on the macro language, so we got part of the programming language idea back.

Lotus 1-2-3 was originally going to include a spreadsheet, graphics, and a word processor. Somewhere along the way we saw the prototype of the Context MBA program. The word processor part of that program was bogging down the whole program. So I thought maybe a database approach would be better than a word processor. Plus a database was a lot easier to do.

All these decisions seem as if they were the result of careful market research, but they weren't. The methodology we used to develop 1-2-3 had a lot to do with the success of the product. For instance, 1-2-3 began with a working program, and it continued to be a working program throughout its development. I was working largely in isolation at the time. I had an office in Hopkinton, where I lived at the time, and I came to the office about once a week and brought in a new version. I fixed any bugs immediately in the next version. Also, people at Lotus were using the program continuously.

This was the exact opposite of the standard method for developing a big program, where you spend a lot of time and work up a functional spec, do a modular decomposition, give each piece to a bunch of people, and integrate the pieces when they're all done. The problem with that method is you don't get a working program until the very end. If you know exactly what you want to do, that method is fine. But when you're doing something new, all kinds of problems crop up that you just don't anticipate. In any case, our method meant that once we had reached a certain point in the development, we could ship if we wanted to. The program may not have had all the features, but we knew it would work.

INTERVIEWER: What are the drawbacks to that sort of development?

SACHS: That approach to programming doesn't work very well with more than one person, or at most three people, working on the program. And those programmers can't be just any three people. If the project gets bigger, then you have to go to the team approach, which is how we did Jazz. I don't have anything against the team approach, but it's just not the way I work best.

INTERVIEWER: Do you still use the same kind of system when you create a program, building it layer upon layer?

SACHS: Yes. That's how I've always done things when I work by myself. I get the program up so that it just begins to work, and then I add features to it.

INTERVIEWER: Did you have any idea 1-2-3 would be as successful as it turned out to be?

SACHS: Mitch had a lot of faith in 1-2-3. My attitude was that if it worked, fine, and if it didn't work, that was okay too. I was still getting a salary; I didn't feel like I was taking a big risk. I remember when Mitch was trying to get the entire capital, he told people that the product was going to set the computer industry on its ear. Frankly, I don't think he believed it; it was sort of hype. But it turned out to be true.

INTERVIEWER: When 1-2-3 really started succeeding, were you in a state of shock or did you just go on to something else?

SACHS: It didn't affect me very much, to tell you the truth. Right after Version 1 came out, in February 1983, I started working on Version 1A, which had drivers so it could be ported to other machines. We hired more programmers to help do the ports, and a couple of the new managers took over many of the everyday operations. A few of us got an office in Littleton and started to work on Symphony there.

INTERVIEWER: *Is that because you wanted to get away from all the other distractions at the Lotus office?*

SACHS: Yes. You can't do the kind of intense programming that Symphony required without a certain amount of quiet, because it takes a lot of concentration. You have to get away from the phones and from people walking in the door. But, I got fed up with the whole thing about halfway through Symphony; I'd had enough of spreadsheets, and I wasn't very happy with the way Symphony was going. It seemed like it was getting too big and too complicated. I like things small and simple. So I went back to the Lotus office in Cambridge and worked on some other projects. Then, at the end of 1984, I left Lotus to start my own company.

INTERVIEWER: *What do you do now?*

SACHS: The only thing I've been involved in that has any commercial value is a word processor. I worked up a prototype in about a month. I didn't really think Lotus would be particularly interested in it, but evidently they are. It started out with a fairly small scope, and as it went along it got larger and larger. Now I've subcontracted out almost all the development to other people and I'm just acting as the architect for the project. Also, I've set up a private foundation to do some environmental work and I'm getting involved in the environmental movement here in New England. That takes up a certain amount of my time. I'm doing more recreational-type computing. I even take vacations now.

INTERVIEWER: *Did you burn out, or did you just need to take a break?*

SACHS: The development of 1-2-3 was ten months of nothing but eating, sleeping, and working. I just had to let go of everything else because there wasn't time for it—I'm still kind of coming out of that. Having an important position in a big company creates a lot of pressure. You just can't unwind. I had worked hard in spurts at MIT, a month or two at a time, but never ten months in a row. Working under that kind of pressure for so many months was very self-destructive in a lot of ways.

INTERVIEWER: *It seems the narrow focus and intense concentration required for programming is bad for a lot of people.*

SACHS: Well, lots of people just aren't temperamentally suited to it. They get restless or uptight.

INTERVIEWER: *Do you like programming or do you prefer being a designer or architect? Do you sit down every day and write code?*

SACHS: I like to do the whole project, the design and implementation. I like to have control over all the pieces. I'm not really much of a team player.

INTERVIEWER: *When you were writing Lotus 1-2-3, what was the biggest problem or the hardest part of the programming?*

SACHS: To tell you the truth, from a technical standpoint, 1-2-3 is not a complicated program. I didn't have to reinvent anything. I salvaged pieces of code and ideas I had used before. The only aspect that had any technical interest at all was the natural order of recalculations and algorithms. I didn't invent that. One summer we hired Rick Ross. It turned out the recalculation problem was analogous to the subject he had done his Ph.D. thesis on; something to do with garbage collection in LISP. He used his previous research to modify the way the 1-2-3 program did recalculations.

> "*I don't like using any tools or programs I didn't write myself or that I don't have some control over.*"

INTERVIEWER: *Why aren't you a mathematics professor at a university?*

SACHS: Math is too hard. I can do mathematics up to the point where I stop being able to visualize the problem. When it gets abstract, I can't do it. But I can do anything that I can make an image of in my head.

INTERVIEWER: *Is that what you do when you are writing your computer programs?*

SACHS: Maybe. After you've been doing something for fifteen years you become unaware of the process.

INTERVIEWER: *Is it easier for you to write programs now than it was fifteen years ago?*

SACHS: Programming doesn't seem to have changed that much in the past fifteen years. Once you get to a certain level of experience, you go from the idea to the program without even thinking about all the intermediate steps; the process becomes automatic.

INTERVIEWER: *What makes a person a good programmer? Is talent or training the key?*

SACHS: It's a combination of talent, temperament, motivation, and hard work. I find quite a lot of people expect to be really good after a short time, but I haven't known too many people who have been successful in doing that. Success comes from doing the same thing over and over again; each time you learn a little bit and you do it a little better the next time. I was extremely fortunate to have a lot of interesting jobs that covered a broad spectrum at the beginning of my career. It's much harder these days for people starting out to get a wide range of experience, because the jobs are already subdivided. People tend to specialize fairly early.

INTERVIEWER: Do you see a great deal of difference between, say, writing a program for a science research project or writing a spreadsheet program?

> *"I'm not a particularly creative person; my real skill is taking ideas and integrating them to make a nice package."*

SACHS: I've found that almost all programming is surprisingly similar. There are a few basic algorithms, and loops and conditionals, but everything comes down to the same process in the end.

INTERVIEWER: Do you generally write a lot of comments in your programs?

SACHS: Over the years I settled on one style of commenting. I break most of my programs up into fairly small modules and I heavily comment the description of the module and its inputs and outputs. That's all I comment on. Once it gets down to that size, there's no point in trying to document all the internal workings of each module. Another programmer should be able to figure it out from there by just looking at the code. I can almost always read code I wrote a long time ago because it's commented that way.

INTERVIEWER: Do you have a set routine?

SACHS: I don't work in binges; I work a little bit every day. With 1-2-3, I worked a lot every day. I work best in the early morning, contrary to the stereotype of programmers.

INTERVIEWER: Do you work in your office or at home?

SACHS: I have worked at home for short periods, but I can work almost anywhere. I can work with noise or without noise, up to a point. I find human voices are incredibly distracting, but I can work with any other kind of sound.

INTERVIEWER: When you look at the code in a program, what do you find aesthetically pleasing or beautiful?

SACHS: If you write in C, I think proper indentation is very important, and naming the variables mnemonically so you can figure out what they are. Programs have a kind of simplicity and symmetry if they're just right.

INTERVIEWER: *Can somebody look at one of your programs and tell that you wrote that program?*

SACHS: Some people could. I think if you get to know someone's style, you can see indicators that tell you who wrote a program.

INTERVIEWER: *How would you describe your approach to programming?*

SACHS: First, I start out with a basic program framework, which I keep adding to. Also, I try not to use many fancy features in a language or a program. For example, the text editor I use is a derivative of one I wrote at MIT fifteen years ago. It has only a few simple commands; but it has everything that I need. It's written in C now, so I take it with me on every new machine. I don't like using any tools or programs I didn't write myself or that I don't have some control over. That way if I don't like some part, I can change it. As a rule, I like to keep programs simple.

Some people are very good at optimizing every instruction. They can make one little piece of code extremely tight. At the other end, some people think only about the algorithm and the actual implementation. I'm somewhere in the middle. I'm not that good at writing extremely tight code. I've found over the years that if you write that way, every time you have to make a change, you have to unravel the whole program and write it over again. But if you back off just a bit, and code very tightly only in a few spots where it's important, its a lot easier to maintain the program once you've finished it.

INTERVIEWER: *Did anyone in particular influence the way you program?*

SACHS: A lot of people. The first person who influenced me a lot was Eric Jensen. He worked on the PDP-1. He's about four or five years older than I am and dates all the way back to the first computers that were on campus. He is an interesting character. I have only been around a few people like him— people who are so advanced at one thing that it's almost scary.

For example, Eric was about the best I've ever seen at making one particular piece of code very small. The early computers had consoles with lots of lights and switches. Eric could enter programs at the switches. He would sit at the console with one hand on a button that inserted the contents of the switches in the next spot in memory. He would flip all the switches up with one hand, and then press them in chords as though he were playing the piano, one chord every few seconds. He was very impressive. I learned a value of aesthetics and a sense of the right and wrong way of doing things from him.

I've also learned a lot from looking at other people's programs. For example, I learned a lot of tricks from reading the IBM Scientific Subroutine Package, which is a huge package of FORTRAN code. I read a lot of books, and I see other people's ideas and absorb them. I'm not a particularly creative person; my real skill is taking ideas and integrating them to make a nice package. It's not that I can't invent new things, but I'm not exceptional at it.

INTERVIEWER: *Do you think computers will continue doing basically what they are doing today?*

SACHS: The rate of innovation is rather slow. There are only a few really new ideas every decade. In fact, people complain about the old days of paper tape and such things, but some of the old technology was really good. And I'm not sure much progress will be made over time.

INTERVIEWER: *Why do you think that?*

SACHS: Well, let's look at the actual speed for one thing. Consider the PDP-9. It had about the same speed as a PC, but it had a fixed-head disk that was very fast. The operating system was very simple. It didn't have some features that are in current operating systems, but it was extremely fast. It could assemble a fairly large program in a few seconds. Even on an AT, I have to wait for several minutes. As the technology has improved, most of the gain has been offset by increased generality and inefficiency in the system. You can still get very good performance if you write in Assembler and take over control of the machine. That's basically how 1-2-3 works.

For example, if 1-2-3 had been written to use only the facilities that were available from the operating system, it would be much, much slower. So all in all, it's not clear that computers are really progressing. In fact, after 1-2-3, I thought there had to be a better programming development environment than the PC or the AT. So we brought in some Sun work stations. I found they were a huge step backward. They didn't compile any faster than an AT. We're seeing all these new processors, but a lot of the power is lost because everyone wants all the features, and that slows everything down.

INTERVIEWER: *Do you think one day just about everybody will have a computer at home?*

SACHS: Yes, as they become smaller and more accessible. A number of hardware companies are rumored to be working on a chip having the power of an IBM PC that would replace all the chips with one big chip. So, yes, I think we'll see computers in every home.

INTERVIEWER: *What do you think about artificial intelligence?*

SACHS: I think the term has been widely abused. You inevitably run up against a brick wall when you try to write intelligent programs. You can develop a lot of the program easily, but you soon reach a point where all of a sudden the going gets incredibly difficult.

For example, MIT wanted to make a computer recognize Morse code. Well, it's just dashes and dots, but when it's sent by a human operator, sometimes the dots are a little long and sometimes the dashes are a little short. People perceive Morse code to be 100 percent accurate, but interpreting the dots and dashes is similar to reading. When you read text, you don't look at each of the letters, which can be flawed or broken. You see words and sentences, and it makes sense as a whole. That's where a huge amount of additional information is brought into play. In Morse code, it's not just a question of trying to figure out what's a dot and what's a dash, but trying to figure out what the sentence says and what the message means. This is an area where there has been no progress, ever. Understanding meaning has always been a major stumbling block in developing intelligent programs, whether it's voice recognition, machine-aided translation of languages, or character recognition. No one knows how to write a program that acquires experience and learns things, in a broad sense.

INTERVIEWER: *How do you perceive computers? Are they just machines, and just giant calculators?*

SACHS: Certainly they're tools. That's what I say objectively. But they're also toys; they're fun. You can interact with a computer. And if you do it just right, you can make wonderful things happen.

Ray Ozzie

BORN ON *November 20, 1955, Ray Ozzie grew up in Park Ridge, near Chicago. He studied computer science at the University of Illinois at Urbana. While there, he worked on PLATO, a computer-based education system connected to nearly a thousand terminals all over the world.*

After finishing college in 1978, Ozzie worked for Jonathan Sachs at Data General near Boston, where they developed a small business system. From Data General, Ozzie moved into the world of microcomputers and software at Software Arts, the creators of VisiCalc. After working at Software Arts for more than a year and a half, Ozzie left to take a job with Jonathan Sachs and Mitch Kapor at Lotus, where he worked on and later became the project leader of Symphony. Since completing that project, Ray Ozzie has started his own company, Iris Associates, which contracts with Lotus to produce software.

Ray and his wife, Dawna Bousquet, and their son Neil now live in a rural suburb of Boston.

Ray Ozzie is a young, bright, enthusiastic fellow. We met at Lotus's new building, though Ray now runs his own business, Iris Associates, which contracts with Lotus. Being in business for himself has been his goal for his entire career. He is emphatic about giving a lot of credit and appreciation to his wife, Dawna Bousquet, who has the patience and understanding to put up with his long, arduous hours. His deep-set eyes, and fine brown hair brushed back off his forehead, coupled with his trim beard, give Ozzie a European look. In his friendly, outspoken manner, Ray Ozzie talked for hours about his programming career, from working the PLATO system when he was in college, to writing Symphony for Lotus, to starting his own company. He had many words of advice for beginning programmers, as well as insights into the future directions of computer software.

INTERVIEWER: Are there techniques for producing good programs?

OZZIE: I believe in a rigorous structure, very consistent and clean. I also believe in highly modular and layered software, and very liberal use of both numbers of files and directories. If you're forced to build pieces separately, then the interfaces stand out more, requiring you to formalize them.

When many people work on a program, it's very important to establish, early in the project, global error-handling, argument-passing, and subroutine-naming conventions (even though everyone may not agree with them). I feel, however, that you should never tell others how to comment their code, how to use braces, or how to indent code. When you're working in somebody else's module, though, you'd better use his or her conventions. It's part of learning to work with others.

The environment for the exchange of ideas should be open. Design sessions should be allowed to be very heated and intense. I have found that many good designers tend to be very opinionated and willing to stand up for what they feel is right, and also know when and how to back down. Good designers do not have the "Not Invented Here" syndrome.

INTERVIEWER: How did you come up with the idea for the project you're working on?

OZZIE: Although I can't comment very openly on my current project, I can say that most products are designed by successive approximation and refinement, and are not just the results of one person's "idea." This project began with a desire to produce a product that would help people use computers more effectively and enjoyably in their businesses.

There is a tendency for people to write programs just to make money and not to solve problems. Instead of being innovative, they look at what already exists and try to copy it thinking, "Gee, I can do a better one of these." A lot of effort and money is being wasted trying to build better spreadsheets, but the world just doesn't need fifty-seven spreadsheets. I think that we've already seen the last wave of people who will make it really big in this industry. Once the seven-figure dreams disappear, people will take the vertical markets more seriously and develop software for specific applications rather than try to shoot for the moon with a product people don't need.

Our product is not a copycat product. I believe that it will be very useful to large numbers of people. But if it makes any number of people happy and more productive, we will have done our job.

INTERVIEWER: When you come up with an idea for a software product, are you confident you can do it and deliver on time?

> *"Software project managers must understand the people working for them."*

OZZIE: Yes, I'm pretty sure that I can. I've had enough experience to know what I'm capable of doing. Complex programming projects run by non-programming managers are often doomed to slip because they don't understand either the intricacies of the project components or programmers' personalities. Software project managers must understand the people who work for them. I know, as best as I can, the family situation, life-style, and working habits of each person who works with me. I know we can't work nine-to-five days and get the project done. I also know I can't push people to work twenty-four hours a day for the entire duration of the project. But I know when it comes to a crunch, I can count on them to work around the clock if it's necessary. I just have to know when to let up.

I also prefer to work with people who are well-seasoned and have been through the process before. I ask the programmer to predict the amount of time it will take him to complete a certain task, and I base my projections on what he says and then bias it by my past experiences with him. Many junior programmers may give me an estimate that is way off. Then, as people become more senior, they learn their own "fudge factor" based upon their steady-state work habits and current motivation level.

INTERVIEWER: It sounds like managing people well is the key to meeting deadlines and creating a high-quality product. How do you do that?

OZZIE: Many managers find programmers difficult to work with. I've seldom had a problem. Problems most often seem to occur when management tries to issue edicts or excessive controls. Programmers are very creative, self-directing, self-motivating people. You have to recognize that up front, and resign yourself to getting in their way only when it's very important to do so. If you go out of your way to make life easy for the team and they know it, they will remember it when it counts.

The environment must be conducive to programming. Different people have different environments that work for them. For us, it's a nice office with the best equipment we can afford, a stereo in each room, and a refrigerator that's always full. At Iris, some members of the group like to work at home, so they have entire machine setups identical to the ones at work.

Programmers shouldn't have to worry about whether they're making as much as their peers (or their management counterparts) because these insecurities can negatively impact motivation. They should feel like they are part of a team; that's why it's important the team be fairly small and not hierarchical, if possible.

INTERVIEWER: You mentioned a minute ago that you prefer people who are well-seasoned. What did you mean by that?

OZZIE: To be well-seasoned you must have worked on a variety of tasks. The best thing you can do after college graduation is work on something intensely for a year or so and then move on to a totally different area in computer science. For example, you might start in operating systems, and then go to networking, graphics, compilers, or databases to get acquainted with different areas. You're more marketable and more useful in the long run as a general programmer.

Many people right out of school lack the breadth of knowledge and experience that is necessary to do significant high-level product design and development independently. A well-seasoned programmer is a generalist, is well in tune with his own abilities and life-style, has the ability to think abstractly, can work well with others, and is both self-motivated and well-motivated.

INTERVIEWER: Tell me how you got into programming.

OZZIE: I started my freshman year of high school in 1969. One of the math teachers brought a programmable calculator to the classroom to show us (it was an Olivetti-Underwood Programma 101), thinking we would get excited about this neat little toy. He invited us to see him if we wanted to play with it. A couple of us did, and we spent a lot of time exploring the capabilities of that calculator.

We also noticed the teachers had their own little toy. The math office had a teletype that was connected with a time-sharing system in the school district, a General Electric model 400. Several of the math teachers played with it, trying to learn how it worked. Of course, we wanted to have a piece of that action too, so we found out how to obtain passwords and had some fun programming in BASIC and FORTRAN. I had a good time, but eventually I lost interest in it as other activities took more time.

INTERVIEWER: *What kinds of other activities?*

OZZIE: I was interested in technical theatre and electronics in high school. I took all the electronics courses offered and worked during the summer as an electronics technician. When I was in college at the University of Illinois at Urbana, I thought I'd study electrical engineering. I spent my freshman and sophomore years in that program.

As I began to take more electrical-engineering courses, I realized it wasn't exactly what I had thought it would be. I enjoyed the tinkering in electronics, but the mathematical theory didn't appeal to me at all. I was casting about for a new major when a friend in computer science convinced me to take a programming course. I loved it. The machine problems assigned to us were fun and easy. Even though I didn't understand all the concepts, I liked programming for the same reason I liked electronics. I could build little things with it—programs instead of gadgets. It was neat.

INTERVIEWER: *So you were hooked?*

OZZIE: The classes were okay, but what really got me hooked was a computer system on campus called PLATO. When I found out, I just had to use it. I discovered that one way to obtain access was to take a computer-science course that used the system. So I signed up and began to play with it.

That was the real beginning of my programming experience. Eventual access to the machine as a systems programmer fed my habit. Every night at 10:00 p.m. the machine became available, and a small clique of people like me would work all night until our time was up at 6:00 a.m. We did this for years. It was great fun.

From the moment I had open access to the computer, schoolwork just couldn't compete for my attention. In fact, the only reason I even thought about school at all was that I had to be enrolled to maintain my habit. If I were kicked out, I wouldn't get to play with the computer anymore. I was not a great student, but I managed to hang on. It took me five and a half years to graduate from college.

INTERVIEWER: *How did you then make the leap after graduation from student to systems programmer?*

OZZIE: I had my first lesson in politics while using PLATO. After nine months of fighting for access as a student, I began to realize it wasn't enough to be good at programming or to enjoy it. You had to play political games to get anywhere. There was a very strict hierarchy of privileges for using the PLATO system because so many people wanted to access it.

INTERVIEWER: *Do you think that happened because so many people wanted to use it, or because PLATO was a sort of mystical object that the university did not want people to touch?*

OZZIE: Probably a little of both. University of Illinois PLATO is a computer-based education system that runs on a massive Control Data mainframe with something less than a thousand terminals connected to it all over the world. The system was designed and implemented by a very small, tightly knit group of people. They were possessive of their invention, particularly when it came to permitting people to do systems programming.

Initially, the only people allowed to do systems programming were the faculty members who had designed it and a few high school and college students who had worked with the inner circle for years and had become friends. Anyone who wasn't in this group had to program in "Tutor," a medium-level interpretive language. I was determined to get into the systems programming, so I managed to politic my way into the circle.

INTERVIEWER: *What did you do on PLATO as a systems programmer?*

OZZIE: While I was using the PLATO system in conjunction with my course, I heard the PLATO hardware group was starting to develop a programmable terminal that was based on the Z80. The PLATO staff hired

> *"I would love to see computer centers made available for kids who want to play but can't afford machines of their own."*

me to develop firmware for the programmable terminal.

I had been working at the time as an electronics technician for the nuclear-engineering department, where I built little custom gadgets for the graduate students.

Later, during my senior year, I was one of three people who started a small company called Urbana Software Enterprises, to develop software for a property-management company. They wanted to build a microcomputer system to be used for their own vertical applications, so they contracted with a hardware group to develop a box based on the Z80, and with us to write a language compiler and interpreter and an operating system.

INTERVIEWER: *Why did it take you over five years to finish college?*

OZZIE: I would sign up each semester for the usual number of courses and then drop two or three of them. I also dropped out for a while. I stuck it out because I was afraid I'd never get a job if I didn't graduate. I was pretty nervous and unsure about the whole process of job hunting. Fortunately, the year I interviewed, 1977, was a very good year to be interviewing because big companies were actively hiring. I interviewed at twelve companies and was well received, primarily because of my practical experience.

INTERVIEWER: *How did you decide who to work for?*

OZZIE: Most of my friends went to the West Coast or to Digital in Maynard, Massachusetts. I was turned down by Digital, which was unfortunate, because I would have liked to have worked with my friends. I thought Digital would be the best place to be because of the potential to work in VAX software development (this was before the VAX was announced).

I took a job with Data General. After I accepted the job, I got another letter from Digital saying they would be interested in talking with me again. But I had already made a commitment to Jonathan Sachs to work at DG. We were to design a new operating system and architecture for a small business system from scratch. The core group consisted of only three people.

INTERVIEWER: *Talk a little more about the system you designed.*

OZZIE: We worked on a low-end small business system. The system was intended to be the replacement for an existing product line and was to have screen I/O performance competitive with Wang word processors.

We came up with a small system based upon micro Nova-based work stations and Eclipse file servers. Each work station had its own processor with 64K of memory (but no mass storage), a keyboard, and a monitor. It was hooked up to the other work stations, file servers, and print servers through a local area network that we developed. I developed the firmware and operating system for the work station while Jon Sachs and Scott Norin did the file server. It took about two years for the system to work well and, at that point, Jon left to start Concentric Data Systems with John Henderson. Scott and I stayed another year and put the final touches on the system. The division was hopping and the product was more or less finished.

INTERVIEWER: *So what did you do then?*

OZZIE: I was beginning to get frustrated at Data General. The process of getting things accomplished at a large company was becoming painful.

So about the time Jon left, I started to talk to a head hunter. I told her I wanted to go to a small company involved with microcomputers. I had been reading magazines and had played with CP/M, so working with microcomputers seemed interesting. But none of the interviews panned out. Most places were doing work on larger computers, not micros. About a year later, I got a call from the head hunter saying she found a little company that might interest me. It turned out to be Software Arts. I interviewed there and immediately liked it. I was hired as employee number 29.

As it turns out, it was a good thing that I left DG when I did—about a month later the project was canceled for political reasons. Data General was trying to unify the entire company under one operating system, and our project was incompatible. It was finished and very close to going out the door. I never had a clue that such a thing would happen.

INTERVIEWER: *What did you do at Software Arts?*

OZZIE: I started out working on the Radio Shack TRS-80 Model 3, on a language interpreter, laying the groundwork for implementation of TK!Solver. I was only there for a few weeks when they brought in a new machine for Visi-Calc development—the IBM PC. I couldn't believe the security. The rooms were locked and we couldn't remove the manuals from the room. The machine obviously was a prototype. After experimenting with it for a few days, I knew that I wanted one.

INTERVIEWER: *Did you think that eventually everyone would want one?*

OZZIE: Absolutely. Well, I thought at least programmers would want them. At the time my market awareness wasn't highly developed. I was still basically a hacker. If IBM came out with a microcomputer, it would mean prices would drop and computers would become more affordable. It would mean programmers like me would no longer be dependent on mainframes.

I was pretty excited about the IBM PC because I felt that it was the first micro powerful enough to compile a program I was working on. I could edit and compile a program, link, and run a test cycle on the same machine. When we first got a hard disk, it was a dream come true. I could just sit in my own office and work to my heart's content. The documentation was atrocious, and uncovering any technical information was just about impossible, but I was too happy to care about that. Even if it was slower, working on the micro-computer was better.

I'm enthusiastic about personal computers because younger people with programming in their blood won't have to fight and play politics to get machine access as we did. I hope parents and schools recognize what a wonder-ful resource PCs are. I would love to see computer centers made available for kids who want to play but can't afford machines of their own.

> *"I come to work because I enjoy playing with computers."*

INTERVIEWER: *It sounds like you were pretty happy at Software Arts. Did you ever think about leaving them?*

OZZIE: I had been at Software Arts for a couple of months when Jon Sachs and I went to lunch together. He had just left Concentric Data Systems and wanted to tell me about a very bright guy he had just met, Mitch Kapor, who had started a small company called Micro Finance Systems. Jon was going to work with him. When I asked what they'd be doing he really couldn't say but led me to believe that it was a VisiCalc clone. He wanted to know if I would be interested in working there.

I didn't know what to say. I had just started at Software Arts and I was happy working on the real VisiCalc; we were just about to show the Radio Shack version. To me that was a big step, it meant VisiCalc would be every-where. Why work on an imitation when you could work on the real thing? I decided to stay. In the meantime, Jon and Mitch did their thing; they built Lotus 1-2-3.

INTERVIEWER: *When did you see Jon next?*

OZZIE: The next time I saw him, and met Mitch for the first time, was at COMDEX where 1-2-3 was announced. By this time I had been working at Software Arts for about a year and a half and TK!Solver was done and had already shipped.

I knew the moment I got off the plane that Mitch and Jon (now Lotus) were doing something right. 1-2-3 was the talk of the show, though I still had no idea at the time it would beat VisiCalc.

I talked to Jon for a long time; he suggested again that I come to work with him. Although 1-2-3 was now out the door, there were still long lists of features that he and Mitch wanted to add to 1-2-3 in the second version. I said that I would give it some serious thought.

INTERVIEWER: *Were you ready to leave Software Arts?*

OZZIE: Leaving Software Arts must have been on my mind more than I realized, because six months before COMDEX I was involved in trying to start a company with three guys from Digital. One of the three had been approached by a representative of National Semiconductor. They were allegedly trying to seed a project to build an inexpensive low-end VAX-like system based upon the 16032 CPU that was about to become available. We were to develop an operating system for the machine that was to emulate VAX/VMS.

It finally fell through because National couldn't make up its mind and come up with the couple of million dollars needed for funding. That didn't stop us. We approached some venture capitalists. It was a sobering experience because they asked a lot of very difficult questions that we had not adequately addressed, specifically about marketing. So we dissolved the company.

INTERVIEWER: *Did you give Jon's offer serious thought then?*

OZZIE: At the time, my wife Dawna was expecting a baby. After Neil was born, we revisited the issue. Still having the urge to start a new company, I had been working on preliminary functional specifications for a new software product. After discussing the situation with Mitch at Lotus, we agreed upon an arrangement under which I would come to Lotus to work on what became Symphony. After the project was completed, we would revisit my functional specs and entrepreneurial desires.

INTERVIEWER: *What was it like working at Lotus?*

OZZIE: Soon after I started, I realized that the one-hour commute from my home to Cambridge took too much time away from work. After talking with Mitch, Jon and I opened a little office in Littleton, a location central to the three people working on the project (Jon, myself, and Barry Spencer).

INTERVIEWER: *So you were going to work on Symphony. Were the ideas all set for Symphony when you came in?*

OZZIE: All that existed was a five- or six-page high-level overview and a never-ending list of features that would be nice to have in the product.

I started working on a major piece, the word processor. Barry Spencer, who had also just started on the project, worked on communications, another big piece. After a few months, Jon seemed to be tired of working on the project. His heart was really not in what he was doing, possibly because he had been working too hard on the same piece of code for too long. So he withdrew and I became the project leader. We brought in a very good programmer, Matt Stern, to bring the team back up to three. Matt initially worked on the database component. For nine more months the three of us worked like mad. I would come into Lotus every two weeks and meet with Mitch to give him an update on the project. He would look at our work, evaluate it, we would re-synchronize our schedules, and then we'd go back and work on it for another couple of weeks.

INTERVIEWER: Was that an effective way for you to work?

OZZIE: Absolutely. Mitch is one of the reasons why Lotus is the best company I'd ever worked for. He has no qualms about delegating authority. He is intensely interested in the details of features, user interface, and the order in which we implement the features. But we are in control of the programming because he's not necessarily interested in algorithms. He doesn't step in every five minutes and change the design around for no good reason.

INTERVIEWER: Why do you think a program as complicated as Symphony came together so easily?

OZZIE: One reason was because such a large part of the company focused its efforts on Symphony. Everyone was very proud of the product and determined to finish it precisely on time. Many of us were also worried, whether we admitted it or not, about the potential competition: Ovation and Framework.

Another reason we met our deadlines was the fact that communication was good. A small development team in an isolated environment communicates very effectively. The moment that communication with the Lotus main office started to become a bottleneck, we responded by closing the branch and moving back to the main office.

Finally, the development team was small. I think product design and implementation should be done by no more than five people, if possible. However, if you are implementing some massive system, like the IRS tax-auditing system, it's obviously impractical to have such a small development group.

But small teams have many advantages, usually.

INTERVIEWER: *How is a smaller team more effective than a larger one?*

OZZIE: I believe that once the team is over five people, communication between individuals begins to break down, and that can cause problems related to product consistency.

Bugs are often characteristic of a bad interface between subsystems, which is frequently a result of inadequate communication among people when they design the subsystems. When a bug is found, there is a tendency to handle it within the subsystem and not look at the program as a whole. Unless you have a couple of people who know how each subsystem works and how it fits in with the whole, you will probably end up with a buggy product.

"Programming is the ultimate field for someone who likes to tinker."

INTERVIEWER: *Are there any other important criteria for a strong program?*

OZZIE: It's important to have a very clean, consistent architectural model of the product as you're working on it. You can change the architecture as you go along, but fixing poor architecture at the end with bug fixes is bad; instead of a couple of minor bugs, you may have to cover up gaping chasms.

1-2-3 is a very well-designed, consistent program. Symphony is a big layer on top of that clean product—a very large-scale program with many interactions between different pieces. It never had significant bugs because everyone involved understood the interactions among the subsystems and the basic 1-2-3 framework.

INTERVIEWER: *After Symphony was complete, what did you do?*

OZZIE: Mitch kept his word. I resurfaced the specs I had written before I started at Lotus and we talked about them. He suggested I work on the specs for a few months to get them to the point where I could describe how the product works, what it's good for, how people use it, and identify how it would be marketed. Barry Spencer took over Symphony's development, enabling me to devote all my energy to the new product.

After I finished the design specs, the vice presidents reviewed them informally. I had to go back and rework the design with no promises they'd be interested. The product had to stand on its own qualifications under scrutiny.

In the end, Lotus agreed to fund my project as a separate company, Iris Associates. I was immediately joined at Iris by two former associates, Tim

Halvorsen and Len Kawell, both from Digital. Since then we've hired two more people.

INTERVIEWER: *What kinds of programs do you think will be on the market in five to ten years?*

OZZIE: I can't wait to see what it will be like. I used to think I could see how it would end up but now I have no idea. Like many others, I mistakenly believed that there was such a thing as a home-computer market.

I used to think that a personal time-management program would be incredibly handy. It turns out that carrying a computer around in my briefcase, opening it up, and booting it up just to see my appointments, is far less convenient than my pocket-sized black book. A black book that my secretary and I could write in simultaneously, however, would be very useful because we could both schedule my time conveniently. I want someone very clever to invent that black book.

INTERVIEWER: *Do you have any particular advice for people who want to develop software?*

OZZIE: There are good opportunities available for those who understand the user in vertical markets. Only a certain number of the mass-market horizontal applications like 1-2-3 can exist. You can probably count them on one hand right now: word processors, spreadsheets, database-management systems. If personal computers are to succeed in the long term, it will be because programs are carefully tailored to meet specific user needs.

Computer-science students who have worked in their parents' businesses have a great opportunity for writing vertical packages. They understand computers and how they might impact a specific business. I think fewer people should be shooting for the moon, and more people should be finding a niche.

INTERVIEWER: *How important is considering the end user's needs when you develop a product?*

OZZIE: I come to work because I enjoy playing with computers, but I design the products as I do because I feel that I can provide the consumer with something useful. It is extremely important to remember that end goal throughout the product-development cycle.

INTERVIEWER: *How do you give the end user what she or he wants?*

OZZIE: First we try to make a profile of who we think will use the product. Then we try to roughly estimate what percentage of the total users will use each feature, so that we have an educated guess about which attributes will be used the most. We try to spend the most time refining features used by the highest percentage of users. If there is an obscure function that's only used by some small fraction of the users, we don't expend as much effort on the design of that function. Only after a product is shipped do we really know if our user profiles were correct.

INTERVIEWER: *Do you ever hear from the users?*

OZZIE: Oh yes. There are lots of stories there. It's fun to get a report from somebody who has used your product daily for a long time and has discovered a bug in some obscure feature. It's great to think there is someone out there with a totally different life-style in a different part of the country using your software, and it's satisfying to know they feel good enough about it to take the time to write a letter and gripe.

My most amazing experience, though, was a phone call I got right after I started Iris, from a surgeon who was using Symphony for real-time data analysis during open heart surgery. It is sobering to think that someone was lying on an operating table, potentially relying upon my program running properly. It reminds one of the real responsibility to the end users.

INTERVIEWER: *Do you consider programming play? When you're writing a program is it painful or pleasurable?*

OZZIE: I wouldn't be doing this if it weren't pleasurable. The painful part is not seeing Dawna and Neil during intense development cycles; I just wish there were a few more hours in a day. I would never be able to do it without Dawna's total support, and the importance of that should not be underestimated.

INTERVIEWER: *What is the fascination with programming? It seems to me a lot of programmers are natural tinkerers or mechanical types who build things and then get into programming later. Why is that?*

OZZIE: Programming is the ultimate field for someone who likes to tinker. Tinkering requires tools. Electrical engineers have various components they can put together to build something. But they're constrained by the availability of physical equipment. With a computer, if you can think about it, you can do it. You can design your own tools or create the parts as you go along. If you don't like something, you can just change it or rewrite it. It's a wide-open tool box, given the resource, the computer. The only limiting factors are the amount of time it takes the computer to do the task and the amount of time it takes you to write the program. You have incredible flexibility.

INTERVIEWER: *How do you guard against burnout?*

OZZIE: By not overscheduling and by taking a reasonable number of breaks from hacking. If I am going to be coding intensely for a period of time, I'll set it up so that I'll spend a minimum of six months doing something like high-level design before I go into that heavy-duty coding mode again. I give myself a break. By the time I get back to programming heavily, I really feel like doing it again.

INTERVIEWER: *Any advice to give young programmers today?*

OZZIE: If you are the kind of person who is pulled into programming, who is compelled to program, I would advise you to be optimistic and program as much and on as many different projects as you can. Spend as much time as possible on the computer but learn to accurately judge your own burnout level, and don't worry if people think you're weird.

This is the main loop for the edit command in our newest version of T/Maker
which also supports Japanese and Chinese (thus the reference to "kanji").

I would say this code is pretty typical in terms of how it looks.


```
edit ()

  { inedit = 1;
    oops[0] = NUL;
    tcsd2 = tcs/2;
    move (tl1,tc1,1);
    pmenu (400);
    if (noimage)  gdraw (0,1,1,1,tl1,tl2);
    else          gdraw (0,1,0,0,tl2-3,tl2);
    error = maccol = maccnt = noprint = mmode = 0;
    inmac = chchin = rinfo = 0;
    chr = 390;
    for (;;) {
          if (rlines) {
              if (ccol >= tc1) ruleone (ccol,0,0);
              else             ruleone (ccol,1,0);
              pblip();
          }
          if (chr == 384) break;
          if (chr < 32 || chr == 127)   ederror(65); else
          if (chr >= 527 && chr <= 529) macro ();   else echar ();
          if (theline[ccol] > SPACE && ccol)
              if (callutl(kanji3,0,theline,&theline[ccol-1]))
                  if (ccol < tc2) fs(0); else bs();
          if (rlines) {
              if (ccol >= tc1) ruleone (ccol,0,1);
              else             ruleone (ccol,1,1);
              pblip();
          }
          if (rinfo++ >= 50) { rinfo = 0; dinfo (1); }
          else            if (lastinfo != cline) dinfo(0);
          if (error) break;
          pblip();
          chr = gfunc ();
    }
    inedit = 0;
    clrbl();
    mmode = 0;
    dinfo (1);
  }
```

Sample code written in C that illustrates Peter Roizen's
style of writing code.

Peter Roizen

A NATIVE Californian, Peter Roizen was raised in Palo Alto. He attended the University of California at Berkeley, where he earned his bachelor's degree in mathematics in 1967. His first job after graduation was as a programmer, although he had very little exposure to programming before that time. Roizen left Berkeley to spend two years in Montreal and Toronto, and then went to Europe, where he worked with the World Health Organization for seven years as a programmer. He later returned to the United States to work for the World Bank in Washington, D.C. In 1980, Roizen started his own company to market and sell the spreadsheet program, T/Maker, which he had worked on in his spare time while employed at the World Bank. In 1985, Roizen moved his small company from Washington D.C. to the San Francisco Bay area. Roizen is 39 years old, married, and has a five-year-old son. He resides in Los Gatos, California.

I made arrangements to meet Peter Roizen at the offices of his company, T/Maker, though the time he spends there is minimal, often as little as one day per week. Indeed, he seemed a little out of place and uncomfortable at the office with ringing phones, many voices speaking at once, and people going about the business of selling software. It was almost as if he had emerged from hibernation to meet with me. Roizen much prefers the solitude of his office at home, where he spends most of his time developing software.

In his late thirties, Roizen is a casual, quiet man with a tousled look, curly dark-brown hair, and an angular face that often breaks into a warm smile. He values his independence, his freedom from the salaried, corporate world, and his ability to earn a living doing what he enjoys doing, programming. He does not put on airs about what it means to be a programmer. He does not exalt his occupation or have great designs on developing a piece of software that will change the world and make him a fortune. Instead, he looks upon himself as very fortunate to have discovered his niche in the world and settled into it.

INTERVIEWER: What do you like about programming?

ROIZEN: Well, I've always enjoyed games like chess and backgammon, because they require strategy to win, and because I always know at the end of the game whether I won or lost. Programming is very much like a game. If I just want to write a program to solve a problem without a lot of fuss, and there aren't many decisions to make, I can usually solve the problem in a fairly straightforward fashion. But there are always different directions to take. Programming is fun because it's challenging to make the best design decisions. One especially neat feature of programming is that it's very clear when you do it well. When I hang wallpaper, if I pay attention I do a decent job, and if I don't, it's lousy, with a few turned corners. If I do a decent job programming, the program runs in a second and accomplishes the task. If I do a lousy job, it runs in ten seconds and one time out of twenty the whole thing dies. I like knowing when I've been successful.

INTERVIEWER: So doing the best you can is a source of satisfaction in programming for you?

ROIZEN: Sure, although I wouldn't blow it out of proportion. There's a big universe out there; a hundred years from now they won't even know what this program was. I'm not expecting to influence the course of the world. I just try to do something every day that's worthwhile, so when I'm finished, I think it was a good way to spend my time.

INTERVIEWER: *Do you feel compelled to program?*

ROIZEN: Not really. I can put it down anytime. I don't feel I have to touch the keyboard at regular intervals or be around computers all the time. Sometimes, when I'm down on programming, I do something else. I used to draw cartoons. I wasn't very good at drawing, so it was difficult to get just the image I wanted, but it was fun anyway. I like to ski, though I'm not an expert. And now taking care of my five-year-old son and helping around the house occupies a lot of my time. But I do get satisfaction out of programming. It's not any better than any other field; it just happens to be a path I followed that has made me happy. So I stick with it.

> *"There's a big universe out there; 100 years from now they won't even know what this program was."*

INTERVIEWER: *How would you describe your approach to programming?*

ROIZEN: I'm very much a "bottoms-up" programmer. I don't worry much about global strategies because I'm never capable of seeing the whole picture until I've done all the specifics. "Top-down" programming is fine when you have to delegate work to various people—obviously you need some concept of how all the pieces are going to fit together. For me, programming is very much an iterative process. I always do small pieces of a program at a time. If I fiddle with the code in one place, I will probably need to change it somewhere else. I just wind my way up or down to a solution that fits.

I'm also very practical. I've seen many intelligent people who are just not practical. They get lost pursuing some academic goal that is totally useless. Being practical is important to good programming. You must be able to guess accurately how long it will take to complete a project, have the ability to calculate what can and cannot be done in that time, and then do it, resisting the temptation to go off and do other things. Practicality is important when you're trying to make every piece of work the best because you always have a limited amount of time to work on it. It's easy to triple the time to complete a project when you're consumed with making it the ultimate in elegance. But if you're still working on it, it doesn't sell too well. You don't have a product, and that makes it difficult to earn a living.

INTERVIEWER: You've been in programming over eighteen years. How did you get into it in the first place?

ROIZEN: After I graduated from Berkeley in 1967 with my degree in mathematics, I went looking for a job and accepted the first one offered, as a programmer, even though my experience with programming was pretty minimal. There wasn't even a computer science department then. I had taken one course in FORTRAN and I was a reader for a class on programming; to help the students and correct their papers I had to stay one bit ahead of them. That was the extent of my experience in the field.

INTERVIEWER: You mean you landed a job programming without ever having programmed?

ROIZEN: The field was new then and employers would hire people who demonstrated an aptitude for programming but had no experience. Like first jobs for a lot of people, it didn't really matter to me what it was. I used FORTRAN and COBOL, reading the manuals as I wrote the programs.

INTERVIEWER: And did you continue to program?

ROIZEN: After that first job, I worked for seven years in Europe with the World Health Organization, and then at the World Bank in Washington D.C. for seven years—both of them big organizations—before I started my own company in 1980.

INTERVIEWER: Do you follow certain principles in developing a program?

ROIZEN: I believe very strongly in using what I've written. Not that I'm the best user of my own programs, but I use them constantly so I'm aware of their shortcomings and can change them if I find something stupid. I remember a program at the World Bank that I was trying to demonstrate for someone. It was someone else's program, and I had never used it before. When the first line came up on the screen and suggested typing HELP to get help, I thought that would be a good first step. So I typed HELP and got the message: FATAL ERROR—SEE COMPUTER ACTIVITIES PROGRAMMING DEPARTMENT. That was a case of a designer who never used his own program enough to follow even the first instruction he put on the screen. That's a very dangerous way to do things.

INTERVIEWER: How does it happen that a programmer never tries out his own program?

ROIZEN: In the old days, lots of companies made a separation between the analyst and the programmer. The analyst made the overall plan using flowcharts, and the programmer filled in the details. Any time you approach the solution of a problem with some people just drawing boxes and others specifying the contents of the boxes, you inevitably end up with a piece of trash that doesn't solve the problem. When I was a programmer, half the plans I got from analysts were totally unworkable. They have the big picture, but they don't have enough detailed information to do their jobs well. Nobody is clever enough to look at the entire picture and also see the details of how the program needs to operate. So I'm for having one person write the whole program from beginning to end.

INTERVIEWER: *Do you think a programmer who works for a company has to compromise?*

ROIZEN: Not necessarily. When someone pays your salary, you have to do what they want you to do, to some extent. Let's face it; money buys influence. It's the rule of the land. But I wouldn't call that compromising. In fact, some companies would call that maturity and positive adjustment. When I worked for those big organizations, I had some assignments that I enjoyed, and I felt satisfied with the outcome; there wasn't anything to compromise.

INTERVIEWER: *How do you approach writing a program?*

ROIZEN: Since I generally program everything myself, I don't have the time to implement features that are very complicated. I have to develop programs that are reasonable in length and can also be finished in a specified amount of time. The people who only write specifications don't think about time very much. There's really a big difference between what we would like to do, and what's possible to get done this afternoon. In some ways, it's a handicap that our company doesn't have the resources of time or money to do exactly what we'd like to do. But in other ways, it's a benefit because it keeps our program relatively trim and useful by not adding great numbers of absolutely useless features.

INTERVIEWER: *Do you write a lot of comments in your code?*

ROIZEN: Almost none. If I need to give somebody a piece of source code for something, I quickly go back and add comments. My own work speaks to me directly. The names and routines are all abbreviations that describe their functions, so commenting is unnecessary and just clutters up the program for me. If I have a structure that I intend to use in five or six places, I might comment on what's in each element. Other than that, I never load a program with comments.

A good memory for detail is important when I read my code, although I don't think I have a particularly good memory overall. I can't remember people's birthdays. I know I went to high school somewhere but I can't remember anything about it. My memory for all that is lousy. But give me a problem, like what would happen if you did this or that, and I could probably remember the piece of code and give a good guess as to what would happen with it. Memory must be quite selective. I know my own memory amazes me sometimes—positively and negatively.

> *"I sit ... with my feet on the desk, reaching out to the keyboard as if I were painting on an easel."*

INTERVIEWER: *Does the source code you write have a particular style?*

ROIZEN: I guess everybody has their own style. My code is very sparse with large white spaces. I try to isolate the functions that need to be used by different routines to economize on the code and improve on speed.

INTERVIEWER: *Do you think there's one right way to create a program?*

ROIZEN: Definitely not. People have to follow their own work styles and habits. I usually sit away from the terminal with my feet on the desk, reaching out to the keyboard as if I were painting on an easel. That's my choice and doesn't mean other people can't sit staring at the keyboard as if they were typing. The only requirement for creating good programs is interest. Obviously, if you're going to do anything well, you need to have a serious interest in it. If you don't care, all the talent in the world will still produce a lousy result. If you do care, you need only one-third the talent to produce something decent.

INTERVIEWER: *What prompted you to leave the World Bank and strike out on your own?*

ROIZEN: My philosophy is to do the best I can in any situation. I felt frustrated because it seemed that good ideas were never pursued and good time was spent cultivating bad ideas. That was true of both the World Health Organization and the World Bank.

INTERVIEWER: *Why do you think good ideas weren't pursued?*

ROIZEN: Big organizations don't create environments that encourage people to think creatively. They reward employees for doing exactly what is requested, and no more. Without incentives, the people who make requests of programmers don't come up with intriguing projects, and the programmers don't spend time thinking of interesting ways to solve problems. In the organizations I worked in, many times we never even worked on the problem because we first did feasibility studies that often took longer to do than the piece of work would have taken.

My father always said, "Your job is no better than your immediate supervisor." That was very true for me. When I had good immediate supervisors, they gave me enough freedom so I could make myself happy at work and go home happy at night. When I had a lousy supervisor, someone who was uninterested in the projects or didn't share any common interests, then it was a lousy job.

I quit, mainly because I got tired of going home every night feeling I wasn't doing anything. I wanted to feel I had earned the money I took home. Instead I was going home every night and saying, "Well, I suffered enough today so I deserve that money as compensation." And that was not a healthy way to live my life.

INTERVIEWER: What did you do to make your life healthier?

ROIZEN: Well, I got a computer and started working on some of my ideas at night. I had about $6,000 in the bank that my wife and I were going to spend on something, possibly a new car or a programmable calculator. Personal computers had just begun to come out at that time. The more I thought about what to buy, a computer seemed to make more sense. So I got a 48K CP/M machine with a terminal. I worked at my job during the day and I worked at home every night and on weekends. I didn't develop the ideas because they would be profitable, but because I wanted to see if they would work. I thought I had a couple of ideas that were worthwhile.

INTERVIEWER: And so that was really the beginning of T/Maker. What inspired the idea?

ROIZEN: At the time, I did a fair amount of programming for budgeting departments whose main function was to total up rows of columns. They would bring us a problem to solve and we would send them away with a big database like Focus that they never really understood. Over the long term, they never got reports like they wanted, and they ran up enormous bills for time sharing. It was an incredible waste of resources, like killing a fly with a sledgehammer.

So I tried to create a simple spreadsheet that would be easy to learn and give the user the results he wanted. I wanted one that would easily calculate totals and subtotals and let the user put text on the screen wherever he wanted it. Initially, I started on it at the World Bank, designing it to be implemented under UNIX, so people would have access to a spreadsheet without mainframe overkill. I wanted to refine the program, but nobody at the Bank was interested. Then I went to several other companies to talk them into making this a facility on their time-sharing systems. No one was interested in the slightest. Everyone thought I was a jerk with a stupid idea.

INTERVIEWER: *But you didn't give up?*

ROIZEN: I decided the only way I was ever going to make any progress was to use my own machine. That was quite a risk for me, because at the time I had the impression you had to be a big company with big resources and organized people to start something like my spreadsheet project. I didn't think a small company could really succeed. It took about a year to get the first version of the product running.

INTERVIEWER: *During that year, were you ever worried about competition—that someone might beat you to it?*

ROIZEN: VisiCalc came out about six months before we got T/Maker finished. The name really frightened me because it sounded like the same product. I didn't even want to look at it because I was so sure it was going to be identical. I don't think I checked it out until I was finished writing T/Maker. Then I realized it was completely different. Of course VisiCalc went on to make millions and T/Maker didn't, but I know that doesn't necessarily say anything about the quality of a product.

INTERVIEWER: *Can you describe what makes your T/Maker spreadsheet different from VisiCalc?*

ROIZEN: T/Maker used a very different approach. Our program uses an empty screen, whereas VisiCalc organizes the screen for the user by creating cells in which you enter numbers and equations. The T/Maker approach is much more relaxed; the calculator part of the program is in the background. When you use it, you feel like you are writing on a blackboard, not like you are running a program.

An interesting feature of T/Maker is that you may write a piece of information, a logical thought, vertically rather than horizontally on the screen. I would not call this a revolutionary concept, but I have never seen another program that does this.

INTERVIEWER: *What were the criteria of your design for T/Maker?*

ROIZEN: First, the emphasis was on keeping the solutions to simple problems simple. If you want to total three rows, you put three plus signs down the left-hand side of the screen as you enter the numbers and then an equal sign underneath to indicate a total. There's nothing easier than that. I didn't try to create a general academic solution that offers so many possibilities that it confuses the user. I chose a solution for people whose work primarily involves adding columns of numbers. With T/Maker, users can define a neat-looking report that meets all of their specifications. Then they can print the report exactly as they see it on screen, because T/Maker syntax allows them to put text anywhere they want on the screen. That's different from most other systems.

> *"I care not only what the code says, but how it looks."*

Another important feature of T/Maker has to do with my style of design. When given a choice between putting in a specific useful function or a general capability, I tend to put in the general capability as long as it doesn't deteriorate the simple uses. Other packages are much more rigid. They assume the user will want to have a two-line heading and a page number on the bottom. In T/Maker, the heading can have a flexible number of lines and the page number can be located anywhere on the page. That does make it harder for the person who just wanted the two line heading, but then the program is stronger for people who use it over a long period of time. Writing a package like T/Maker requires an incredible number of judgment calls. I like to believe most of these are well made in T/Maker.

INTERVIEWER: *What was it like working on T/Maker?*

ROIZEN: It was fun. I was thrilled every time I compiled it and some new feature worked. It was exciting when someone looked at it and thought it was decent enough to sell. Even more exciting, of course, was when the checks started coming in and I actually made a living doing something that was so satisfying to me.

INTERVIEWER: *What was the greatest problem you faced when you were writing the program?*

ROIZEN: Having only one computer was difficult. It would invariably break down the day before I was going to demonstrate some facet of the product. Also, I had to write a screen editor, as T/Maker uses a visual-type syntax. I had never done anything like that before, and it was a bit complicated.

INTERVIEWER: What language did you use to write the program?

ROIZEN: I wrote the first version in CBASIC because there was nothing else at the time. In retrospect, I'm rather pleased. It not only worked, but was relatively fast. When I was finally able to use C (BDS C), everything ran ten times faster. To this day, getting a screen editor to work in CBASIC and have it be reasonably quick is an accomplishment I'm proud of.

INTERVIEWER: Did anything unexpected develop from writing the spreadsheet program?

ROIZEN: Contact with users has been terrific fun. Fans occasionally write us letters and some of the mail is very touching. Once we gave a free copy of T/Maker to a prison. Someone there wrote to tell us how much they enjoyed using it and how appreciative they were that someone would care about prisoners. A fellow in Southern California sent us a box of avocados because he uses T/Maker to run his ranch. It's like having an extended family. Even though you've never met, talking on the phone and writing one or two letters is enough to make users part of the family. It's a very nice side effect of having this business.

INTERVIEWER: Has your life changed much since you wrote T/Maker?

ROIZEN: My life's changed a lot, particularly my perspective on my job and salary. When I worked for someone else, I thought I always had to get a job that paid at least five percent more than the previous one, and I was adverse to taking risks. I was always thinking about salary and the next payday, because I might want to buy a new TV or stereo. When I worked at those early jobs I often wondered why anyone paid me such a good salary for doing nothing that contributed to the benefit of the world—sitting around and drinking coffee with other people, writing feasibility studies that were never implemented and programs no one could use. My job didn't really benefit anyone other than me, and the only benefit was my salary. After a while, I began to feel I was worthless because I wasn't doing anything useful.

Now I have the feeling that I have some reasonable skills that are useful. I get satisfaction out of my work, so I'm not very conscious of the salary. If I had the choice to make half as much money and do what I want, or twice as much money and do what somebody else told me to do, I'd choose the lower salary and the freedom. When I'm basically happy at work, I don't need to drive a Porsche because it's not an important part of my life. Working at what I like has become a large part of my life.

INTERVIEWER: What are you working on now?

ROIZEN: I'm working on a revision of T/Maker. Having fiddled with the program for five years, I see lots of areas where T/Maker can be improved. I see problems I couldn't see when I was writing the program. Until you actually try something and use it heavily over a period of time, you don't see the holes in it. You don't see the forest for the trees. There are trees in T/Maker that could be grouped together in a better forest than they are now.

The old product doesn't make many concessions to people who don't read the manual or who aren't familiar with computer jargon. That was an area I wasn't particularly sensitive to because I use computers every day, all day long. If there's a keystroke to learn, I learn it. I can make it easier to use for the person who uses the program less frequently, like on weekends. It's difficult to remember from one Sunday to the next how to operate the program.

INTERVIEWER: Have you ever considered doing anything entirely different from T/Maker?

ROIZEN: I wouldn't mind trying something else. But I have so much time, code, and effort invested, it's difficult to quit and try a new idea. There is a fair amount of startup time in any new project. And T/Maker is always open to adding new modules. I also have the help now of a programmer who understands the machine better than I do so that opens some new doors.

INTERVIEWER: Would you consider programming an art, a science, a trade, or a skill?

ROIZEN: I definitely consider it to be an art. I believe anything done well can become art because all jobs can be done with a certain amount of taste or artistic talent. In my own work, I care not only what the code says but how it looks. I frequently go back over code just to adjust it so it looks better.

INTERVIEWER: Would you compare programming to any other art—composing music, painting, or writing?

ROIZEN: It's difficult to make comparisons when I only know one of those things well. I have no idea what a composer is looking for when he's trying to write a piece of music. The art lies in being interested in whatever you're doing and trying to do a quality job. I don't put on a special programming suit to program and put on another suit to hang wallpaper in my house.

INTERVIEWER: Do you consider computer science to be a true science?

ROIZEN: I'm not a big believer that studying computer science makes good programmers. Obviously, you have to learn how to develop a hash table or a few algorithms. But maybe you're better off learning that information on your own, like I did. Well, I had to teach myself, because there weren't any reference books or classes at the time. I'm saying this because most of the problems that occur don't fall into the categories you learn in a book or a class. You can't turn to page five in a book and find a solution to one part of the problem and look on page six for the solution to the next part and put the two together to resolve the whole problem. Those kinds of solutions never work.

The biggest and most difficult part of any problem is just deciding what direction to take. When I fiddle with something enough, I figure out what the plan should be, and then the actual programming isn't that tough. Learning ten different sorting algorithms in computer science doesn't really help very much in figuring out how to design a solution.

> *"A fellow in California sent us a box of avocados because he uses T/Maker to run his ranch."*

INTERVIEWER: *You're giving advice here to the new generation of programmers. Has anyone in particular influenced you?*

ROIZEN: No one in particular. I did enjoy *Zen and the Art of Motorcycle Maintenance.* Although I probably didn't understand three-quarters of it, the few lines I did understand had a big impact on me. When I read the book, I started to think a little bit more about quality and doing things well, even when it seemed no one cared. The author described a motorcyclist who took his bike to the shop to be repaired. Without thinking, the mechanic grabbed a tool, the wrong one, and immediately stripped a nut. You find some people like that, who look at work as an unthinking activity. The author's description of the pleasure in doing things well was influential.

INTERVIEWER: *Do you interact much with other programmers?*

ROIZEN: Not much. I prefer to pursue my own ideas. I don't know how other programmers work, but I don't think they're very interested in my ideas. My experience in trying to sell people on the idea of T/Maker confirmed that.

One of the great things about programming is you can own the equipment and do the work yourself. You don't need the cooperation of other people to do something. You can be quite independent. In the company, I've reduced my visits to the office now to about one a week. I don't enjoy tasks that have to be done in the office, such as planning marketing strategy, or sitting in meetings. It brings me no satisfaction. I prefer to work alone at home.

202

INTERVIEWER: *What do you think makes a good programmer?*

ROIZEN: A good programmer is a good worker who has a degree of interest in what he's doing. His objective is to produce a product that is the best it can be, like the Army ads say, no matter how difficult it is to meet that objective. He also needs a good memory for detail. I can pick up a piece of code I wrote a couple of years ago and generally quickly grasp what I was doing.

INTERVIEWER: *If a programmer writes a program that's excellent, is it sure to succeed?*

ROIZEN: I used to think so. But now I don't really know. It depends on how you define success. I define success as doing what I want during the day and paying the bills at the end of the month. That kind of success is not very hard to achieve. You could do most anything and reach that level of success. But I also know you can't displace a very successful product like Lotus even if you wrote a package that was ten times better. Not only that, good ideas are hard to come by. It's not like I can sit down and say, "Gee I'm going to have a good idea today." Or you can't just get ten people to come up with fifty ideas. In my whole life I've had possibly three or four ideas decent enough to develop into useful projects. One of them was T/Maker, but because I didn't pursue any of the others, I don't remember what they were.

INTERVIEWER: *What do you think is going to happen to the computer industry in the next couple of years?*

ROIZEN: I don't know. I'm one of the worst people to ask, because I don't follow the trends. When I do pick up a personal computer magazine and thumb through it I feel depressed. There are so many slick products. I see the glossy pictures of their fancy screens, and I inevitably get the feeling ours must be inferior. One solution to that depression is simply to avoid the magazines. Consequently, I don't keep up with what other people are doing. But I don't worry as long as we have customers. We continue to improve T/Maker and they continue to buy the updates. We have some OEM customers who are particularly regular and if we give them something better now and then, I think they'll continue to be our customers.

INTERVIEWER: *Do you think a computer will ever be a smart machine?*

ROIZEN: The computer is a very sophisticated, very fast, and usually very stupid machine. It is also incredibly handy for doing all the tasks that take lots of time and are very boring to do. The machine can do them because it doesn't get bored. It doesn't get up in the morning and say, "I'm tired of adding numbers; I'm tired of doing this." The computer just does it. It's a tool just like a screwdriver. If you use it properly you can save yourself from doing a great deal of tedious work.

For many tasks an algorithm could be developed which would give a better result than could be developed intuitively. For example, a computer may be able to deliver a better diagnosis more quickly than a doctor for a simple case like tonsillitis or a type of fracture. Applications that require speed would be extremely impressive. Medical diagnoses could make the computer seem intelligent because it is very fast and doesn't make logical mistakes. But if the subject matter requires more thought—say the diagnosis of a more complex or rare disease, like certain cancers or viral infections—where we don't know all the clues that lead to the solution, I think it is unlikely the computer will ever do an adequate job of solving those problems.

INTERVIEWER: Do you care about the role of the computer in society?

ROIZEN: Not really. I'm not that concerned with the industry or the world. I'm concerned with the world to the extent that I would like it to be a peaceful place and I'd like to do my part to make it peaceful. But as far as my work is concerned, I'm not concerned with whether there's a good marketing strategy for the programs I write, whether the computer industry is about to go into a slump, or if it's a good time to be doing a particular project. I don't care about those things. I could spend all my time figuring out whether I should be doing something, leaving no time to get anything done. It's like taxes. I like to pay my taxes, because it's a contribution to society, and if there were no society I wouldn't be making any money. I know people who could make quite a lot of money in the time they spend worrying about their taxes.

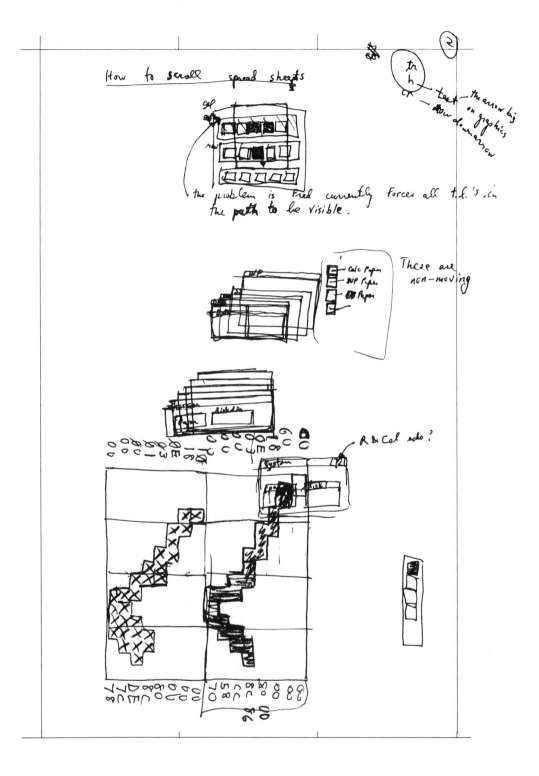

How to scroll spread sheets

the problem is Fred currently forces all t.f.'s in the path to be visible.

These are non-moving

R & Col echo ?

Carr made use of these "spreadsheet wanderings" to help him design Framework. More sketches and notes are found in the Appendix (pages 334-347).

Bob Carr

AS THE CHIEF Scientist
at Ashton-Tate, Robert Carr, 29, is responsible for directing research in new
products and technologies. One of the pioneers in the field of integrated software, Carr is the designer and principal developer of Framework and its suc-
cessor, Framework II.

Previously, Carr was chairman of Forefront Corporation, a company he
co-founded in July 1983 to complete the development of Framework, a program he had started on his own fifteen months earlier. Ashton-Tate agreed to
finance Forefront in return for marketing rights to Framework. In July 1985,
Ashton-Tate purchased the company.

Before developing Framework and co-founding Forefront, Carr worked as
a programming consultant on the development of Context MBA, one of the
first integrated software packages. Previously, Carr worked at Xerox PARC on
predecessors of the Xerox Star and SmallTalk products. He holds both a bachelor's and a master's degree in computer science from Stanford University.

Forefront is a small operation with a core group of programmers working together in a cooperative style. Bob Carr is young, full of energy, modest, and astute. He serves as the technical leader of this devoted group.

Carr was dressed neatly, wearing round tortoise-shell glasses, corduroy pants, and an oxford cloth shirt. As we talked, Carr gesticulated and drew diagrams on the whiteboard. He spoke with great intensity and thoughtful deliberation in well-constructed sentences. He reflected upon his past and on his approach to program design, as exemplified in his most ambitious project, the creation of Framework.

INTERVIEWER: *Did you always intend to be a programmer?*

CARR: At Stanford I was torn between my first love, the humanities, and my more practical side, which leaned towards engineering. I straddled them both, dividing my course time to keep the two options open.

I enjoy writing, and I think I'm literate. I still toy with the idea of being a writer of fiction. Writing English and software are far more than just acts of capturing something in code or on paper. They are processes that help evolve your thinking tremendously. When you're forced to write something down, you think the idea through two or three steps further.

Halfway through my junior year I made the great compromise. I said, "I've got it! I love writing, so I'll make that my living, but I'll be practical and be a technical writer. Then I can bring the bread home, and I can still do inventive and creative writing as well." I spoke to a couple of journalism professors who pointed out that to get a good technical writing job, nothing beats having a technical degree, so I decided to pursue it. But then I found I didn't like engineering: mechanical engineering—yuck; electrical engineering was interesting but I couldn't hack it; chemical engineering; none of them was an option.

During the same quarter, I took a beginning programming class. I had to use punch cards on the big mainframe to program in ALGOL W. I loved it. I also had a job that quarter as a night security guard at the new timesharing system at Stanford called LOTS. They had a DEC 20 with thirty terminals, and the place was open all night. I sat at the front desk to make sure no one walked off with the equipment.

I couldn't touch the machines, but Ralph Gorin, bless his heart, put a terminal on the guard's desk, so I learned word processing and began to do a little programming. I'd never touched a computer before then, but I decided right then to pursue my technical degree in computer science. There was one hurdle, though; Stanford didn't offer an undergraduate degree in computer science. But I wasn't going to let bureaucracy stop me. I learned of an engineering degree called general engineering, in which you could design your own specialization or "depth portion." I designed my depth portion in computer science and called it computer engineering. Over the next four quarters I ripped through a bachelor's degree and loved it. By then it was clear that I would rather do the programming than write about it.

"The key to the craft of computer science, and I say craft because it certainly isn't a science yet, is to find rules."

INTERVIEWER: *So in 1978, armed with a bachelor's degree, you entered the professional marketplace?*

CARR: Right. I had the tremendous good fortune of latching onto Xerox PARC at a time when an offshoot called Advanced Systems Department (ASD) was splitting from the main research center. ASD set up offices right next door to Stanford. At the time, Xerox was the world leader in many ways, and ASD was a hotbed of research with some of the greatest people around. People like Charles Simonyi; Harvard professors like Ben Wegbreit and Jay Spitzen, both of whom went on to help found Convergent Technologies; Doug Brotz, now one of the key programmers with Adobe Systems; and John Ellenby, who founded GRiD Systems.

INTERVIEWER: *What purpose within Xerox did ASD serve?*

CARR: Xerox PARC was having problems transferring their terrific technology-development work to the product-development stage. The charter of ASD was to take this technology and turn it into real-world systems, but not into final market products. ASD was a middleman between the initial development and the final product division in Los Angeles, which, for instance, did the Xerox Star. ASD developed prototypes to probe the market.

I was a grunt programmer. I worked with a group that developed integrated office systems, doing word processing, database, and calendar-oriented tasks. It was all to be based on top of a single database.

INTERVIEWER: *Did your experiences at Xerox and ASD teach you anything about management and the creative workplace?*

CARR: Yes, since then, and especially here at Forefront, I've tried to surround myself with people who are better than I am. A lot of the people I hired for Forefront are better programmers than I am, and I've learned a lot from them. ASD also showed me that great software development is largely composed of good initial design and, thereafter, a lot of very solid engineering.

INTERVIEWER: *What eventually became of ASD?*

CARR: Xerox went through a change of management, shot ASD down and folded the group back into the rest of Xerox. Many people left then. I went back to school to finish my master's degree. I was quite disenchanted with computer science and very unhappy. Programming was giving me zero vent for my creativity. I felt like a very small fish in a pond full of very big fish. On the one hand, it was a terrific opportunity to learn, but on the other, I was not creating or designing anything myself. You have to serve an apprenticeship, but I wasn't dedicated enough to see it that way.

Finishing my master's was an easy way out. What I decided to do next was to make a clean break with my life, make a fresh start and see where I would land. I sold my car and, with $2,000, went off to Latin America. I'd always felt that living in another country and learning another language would be a fundamentally good thing, so I thought I'd travel and settle in some foreign place and look for a job, probably as a programmer.

I planned to get all the way to South America, but never made it past Mexico because I liked it so much. In Mexico City, I worked as a volunteer in a youth hostel for six months and lived with the couple who ran it. At the end of this period, I felt ready to work again, and so I went back to Los Angeles to look for work.

I ended up with a short job programming on the HP 41C, a programmable calculator. The software I wrote was intended to analyze whether it was profitable for my client, an oil magnate, to build certain refineries. While doing this, I found out about a company starting in the neighborhood that needed programmers. The company was Context Management Systems; they were the people doing Context MBA.

INTERVIEWER: *Wasn't the Context MBA program a competitor to VisiCalc and Lotus 1-2-3?*

CARR: Context MBA was an idea for a better mousetrap. It was a single program that would have a giant, powerful spreadsheet, far more powerful than VisiCalc, which was the best-seller at the time. It would do database or data-management operations within the spreadsheet, graphics, and word-processing applications. It was a lot like Lotus 1-2-3.

I worked about a year until we finished the program. It shipped in July 1982, six months before Lotus. The company had high hopes, on a par with what ultimately happened to Lotus 1-2-3. Namely, tremendous success beyond the hopes of any mortal. But Context MBA did not experience success. Lotus 1-2-3 came along and stole the show, for good reasons. Lotus had superior marketing, and although their product was not as feature-rich as Context, it was much faster. Context had bet that a multitude of incompatible PC hardware would exist and, therefore, portability would be a key competitive edge. So they went with the UCSD operating system, which is a very portable environment but painfully slow. They lost their bet because the IBM PC set the standard. Writing in assembly language and tailoring specifically for the IBM PC was the winning route to go. Lotus 1-2-3 got the stars and Context went out of business.

INTERVIEWER: I take it your work at Context rekindled your interest in programming?

CARR: Working in computers again really fired me up. The vice president of software at Context was incredibly good, and I had a lot of software training in areas germane to the problem at hand. So here, all of a sudden, I was more of a medium-size fish in the pond. I could make a difference. This experience gave me great satisfaction, and showed me that I could really enjoy programming computers.

At the same time I watched this company grow from four individuals to twenty-five in the space of a year. I watched the startup process. It's just many, many decisions and tasks and little joblets each done, in their own time, one step at a time.

INTERVIEWER: During this early period, did you work with anyone who influenced your style of programming?

CARR: There have been about three or so programmers whom I have learned from. The first was Clark Wilcox. He was developing a language called Mainsail when I was at Stanford. He's an incredibly prolific programmer. Clark was always very careful about editing his program. If he ever added a begin statement, right away he would go down a few lines and add an end statement. Back then, to my way of thinking, that was a pain. And yet, that's a habit I now see as a very important part of practicing my craft. I am absolutely meticulous about doing it that way.

Then at Xerox, Jay Spitzen; and at Context, Jim Peterson. From each of them, I've learned a lot about designing software. They were working on the architecture, designing parts of it, and I was helping to implement it, so I learned a lot from the judgments they exercised.

INTERVIEWER: *When was the idea of Framework born?*

CARR: As I was nearing the end of my contract with Context, I started thinking about providing multiple functions to users. I also began to realize that basing all this functionality on a single giant spreadsheet was wrong.

> "From an artistic standpoint, the best software comes from the realm of intuition."

One day I considered what would happen if you had a spreadsheet cell that you could open up and inside find another spreadsheet, and inside of that find yet another. I made a simple drawing of a square inside of a square inside of a square, to express this notion of information inside of information. Then one day I mentioned to a friend that, although Context MBA was an exciting product, I thought there was a much better way to do it. Then he asked the very simple question that set me on fire, and became the catalyst for Framework: "Well," he asked me, "how would you do it?"

I needed to test myself. I felt bad about several projects elsewhere in my life that I hadn't completed. From then on, my vague feeling of a better way to solve a problem turned into a torrent of ideas flowing into a single concept, of squares nesting inside of squares, windows inside of windows.

I worked on Framework in the mornings and evenings, just scribbling notes. I was still programming during the day. After four months of brainstorming on paper, I had a direction to pursue. I spoke to the Context management about it. They were excited, but already had plans for the evolution of their company and product line. The chances of my visions being implemented there were minimal, so I broke ties with them and moved to San Francisco, where I wouldn't be tempted to go back to work for them. They were great people. I lived off my savings and continued designing, thinking that if it turned out to be a viable program, I could turn it into a business opportunity. I was obsessed. My emotions rode with the progress of the idea, and I worked on it harder than I had ever worked on anything.

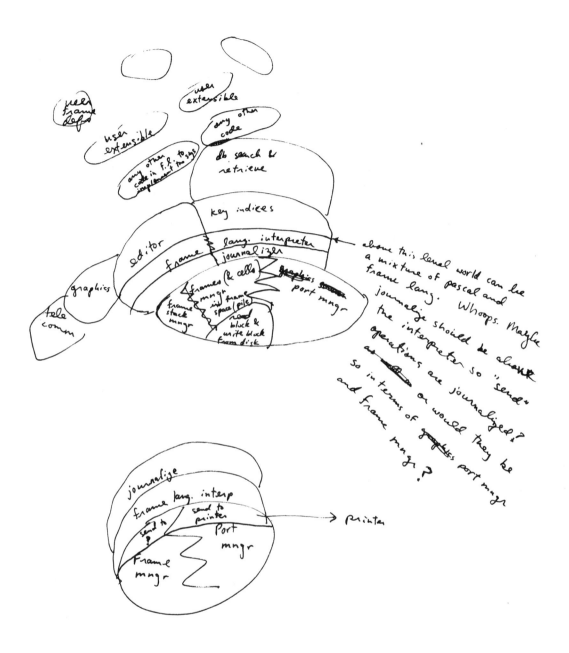

The handwritten labels in the diagram read:

user frame defs

user extensible

user extensible

any other code

any other code in f.l. to sys implement.

db. search & retrieve

key indices

lang. interpreter

editor

frame

journalizer

graphics

frames (& cells)

graphics

port mngr

tele comm

frame stack mngr

frame mngr in frame space (pile)

read block & write block from disk

above this level world can be a mixture of pascal and frame lang. Whoops. Maybe journalize should be above the interpreter so "send" operations are journalized? or would they be as in terms of graphics port mngr so in terms of frame mngr.?

journalize

frame lang. interp

send to ?

send to printer

frame mngr

port mngr

→ printer

These layered circles represent Carr's "very early groping towards structure" during development of Framework.

INTERVIEWER: What goals and work rules did you set when you were working on Framework?

CARR: One piece of advice I had been given was to hold off programming for as long as possible. Once you get a corpus of code building up, it's hard to change direction. It sets like concrete. So I held off for as long as I could, but I couldn't hold the design in my head forever.

Originally I conceived Framework as being a multifunction product with word processing, spreadsheets, graphics, and a database. Further still, I had the ambitious concept to implement bootstrapping; in other words, at a low level, you implement a system or language upon which the rest of the system is built. I wanted to come up with this magical, trendy machine that could be Framework's language and system. And I got rather depressed because I just couldn't lick that beast. So I scaled down my plans.

One of my other goals was to simplify the core design and architecture as much as possible, by implementing a single universal data object. The reason for this is that when you implement layer upon layer of detailed features which absorb memory, you need an utterly simple scheme on the internals, or you're doomed to have a big complex pig of a program.

I finally gave up on the goal of implementing a low-level language, and chose to write the code in C. Unfortunately, the compiler I used was a buggy compiler, and I soon found that I wasn't going to get anywhere with it. So I decided to write in assembly language, because it has some real advantages in dealing with memory management on the 8086 architecture.

In January 1983 I started programming the idea. It was based on this single data object, which I called a frame, and on which the whole system would be implemented. It was quite a gamble. If it worked, I'd be able to get a system up and running in a short time. If it failed, I'd go nowhere.

It turned out to be tremendously successful. Within a few months I had a lot of the user interface working, and within six months I had a very efficient working prototype. This was the system I was looking for, but it was only one-fifth complete. It provided the desktop, frames nesting inside each other, word processing, filing, printing, and pull-down menus. You could create spreadsheets, though the language was missing, and create databases and sort them. I did all these features in six months, working on my own.

INTERVIEWER: Explain further your concept for a single data object, or a "frame," as you termed it.

CARR: There are different kinds of frames, with different properties. One property could be a row-oriented frame. Another property could be a column-oriented frame. So, if you put some row-oriented frames next to each other inside of a column-oriented frame, you would have a spreadsheet. The spreadsheet was implemented out of the same building blocks as everything else in the system, as was the database. Consequently, we got a lot of leverage out of using the same code over and over again, and hence a lot of functionality from the program.

For instance, all of Framework's word-processing capabilities are fully available in the spreadsheet. To achieve this functionality in a window-style environment, you have to build a 200K spreadsheet module, and another word-processing module in another window. If you want the spreadsheet to have word-processing capabilities, you've got to add on another 50K to do boldfacing, italics, wordwrap, search and replace, and all those other things.

INTERVIEWER: *As Framework progressed toward the final product, did new features appear?*

CARR: We added new features and more robustness. There were whole new areas of functionality that we and Ashton-Tate decided to add. Probably the two biggest are that the spreadsheet was not originally intended to be a full-powered spreadsheet, yet it certainly grew into one; secondly, we added telecommunications capability to compete with Symphony.

Your best design work comes when you start from an elegant, good design, get it up and running, and then react to other ideas which only occur during its use. This approach is costly. Often you must do a major rewrite, or come close to throwing out whole sections of code. Doing this takes what I call heroics on the part of the programmers. For example, on Framework, I had a functioning word processor before any programmer joined me. Then Dan Altman came along and, over the next year, literally rewrote the word processor three times.

And with Framework II, he's done major reimplementations to make it more memory-efficient. Sure, he's getting paid for his work, but it takes more than just doing your job to be able to go back and redo something when you've already given your best effort. That's why I call it heroics.

INTERVIEWER: *What's it like to create both the company and the product?*

CARR: It's hard. I think I've had it better than most because our company has focused on just one path of software development. The charter we set ourselves was to create an ideal programmer's environment. The company isn't perfect, but everyone here has vouched that this is the best job they've had, myself included.

It's also scary, because I'm always concerned about losing our environment. The better off I am, the more I worry that it has to end sometime. In our case, we've merged with Ashton-Tate and that brings some changes. My partner and I had to worry about the payroll, health insurance, office space, how long a lease we could commit to. We had to worry about our contracts with Ashton-Tate. Are we going to get enough money? Are they going to sue us? Are we going to sue them? Are we going to be successful? What if Framework fails? All these questions are part and parcel of having your own company. It's a relief all those issues and concerns are under the bridge, so now, once again, all I have to concern myself with is software development.

"Users should be able to forget that there is a program between them and their information."

INTERVIEWER: *So the decision to merge with Ashton-Tate was so you could return to programming?*

CARR: Freeing my time for programming was one reason for the merger. Being a separate company and having all those managerial concerns took me away from programming. With the original Framework product, I was very much in the center of the storm. I programmed for a year, and spent more time than that on design. Then five programmers and a documentation designer joined the project, and we worked day and night for ten months. But with Framework II, I wasn't in the front-line trenches with the programming effort. I was more concerned with the direction of our company, Forefront.

INTERVIEWER: *Describe the "ideal environment" for programmers. And what was your role in creating it at Forefront?*

CARR: A very important part of our work is our interaction in a consensus-oriented design approach where we work together; that means the team must be small, say, no more than seven or eight people. We work closely on evolving a design, doing a lot of whiteboarding, and no single individual really plays a dictatorial role. There is an arbiter, in case the group gets stuck, which in our case isn't very often.

My role is one of facilitator, drawing out the design ideas and helping the group toward a conclusion. Not my conclusion, but one evolved by the group.

We try an idea out by implementing it and reacting to it, and then get new and better ideas. In group dynamics, you need someone who's good at drawing out the ideas and then prodding everyone along. Occasionally, there will be a situation where we just can't get a consensus, so we step back and examine the time constraints, money constraints, or space constraints, and then decide from there. The original Framework process was a very iterative and evolutionary one.

INTERVIEWER: *It sounds as if you're more attached to the programming process than to the business end of things.*

CARR: Yes, I like the programming, but more importantly, I like being able to focus on things. I can't divide my time between four different projects and give my all to each project. I function better when my time is devoted to a single project. Trying to play the lead technical role and help run the company split my time 50-50.

INTERVIEWER: *Where did you learn the techniques you use?*

CARR: From experience and also introspection. I tend to reduce things to a fairly simple framework, if you'll excuse the term, and then expand it back out to apply to the real world. And I'm forgiving; I don't expect the framework to fit perfectly what I'm applying it to, but I expect it to provide insight and guidance to whatever topic I bring it to.

I'm horrible at math but I might have been happy as a physicist, because I believe that they do what I do: They reduce all of physical reality to a relatively small number of theorems and rules they can use to predict and interpret physical reality. I'm doing the same thing with software—trying to come up with some theorems.

INTERVIEWER: *Do you think adherence to these techniques makes a good programmer or program?*

CARR: Yes, I think the key to the craft of computer science, and I call it a craft because it certainly is not a science yet, is to find rules. There is a classical discipline of computer science that embodies a couple of the major rules to be found, and your best programmers are usually aware of those several universal rules.

INTERVIEWER: *You referred to programming as a craft. Why do you consider it a craft rather than an art or a science?*

CARR: It's a combination of both. I feel very secure in making this assertion. There are certainly some very scientific, well-grounded principles that are tremendously important for software development, but good software ends up beyond that. For instance, if you look at the sketch of the decision-tree which led to the design of Framework, you will see I spent a lot of time thinking, scribbling—a lot of subconscious activity. (See the sketch at the beginning of this interview.) That's where the art is. In art, you can't explicate how the end result was achieved. From an artistic standpoint, the best software comes from the realm of intuition.

INTERVIEWER: Intuition aside, have you developed some concrete rules in program design?

CARR: First, the granularity of anything you do is very important, and the granularity should be flexible. This rule can be found again and again in the universe. In investments, it's expressed by the rule of diversification: You don't want to put all your eggs in one basket, nor do you want to spread your investments over three thousand different areas so you can't manage them intelligently. For software, users must be able to break their work, and the program, into separate pieces rather than dealing with a single, giant entity.

Second, granularity runs into another one of my rules, homogeneity. Architecture should be homogeneous; it should not have a lot of exceptions or special cases. If you design a system to deal efficiently with memory objects that are megabytes in size, as well as objects that are bytes, you'll end up with tremendous complexity. It's better to deal with either one or the other; that's what I call homogeneity.

Another global rule deals with recursion—it is one of the top three or so brilliant, powerful levers that computer science has brought into software. The most powerful software usually applies recursion internally and often provides recursive capabilities to users.

Memory management is the most important aspect of the internal architecture of a program. One rule in this area is never copy the same data twice. With some programs—one of them Context MBA—the same data appears twice again and again, different modules of code would copy data and place it in a buffer where it could be worked on, then the data would end up sprinkled throughout memory. This is an evil for several reasons. It bloats your memory requirements because you need all these temporary buffers. But that's the least of the evils. It also bloats your development time and costs because it takes more time to develop and debug. The most damning problem with this idea is that when you shove data from one buffer to another, you end up losing flexibility and functionality because you can only do one thing to the data when it's in that particular buffer, such as word process only in the buffer that word processing owns. In contrast, when you have one representation and place for the data, you get a lot more flexibility.

INTERVIEWER: *Do you have any rules or guidelines you follow in the design of a user interface?*

CARR: One of the most important qualities to achieve is what I call transparency. Users should be able to forget that there is a program between them and their information. In fact, as they get used to the software, their minds should be filled only with the task at hand; they shouldn't have to stop and think about what command they need. Consistency and predictability of commands and their actions are two of the most important factors in creating transparency.

> *"We all know sensual pleasures taken to excess are a curse... it's the same with menus."*

INTERVIEWER: *How did you translate simplicity and clarity into the user interface of Framework, yet retain a richness of functionality and performance?*

CARR: We developed a menu scheme with restraint and discipline. We all know that sensual pleasures taken to excess are a curse rather than a blessing; it's the same with menus. They require great discipline.

Menus are the best way to present a choice of commands to the user. But there are menu systems that branch so much that they become monstrosities. Then there are the less monstrous systems which have reputations of being very complex and extremely difficult to learn, largely because they have such extensive menus.

With Framework we exercised discipline in our menus and ended up with only nine menus and four submenus. We used pull-down menu technology so that it is always very clear where you are. I decided to use pull-down menus instead of the Lotus 1-2-3 style, because in 1-2-3 you can't tell where a menu comes from; the new menu overwrites the line that had the old menu. Pull-down menus hog screen space but the users always know where they are. In all of those menus we had only 100 commands. Wordstar has more than 130, Lotus 1-2-3 has 300, Symphony has 600.

INTERVIEWER: *Did you sacrifice functionality to achieve this simplicity?*

CARR: Design in every arena from architecture to furniture has settled on some principles in which minimalism is a real benefit and virtue. In a few specific cases we sacrificed functionality; but in terms of overall functionality, no. Framework has an overriding, overlapping set of multiple functionalities in a single command. I came up with ten or so operations that are fundamental to all applications, such as copy, move, delete, create, and find; I decided, for example, I should have the same copy command for the word processor and the spreadsheet.

To provide functionality in the different areas, I had to steal a terrific design notion Xerox originated: All commands should act on data already selected or highlighted by the user. It is called the object-verb design, versus the verb-object design.

A verb-object design would have you press the copy command and the software would then prompt you by asking, "What do you want to copy?" You would highlight some text and it would ask, "Where do you want to copy it to?" And you'd go there. This design is very prompt-driven and puts the user in a reactive mode, which is successful to a certain degree, especially in guiding neophyte users.

On the other hand, our object-verb commands are often the equivalent of ten commands in another application. A word processor may traditionally have separate commands for copy word, copy sentence, copy character. But we only had one copy command, because Framework has a very powerful selection capability that's very efficient in using cursor commands.

INTERVIEWER: Are there other fields such as psychology or graphic design that you feel may be helpful in software design?

CARR: I think one area is linguistics. We need to look more at this to see what it has to offer in software design. Presently, the products use cryptic presentations, icons, or a word on a command menu to present concepts, information, or signposts to the user. Hence, we need to study the science of signposts, whatever that is. We have tried to address this area at Forefront. We have several nonprogrammers who have psychological and instructional training backgrounds, and they've brought tremendous wealth to our design.

INTERVIEWER: Could you keep working on a program forever, rewriting, refining, changing?

CARR: We wouldn't, though there are endless possible variations of a program. At some point, the original structure or internal architecture becomes more concluded, more Byzantine, because of all the changes being wrought on it. Beyond this, it becomes too complex and less efficient to re-work the program.

To be frank, with Framework II, we'd be real smart to move on to new implementations and not mess with the existing body of code, because it's a very large program. It's gone through a lot of iterations in two years. Next time around, it would be more efficient to start over and take what we have learned and come up with a new architecture.

INTERVIEWER: *You constantly refer to internal and external architecture. Could you elaborate?*

CARR: The external user interface of any product has an architecture, or structure. It has its little routes and byways. The internal structure of the program can also be described as an architecture. Those two architectures are the most important things about any program. By looking at how they re-late to each other and how they may or may not mirror each other, you can predict a lot about the ultimate success of a program.

The best programs have an external architecture that mirrors the inter-nal architecture. The best example is spreadsheets. Usually they are imple-mented as a grid of cells in the memory. The user also deals with a grid of cells; so the two architectures mirror each other perfectly. They are "con-gruent." Spreadsheets can be very efficient, fast, and fluid because of those virtues, and as a result they've been very successful on the market.

But what happens when you try to implement a word processor on top of a spreadsheet, where internally you have one architecture, but externally you are trying to provide a very different structure, namely, a long, scrolling papyrus roll of text? You end up getting relatively poor performance with a bulky user interface. In fact, there have been no successful word processors implemented on top of spreadsheets.

So with Framework one of my cardinal rules was to come up with an internal structure that mirrored exactly the external. The notion of frames within frames would probably be recognized by any programmer as a hier-archy for a tree. Framework is simply a tree-structured data structure, where each frame points to its son and daughter frames in turn. It's a very simple, straightforward architecture.

INTERVIEWER: *What do you think of the general concept of integrated soft-ware programs?*

CARR: It's a great topic for conversation. There are a lot of levels on which to talk about integrated software. One facet of integration, the one most people think of, is multifunction software, where one piece of software does the equivalent of several stand-alone packages, such as spreadsheets, graphics, and word processing. Just having several functions available at once in an integrated package, versus an integrating environment such as Microsoft Windows, has nothing more to offer than the ability to merely present multiple functions at the same time. You need more. You'd also like to have an ability to share data among the different functions and an ability to easily use the different applications interchangeably. That's called learning transference, or command consistency.

"The only way you can get semantic consistency is through . . . good designers and programmers working very closely together."

Today at least, an integrated package has a compelling advantage over an integrating environment. In ease of use and ease of learning, integrated packages have an advantage in user interface that stems from the nature of user interfaces being split into two levels.

The two levels in user interface are syntax and semantics. Every user interface has its syntax, and those are the rules or the aspects that govern how you interact with the commands themselves—how the commands are presented, how you issue commands, and the responses or actions of the commands. The Macintosh computer with the Toolbox in ROM, Microsoft Windows, Gem; all those products do a superb job of addressing consistency among the syntax of commands. Typically, you'll find all commands are issued in a similar manner. You issue the command in the same fashion, with a certain keystroke or a mouse click. So, syntax is very consistent across the different functions.

But there's another layer that's as important for ease of use; this is the semantic layer and it pertains to the meaning of the command or what it will actually do to the information. Most environments don't address semantic consistency. Today on the Macintosh there are lots of databases, many of which work very differntly from other database products. There is no semantic consistency. One database product inserts the record before the mouse cursor, the other appends it after the mouse cursor. Another doesn't even use a mouse cursor, but has the command in the menu. Semantics vary widely; as a result, there is a low level of learning transference whenever you go from one database product to the other, even though there is usually a high level of syntactic consistency.

INTERVIEWER: Is there any way to get this semantic consistency across multiple functions?

CARR: I strongly argue that there is no technological solution today. There is no set of compilers or well-structured, object-oriented interfaces, library modules, or even rules on paper that result in semantic consistency. The only way you can get semantic consistency is through what I would call the organizational solution—a human organization of good designers and programmers working very closely together.

We did that with Framework. The product has been reviewed as being number one in ease of use and ease of learning. It's because we were working together as a single unit, pretty much with a single mind.

In the future we may see a trend toward what I call "component software." It may be possible that future operating systems will support more modular software to let different modules link themselves together. We may see an ability to get modules on the shelf in separate packages which users can buy one at a time, and which have deep semantic consistency. For at least several more years, those modules will still have to come from the same human organization.

It will be some time before you can buy an integrating environment, and then buy your spreadsheet from one vendor, your word processor from another vendor, your database from yet another, and get learning transference between them at a meaningful level.

INTERVIEWER: Why not standardize? Would that solve the problem of semantic inconsistency?

CARR: First, there's no best way to do any one of the individual functions, be it spreadsheet or database. And it gets even more complex when you try to come up with a consistent design for the commands and their actions across a database, a spreadsheet, a word processor, and graphics. Each of those areas has its own needs and stresses. You need to come up with a command design and a user-interface design that is the best solution for all of them at once.

Data integration is the other area integrated software can address that the environments have not addressed. There are two aspects of data integration. The first is cutting and pasting, or transferring information from one module to another. I think the environments do a good job of cutting and pasting. They usually specify how to do it, and if the modules have been written with cutting and pasting in mind, they can take numbers from the spreadsheet and put them into the word processor or into the graphics. Integrated software does this already.

The other important aspect of data integration is getting different kinds of data to live together in their live formats. Can you, in a single document, have a live spreadsheet, live word processing on both sides of the spreadsheet, and a live graph? As humans, we deal with logical entities. We don't care if a report mixes numbers, graphics, and text. To us the report is a single logical entity—a report on the profitability of a market segment requires different data types to convey the information accurately.

Why should the user have to break up the report into two different files from his spreadsheet, three from his graphics program for each graph, and two from his word-processing program? Why not have just one file called "Marketing Report"? This is an example of live data integration, perhaps the fundamental driving point for Framework. I felt that users needed to be able to break their information into separate chunks, and those separate chunks had to be diffent types of data. In Framework, the software worries about how it's done, letting the user think of a report as a single, logical entity.

INTERVIEWER: What about the future of computers? Where are they going and where will they be in five or ten years? Do you think we'll be working with the same tools, the same languages?

CARR: The productivity tools we know today will be with us for a long time; they work well and that's why they're out there. We still start from scratch with all the systems we build. One future challenge should be to come up with a better way to mix and match modules and build up a base of flexible building blocks. Operating environments are a stride in this direction. They relieve the necessity of reimplementing a lot of the syntactic user interface in each product. For this reason, I think the existing operating systems are here to stay.

I hope we can move toward component software. Then the user will be able to replace a piece of a program with a plug-in module from a software house that knows how to do floating-point arithmetic or word processing better. This will be a trend over the next ten years. But it's a tough goal because we're talking about interfaces between separate modules of software, one of the least understood areas in software design. I don't think many of us are very good at designing and implementing good, clean interfaces.

I also look forward to the day, years from now, then we're no longer cursed by the segmented architecture of the Intel 8086 chip. Perhaps the 80386 might be it. I think the 8086 has its benefits, but I've mostly felt its curses. During the development of Framework, it literally added 30 percent to our development time and costs, just wrestling with the way it fragments memory into different segments, rather than being one long, continuous stream.

Do you think you'll always be in programming?

CARR: No, I hope I can make a major change to something else. Programming can be addictive. One of my big concerns in bringing Framework to the market was that I, for the first time, became a workaholic. During

"Programming can be addictive."

Framework's development I knew I was a workaholic because I wanted to be a workaholic. I was striving for a goal I had set for myself, and being a workaholic and letting that consume my life and relationships was part of getting there. But I don't want to be a workaholic forever.

Since I finished the original Framework, I've been able to back away, but I hope to get consumed again by programming or some other endeavor. I've got a lot of years left in this field—I'm twenty-nine now. Five or eight years from now—then will be the time to make a major change. My skills seem to focus on what I can do beyond programming. I'm fairly verbal and literate, and I'm able to communicate with other people, much more so than a lot of other programmers. This has a lot of value not only in management, but in salesmanship as well.

With an idea as innovative as Framework, from day one I had to sell, sell, sell. Not overt salesmanship, but I had to present the idea, clearly and concisely, again and again. Every person I showed the program had to have it explained why it was different and better. One of the reasons we were successful with Framework is because both I and my co-founder and partner, Marty Mazner, who is more of a marketer, were able to combine a compelling presentation of the concept with the underlying technological innovation.

```
          SYMMETRICAL AIRFOIL GENERATION PROGRAM.   JEF RASKIN, 1984

        While this program is nothing that experienced programmers will learn much
    about coding from, it demonstrates the power of being able to embed executeable
    code into the text produced by a word processor.   What this does is to make
    the mechanics of documentation simple.  Using a typical program editor for
    extended text is usually bothersome enough a chore so that our program comments
    become terse and more difficult to read.  I have observed that when I document
    a program in this thorough fashion, it often runs on the second or third try,
    whereas when I do not document carefully, much more debugging is required.

        Please note that this text you are reading is part of the program (or,
    equivalently, that the program is part of the text).

        The program itself plots, on an Apple II, given Information Appliance's
    SwyftWare environment, a family of airfoils that I am developing for my
    aerobatic model airplanes.  It does it by a transformation of a circle, much as
    the Joukowsky transformation does.  This permits relatively easy calculation of
    the lifting characteristics of the airfoil, although a program to do that is
    not shown here.

        The program begins by setting up graphics mode and a few constants.
    First, for graphics mode:

            90 HGR

    The constants include

            100 pi = 3.1415926

    and one that determines how much the airfoil will "cusp" or be concave toward
    the rear.

            110 c = .81

    Another important variable controls the thickness ratio of the airfoil.

            120 f = .22

        The program works by using the usual pair of formulae

            x = r cos t       y = r sin t

    to generate a circle parametrically by letting t vary from 0 to 2 * pi in
    convenient steps.  r is chosen to be .5 so that a circle of diameter 1 results.

            130 FOR t = 0 TO 2 * pi STEP .04
            140 x = .5 * cos(t)
            150 y = .5 * sin(t)

    The circle is centered on the origin, and we first move it to the right by .5
    so that all the x-values are positive, and are, in fact, in the range (0,1).

            160 x = x + .5
```

```
        To understand how this transforms a circle into an airfoil rounded at one
    end and pointed at the other, note that if we multiply each y-value by  the
    corresponding x-value we will, near x=0, have very small y-values, yielding a
    point.  But as we approach x=1 the curve approaches a circle.

            200 y = y * x^c

        The exponent of x changes x's effect.  Many functions of x will do for
    this role.

        Airfoils tend to be long and thin.  Thus we want to squash the shape in
    the y-direction.  The thickness ratio is thus applied to y.  This could have
    been done in the previous line of code, but it is separated out for clarity.

            210 y = y * f

        We now have -f < y < f and  0 <= x <=1.  This has to be translated to
    Apple screen coordinates where 0 <= x <  280.  Again, these transformations
    could have been included in some of the earlier program statements, but for
    clarity the plotting is separated from the generation of the foils.  The 250 is
    chosen as conveniently large for the screen.  This will make x vary from 0 to
    250

            400 x = x * 250

    and to keep things square, we apply the same scaling to y, remembering that y
    has already been decreased by the f factor.  We also have to make y always
    positive.  Obviously, we will go off-screen if f is too large, but we will
    assume smart users who read this documentation and behave accordingly rather
    than bother with too much error checking.

            410 y = y * 250 + 100

        Now to plot these points, and close the loop, and then go into an infinite
    loop so that the computer will not mess up the screen with messages.

            500 HPLOT x,y
            510 NEXT t
            520 GOTO 520

        All that's left is to type and use the CALC command on "run".  You will
    have to modify the program to run on systems other than SwyftWare-equipped
    Apple II's.
```

This program demonstrates how Raskin embeds executable code into text that is produced by a word processor.

Jef Raskin

APPLE COMPUTER'S

Macintosh project creator, Jef Raskin, is a man of many talents. He is also a past conductor of the San Francisco Chamber Opera Company; a holder of patents in packaging design, aircraft structures, and electronics; an artist whose work has been exhibited in the New York Museum of Modern Art and the Los Angeles County Museum; and currently chief executive officer of Information Appliance Inc. He was born in New York City in 1943—as he puts it, about the time the digital computer was born.

At the State University of New York at Stony Brook, he studied mathematics, physics, philosophy, and music, while earning a number of scholarships and a National Science Foundation grant along the way. After five years of study, he graduated with a bachelor's degree in philosophy. He received a master's degree in computer science from Pennsylvania State University, and later became a professor of Visual Art at the University of California at San Diego (UCSD). He taught at UCSD for five years, and was also director of the Third College Computer Center.

He resigned from UCSD with the gesture of flying over the Chancellor's house in a hot air balloon, which, he says, is all anyone needs to know about his reasons for leaving. He then became a professional musician, doing both teaching and conducting. When the 8080 microprocessor was introduced, Raskin founded Bannister & Crun to exploit the new technology. The company found a profitable niche by writing manuals and software for Heath, Apple, National Semiconductor, and other companies.

In 1978, he became Apple Computer's thirty-first employee and manager of publications. He later became manager of advanced systems and formed the group that created the Macintosh. After leaving Apple in 1982, he taught at the Dansk Datamatik Institute in Denmark before returning to Silicon Valley to found Information Appliance Inc.

When told the title of this book, Jef Raskin was quick to point out that he wasn't a programmer per se, but rather a designer or a "metaprogrammer," and that his company is not involved with traditional software. Jef Raskin is a person who strives to distinguish himself from the crowd. He is an inventor with original ideas for new software and innovative ways to make microcomputers perform. He is not the person who sits down at the computer and writes the source code. This distinction between a programmer and a software or systems designer is becoming more and more prevalent as software becomes more complex, and as more people are trained in the techniques of translating specifications into code.

The office of Raskin's new startup company is on University Avenue in Palo Alto, the town that seems to have become the center of activity for many defectors from Apple Computer. The offices of Information Appliance were not like the elegant, ostentatious offices of many other software companies; they were, in fact, relatively small, somewhat dingy, and just plain ordinary. They could have been the offices of a small appliance company, and I presumed this was all part of Jef Raskin's microcomputer philosophy.

Raskin, with his graying beard, slightly balding head, and alert, darting eyes, had the look of a seasoned professor. He greeted me somewhat breathlessly, explaining he had been in a bicycle accident on the way to work, which made him late. He appeared in a somewhat unsettled state. He ushered me into his small office and proceeded to straighten things up a bit. Behind his desk to one side was an Apple IIe computer. Against the other wall was a Yamaha keyboard synthesizer. Behind me was a ten-speed bicycle and a bicycle pump, and what appeared to be a small oriental shrine.

Raskin is a very animated, excited, and excitable fellow. At certain moments, I felt I was in the midst of an amusement park; one minute Raskin would give an impressive demo of his new product as if performing magic tricks; a little later he would break into a juggling act; next, he would swing around and play a song on his synthesizer; and then he would send a little model car whizzing around on his desk, all the while discussing the past, present, and future of microcomputers.

He has a vision of the role microcomputers should play: not one of glorious, mysterious, elusive machines, but one of invisible, easy-to-use, practical appliances.

INTERVIEWER: *You're best known for having created Macintosh at Apple. What role did you play?*

RASKIN: In 1979, Apple was working on the Lisa. Believe it or not, it started as a character-generator machine. I was manager of advanced systems at Apple, and I was really unhappy with the Lisa. It was very expensive, and I thought Apple was foolish to tackle DEC, Data General, and IBM in the minicomputer price range.

When I was a visiting scholar at the Stanford Artificial Intelligence Laboratory in the early seventies, I spent a lot of time at Xerox's Palo Alto Research Center. I thought the work Xerox PARC was doing with bit-mapped screens, generalized keyboards, and graphics was wonderful. So I lobbied hard and got Apple to change Lisa to a bit-map machine. I helped put Xerox and Apple together. At one time Xerox owned about 10 percent of Apple stock.

What I proposed was a computer that would be easy to use, mix text and graphics, and sell for about $1,000. Steve Jobs said that it was a crazy idea, that it would never sell, and we didn't want anything like it. He tried to shoot the project down.

So I kept out of Jobs' way and went to then-chairman Mike Markkula and talked over every detail of my idea. Fortunately, both Markkula and then-president Mike Scott told Jobs to leave me alone.

I hired the original people: Bud Tribble, Brian Howard, and Burrell

Smith. We went off to a different building and built prototypes of the Macintosh and its software, and got it up and running.

Later, after he took over, Jobs came up with the story about the Mac project being a "pirate operation." We weren't trying to keep the project away from Apple, as he later said; we had very good ties with the rest of Apple. We were trying to keep the project away from Jobs' meddling. For the first two years, Jobs wanted to kill the project because he didn't understand what it was really all about.

The original Macintosh was a careful, rational design. Eventually, everyone at Apple realized it was Apple's main hope for a product to follow Apple II. Then Jobs took over. He simply came in and said, "I'm taking over Macintosh hardware; you can have software and publications." He threw out the software design, made the Macintosh software compatible with the Lisa, and insisted on using the mouse. The machine became much larger, more complicated, and much more expensive. It now runs like a tub of molasses. Have you ever used MacWrite? We call it MacWait around here. And then a few months later Jobs said, "I'm taking over software; you can have publications." So I said, "You can have publications too," and left. That was in May of 1982. He and Markkula said, "Please don't leave. Give us another month and we'll make you an offer you can't refuse." So I gave Apple a month; they made me an offer, and I refused.

INTERVIEWER: *But the machine was a success. Jobs must have contributed something.*

RASKIN: He did do some very important things, especially in the early days of Apple, which made the difference between Apple being just another little computer company and the great company that it became. He had good ideas: putting the Apple II in a nice one-piece case, marketing it, going out and getting really good people, and seeing that it had good manuals.

INTERVIEWER: *You seem rather sensitive on the issue of getting credit for your work.*

RASKIN: It's not my intention to take all the credit for Macintosh; it was a team effort. If Jobs would only take credit for what he really did for the industry, that would be more than enough. But he also insists on taking credit away from everybody else for what they did, which I think is unfortunate.

I was very much amused by the recent *Newsweek* article where he said, "I have a few good designs in me still." He never had any designs. He has not designed a single product. Woz (Steve Wozniak) designed the Apple II. Ken Rothmuller and others designed Lisa. My team and I designed the Macintosh. Wendell Sanders designed the Apple III. What did Jobs design? Nothing.

INTERVIEWER: *Would you say your experience at Apple was a bad one?*

RASKIN: No. The first few years, '76 to '80, were wonderful. I had a great time and have no regrets. In the early days, Jobs and Wozniak were a joy to work with. But then from late 1980 through '82, working at Apple became a real nightmare for me.

INTERVIEWER: *When you left Apple, did you think you'd go back into business again?*

RASKIN: I thought I'd never do that, or anything dumb, like work in Silicon Valley again. I was tired of working seven days a week.

After leaving Apple, I went back to teaching, in Denmark. I'd just gotten married, and was still on my honeymoon when I had this idea. I realized that what I'd been trying to do all those years was wrong. I'd been trying to design a better computer and I didn't want a computer at all. I wanted something that worked like an appliance. And my idea seemed too good not to share.

> *"I didn't want a computer. I wanted something that worked like an appliance."*

INTERVIEWER: *And this was the idea that inspired you to create a new company, Information Appliance. How does the word "appliance" reflect the products you are developing here?*

RASKIN: Have you ever noticed that there are no Maytag user groups? Nobody needs a mutual support group to run a washing machine. You just put the clothes in, punch the button, and they get clean. To do information processing, I don't want hardware and software; what I really want is an appliance to do my tasks. And what tasks do I do? Surveys show that 85 percent of all personal computer users use word processing, so I need a word processor, a wonderful word processor—the best in the world. But I am sort of simpleminded. I can only remember ten or fifteen commands. That's why the system I use has only five. That way I can wake up at 3:00 a.m., get out of bed, go over to the computer, and just type out an idea.

INTERVIEWER: *You mean you've tried to simplify a system?*

RASKIN: Right. Let's consider what it would be like if a computer company had designed a toaster. You wake up and you want a piece of toast for breakfast. The first thing you do is switch the toaster on. If it was designed by General Electric, you'd put the toast in and off you'd go, but no, this toaster was designed by a computer company. So what happens? First of all, it does a two-minute toaster check. Then you put in the system disk and boot the system. After that you put in your breakfast disk and then you type "Load TOASTED.CODE."

So, what happens next? Up comes the menu. It asks, "What kind of bread are you going to have?" If it is a California program, it'll say croissant, bagel, English muffin, whole wheat, and at the bottom, of course, white bread.

They're labeled A, B, C, D, E, so you hit C because you feel like a muffin this morning. Nothing happens because you forgot to hit return. You'd think the machine would be smart enough to respond to C, but you have to hit return anyway.

Do you think it does anything now?

INTERVIEWER: *Well ... ?*

RASKIN: Of course not. It's designed by a computer company. It says "Are you sure?" Now you're ready to throw it through the wall. Are you mad yet? Haven't you been mad at computers for years? But because you spent a couple of thousand dollars on it, you put up with all this stupidity, and so does the rest of the world. Millions of people go through nonsense like this every time they use a computer.

So you type "Yes" and hit return, but get an error message because you were supposed to hit something else. You consult the manual, but it tells you nothing because the people who wrote it were describing a prototype system that has changed. Finally, you put the bread in slot two, indicate whether you want light, tan, or seriously burnt bread and the computer asks, "Do you want to save this breakfast so you don't have to redo this again?" So you type "Yes," and it tells you to place a disk in slot one, but you discover that you're out of formatted disks.

You call up the dealer and ask if there's any way to save this while formatting the disk without losing everything you've already done this morning? He says, "Yeah, just buy this $3,000 hard-disk system with MS-DOS 9.8 and that will solve all your problems. It comes with a manual and a handtruck." The handtruck is for moving the manual. And you're already late for work . . . . But that's the way things are. Our product says a lot about this kind of dilemma. Let's move over to my computer.

[We seat ourselves before an Apple IIe equipped with a SwyftCard and keyboard labels.]

Watch this. There is no disk in the drive, and I want to type a message, "Remember to bring home some milk." How do you like that? I turn it on and start typing. No need for commands, no insert, no getting to the editor, I can just start typing.

Now I want to print the message and put it in my pocket, so I can use it later. I press a single key, and it prints. Isn't that convenient?

INTERVIEWER: *Can you make toast on this?*

RASKIN: No, the crumbs get into the disk drive.

INTERVIEWER: *What else can users do on this appliance?*

RASKIN: We can do calculations easily. Before, whenever I was using the word processor and wanted to do a calculation, I'd get out my pocket calculator and have to use a separate calculating program, or get up SideKick; on the Mac, you call up the calculator and paste it into your document. We also have telecommunications capability.

INTERVIEWER: *All in the same program?*

RASKIN: Sure. There is no difference between all the applications. What's a word processor? You use it to generate text, move it around, change it if you make a mistake, and find things. What's a telecommunications package? You use it to generate text, or receive text generated by someone else. Instead of it coming in from a keyboard or out from a printer, it comes in or out over a telephone line. And what's a calculator? You use it to generate numbers, which are just text, and the answer should come back into your text. So, one day it dawned on me, if these applications do the same thing, why not have one little program that does them all?

INTERVIEWER: *Well, what is this product you've developed to cover all of these features?*

[Raskin holds up a simple card.]

RASKIN: It's called a SwyftCard. It's a board for the Apple IIe. Not much to it, eh? That's why we can sell it for $89.95. It's so friendly, so simple, that we've actually had people tell us that they sold their IBMs or Macintoshes and bought an Apple IIe with a SwyftCard after seeing this.

INTERVIEWER: *Does this only work on the Apple IIe?*

RASKIN: The SwyftCard works only on the Apple IIe now. We will soon have identical software in a product called SwyftDisk for the Apple IIc. The

SwyftDisk will probably be available in early March.

INTERVIEWER: *Do you have plans to implement it on other computers?*

RASKIN: One of the things about our company is that we never say anything until we have something already done. The first time you read about this product, you could order it. But let me show you some other advantages to this system . . . . [Raskin returns to the computer screen.] If you forget to save some text and you load in another file, normally you'd lose that text. This system is smart enough so that it never loses anything. But I'll do something

"Have you ever noticed that there are no Maytag user groups? Nobody needs a mutual support group to run a washing machine."

even more outrageous. [Raskin gets up from his computer and places a disk on a giant magnet hanging on the wall.] This is now a totally unformatted blank disk. I'll apply this very powerful magnet to it to prove that it is blank. I'll insert it into the disk drive and type some text and use the DISK command [the disk whirs for four seconds]. Now I'll do something even worse; I'll switch the machine off. Still, I guarantee that when I switch the machine back on, the text will have been saved. [He turns the machine back on; in four seconds the text appears on screen.] See? The system saved the text on a totally unformatted blank disk in just four seconds. DOS can even format a disk in less than half a minute. Not only that, but when we turned it on, even the cursor was exactly where we left it.

INTERVIEWER: *Okay, it's smart, but is it fast?*

RASKIN: It will keep up with typing much faster than any human can type, and it automatically word wraps, formats, and paginates as you type. The cursor-moving technique is faster than the mouse. Not only is it inherently fast, but you will use it faster because you don't get tripped up by it.

INTERVIEWER: *How did you get the speed?*

RASKIN: Very, very clean design. This system neither drinks nor smokes. It exemplifies the kinds of things I'm working on these days.

INTERVIEWER: *Most users are dazzled by the mouse; it has market acceptance. Why do you dislike it?*

RASKIN: I hate mice. The mouse involves you in arm motions that slow you down. I didn't want it on the Macintosh, but Jobs insisted. In those days, what he said went, good idea or not.

INTERVIEWER: Your whole approach seems counter to the industry trend to make bigger computers to accommodate bigger programs . . .

RASKIN: Yes. Instead of saying bigger, bigger, we're saying better, better. When I told our investors about this project, I said, "We're going to have a word processor, information retrieval, and telecommunications package with only fifteen commands and 64 bytes of code." All the other companies were talking hundreds of commands and hundreds of bytes of code. The company (Information Appliance) was surprised that it came down to five commands. It's the only project I've ever been on that got simpler with time instead of bigger or more complicated.

We have a whole valley full of people talking UNIX versus MS-DOS. What do you need *any* of that for? Just throw it all out; get rid of all that nonsense. Maybe you need it for computer scientists, but for people who want to get something done, no. Do you need an operating system? No. We threw out that whole concept. Applications like VisiOn, Gem, and Windows are just cosmetic treatments on hidden operating systems, but we have no operating system beneath this. You know what happens when you apply heavy cosmetics to something? You get that heavy cosmetic look.

So here is a program that runs on an ancient Apple IIe, a one-megahertz processor, and from the user's point of view it runs faster than IBM, Macintosh, mainframes, SuperVax, or anything.

INTERVIEWER: Was your motivation on this project different from what motivated you to design the Macintosh?

RASKIN: Some of the motivation was the same, some of it different. With the Mac, I was trying to make the best compuuter I knew how to make. When I created Information Appliance, I was no longer trying to make computers. I just wanted to make the benefits of computer technology easily available to everyone.

That idea goes back to when I was an interdisciplinary professor at the University of California at San Diego in the sixties, teaching in the visual arts department. I was an artist and a musician as much as a computer scientist, and I loved teaching computer programming to people in the arts and humanities. I also taught computer programming, computer art, and computer movie making to people who normally didn't work with those fields: a class of Mother Superiors, or a class of third or fourth graders.

INTERVIEWER: Prior to Apple, you were very involved in academia. What exactly was your background in those pre-Apple days?

RASKIN: Well, my sixth grade project was a digital computer that I built with relays and big switches. I studied mathematics, philosophy, music, and physics at SUNY (State University of New York), Stony Brook. At Penn State I began a Ph.D. in philosophy, but got a master's in computer science instead. At U.C. San Diego I began a Ph.D. in music, but became an art professor instead. I was a professor for five years, and then I became a visiting scholar at Stanford at their Artificial Intelligence Lab.

Next, I was a conductor of the San Francisco Chamber Opera Company, and taught music in San Francisco. Then along came the personal computer, and I thought, "Hey, computers interest me again." I bought one of the first Altair kits and built that. I thought the manuals were dreadful, so I formed a documentation company called Bannister & Crun, named after two characters out of an old English radio program called the Goon Show. I wrote manuals for Heath, National Semiconductor, and Apple. I started a model airplane company, too.

INTERVIEWER: Do you feel there is any parallel between music, the arts, and the computer?

RASKIN: Not a parallel. But I'm definitely trying to do things that will make people happy. One of the reasons I liked being a musician is that musicians have rarely done anything bad in the world. If you're a physicist, you might invent something that explodes. But musicians never do. Artists can create propaganda posters but with musicians, it's usually pretty neutral stuff. I have always been interested in doing something that would make lots of people happy.

People who use the SwyftCard won't lose files, will spend a lot less time working, and be less frustrated. They're going to be happier people than they would have been using something else. I'm trying to do genuine good in this world. Another fact: This system is usable by blind people because of the way the cursor is moved. Visually oriented systems like the Macintosh are totally unusable by blind people.

We currently have our systems at the Veteran's Administration, Western Rehabilitation Center, and the Sensory Aids Foundation, and they're reporting back to us, saying, "Hey, this works with blind people." So here I'm doing something that will enfranchise a large block of people.

INTERVIEWER: Do you still find time to pursue the arts?

RASKIN: I don't do visual arts, but I'm still a musician, though I don't perform very much any more. I don't have enough time to practice now that I'm running the company. Occasionally, I'm asked to play at a friend's wedding. That's how I worked my way through graduate school: playing in bars and nightclubs. Every Wednesday night at Penn State, I'd play the piano for the old-time movies. At home I have a nine-foot concert grand. I like to play Bach and Mozart.

INTERVIEWER: *Such a heavy academic background must have made you a hot property at Apple . . . .*

RASKIN: During Apple's first few years, I was the only person with a degree in computer science in the whole company. And I didn't tell people, because if they had known I had actually been a professor and a computer center director, they might not have let me in the company.

INTERVIEWER: *Why?*

RASKIN: Because there was an anti-academic bias in the early Apple days. I was able to come in and write good manuals because I said to Woz, "You're an expert in hardware," or to Randy, "You're an expert in software." Then I'd tell them, "Well, I don't know much of that stuff, I just know how to write, so I don't bother you, you don't bother me."

INTERVIEWER: *How long did the SwyftCard take to develop?*

RASKIN: The company's been here for about three years, but we are doing other things too, so it's hard to say how long. We didn't get into business to produce a board for the Apple IIe, but it seemed like such a good idea that I would have felt very bad not to have released the product. I saw a lot of good products at Apple and Xerox pass from desktop to desktop, and never get to the market.

INTERVIEWER: *Was it difficult to find the backing to start Information Appliance, or did the strength of a good idea and your fame from the Macintosh carry you through?*

RASKIN: After I laid out the details of what the SwyftCard was going to do, I swore some friends from Apple and Xerox PARC to secrecy and showed them the specs. They took one look at it and said, "No way; it won't work; we've been trying to do that for decades." Then they all called me up next day and said, "Hey, you know, it looks like it'll work." So I decided to hire a few programmers, just with my own money, to see if I could implement my idea. I decided to implement it in FORTH, because FORTH is a rather compact language and is inexpensive to implement. It's not my favorite language, but I thought it was suitable for this particular application. I always believe you should use the right tool for the job.

I went out and hired a FORTH programmer and a few other people, mostly personal friends of mine. Nobody from Apple. I didn't touch the company. I didn't want to get into any legal hassles, and Apple was nasty enough then that I worried about such things.

INTERVIEWER: Did you embark on a heavy marketing campaign to promote your product?

RASKIN: We didn't have much budget for marketing. We just took a little bit of money and ran a few ads to get the message out to those people who wanted it. The reaction we've gotten is that this is a great product, and sales are climbing much faster than we anticipated.

INTERVIEWER: Are you wary of aggressive marketing and hype? Do you think it has caused problems in the industry?

RASKIN: It sure has. I saw a full-page color ad in a magazine for an LCD screen for an Apple IIc and so I called the company. They told me, "We expect to have them ready in ten months." A full-page color ad! I think they're wasting their money.

INTERVIEWER: As a professor on campus, a reporter for magazines, a writer of manuals, and a designer of computers, you have carried a message— namely that computer benefits are accessible to the masses. Is Information Appliance simply another vehicle for your message?

RASKIN: If this company is at all successful, I'll again be reaching millions of people. What's going to get the message out is the product. If the company makes a lot of money, everybody will listen to my message. So, the way to carry a message in this world is, unfortunately, to make money.

If I wanted to tell the world that bit-mapped screens are great, no matter how many articles I wrote, nothing would happen. Xerox wrote dozens of articles, and who was listening? But get Macintosh out there, at a reasonable price, sell a few tens of thousands, and guess what? Everybody who buys one or reads about it discovers the whole idea of bit-mapped screens, graphics, and the fact that you don't need separate graphics and text mode, that letters are just another example of graphics, and that you can do fancy fonts without additional hardware.

It's absolutely ugly, but unfortunately quite true of the world today; the more money you make, the more people tend to listen to you. If you're not quoted in *Fortune* or *Forbes* or the *Wall Street Journal*, then nobody listens. If you say something that makes a lot of money, whether what you said is true or not, people listen.

INTERVIEWER: *Speaking as one who has seen both ends of the corporate spectrum, what do you think of the big company versus the small company?*

RASKIN: You should have heard what Jobs thought about what he was going to make happen when Apple grew large. He forgot his ideals so fast. Woz kept his a heck of a lot better. There's a person at Apple who is one of the few people who made a bit of money and has not changed at all, and that's Brian Howard. He's a wonderful person. I don't know how much he's worth, but he still drives the same car I sold him for $75 ten years ago.

> "Are you mad yet? Haven't you been mad at computers for years?"

INTERVIEWER: *What do you think is the biggest problem your business faces?*

RASKIN: How in the world do you sell something that's different? That's the biggest problem. The world's not quite ready to believe. It's like in the early days at Apple, they said, "What's it good for?" We couldn't give a really good answer so they assumed the machine wasn't going to sell. But I do know the way I plan to sell my product is by word of mouth. Some people will try it and say, "This product really gets my job done. It doesn't have fifteen fonts. I can't print it out in old gothic banners five feet long, but I sure got that article finished under the deadline." That's how I can sell it. Later, people will understand it.

This is like when I first started Macintosh, nobody, not even Jobs, knew what icons or bit-mapped screens were. Now they are in everybody's vocabulary in this industry. I've done it before and I'll do it again.

INTERVIEWER: *What do you think about the current lull in the computer industry?*

RASKIN: I think that's why we're going to make a lot of money. The reason for the downturn, in my opinion, is that everybody who's going to buy one of these really hard-to-use machines has done so, and they are only selling to people now who are pretty much forced into it. Forced into it by the fact that they have to work with it, or because someone else tells them they have to. Or because the Joneses down the street have one. Right now, there's a lot of room for a product that is genuinely easy and fun. I think the market is saturated with complex machines and I think this company's going to open up a whole new marketplace.

After you've seen our system and go back and use your system, every time you use your computer you're going to say: "If I were working with an Information Appliance, I'd be done by now. I wouldn't be sitting here waiting, twiddling my thumbs, I wouldn't have lost that idea or that nice sentence I'd thought of." I'm trying to sell a system that makes people happier. You can get more work done and you'll spend less time being bothered if you use one of our products.

INTERVIEWER: Do you think the computer will eventually do other things besides word processing, spreadsheets, and things like that? What about all those promises people made about running your home?

RASKIN: I've never believed those very much, and I'll tell you why. First of all, there will be special-purpose systems which have microcomputers and do various tasks around the house. There already are, but you don't think about them as computers: they're appliances. When you use a fancy micro-wave oven, do you think about the fact that it actually has a microcomputer inside with a little bit of RAM and ROM, and it runs programs? Does anyone ever think about any of that? All you do is punch the time, put in the food, and get it warm for breakfast. That's a hidden microprocessor. We have lots of hidden ones. But are computers going to do that? No way. First of all, have you ever seen any two computer products that are really compatible? Do you think that the XYZ Company that's making automatic electric windows is going to make their product compatible with Company G's computers? You know what a mess it is trying to run other manufacturers' printers with your computer. It doesn't work; it won't happen.

INTERVIEWER: Besides your work in computers, do you have other creative projects?

RASKIN: All kinds. I'm a typical inventor. I've got projects coming out of my ears in all directions. For example, I have a company that makes radio-controlled model airplanes. I'm also working on a new design for a piano. It will probably be as successful as other piano innovations of the last hundred years: namely, a total failure. My new piano sounds lovely, but I don't know if it is ever going to sell.

I'm working on a numerically controlled milling machine that will sell for under $5,000, so small shops can have them. Right now the only ones available cost $30,000 to $100,000. I've got one of mine working at home now.

INTERVIEWER: In looking through the manual for your product I noticed two things: First, it's very thick for such a simplicity-oriented product, and second, it's very comprehensive and easy to read. Does this book reflect any of your feelings on computer literature?

RASKIN: The whole attitude of this manual is different. The attitude is that the people who are going to use this manual are real human beings, just like me and you. We don't want to reference a hundred manuals to find an answer, and we also like to read English. So when I started this project, I set out to write the simplest, neatest, nicest manual possible.

Before we published this manual, we went to the trouble of writing and typesetting a first-draft manual, which we knew was not going out to the world, yet looked really good, so people didn't feel they were getting a preliminary manual. Why? To have people try it and learn from it. We wanted them to feel they were getting a real, finished system. We did not write the final manual until we had the actual product. When you run your own company, you have a chance to try to do things right. I've never been any place where they would let me write a manual first, throw it out, and then rewrite it. We also did all those silly little things that too few companies in the industry do, like giving credit to everybody who worked on the project.

There's a reason for the manual's size. Our idea is that if you have this manual, and also have other equipment, you won't have to look at the other manuals to get the answers. Our manual has most of the answers, not only for our equipment, but for almost everything else you're likely to hook up to. We think that's different from most manuals. If you want to know why the product is so simple, you can read the schematic, and the "Hardware Theory of Operations." No secrets. If you want to know why it's so fast, you can read the "Software Theory of Operations." There's also a "User Interface Theory of Operations." I've never seen that anywhere else. The manual has a long glossary, which can help teach you about the industry. Every term we use is defined. It's not just one or two pages, it's a real glossary. And there is a cross-referenced index that goes on for pages and pages.

INTERVIEWER: Do I detect a contempt for user-interface systems and manuals that don't use simple English commands and text?

RASKIN: I usually can't figure out what icons mean, but I can figure out what English words mean. It's easier for me to translate English into Spanish and French than it is to make up icons that can be understood by everyone everywhere in the world.

I've been working in this direction for a long time. It wasn't until I got away from Silicon Valley and let my head clear for six months that I suddenly saw I'd been simply barking up the wrong tree.

INTERVIEWER: *You mean you had been swept into a whirlpool of complexity there?*

> *"I learned a lot about the world in a Rolls Royce. After I left Apple, I sold the Rolls."*

RASKIN: Icons, windows, mice, big operating systems, huge programs, integrated packages.... I would like to remind the world that just because two things are on the same menu doesn't mean they taste good together.

INTERVIEWER: *Is that your message to Silicon Valley? To show the creators of complex systems that there is a simple alternative?*

RASKIN: Yes.

INTERVIEWER: *Would you say that this manual is the high point of your career as a technical writer?*

RASKIN: I entered the computer industry as a freelance reporter for *Doctor Dobbs, Byte* magazine, and a now defunct magazine called the *Silicon Valley Gazette.*

I became manager of publications at Apple and wrote some manuals that were highly rated, but this manual is beyond anything I'd even come close to writing. But I didn't write it myself. The lead author is David Alzofon; I wrote less than half of it.

The whole system is based on a few rules, a few psychological principles that make an easy-to-use system. If you read the "Theory of Operations" sections in the manual, you find out that the company has a theory of how human beings work, and this enabled us to design our product.

INTERVIEWER: *What is the theory?*

RASKIN: It's relatively simple. I asked myself the question: "What makes people form habits?" When I'm using a system, I'm happiest if I can keep my mind on what I'm trying to do, rather than on the system itself. The system should not intrude. When I'm tying my shoes, according to habit, I don't really think about it. I'm not putting my attention on tying my shoe. I wanted my system to be so simple that it would not distract users from their main task; I wanted using my system to be natural, like a habit. So I asked, "What are those things that make for habit?"

Well, the psychology books I read usually say a habit is something that you do the same way repeatedly, and that you're likely to do the same way again. There are some immediate implications from this. Picture yourself driving your car. Let's say that every Thursday the gas pedal and the brake pedal are interchanged. It would drive you up the wall, or through it. You couldn't live with it. Yet our computers change things around all the time by using "modes." A system should be "modeless." The same user action should always have the same effect.

SwyftWare is essentially modeless. Most computer designers, for some reason, delight in providing many ways of doing something. If there are fifteen ways to do something, they think it gives you freedom. The fact is that most users don't use the majority of the commands on their word processors. There are a few that everyone always uses. And even though they've read the manual and know it might be a little more efficient to use a special technique, they don't bother. They use the same ones every time.

On Macintosh, there is a backup of keyboard commands for all mouse commands because nobody's going to use the stupid mouse all the time. Okay, but whenever there's more than one way, there's that moment of hesitation while you think about the manual. Even after you've developed the habit, sometimes you're doing some work and think, "Gee, isn't there a faster way?"

So not only should one action do only one thing, but there should be only one path to a particular goal. That way you always use it, and you never have to think about it. We call that "monotony." My system is not perfectly monotonous, but it is as close as I know how to make it. [Laughs] Maybe some day I'll learn how to make a system totally monotonous.

INTERVIEWER: What do you feel artificial-intelligence programs can contribute to society?

RASKIN: Artificial intelligence teaches us a lot about ourselves and about knowledge. Any reasonable artificial-intelligence program will not fit on a very inexpensive machine, at least not these days.

Real artificial intelligence is something like religion. People used to say that just above the sky were heaven and angels. Then you get a rocket ship out there, and now you know that's not true. So they change their tune. As soon as you accomplish something, it is no longer artificial intelligence.

At one point, it was thought that chess-playing programs encompassed artificial intelligence. When I was a graduate student, you could get a Ph.D. in artificial intelligence by learning to program chess. Now you can buy a chess player for $29.95 and nobody calls it artificial intelligence. It's just a little algorithm that plays chess.

First, there's a problem of definition. Then it gets more complicated. People say that programs should understand natural language, but our utterances are too inexact for a computer, or anybody, to figure out what is meant to be done; that's why we have programming languages. If anyone's ever worked from a spec prepared in English, they know that you can't write a program from it because it's not exact. So if human beings can't do it, there is almost no way we can expect to make a machine do that kind of thing. When you're dealing with so-called artificial-intelligence programs, the computers have got to learn a vocabulary. Let's say you have five commands and you want the machine to understand any possible English equivalent to them. But it won't understand any English equivalent: One person might say, "Get employee number," while an Englishman might say, "Would you be so kind as to locate the numerical designation for our employee." That's exactly the complaint AI people are trying to solve.

A lot of the promise of artificial intelligence is misunderstood. What artificial intelligence has already taught us about the nature of languages is wonderful. So, do I think artificial intelligence is worthwhile? Absolutely. Do I think it's going to turn out great products? A few. Do I think it's going to fulfill the promise that you read about in the popular press? Not at all. Will I be putting a lot of money into artificial intelligence? Nope.

INTERVIEWER: Before, you equated power and prestige with money. Having tasted success, what changes have been forced on you?

RASKIN: Let me tell you a funny story. I used to have an old orange truck that I bought in 1970. An International Harvester. It had been across the country a couple of times, held everything, and you could sleep in the back. Wonderful truck. And here I was an executive at Apple, taking people out to lunch in this old orange truck. But I was too busy to keep up with the latest things in cars. I hadn't been in a "toy store" for months. Eventually, little hints began to be dropped. "Why don't you get a good car?" Well, okay, I'm a responsible employee.

Everybody was driving around in these Porsche 928s or Mercedes

Benzes and I just never wanted a luxury car of any kind. But they really wanted me to have something that was respectable. So my brother and I put our heads together and he came up with the idea. He said, "You know for about the same price as a new Mercedes or Porsche, you could buy a used Rolls Royce in absolutely magnificent condition. That way nobody could ever complain that you don't have an appropriate car, and you wouldn't have done what they expect you to do." So I got a used Rolls Royce. It's funny. Some people in the company had never spoken to me before, but they were very happy to talk to me then.

Anyway, I discovered a lot about this little democracy we have. When I went into a gas station, all of a sudden they carefully wiped off the window and called me "sir." And I could park out in front of a restaurant in a no-parking area and they would say, "sir" and "thank you," and "We're glad you parked your car right in front of our marquee where everybody can see that a Rolls Royce customer comes to eat here." It was always fun to go to the drive-through at MacDonald's, too.

I learned a lot about the world in a Rolls Royce. I went to the airport and five guys came over and opened up the door and said, "Welcome to San Francisco International Airport, sir." That never happened when I drove anything else there. They expected a huge tip. It was also a lot of fun driving in downtown San Jose among the low riders. They respect heavy iron as much as I love their cars.

I could go right up to big plants like Kaiser, where they have all those guards, and just drive on through. I always wanted to take a tour inside but could never get permission. In the Rolls, I just drove up and said, "I have an appointment with Mr. Mumford." "Thank you very much. Drive on through."

After I left Apple, I sold the Rolls.

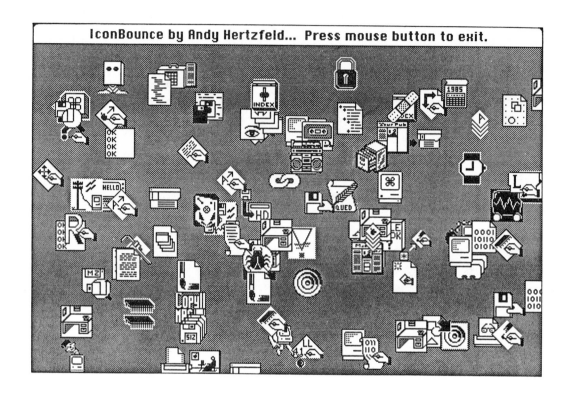

Icons will bounce on your Macintosh screen with a program written by Andy Hertzfeld. Just key in the program found in the Appendix (pages 361-369).

Andy Hertzfeld

BORN ON *April 6, 1953, Andy Hertzfeld grew up in the western suburbs of Philadelphia. Hertzfeld became intrigued with computers in high school, where one of the first programs he wrote was a dating program for a school dance. He went on to study physics, mathematics, and computer science at Brown University, eventually earning his degree in computer science in 1975. Hertzfeld later earned his master's degree in computer science at the University of California at Berkeley in 1979. After receiving his graduate degree, Hertzfeld went to Apple Computer, where he worked on the Silentype printer, the Apple III operating system, and other products. In February 1981 he joined the Macintosh development group as the second programmer to work on the project, and became the principal developer of the Macintosh operating system. Recently, Hertzfeld left Apple to work independently. He has since developed a program called Switcher for the Macintosh and a low-cost, high-resolution digitizer called ThunderScan.*

The door was open at dusk when I walked up to Andy Hertzfeld's small, cottage-style house on a side street close to downtown Palo Alto. I walked into a dimly lit room where I heard Andy talking on the phone. He spoke in an animated, upbeat voice while he sat on the sofa, barefoot, clad in jeans and a T-shirt, with one leg tucked underneath him. He was a short, heavy-set, slightly tousled young man with a friendly, relaxed demeanor. He smiled and waved me into the room, pointing toward a chair, all the while talking to the person on the other end of the line.

"A computer gives an amazing feeling of control and power to a kid."

I took a seat and observed my surroundings. We sat in a rather large, open, front room furnished with a large sofa and one chair. I tried to turn on the lamp next to me, but it did not work; so we sat more or less in increasing darkness as the sun set. Two bookshelves filled to the brim with books stacked both upright and sideways, a synthesizer, a Macintosh, and a stereo stood against the walls. The room was slightly unkempt but in no way dirty. Andy later explained that he is extremely messy but I was lucky because I happened to come on the one day the house is clean, the day the cleaning lady comes. With little delay, Andy hung up the phone. In his talkative, friendly manner, he discussed candidly his career as a programmer, delving into both the good and bad times at Apple, and explaining his approach to programming. More than anything else, Andy stressed that he programs because it is fun, and when it is no longer fun he will move on to something else.

INTERVIEWER: *Can you pinpoint the period in your career when you became enamored of personal computers?*

HERTZFELD: The big event for me occurred in March 1977 at the first West Coast Computer Faire. It was very exciting because it was the first real gathering of the clans in an industry that was just starting out in the area. I saw the Apple II for the first time, and I said, "That's the one I want." It was real sexy. A computer with graphics would have been enough, but the Apple II had color graphics, and that blew my mind. Unfortunately, those Apple II's were kind of expensive and I couldn't afford one. Finally, in January 1978, Apple had a "$400.00 off" sale, so I bought one. It's usually true that reality can't fulfill expectations, but the Apple II was twice as good as I ever thought it could be. Buying that machine was the best single purchase of my life.

I tried to make personal computers the topic of my graduate-school research, because to me they were the most exciting machines in the world. I was amazed that almost every professor in the department thought personal computers were the worst thing that ever happened to computer science. So I lost interest in my courses during my second year of grad school. I just wanted to play with my Apple.

INTERVIEWER: Why were the professors against personal computers?

HERTZFELD: Because personal computers were less powerful and had less memory than the big computers they were programming. They thought personal computers were moving computing back twenty years. They just hadn't caught on to the thrills that ordinary people can have on these machines. Suddenly, computers were within the reach of everyone. I guess a lot of academics couldn't have cared less. I didn't care that personal computers had 1/100th of the memory that the bigger computers had. They were so much more fascinating, and they only cost a thousand to two thousand bucks. And so I started teaching myself about the Apple II. In April 1978, I became a charter member of the first Apple users club in the Bay area. That was a place to show off your programs and get other people's programs.

INTERVIEWER: What kind of programs were you writing then?

HERTZFELD: The very first program I gave to the club was a general-purpose music editor. It played a Rolling Stones song, "Mother's Little Helper," on the Apple II. The second program I gave away was an I Ching program that used the Apple II graphics to interact with the user. To simulate a throw of the yarrow stocks in my program, I flashed a line on the screen on and off hundreds of times a second. When I hit the Apple III paddle the flashing would stop. I'd do that six times and get a hexagram, and then the interpretation of the hexagram would be displayed. I was intrigued by how the digital nature of I Ching matched the digital nature of the computer. These early programs were written in BASIC because that was all there was then, really. Later I started using assembly language because I knew that was the only way to write good programs.

INTERVIEWER: At what age did you initially get into programming?

HERTZFELD: When I was a high school kid, I was lucky enough to go to a school that had a clunky old Western Electric teletype hooked up to a GE time-sharing computer. In my junior year, in 1969, I learned to program in BASIC and FORTRAN and then PL/1. I was sixteen years old at that time.

INTERVIEWER: *Was that the beginning of an obsession?*

HERTZFELD: Yes, pretty much. Like a lot of people, I hadn't even heard about computers until a friend told me they existed. He showed me some listings but even then I didn't have a clear idea of what a computer actually was until I took a class the following year. Then it clicked in my mind and I fell in love with them. Today the computer is everywhere. We're bombarded with computer this, computer that.

I found I had a talent for programming. A computer gives an amazing feeling of control and power to a kid. To think of something, and then get the computer to do what you thought of, was such a great feeling. It always has been. That's what attracted me to the field. Learning to program is like learning to ride a bicycle; you can't read books about it. You have to do it.

One of the first programs I wrote was a class dating program that was actually used at a spring dance. Since I was a totally self-taught programmer, the dance program didn't work too well. I had gotten a whole bunch of students to gather around and watch the program run. But I didn't take into account that the same girl would get assigned to all the different men. One girl just kept getting matched with every guy and I realized that what I'd forgotten to do was eliminate a person once they were assigned. Even worse, she was a really weird girl.

INTERVIEWER: *When did you start taking programming seriously?*

HERTZFELD: It wasn't until I was in my junior year in college, majoring first in physics and later in math, that I started thinking, "Oh my God, I'm going to have to choose what to do with my life." I didn't want to wear coats and ties and be a part of the corporate structure. Then, for a while it was a case of, "Oh my God, I'll never be able to find a job doing anything." Then, when I found that the graduate math courses were really hard, it became, "Oh my God, I hate my major," and my intended career as a math professor started sinking out of sight. Programming didn't occur to me as a career choice. It wasn't a career in those days.

I got more involved with computers through summer programming jobs and consulting for $3.00 an hour at the student computing facilities. Then I took some more advanced computer courses in my senior year at Brown. I decided to be a computer-science grad student, but still I didn't think of computer programming as a career that I would pursue.

It was different in those days. That was 1975, when awareness about computers and programming was different than today. Personal computers hadn't yet brought computing to everyone's attention.

INTERVIEWER: *What was the meaning of programming then, and what has it become today?*

HERTZFELD: In 1975, a programmer was someone who worked for a bank or maybe NASA, something a little more glamorous, but the career was really obscure. There was no reason your average teenager would want to be a programmer. The concept of the computer had not reached the average person, except in a science fiction sort of way. In 1975, no person could afford to buy a computer. In fact, the personal-computer revolution was just beginning then. That fall the Altair kit was put on the market, and I began to see articles in magazines about microcomputers. That development was very important to me.

"The Apple II disk is amazingly unusual. It's a crazy, twisted, brilliant piece of engineering."

You see, as a programmer I always liked getting to the bottom of things, working my way down to the most fundamental level and understanding everything about the way a computer works on that level. My interest was in operating systems, but I was really frustrated by all the computers I'd ever programmed. I never could get down to their lowest level because the computers were always shared by a number of people and I was not one of the people they allowed to do the essential programming. I couldn't experiment. I thought if I got my own computer I could do whatever I wanted with it. But the Altair kit was not for me because I didn't like soldering and putting things together. I knew immediately, though, that the personal computer was for me.

INTERVIEWER: *What were some things you really loved about computers and programming?*

HERTZFELD: I really loved graphics on the computer. Minicomputers and mainframes didn't especially appeal to me because they didn't interact with people very much. More than anything, I loved impressing people. I could show my friends something and watch their mouths drop as they said "Oh, wow." Graphics and sound were two things most people took an interest in. I guess I wanted to impress myself more than anyone.

INTERVIEWER: *Back to your job hunt. What company was interested in hiring you as a computer programmer?*

HERTZFELD: This guy flew me out to Texas to interview me, and he liked me, so he offered me a job. The job was with the largest insurance company in Galveston, Texas, which is about as strange a city as there is in the United States. It's a resort town past its prime, full of hotels, and with a weird combination of ultra-macho tattooed shrimp-boat guys, oil guys, and cattle guys. They were cultures that I just didn't fit in with at all.

Before I went to this big insurance company, it had a really bad guy in charge of all their computer services. He was on some sort of power trip. You see, when you're in charge of a computer facility, you want to be in charge of the biggest possible computing facility. It looks better on your resume and you get more money; typically, your salary is proportional to how many computers there are in your facility. So this guy talked the company into buying literally four times the amount of computing power they could possibly use. They had two enormously expensive, $15 million IBM computers. When they found they were only using 15 percent of their power, they fired the guy, but they were stuck with all the computers. Well, just 20 miles from Galveston is NASA, and they needed as much computing power as they could get, so my boss convinced NASA to buy 50 percent of the computer time that the insurance company didn't need. The connection with NASA made the job fun for me. My job was to maintain and enhance an APL system that NASA was using. I learned a lot about operating systems at that company before I left to start grad school at Berkeley.

I arrived at Berkeley in September 1976. I actually discovered the first computer store right in Berkeley; it was a byte shop on University Avenue. I would hang out there and look at the computers. Most of them still had lights and switches. I was fascinated.

INTERVIEWER: *You said earlier that after your second year in grad school, your interest in the Apple II was greater than your interest in coursework. What were you doing in school at this point?*

HERTZFELD: I had spiritually dropped out of school, but I still went to my courses. Five thousand Apple II's had been sold, so I thought there was a market. It didn't occur to me to sell programs for it until I met the legendary Apple II programmer, Bob Bishop. He had bought his Apple six months before I bought mine, and by the time I was getting it figured out, he was already

writing good assembly-language programs and games. He was the first programmer to have his programs marketed for the Apple II in 1978. I had met
him at one of the Apple II users group meetings. He told me he was making
$6,000 a month. I thought that was amazing; I was making $7,000 a year as a
teaching assistant.

I started writing more programs. I gravitated toward systems programs
and wrote an ambitious program; a character generator that used the graphics of the Apple II to give it lowercase letters, which the machine lacked at the
time. It was an intricate little systems program. I had also started publishing
articles and some of my programs in magazines, such as *Doctor Dobb's Journal* and *Micro*. I was about to send my character-generator program away to a
magazine when I met a friend who was also an Apple II user. His name was
Barney, and he said, "Are you crazy? You can make $50,000, or maybe
$100,000." I thought about it and we went into business. The idea was that
we'd split profits fifty-fifty. I would create the product and have no other responsibilities. He would do the manufacturing, write the manual, and run the
business. This was in the days when there were six or seven thousand Apple
II's in the world.

Barney started showing the program to other companies. We ended up
taking it to Apple in December 1978. I had met a few Apple people at the club,
including my hero, Steve Wozniak (nicknamed "Woz"), who was the exact
ideal of what I wanted to be. The person we had to talk to at Apple was Steve
Jobs. We were scared to death of this meeting because we had met two early
Apple employees who said, "Steve Jobs is an ogre, he'll just rip you to shreds.
You're taking your life in your hands showing him this product." But it turned
out he was ultra nice to us, as nice as he could possibly be. Getting Apple to
sell our program was the ultimate. We made a deal with him. They were
going to give us $5.00 for each program they sold. We made an appointment
to visit Apple the next week to go over the details, and to explain to the engineering staff how the program worked. Then Jobs said, "I've changed my
mind. Your program doesn't fit in with our product line." I wasn't too upset
because I knew we could sell it to someone else. Mountain Hardware (now
called Mountain Computer) ended up taking it to market.

In a few months I made $40,000. I decided I didn't need school if I could
write programs that made money like that. Then, in January, Steve Jobs
called me and offered me a job as a programmer. He had a particular project

that he wanted me to do. I hesitated for a few months, but when I ran into him again at the fifth West Coast Computer Faire in 1979, he said, "Well, why haven't you come to work?" So I went down for an interview. After the interview, I almost decided I didn't want to work there.

INTERVIEWER: *Why weren't you interested in working there? It seems like it would be a dream come true.*

HERTZFELD: Because Apple had hired all these Hewlett-Packard people who were running the Apple II engineering, and they didn't know anything

"I expected to go to Apple and learn profound secrets, ... I knew more about Apple II than most people there."

about the Apple II. Apple went through various fads where it would hire engineers from a certain company. It had an HP period, a Xerox period, a DEC period, but HP was the dominant one in the early days. There were a few Apple II hobbyists like me, Bob Bishop, Charlie Kellner, and Rick Auricchio, who had bought Apple II's and became so obsessed with them that they naturally migrated to Apple. But, they also hired all these guys who didn't even know what an Apple II was when they started working there. To me that was totally incomprehensible. Why work at Apple if you don't even like the Apple II? It was a bad business decision.

Half the people I originally interviewed with didn't want to talk about the Apple II. They wanted to talk about UNIX, which I could talk about because that's what I was doing at Berkeley. Apple had the greatest product in the world and these guys didn't even like it. The last guy I talked to in my interview got me, though. His name was Dick Huston; he was the guy who wrote the Apple II boot ROM. We talked about Apple II details concerning how the disk drive worked, which I didn't know but was dying to find out about. In ten minutes I learned something I'd been trying to figure out for months. The Apple II disk is amazingly unusual. It's a crazy, twisted, brilliant piece of engineering. Most computer disk-controller cards usually had something like thirty chips, including some expensive LSI chips. Woz's disk-controller card had five tiny cheap chips, and furthermore, it worked better than any of the expensive ones. I later became an expert in the little details of how the disk drive worked, which was exactly the knowledge I needed to break copy-protected programs. If someone would get a new game program in, they'd bring it over to me. I'd compete with one or two other people at Apple to see who could break the copy protection first.

I started working at Apple in the summer of 1979. The first product I created was called the Silentype printer. I had expected to go to Apple and learn incredibly profound computer-science secrets, as well as the details of the Apple II, but I quickly found out that I knew more about the Apple II than most of the people there. What I started learning the most about was stock options. That was all anyone talked about. My job offer was $24,000 a year and a thousand shares of stock options, which was later raised to two thousand. I didn't think anything of the stock options. I thought a thousand shares was nothing.

Meanwhile, the Apple III was being designed. It was called the "Sara" in those days, but people thought of it as the Apple III. I thought there would be guards with machine guns around it, but the machine was just sitting there; I was amazed crowds weren't around it all the time. Except for the guys that were working on it, most people didn't think it was that exciting. In my spare time I wrote demo programs to try out its new features. That was thrilling because it was brand new hardware that wasn't doing anything yet.

INTERVIEWER: *Were others at Apple taking that kind of opportunity to do personal projects and research?*

HERTZFELD: Two or three people were like that at Apple. Bob Bishop was one of them. He gave the Apple II speech recognition, with no extra hardware at all, by sticking a microphone into the cassette port. In those days, Woz was still there, and I remember that I got a desk near him, which was very exciting for me. I actually had a desk right next to my hero. I could talk to him every day. I could eat lunch with him. I was in heaven.

Woz was doing various projects. One used the total amount of memory of an Apple II to calculate the mathematical constant E to a hundred thousand decimal digits of accuracy. That was a very hard thing to do, because the Apple II didn't have much memory. He had to use every single piece of memory, including the memory on the display screen, to hold this big number. And he didn't have any intermediate results because all the memory was holding just one number. This program took fourteen days to run. He just sat around, for fourteen days, waiting for the moment when it would be finished. Often, six days into the experiment his Apple II would flake out and crash. He'd start over from the beginning. He'd do all kinds of goofy projects like that.

INTERVIEWER: *What was happening financially to the company during this period? Wasn't this just before Apple went public?*

HERTZFELD: Apple sales were taking off like a skyrocket. Starting in the fall of 1979, and all through 1980, sales soared. Then Apple went public toward the end of 1980. All of a sudden, all these people I was working with were millionaires.

I gradually learned that the stock was incredibly inequitably distributed. You would like to think that the people who contributed the most to the company would have the most stock. Not at all. The people who cared about having the most stock had the most stock. There were engineers who spent their time plotting how to get more stock, to the extent of being criminal; while other people who were programming their hearts out and working fifteen hours a day for the company didn't get any. Everyone was conscious of this, but going public really turned the light switch on. When you wake up after the party and some guys are worth $5 million and others are still just earning their $30,000 a year salaries, you certainly notice. There were some bitter feelings.

There is a story about Woz, who of course got a lot of stock because he founded the company. He felt it was very unfair that some people didn't get any stock and other people got so much, so he took his personal stock and sold up to twenty-five hundred shares to anybody who had been working at Apple before a certain time. Woz had the best intentions, but that became an incredible field day for the bad people. What happened was that a lot of employees who didn't care about money didn't use their right to buy the stock, so the greedy people said, "Well, I'll give you the money and I'll buy your shares for you." Some guys stopped doing their work and became stock purchasers; they were horrible people, bad personalities, bad engineers, dripping with greed. In a month, one guy made hundreds of thousands of dollars by doing that. It was basically stealing money from Woz. But that was all part of Apple going public.

By the end of 1980, Apple was less of a fun place to work. Often your boss was hired from another company and knew nothing about the product. Finally, Mike Scott realized that Apple had hired all these dummies to manage everything and in February 1981, he fired them all on the same day. He fired forty people out of a ninety-person engineering group. That day in Apple history is called "Black Wednesday." People were stunned.

INTERVIEWER: How did you become involved with the Macintosh project?

HERTZFELD: I used to do all kinds of demos on new hardware in my spare time after I finished my regular projects. I would go into the hardware lab and help out the guys working there. One really young crazy guy, named Burrell Smith, was actually working in the service department as a computer repairman, but he would hang out in the hardware lab where the real engineers were and ask questions and learn everything possible. At the end of 1979, Jef Raskin, another legendary Apple character, was working on a project to make a new computer called Macintosh. He found Burrell in the service department, and had him design this little computer. Although Burrell's machine was actually very different from what eventually became the Macintosh, it looked like a really neat computer.

"Then Apple went public toward the end of 1980. All of a sudden, people I was working with were millionaires."

No one had ever programmed it before, so I spent my spare time doing little demos on it as it came together. The very first day he got it working, I stayed at work really late getting a picture of Scrooge McDuck up on the screen to prove that the video worked right. It was a beautiful little picture. Right before "Black Wednesday," Steve Jobs had sort of taken over the project and moved the four people working on it to this remote place, so I never got to see it any more. And I thought, "Hey, all these bozos around here are doing ordinary stuff. I want to work over there on the Macintosh project with those guys." So I told Mike Scott. That afternoon I was sitting in my cubicle and Steve Jobs came over and said, "Andy, you're working on Macintosh now." I said, "But I've got this Apple II stuff to finish up here." "No, you don't, you're moving to the Macintosh project now," he said, and he picked up my gear and carried it to the car.

I was very lucky because I was the fifth person to work on the Macintosh. All the people working on it were mavericks, people who didn't like working in organizations. It was a thrilling project: a machine that would be incredibly cheap to manufacture; a machine that was literally ten times more powerful than an Apple II. Steve let all the smart people work together with no managers. In a way, the management structure was turned upside down, because Steve Jobs was one of us.

INTERVIEWER: Who were some of the other principal players who worked

257

on the Macintosh project?

HERTZFELD: There were basically five people who wrote the system software: myself, Steve Capps, Bruce Horn, Larry Kenyon, and Bill Atkinson, who brought his expertise from Lisa. The first Macintosh programmer, brought there by Jef Raskin, was Bud Tribble, who is very talented. He had to quit the project in December 1981 to go back to medical school. He now holds an M.D. and a Ph.D. in neural science. Larry Kenyon had worked with me on the Apple II peripherals, so I knew he was great. Bruce Horn was another important contributor, too. He practically grew up at Xerox PARC, having started working there when he was fourteen, and by the time he was twenty-two, he was working on the Macintosh. Then, in January 1983, Steve Capps, a fantastic programmer, joined our group. There were some other people who helped, but these five wrote virtually all of the ROM for the Macintosh.

"More than anything else, what motivates me is that I want as many people as possible to use my programs."

INTERVIEWER: *What kind of strategies were used to develop the Macintosh?*

HERTZFELD: I think the only way to do good work is when the designers and the implementers are one and the same. The person who wrote the code was the person who designed the code.

INTERVIEWER: *When you were working on the Macintosh, did you know it would be a real success?*

HERTZFELD: Absolutely. We thought it was so much better than anything else that it was ridiculous. We thought it was the perfect computer. But while we were working on it throughout 1981, we were total nonentities at Apple. Less than twenty people worked on it, and it was not part of Apple's product plans. Everyone thought Steve Jobs was crazy and that Macintosh was Steve's back-to-the-garage fantasy. Everyone knew it took a hundred engineers to create a new computer. You can't do it with six guys. But in early 1982, after we got the computer working, people said, "Hey, maybe this has something to it." By 1983, Apple knew that the Macintosh was going to happen.

Another unusual thing was that Steve wanted to give credit to the people who actually did the work. The idea came from something that happened when Lisa came out: Lisa had a lot of publicity, and Bill Atkinson had done

110 percent of the important work. He literally created Lisa. But, in articles that came out about the computer he didn't get any credit for it. That was because the Lisa project was as incredibly bureaucratic as the Macintosh project was free and loose. Lisa had a complicated organization, with six levels of management and a hundred programmers. The magazines talked to the managers, and the managers considered themselves the architects of Lisa, even though it was mostly Bill's creation.

Bill felt awful. Something like that had happened to him when he was in college. He did some landmark work, a computer-graphics movie about the brain, which made the cover of *Scientific American*. The professor he did it for took all the credit, while Bill had done all the work. He was so distraught that he was ready to quit. Apple ended up naming him an Apple fellow to make him happy.

So, Steve Jobs promised us credit for Macintosh. The publicity culminated in the Macintosh introduction. Of course we thought it was the best computer in the world, and it turned out other people really liked it. I got my picture in *Newsweek* and *Rolling Stone* magazines. I'd been reading *Rolling Stone* since I was sixteen years old.

INTERVIEWER: When and why did you leave Apple?

HERTZFELD: I left Apple after Mac shipped and the Mac group started building up their bureaucracy. I clashed with the new engineering manager, whom I initially interviewed and approved, and who turned out to be a control and authority freak. The guy thought I was too big for my britches and figured he could break my spirit by giving me bad reviews. I was shocked. Here I was devoting my life to this company, doing the best work I'd ever done, and working fifteen hours a day to get the project out. Macintosh wasn't supposed to be like that, but this guy came in and made it like that. So I had to quit, but I'd put two years of my life into Macintosh; I cared about that more than I cared about anything. So I stayed until Mac shipped, and then I left to work for myself.

INTERVIEWER: What do you like about programming?

HERTZFELD: It's the only job I can think of where I get to be both an engineer and an artist. There's an incredible, rigorous, technical element to it, which I like because you have to do very precise thinking. On the other hand, it has a wildly creative side where the boundaries of imagination are the only real limitation. The marriage of those two elements is what makes programming unique. You get to be both an artist and a scientist. I like that. I love creating the magic trick at the center that is the real foundation for writing the program. Seeing that magic trick, that essence of your program, working correctly for the first time, is the most thrilling part of writing a program.

INTERVIEWER: *Do you think you'll always program?*

HERTZFELD: I think I'll always program, but I don't expect to always be as good a programmer as I am now.

INTERVIEWER: *With so much experience, it seems it would become easier to program as time goes on.*

HERTZFELD: To do the kind of programming I do takes incredible concentration and focus. Just keeping all the different connections in your brain at once is a skill that people lose as they get older. Concentration is a gift of youth. As you age, you become wiser. You get more experienced. You become better at living. But I don't think that when I get older I'll have the edge I do now. Right now I think I'm better than I ever was, but I don't expect that to continue. I still think I have a few years of my best work ahead. I don't think my forties will be as good as my thirties, but I expect my thirties to be better than my twenties.

INTERVIEWER: *What do you think will be happening in ten years in the computer world?*

HERTZFELD: Who knows? What I'd like to do is write a novel. I've always wanted to do that. As a kid I was a voracious reader, and I loved modern fiction. Some of my heroes are writers like Thomas Pynchon.

INTERVIEWER: *How would you describe your work habits?*

HERTZFELD: I've always had very flexible work habits. I work differently on different projects. The first six months of this year, I did a big complicated program for the Macintosh, called Switcher, and that was one of those projects that was very difficult to finish. The core work lasted six weeks and the entire project lasted eight months. When I'm really working hard on something, I do most of my work at night. I never used to go home from Apple until about ten at night, just when the body decides it's a nice time to quit. Usually I do the the bulk of my really good programming after dinner, from 8:30 in the evening until two or three in the morning. If I'm really cranking on something, it becomes more important than everything else.

I'm also very lazy, and I have no self discipline. The only reason this place isn't sloppy is that I have a cleaning lady who was in yesterday. What makes me program is my enthusiasm. I'm only good at doing the things I like to do. Fortunately I like programming, but if I ever lose my enthusiasm, I won't be able to program.

INTERVIEWER: *Do you think you'll ever run out of good program ideas?*

HERTZFELD: No, only because computers are still in their infancy, and essentially everything gets reinvented every five years. Suddenly you have five times as much memory to work with, if not ten times as much, and the rules start to change.

INTERVIEWER: *Well, you've certainly made some contributions to the computer industry. Is there a feeling of satisfaction that comes from that?*

HERTZFELD: I see so many people using my work now. I wrote a lot of the core software for the Macintosh. Any time you see anything done on the Macintosh, someone has used some of my instructions. That's an incredible thrill. More than anything else, what motivates me is that I want as many people as possible to use my programs.

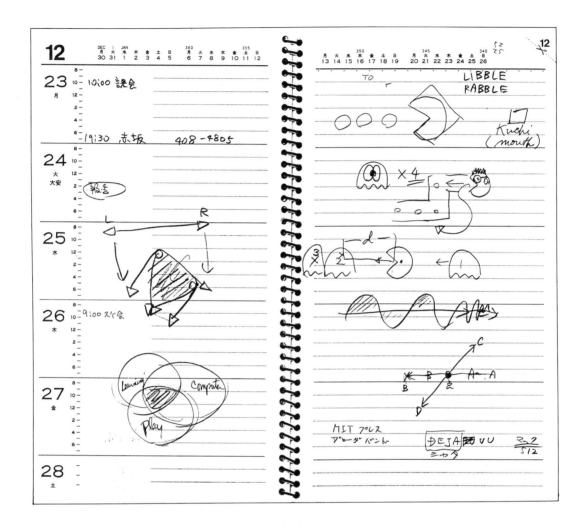

During the course of the interview Iwatani drew these sketches and diagrams in his calendar notebook. They illustrate how the shape of Pac Man evolved and how the ghosts move in relation to Pac Man.

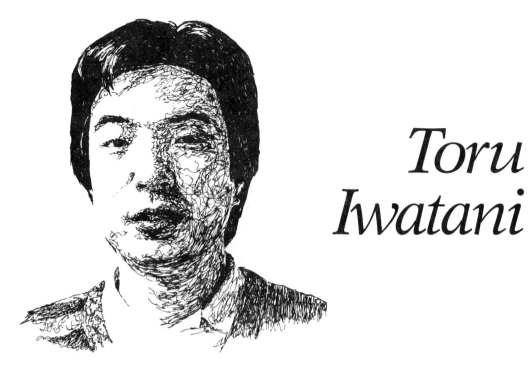

Toru Iwatani

GAME DESIGNER *Toru Iwatani was born on January 25, 1955 in the Meguro Ward of Tokyo, Japan. He is totally self-taught, without any formal training in computers, visual arts, or graphic design. In 1977, at the age of 22, Iwatani joined NAMCO LIMITED, a computer software company in Tokyo that produces video games. Once within the company, Iwatani eventually found his place designing games. He completed Pac Man with the help of four others, after working on it for a year and five months, taking it from concept to finished product.*

The game was first introduced in Japan, where it was very successful. When the game was exported, Pac Man captured the imaginations of Americans and Europeans as well. Iwatani went on to design more games, his favorite being Libble Rabble, which he designed after finishing the Pac Man project. Lately, Iwatani has become more involved in the administration of NAMCO LIMITED.

Geoff Leach, a friend and associate in Tokyo, sent me a lively telex one day, saying he had learned the name of the designer of Pac Man through his boss, Mr. Imaizumi, who happened to be in a study group with the designer. He thought he might be able to arrange an interview for me. I fired back a telex, expressing my delight at the prospect.

In Japan, the individual responsible for creating or designing a product is often not singled out and recognized. The group or company receives the credit, and the individual, although known in certain circles, remains inaccessible and unidentified. In this case, due to the personal nature of the contact, the interview was granted.

Mr. Leach and I took the subway to the outskirts of Tokyo to the offices of NAMCO. After reaching our stop, we wandered down narrow, busy streets in a shop-filled neighborhood until we came upon a striking brown marble building. The success of Pac Man had obviously served the company well.

We pushed through a set of double doors to enter the large white-marble lobby, where we were immediately welcomed by a gesticulating lady robot receptionist. She was decorated in pink and cream colors, with a nice pink helmet-like hat and blue eyes, and she had a shapely feminine figure. There was not another soul around. We paused, looking at her from a distance behind the counter. As we moved further into the lobby, she motioned us up to the counter. A computer terminal on the counter next to her flashed "WELCOME TO NAMCO," and prompted us to look through a telephone directory and call the person we wished to see. We stood at the counter quite amused and somewhat baffled by all this, when the public relations director came up to greet us and ushered us into a conference room where we were served tea while we waited for Mr. Iwatani to arrive.

He entered the room and we all stood and greeted, bowed, and exchanged business cards. Mr. Iwatani was a tall, striking man with a quiet, yet forceful, manner. He wore a light yellow polo shirt and wide-wale corduroy slacks. It was explained that the interview would be conducted in Japanese, with Mr. Leach acting as the interpreter. Iwatani spoke carefully and thoughtfully in his deep voice, and as he expressed his thoughts, he scribbled notes and sketches in his calendar notebook to illustrate his points.

INTERVIEWER: *How did you first become interested in computers?*

IWATANI: I must tell you, I don't have any particular interest in them. I'm interested in creating images that communicate with people. A computer is not the only medium that uses images; I could use the movies or television or any other visual medium. It just so happens I use the computer.

There's a limit to what you can do with a computer. Hardware limitations become my limitations. They restrict me, and I'm no different from any artist—I don't like constraints. I'm also limited because the only place the end result appears is on the screen. Turn the computer off, and the images vanish.

INTERVIEWER: *How did you choose video games as a way of communicating with people?*

IWATANI: I entered this company, NAMCO, in 1977. I hadn't yet established my own personal vision of what I would do here. My contribution to the company just happened to take the form of video games.

INTERVIEWER: *Had you ever studied game design or design in general?*

> *"I'm interested in creating images that communicate with people."*

IWATANI: I had no special training at all; I am completely self-taught. I don't fit the mold of a visual arts designer or a graphic designer. I just had a strong concept about what a game designer is—someone who designs projects to make people happy. That's his purpose.

It's important for you to understand that I'm not a programmer. I developed the specs and designed the features, but other people who worked with me wrote the program.

INTERVIEWER: *What was the thinking behind the design of Pac Man?*

IWATANI: First of all, the kanji word "taberu," to eat, came to mind. Game design, you see, often begins with words. I started playing with the word, making sketches in my notebook. All the computer games available at the time were of the violent type—war games and space invader types. There were no games that everyone could enjoy, and especially none for women. I wanted to come up with a "comical" game women could enjoy.

The story I like to tell about the origin of Pac Man is that one lunch time I was quite hungry and I ordered a whole pizza. I helped myself to a wedge and what was left was the idea for the Pac Man shape.

INTERVIEWER: *Is the story about the pizza really true?*

IWATANI: Well, it's half true. In Japanese the character for mouth (kuchi) is a square shape. It's not circular like the pizza, but I decided to round it out. (See Iwatani's illustrations at the beginning of this interview.) There was the temptation to make the Pac Man shape less simple. While I was designing this game, someone suggested we add eyes. But we eventually discarded that idea because once we added eyes, we would want to add glasses and maybe a moustache. There would just be no end to it.

Food is the other part of the basic concept. In my initial design I had put the player in the midst of food all over the screen. As I thought about it, I realized the player wouldn't know exactly what to do; the purpose of the game would be obscure. So I created a maze and put the food in it. Then whoever played the game would have some structure by moving through the maze.

The Japanese have a slang word—paku paku—they use to describe the motion of the mouth opening and closing while one eats. The name Pac Man came from that word.

INTERVIEWER: *Once you decided Pac Man would be a game of food and eating, what was the next step?*

IWATANI: Well, there's not much entertainment in a game of eating, so we decided to create enemies to inject a little excitement and tension. The player had to fight the enemies to get the food. And each of the enemies has its own character. The enemies are four little ghost-shaped monsters, each of them a different color—blue, yellow, pink, and red. I used four different colors mostly to please the women who play—I thought they would like the pretty colors.

To give the game some tension, I wanted the monsters to surround Pac Man at some stage of the game. But I felt it would be too stressful for a human being like Pac Man to be continually surrounded and hunted down. So I created the monsters' invasions to come in waves. They'd attack and then they'd retreat. As time went by they would regroup, attack, and disperse again. It seemed more natural than having constant attack.

Then there was the design of the spirit (kokoro), or the energy forces of Pac Man. If you've played the game, you know that Pac Man had some ammunition of his own. If he eats an energizer at one of the four corners of the screen, he can retaliate by eating the enemy. This gives Pac Man the opportunity to be the hunter as well as the hunted.

INTERVIEWER: *What did you intend the character of Pac Man to be like?*

IWATANI: Pac Man's character is difficult to explain even to the Japanese—he is an innocent character. He hasn't been educated to discern between good and evil. He acts more like a small child than a grown-up person. Think of him as a child learning in the course of his daily activities. If someone tells him guns are evil, he would be the type to rush out and eat guns. But he would most probably eat any gun, even the pistols of policemen who need them. He's indiscriminate because he's naive. But he learns from experience that some people, like policemen, should have pistols and that he can't eat just any pistol in sight.

(Iwatani begins sketching diagrams of curves with points on his calendar notebook. See the illustrations at the beginning of this interview.)

INTERVIEWER: *What was the most difficult part of designing the game?*

IWATANI: The algorithm for the four ghosts who are the enemies of the Pac Man—getting all the movements lined up correctly. It was tricky because the monster movements are quite complex. This is the heart of the game. I wanted each ghostly enemy to have a specific character and its own particular movements, so they weren't all just chasing after Pac Man in single file, which would have been tiresome and flat. One of them, the red one called Blinky, did chase directly after Pac Man. The second ghost is positioned at a point a few dots in front of Pac Man's mouth. That is his position. If Pac Man is in the center then Monster A and Monster B are equidistant from him, but each moves independently, almost "sandwiching" him. The other ghosts move more at random. That way they get closer to Pac Man in a natural way.

When a human being is constantly under attack like this, he becomes discouraged. So we developed the wave-patterned attack—attack then disperse; as time goes by the ghosts regroup and attack again. Gradually the peaks and valleys in the curve of the wave become less pronounced so that the ghosts attack more frequently.

INTERVIEWER: *Were there any other people working on the Pac Man design team with you?*

IWATANI: There was one hardware engineer, one person who wrote the music, and the package designer—approximately five people actually worked on it, counting the programmer and me.

From the concept to the time the game was on the market was about one year and five months—rather longer than usual. We tried out each feature as we went along. If it wasn't fun or didn't add anything to the game's complexity, we dropped it.

INTERVIEWER: *Was Pac Man as popular with women as you had expected him to be?*

IWATANI: Yes. Not only was Pac Man successful with women, but all the other versions like Ms. Pac Man were successful, too. And Pac Man was more popular in other parts of the world than I expected. I was confident the game would sell reasonably well in Japan, but I was quite surprised to see how well it sold in the United States and other countries.

INTERVIEWER: *Are there any aspects of Pac Man you now wish that you could change?*

IWATANI: Pac Man was something I accomplished a long time ago. When I was designing it, I felt I'd taken myself to the limits of my own skill and what others were doing. I was satisfied then. But it doesn't really have very much to do with who I am or what I am doing today.

There was another game I developed after Pac Man, called Libble Rabble. The game concepts make it quite an interesting game—even better than Pac Man. But it didn't do as well as I expected.

INTERVIEWER: *How has your life changed since you designed Pac Man?*

IWATANI: My life hasn't changed in any big way, although my ideas about what I want to achieve have. Recently I've felt I would like to make the people who enjoy playing games cry—give them an emotion different from the ones they're used to when they play video games. I'd like to come up with some kind of very dramatic game. I want them to have the opportunity to experience other emotions, like sadness. They're not going to cry because they are hurt. They will cry when they play my game for the same reasons people cry when they see a movie like E.T., because it touches them. They go to sad movies of their own free will because they like to be moved, even though it's a sad feeling. I'd like to create a game that would affect people that way.

INTERVIEWER: *Do you think it's more difficult to make people sad than it is to make them happy?*

IWATANI: Much more difficult. It's possible to induce laughter in a short

> *"The Japanese have a slang word—paku paku—they use to describe... the mouth opening and closing while one eats. The name Pac Man came from that word."*

time with jokes, but getting people to cry requires creating a special situation, and that takes more time. A film such as E.T. where one laughs and cries is quite difficult.

INTERVIEWER: *Do you ever tire of developing games?*

IWATANI: Right now, I'm getting away from the design process and am more involved in administration. That's nice, because I can have my staff do things I don't like to do very much and avoid the frustrations I had before. Also I'm able to do the things I want to do—no one tells me not to, and that's very comfortable.

INTERVIEWER: *Do you design other things besides games?*

IWATANI: One's actions are all designs, I feel. For example, if you are seeing a woman, you think of ways to please her. Should you give her a present? What kind of present? When should you give it to her? You come up with some kind of strategy or game plan. Just as in game design, you must derive pleasure from seeing the expression of happiness on another's face.

I belong to a study group of about 40 people, in which we talk about new media, including educational software and the problems of education it can address. It's an area we have to work on because it is an embarrassing fact that the Japanese educational system is the worst. Frankly, I think that unless education is fun and entertaining, people won't learn.

My specialty, of course, is entertaining people. If there is a learning objective that can be expressed in a fun way, it could be the basis for a good game. I'm also interested in educational software and computer-assisted instruction (CAI) for reasons of economic survival. Companies concentrating only on game design do not have a secure future. And there are many people with enough interest to pay good money for educational software.

INTERVIEWER: *What kind of skills or philosophy must a game designer have to be successful?*

IWATANI: You must understand people's souls (kokoro) and be creative enough to imagine things that can't be thought or imagined by others. You must be compelled to do something a little bit different than the rest of the crowd and enjoy being different. You must also be able to visualize the images that will make up the game, and you shouldn't compromise with the first easy idea that comes to mind. In the last analysis, you must enjoy making people happy. That's the basis of being a good game designer, and leads to great game design.

INTERVIEWER: Which game do you think is the best?

IWATANI: Well, not to toot my own horn, but Libble Rabble is number one. Among other companies' products though, Atari's games also seem good.

INTERVIEWER: What do you think game design will be like in ten years?

IWATANI: It will be closer to the movies—that's happening even now as we see the development of large-scale games. Also, there will be an increase in multi-player, network games like Mega War—the fascination of fighting the unknown. It's intriguing to think of playing not only with another person, but with someone you don't know and can't see.

©1981 Scott Kim

In this sketch, numbers plot points along curves and
letters plan the composition of pieces into character
shapes. Because of the symmetries among shapes,
many pieces repeat. Shapes were planned on paper
first, then tuned interactively on the screen. The final
image was produced on a laser printer. The Appendix
(page 372) contains more sketches from Kim.

Scott Kim

LOS ANGELES native

Scott Kim was born on October 27, 1955. He studied mathematics, computer science, and music at Stanford University, earning a B.A. in music in 1977. In 1975, after taking a graphic-design course, Kim began working on his "inversions," the term he uses to describe his artistic renditions of words that can be read from many different directions, similar to palindromes and anagrams. In 1981, Scott Kim published the book Inversions. *Contributors to the book include many of the outstanding personalities in the computer field. The book includes a foreword by Douglas Hofstadter, Kim's professor and friend. John Warnock helped program the images. Donald Knuth and David Fuchs helped with typesetting, and Jef Raskin wrote the "backword." To go along with his book, Kim has recently developed a piece of fourth-party software, Inversions for the Macintosh. This software runs on top of MacPaint and includes many exercises, techniques, and games for creating inversions.*

Kim has applied his intimate knowledge of graphic design and typefaces to his work in computer science. Currently he is researching a radically new user-interface design for his Ph.D. work at Stanford. In conjunction with his studies, Kim has worked at Xerox PARC as an unpaid consultant since his undergraduate years. He also works at Information Appliance in Palo Alto. In addition, he has his own company, LOOK TWICE.

Sitting next to a Macintosh at a large conference table, Kim and I talked for hours about his work and philosophy. Scott Kim is a soft-spoken, deliberate thinker; a dedicated student of the problem of how to change the computer so that it can be a much more direct, effective tool for everyone to use. His unusual background in graphic design, mathematics, and music helps him approach the problem from a visual perspective, a far different view than that of most engineers. Kim is a visual thinker above all. His inversions, which he can create on the spot at a moment's notice, are a testament to his mental dexterity and flexibility. And one day he will also succeed in bringing to reality his vision of the computer that will work in a direct manner, with the same notation on screen and in the computer's memory.

INTERVIEWER: *What made you want to publish your inversions artwork in a book?*

KIM: While I was an undergraduate student at Stanford, three major things happened that all came together to inspire me to do this book: I started working with computers, I met Douglas Hofstadter, and I took a graphic-design course.

In 1975, I started a sequence of computer-music courses taught in the music department and what was important, besides its being a good class, was that it was taught at the Stanford Artificial Intelligence Lab. It's probably a common story that people tend to learn about computers not so much through classes as through some network of friends and people helping each other. And in my case, my breeding ground was the AI lab. It was a wonderful environment to learn in. It was physically isolated from the rest of the campus, situated in a run-down building in the foothills a few miles away. When you looked out, all you saw were hills and trees and blue sky.

INTERVIEWER: *So was this CCRMA (Center for Computer Research in Music and Acoustics)?*

KIM: Right. CCRMA at the time was the same as the Stanford AI lab. The music people used to be just a little appendage on the edge.

INTERVIEWER: *So, is it true that you were introduced to computers through music, basically?*

KIM: Actually, my first experience with computers was in high school, but at Stanford I really started learning a lot about them. The sequence of computer-music courses gave me access to this wonderful community of people who were just out there hacking their hearts out for the pure love of it, and who would, at the drop of a hat, just spend the whole afternoon telling you what they were doing. That was a wonderful way to learn.

What also was exciting was discovering the word processors and video games they had there. Those weren't commonly available at the time. The AI lab had early versions of Space War, so we would sneak out to the foothills to play the games. This was back in the days before people had computers at home, let alone video games or anything like that. It was a really magical time. This was during the first year I arrived at Stanford.

INTERVIEWER: At that point did you get obsessed? Did you study everything there was to study?

KIM: Yes, to a certain extent. I started taking computer courses like crazy. I took a LISP course at the end of my first year. The second year I took Knuth's sequence of courses in data structures. I learned all the languages. I got most of my computer-science education the first two years, so that by 1975 when I went to study computer music I was already an old hand, or at least I felt like it.

> *"My experience with programming is generally that I would rather avoid it, if I can."*

INTERVIEWER: So when did you get the idea of doing inversions?

KIM: In 1975 I took the one and only art class I ever took as an undergraduate at Stanford. It was a basic design course, and it was formative in a couple of ways. It sparked my interest in the visual side of things. I've always been interested in visual play; animation in particular has always captured my interest, but it was always a hobby. For an assignment in the course, I created an inversion.

That school year I also met Doug Hofstadter. He was in the middle of writing a monumentally fascinating book entitled *Gödel, Escher and Bach*. I had the great privilege of working with him for a couple of years while he wrote the book.

INTERVIEWER: What did you do for Doug Hofstadter?

KIM: We became friends, and from then on we just worked side by side. We would stay up all night in the terminal room and we'd talk out ideas, then he'd print out the latest version of a dialogue and we would bat around more ideas. We were like colleagues. And working on his book really gave me the

275

confidence to do my own book. Doug's book is wonderfully personal. He didn't hold anything back. Besides writing the book, he even went to the trouble of typesetting it himself.

INTERVIEWER: Yes, I noticed. For your book, I understand John Warnock did the images.

KIM: John Warnock helped me there. Of course, now he's associated with Adobe, but at the time he was my mentor at Xerox.

While I was a student at Stanford I was an unpaid consultant at Xerox PARC. Stanford has a close relationship with their research lab. Originally I went to Xerox PARC to fool around with Metafont, a typeface design language. Eventually I started doing images in Warnock's language, JaM, the predeccessor of PostScript. JaM stands for John and Martin, John Warnock and Martin Newell, the developers.

As I got into producing illustrations for my book *Inversions,* I explored the possibility of using JaM to create the images. I didn't have to use a computer for these designs, and in fact, for two-thirds of them I didn't. But for some of the designs—for instance, the infinity spiral—I knew that if I went to the trouble of computerizing it, at the very least it would be interesting to find out what would happen. Since I was comfortable with programming, it was no problem. In the case of the infinity spiral, I wrote the program that created the letters. I first worked it out on graph paper, did all the sketches, numbered the points, and wrote a short program to create the word "infinity" as I had designed it. Then I described to John Warnock what I wanted him to do, and he wrote programs that transformed the straight lines into spirals. It's wonderful working with him because he has a great graphic design sense. The programs created images that would have been difficult without the computer. Since that time I've been pushing myself to see what can be done that is appropriate to computers and to visual expression.

INTERVIEWER: Now, you are creating a piece of software that deals with inversions and helps people learn how to create them. How did you go about developing this software?

KIM: It's called Inversions for the Macintosh and it's software that goes along with the book. The two will be packaged together. The basic question I posed was, "What can I do on the Macintosh that would enhance this book?" Now, my instincts are never to just present something, saying, "Look at this, isn't this neat." It's always, "Look at this and here's how you can do it too." And that's what Inversions on the Macintosh does. I developed the software to run on top of MacPaint.

I can program easily, but I decided in developing this software that I would take the unusual strategy and not write any programs. After experimenting with MacPaint for a while, I realized that I really didn't have to write a program. And my feeling about programming is that I would generally rather avoid it, if I can.

INTERVIEWER: Why would you rather avoid programming?

KIM: Because the act of writing a large complex program is indirect. If I could do it more directly, I would prefer to. I consider it a challenge. What could I do on a computer that would be interactive without a program?

Inversions on the Macintosh is what I call "fourth-party software." There are plenty of examples already. There are templates for spreadsheets and within MacPaint there's clip art. Templates are a nice direct response to something that somebody actually needs. Clip art is a carryover from another medium. It's useful, but it's certainly not making use of the medium in a really new way.

My software is just MacPaint files and fonts. It was created exactly like anybody else would create files with MacPaint, by typing and drawing. The files contain visual puzzles and exercises that start simple and become increasingly difficult as you move through them. But my software is only half MacPaint; the rest is what you can imagine in your head. I'm really encouraging people to develop mental flexibility, to try to imagine what's going to happen before they do something. That sort of skill, imagining what will happen, is something not usually taught in school. By playing with blocks at home, children get to imagine space, but it's just not taught in school.

INTERVIEWER: You mentioned fourth-party software. Describe it and what you like about it.

KIM: Third-party software is software created by companies using conventional programming languages. Fourth-party software is created by users themselves, without programming, at least in the usual sense. It's built on top of third-party software. This requires that there be good rich third-party software around.

Today there are problems with software. Most software is very expensive. The prices really don't make sense over the long run, but there are a lot of forces that keep prices high now. The market is not yet enormous; software production costs are high—there are a number of other circular arguments.

The great thing about fourth-party software is that anyone who has a computer can create it. You can build on top of existing programs. Some are specifically designed for this—Pinball Construction Set is an example.

The software available today was written by programmers. Let's compare that to the book industry. If the only people who wrote books were paper manufacturers and printers, we'd get instructional texts and reference books, but few novels and personal essays. The solution would be not to teach everyone how to print their own books, but to make printing cheap and available so authors could concentrate on content. Programming should be so simple that all users can build their own personalized software.

> *"The computer is a very alluring machine, it always tempts you to do one more thing."*

INTERVIEWER: *Do you think the process of creating software will simplify so almost anyone with a computer can create their own?*

KIM: Basically, I expect the nature of programming to change. Now, you keep all these thoughts and algorithms in your head and you're off in a corner trying to sort through them and put them together in a giant puzzle, working long nights. In a few years I expect a lot of pieces needed to build programs, at least the ones that are frequently used, will be available. For instance, if you want to build your own program, you will go down to a store like Radio Shack and buy premade parts for building it.

For the most part, I expect that most people will not program in the usual sense as we understand it today. Even now, I believe there is no fundamental difference between programming a computer and using a computer. They're very different activities, but they are on a continuum. When you type your name into a computer, that's programming of a sort. The other type of programming through languages available today is a much more indirect activity. When more direct programming languages are available, then almost anyone will be able to build a program; it won't feel much like programming any more. You won't call them languages either.

INTERVIEWER: *Okay, what will you call computer languages then? Or is it that you won't even recognize them as computer languages, won't even be conscious of these languages? Will they become like English?*

KIM: The words we now use to describe all this will change. Alan Kay's vision is that computers will be successful when we stop using the word computer. He would often say that in the early days of electricity, a common belief was that some day everyone would have an electric motor in their house. That's like computers today. When computers get small enough and cheap enough, they will disappear into the environment. You won't even point your finger and say, "that's a computer," since they will be all over the place. The computer is not successful until it disappears.

INTERVIEWER: *Is your work with inversions connected in any way with your Ph.D. research?*

KIM: I am working on several projects at the same time. Inversions, only in the sense that it deals with the graphic images presented in a computer medium, relates indirectly to my research. For my Ph.D. thesis, I'm really thinking about graphic-interface design in the spirit of Alan Kay, but in a different direction.

My focus is very fundamental. I'm saying, "Suppose we really start from scratch, throw out everything we know about computers, and design a computer from the ground up that would really fit the way a visually oriented person would like to operate." I want a computer that is like a piece of paper. As a starting point, that means eight and a half inches wide, eleven inches tall, about this thin, about that shape. Not all of the metaphor would necessarily fit, but what's really lovely about paper is that you don't have to think as you do with a computer: "How can I get to text modes, what do I have to push to do this?" Paper is very direct. What you see on the surface of the paper is what there is, whereas with a computer you have to think about what's behind the page, what's acting behind the screen. The computer is like a piece of paper with wires and hardware hidden behind it.

INTERVIEWER: *How do you approach the problem of making the computer into a piece of paper?*

KIM: I'm starting to think about what I don't like about computers as they are. Then I think about graphic design and working with images, and about what I do like about that, and then I look for ways for the two to meet. There are visual artists working with computers, that's for sure. Most of them use painting programs. Painting programs are really direct, very much like paper, but the computer adds nice features. You can change a color after you've already put it down. Everything's fluid; you can always combine images. The piece never has to be finished.

Musicians are, as a lot, not averse to programming; a lot more musicians program than artists. Musicians, at least classically trained ones, are accustomed to working with an abstract notation, they're used to an indirect process. It's not merely that the notation is different from the music, it's also that the conception in their head is different. They work out things in their heads, then they work them out on paper.

On the other hand, an artist is used to working much more directly; and for that matter, a musician who improvises primarily would be in the camp of visual artists also. It has less to do with visual and audio than it does with the style of working. There are also visual artists who are very indirect. A graphic designer is less direct than a painter because a graphic designer has to go through typesetters and give instructions to other people. But most visual artists are not used to working indirectly and they care about how something looks. Computers, as designed, do not give you the feeling that the person or the people who designed them cared about how a thing looked.

On the most basic level, I'm thinking about what a computer is and why we inflict computers on ourselves, anyway. There are a lot of problems with computers today. I don't necessarily know the solutions for them right now, I'm just trying to critically examine computers again, because I also think there's a lot of promise here to bring to the surface.

INTERVIEWER: So are you thinking about a computer that would be used by everyone, or would it be specifically for the artist?

KIM: The artist is part of the inspiration, but ultimately I'm thinking about something for everyone. There's no single direction. The way I work is to get involved with several projects that are slightly different but overlap in different ways, and then I let the whole thing boil.

For my thesis, I was originally going to build a visual programming language. I thought that might make it more direct. I built little tiny projects to test out particular ideas. The first thing that came to mind was this language that was sort of like strings of words except it used symbols arranged in something like a flowchart. Most visual programming languages have a sort of circuit analogy. But all along I had a very queasy feeling that it wasn't right. My gut reaction was, I might as well write in Pascal.

I had long talks with many people about the subject, but eventually I had a conversation with Larry Tessler, who at the time was writing an article on programming languages that was published a year ago in the software issue of *Scientific American*. He is an expert programmer and did a lot of the work on Apple's Lisa computer. He gave me some good advice when he said to me, "As a programmer you get to a point where you say to yourself, 'Oh no, I gotta write another program.'" It's like you're barreling down the road with your idea and then you've got to take this big detour, you've got to go back to home. Programming is still an interesting activity, but it's generally not what I actually want to do. That's my feeling.

It's taken me a while to realize how much I didn't like programming, because I couldn't imagine it being otherwise, but now I can imagine it, and I am insisting that it be otherwise.

> "My software is only half MacPaint; the rest is what you can imagine in your head."

INTERVIEWER: *What's it feel like when you realize it could be otherwise?*

KIM: In a way you get impatient. You start saying to everybody "Come on, I want to see some people doing some innovative things here." I tell people, "Don't accept things the way they are, they don't have to be this way." I have become much more reluctant to actually program, except in very mediated doses. The computer is a very alluring machine, it always tempts you to do one more thing. If you're word processing, you want to get every last typo correct; if you're programming, you want to put every last feature in. It's good to know when to stop.

INTERVIEWER: *Has any one person in particular influenced you in what you do and how you do it?*

KIM: Well, let's see. In thinking about software, there are three people who have influenced me. They are Jef Raskin, David Thornburg (who also worked with me on Inversions for the Macintosh) and Ted Nelson. The three of them believe in simplicity—boy, do they believe in simplicity. When they say simplicity, they mean it. For instance, five is the largest number of anything you're allowed to have.

David Thornburg is the one who's written it out most clearly. He has a little book called *Zero Mass Design*, the premise of which is that if you're going to work on something—for instance, you're going to write a book, or you want to write some software, or you are about to embark on any other project that requires planning—start with a very simple design. But it's more extreme than just keeping it simple; you start with a design that's so simple that it won't work. That requires a great deal of discipline because you go into the project with the premise that you will fail; until you've tried something and actually seen it fail, you don't know how simple you can get.

Dave Thornburg's example, from James Adams' book *Conceptual Block-busting*, is the Mariner IV spacecraft. It had large solar-cell panels that unfolded. The problem, as stated, was to have a mechanism that slowed down the panels as they unfolded so that they wouldn't break when deployed. So they tried oil, but that was sort of messy, and they tried springs; they did all sorts of things. The day for the launch was coming nearer and nearer. What were they going to do? Remember, the problem as stated was to find a way to slow down the panels, or to find a braking mechanism. Finally, somebody had the brilliant idea to try it with nothing, so they tried it and the panels shook and shivered but nothing broke. If you state the problem with assumptions, you're going to get them. You've got to pare back and pare back and pare back. Starting with a very simple design has wonderful advantages, but it requires a psychological twist; you have to expect that it will fail and enjoy that.

INTERVIEWER: *So with zero mass design in mind, how will you get to the point where the computer is like a piece of paper?*

KIM: The key insight in my thesis is that there is this presumption in computer science. It took me a very long time to notice it because it is so subtle. What you see on the screen is, as Alan Kay calls it, "the user illusion." The screen is a pretty faithful representation, but what is really there are the data structures off in the computer's memory. The computer is really looking at that, not at you. It also gives you a picture on the screen, and you've got to look at that and imagine what the computer's thinking behind the screen. The MacPaint system is pretty nice; you can see exactly—that pixel stands for that pixel, so in some cases the illusion is very good, very close to reality. Let me draw a diagram.

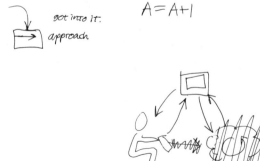

$$A = A + 1$$

got into it.
approach

Here is the user with the keyboard, the computer screen, and the memory. There's this little triangle of interaction. You type and the information goes into the computer, which stores it and then feeds back the picture on the screen, which you see. And the computer's thinking here in the memory, but what you see on the screen is different from what the computer's thinking.

Everybody who's thinking about visual programming is actually thinking about a visual representation of programming. The programming itself stays the same, but you put pictures on top of it. I think that is just dressing up the surface, but it's not dealing with the substance. The missing link is here, between the computer and you. The computer is not seeing what you're seeing on the screen. If the computer had to deal with the screen exactly the way the user did, then the interaction would be direct. I would like the computer to think visually, and the way for it to do that is to deal with exactly what the user is dealing with.

I've discovered that this is such a weird idea that I've had to build a working example at Xerox in order to explain it.

INTERVIEWER: *How can you possibly put everything on the screen?*

KIM: Well, you'd certainly run out of room quickly, so in the most real sense you can't. For the moment, I'm building only a very simple program so that you can literally put everything on screen.

Before you can have a program, you have to have an environment in which it can live. What I built was a very, very simple text and graphics editor. It's in the same category, generally, as MacPaint, but it's a lot simpler. In Mac-Paint, once you've typed a word you can't edit it. You lose the ability to rework it because the letters in the words you typed are stored as bits, not characters.

MacPaint represents the picture on the screen literally by what bits are there. To edit, you can take anything here, even if it's half a letter, and move it around. You're able to forget those are letters and just treat them as pictures, which is a lovely thing in MacPaint. What's missing is that you cannot go from the bits on the screen back to what the letters were.

INTERVIEWER: *What do you think having everything represented on the screen will achieve? Will it make the computer less complex for the user?*

KIM: The prototype I built is not the answer to that question. It's merely a step along the way to getting there. I'm asking a "what if" question: What if everything is on the screen? I don't think my prototype is really the answer. But, again, people have given up without even considering it as a possibility.

The computer programmer typically makes the assumption that what's on the screen is not what's real. The screen representation, the documention, all those things are a side effect. What's real is the algorithms, the program that runs behind the scenes. It's real tricky because when you program, you fall in love with the fact that you can handle all of these complex abstract elements. You think that it has to be that way. I don't believe that. Dealing in graphic design helped me realize it doesn't have to be this way. When you talk to a graphic designer, you don't talk, you show pictures because that's the real

"The computer is like a piece of paper with wires and hardware hidden behind it."

stuff, that's what is important. When you meet a graphic designer, the first thing said is, "Okay, let's see your portfolio." What's important is not all the abstract concepts that fed into the items in your portfolio. And that's not what is there either. What's there is what is on the paper.

INTERVIEWER: What about music? Music has never gotten away from an abstract way of going about things, has it? Notation will never disappear, will it?

KIM: Well, most music doesn't use notation. Actually, I think I'm crippled as a musician because of my academic training. I'm stuck in the rigors of music theory, technique, and notation. I can't improvise as a lot of people can. I really envy them. They can directly think about all of those things at the same time they are playing.

In the early fifties, Grace Hopper, who's the mother of high-level programming languages, went around saying people shouldn't write in assembly language, they should write in something that looks more like English. She was told that computers can't understand English, so it's impossible. But that's not the point. Pascal is not English. It's a compromise between what a computer can understand and what a human can understand.

I would like people to be able to work with computers in something that looks more like pictures. That doesn't mean I'm opposed to abstract notations. Instead, I would like to include words and symbols as special sorts of pictures. In order to do this, the computer has to be able to make the transition from the bits on the screen to the letters, somewhat like optical character recognition.

INTERVIEWER: What did Inversions *have to do with this idea?*

KIM: Well, there is actually a nice connection. One very peculiar thing about this book is that it's not serious. It's downright silly. I like playing; that's where a lot of new ideas come from. Another thing about this book is the question, "Are these pictures or are these words?" It's difficult to tell. They're a little bit of both. Most people forget that these little black and white things on the page, these characters, were actually drawn by somebody. The originals of this typeface were drawn by somebody. Letters are shapes, but you forget that, you think they're somehow different. And you forget it because the way you produce them is different. To do typesetting and to do illustrations you must use very different tools, and they are all united at the very end of the book-publishing process.

Before Gutenberg, illustration and type were one and the same; they were inseparable. But afterward, the two disciplines became separate and diverged. Now that we've got the Macintosh, I can see a medium where they come back together again. In MacPaint there is no distinction between words and pictures.

The characters in our alphabet actually started out as pictures. They are a human-made object. They did not come from nowhere and get fixed in stone. They have changed and evolved over the centuries. It is important to realize that all notations, whether music, or language, or computer languages, are just made up. They are symbols that can be changed. There is a choice. The ability to change notation empowers human beings.

Jaron Lanier

FROM NEW Mexico and West Texas where Jaron Lanier grew up, he moved to California in 1981 with the intention of carving out, as he says, "some sort of hippie-like lifestyle in Santa Cruz, playing flute in the mall." But it never worked out. Instead, at the age of 25, Lanier finds himself running his own company called Visual Programming Languages, and developing products most of us never dream could exist. He initially entered the computer world by programming the sound portion of video games. Eventually, he developed whole video games while working at Atari. His most successful video game was Moon Dust, which made the Omni top ten in 1983. Currently, his work as a programmer centers on the development of a language Lanier believes could revolutionize the computer industry. He resides in Palo Alto, California.

After some searching, I found Jaron Lanier's house on a small, rather obscure dirt road off El Camino Way, a small circular road branching off from the well-traveled El Camino Real in Palo Alto. I parked my car behind several others in the driveway and wandered up a short path to the small cottage-style house, painted white with blue trim. Overgrown bushes graced the house and gave a comfortable, unkempt air, a lived-in look. I paused on the porch at the front door, wondering what I would find inside, and then I knocked, expecting the unexpected.

Hundreds of old musical instruments, many of them exotic, filled the front room where I waited. Strewn on top of the coffee table were flutes and recorders of various sizes, most made from bamboo. A variety of lute instruments, including mandolins, hung on the walls. Tacked up on the wall across from me was a batik fabric. It was not centered nor especially straight. In one corner stood an upright piano with the box opened so that the strings were exposed. Against the adjoining wall stood a Yamaha synthesizer, and next to it was a Macintosh computer. These were the most modern instruments in the room. Directly across from where I sat was a bookshelf that was filled with books on a wide range of topics from Buddhism to Small Talk.

Jaron bounded into the room wearing sandals and a short-sleeved royal blue shirt with the collar unbuttoned and the shirttail outside his pants. He was a big, heavy-set young fellow with curly light-brown hair, a beard, and big alert hazel eyes. He smiled widely and greeted me with an excited, animated voice, and then sat down in a chair next to the futon sofa where I sat. After we talked a while, I got the distinct impression Jaron was a free-thinking, unpredictable sort of guy who was always full of ideas and whimsy. When I remarked, gesturing to the instruments, about Jaron's obvious love of music, he quipped that he was a member of the musical-instrument-of-the-week club.

Throughout the interview, Jaron seemed to instill the computer with a mystery and an offbeat future that most people within the industry had not envisioned. He posed the question, "What if the computer affected your reality and the way you perceive things?"

INTERVIEWER: *What are you doing with programming languages now?*

LANIER: Well, basically, I'm working on a programming language that's much easier to use.

INTERVIEWER: *Easier because it uses symbols and graphics?*

LANIER: It needs text, too. It's not exclusively graphics. With a regular language, you tell the computer what to do and it does it. On the surface, that sounds perfectly reasonable. But in order to write instructions (programs) for the computer, you have to simulate in your head an enormous, elaborate structure. Anytime there's a flaw in this great mental simulation, it turns into a bug in the program. It's hard for people to simulate that enormous structure in their heads. Now, what I am doing is building very visual, concrete models of what goes on inside the computer. In this way, you can see the program while you're creating it. You can mold it directly and alter it when you want. You will no longer have to simulate the program in your head.

INTERVIEWER: *Where did you get the inspiration to create this particular programming language?*

LANIER: When I was doing video games, I realized programs could be a lot of things. They could be forms of expression, teaching tools—many things. And I thought that ordinary people should be able to make them, that hackers shouldn't have the exclusive ability to write programs. People should be able to speak and breathe programs just like they talk now. Making little worlds inside the computer should be as easy as saying hello to your friends in the morning. I really believe we're going to get to that point, and that it will be a very profound type of communication.

INTERVIEWER: *Do you mean people will be able to communicate through programs in the future?*

LANIER: Sure. Imagine we're cave people, and someone comes along and somehow communicates to us that there's this thing called language that we can speak. And you ask him, "What's that for?" We're in a similar situation today. Now we use symbols, called words, that when spoken invoke meanings in our minds. But what is more interesting to me is that you can actually build full models of concepts instead of just giving them names. For example, we can say "solar system" and we can say "planets go around," and we can describe it. But with a computer you can actually build one, an actual simulation of the concept you're talking about. I think this capacity to make models, as opposed to just giving concepts names, will be the most worthwhile contribution computers will make for humanity. It will eventually allow people to really communicate ideas they can barely communicate now.

INTERVIEWER: *What kind of progress are you making?*

LANIER: Oh, great. The biggest problem we've had is a hardware problem. One of the major problems with the computer world right now is that when you start working with a particular machine, by the time you finish the project, the machine isn't around anymore. That's set us back a bit. The full-blown, professional version of what we're working on won't reach the world for a couple of years yet. But when it does, it will really change the way people think about programming. Everyone will program. I'm serious. You'll like programming because it will be fun.

INTERVIEWER: *Are you aiming at the mass audience? Are you trying to replace the programming languages that are in use today?*

> *"Computers right now are ridiculous. They hardly do anything for people."*

LANIER: None of those are reaching the mass audience, despite Turbo Pascal selling half a million or whatever. That's hardly a mass audience. So, yes, I am aiming at the mass audience that programming languages have never reached before. But I'm also aiming at those people already using programming languages. One of the characteristics of my language is that it has a rather chameleon-like form to it. I can't explain too much about it technically. It can mimic a traditional language, or it can take on the appearance of C, for example, for people who are used to that language. It will be very graceful. People will be able to adapt to it gradually without feeling a sudden change.

INTERVIEWER: *So why can't you explain very much now about the language technically?*

LANIER: Because there's a company involved and, you know, the usual big black wall of trade secrets.

INTERVIEWER: *Your company is Visual Programming Languages, VPL. How did you go about starting a company?*

LANIER: Oh, well, when you get right down to it, it really just happened. I was doing this work on languages, and various people were very supportive of me. I came to a point where I ran out of money and they said, "Let's invest in it." And, "ta-da," there was the company.

INTERVIEWER: *What originally brought you to programming?*

LANIER: I once saw someone using a word processor and I thought, "What an amazing thing. If you could make one of those for music, wouldn't it be great!" I was a composer at the time. That was five or six years ago. I thought it was a great idea, but I never built one. I put it off to build this more general, more powerful tool. With what we are working on, it will be much easier to build a word processor for music, or a hundred other tools.

INTERVIEWER: *Did you study programming in school?*

LANIER: No. I didn't think it made sense. I was more interested in the computer conceptually. So I began to track down many of the people who invented computers. They're all still alive and they're even accessible. You can just call them up. I learned what they thought about computers in the old days. Nobody really sat down in the beginning and thought about what a computer would be like. Initially, people thought of them in terms of different metaphors, mostly in mathematical terms. The impression I got was that the whole process of developing computers was kind of random. That's not to belittle the people who invented them, because they did a wonderful, wonderful thing. But it's just not possible to see the future. Today, we're using computers to do tasks they were never originally designed to do. What I mean is, the idea of what a programming language is doesn't really relate very well to using them to process words. Programming languages were invented by people who thought mathematically, and word processing was invented by those who thought about business and offices; two separate worlds. Different people look at the same idea in different ways.

INTERVIEWER: *Do you mean the original idea went through changes in the process of becoming reality?*

LANIER: See, what I'm doing goes way back to the fifties. I'm going back and taking a fork in the road that everyone passed by. Everyone in programming today is talking about different ways of telling the computer what to do. My programming language doesn't do that. With mine, you actually look at what the program is doing and you mess with it until it's right. It's really a different process.

For example, you have a recipe, which a person follows to make a cake or something. That's what current programming is like. On the other hand, there's tuning your car's engine. You watch the thing running and see what it does and change it until it works the way you want it to. My programming language is more like the latter.

INTERVIEWER: *Are you saying there's not much creativity in the way people program today?*

LANIER: No, no. The way people program is great. There are a lot of great programmers around. I'm saying that the languages they use are awkward. They're being impaired. And in particular, a lot of people who should be making interesting programs aren't, because the languages are too difficult for them to even consider it. With my programming language, people who are trying to convey ideas in any field—history, philosophy, politics, psychology, and certainly in the sciences and mathematics—will be able to create their own programs.

INTERVIEWER: *Which programmers do you especially admire?*

LANIER: Oh, gosh, there are a lot of brilliant people. Just this morning I was talking to Dan Ingels, who is one of the original SmallTalk crew. He's a very inspiring person. And some of the generation who invented computers are just really wonderful, like Doug Ingelbart. He came up with the mouse and windows, among other things; the whole world that Xerox and the Macintosh were based on. He's still around. He lives in Menlo Park. There's Marvin Minsky. He kind of invented artificial intelligence. He's an inspiring guy.

INTERVIEWER: *What do you think of artificial intelligence?*

LANIER: I think the term is an odd one. Calling it artificial intelligence is pretty strange. People are associating consciousness with behavior, that is, the displayed ability to accomplish certain tasks. I don't see them being connected at all. It seems clear that you can get computers to behave in any way you can program them to behave. Some programs might be so complicated that you want to call them intelligent, but it's kind of a meaningless term to me. What they are doing at MIT is really quite interesting: teaching a program to recognize a certain picture. But all the expert systems are bogus. There's no content whatsoever in a lot of the commercial products that are called AI. Artificial intelligence means different things to different people.

INTERVIEWER: *Do you see your language being used commercially?*

LANIER: Oh, sure. It will have a profound effect commercially. It will make developing software much faster, and therefore cheaper. It will also totally change the way people choose software and the way they design software. Right now, because the technology is so new, you can sell software based on the sole attribute that it works. In the future, software standards will be much higher. People will say, "Of course it works. I can make it work." And they will ask, "Does it make me feel good? Does it help me think in the way I want to? Does it, in some way, match the way I write?" I think that computer programming will soon be judged a little more on its quality and aesthetic content, and a little less on just the basis of whether it works or not.

INTERVIEWER: Will your visual programming language look beautiful? What exactly will it look like?

LANIER: What is aesthetics in programming all about? Well, it depends on the program. One very important kind of program is an editor, which helps you make text. A graphics program like MacPaint helps you make pictures. And there are programs to help you make music. Now, if you observe these programs at work, you will notice that they all have assumptions built in about what you are going to do with them. With word processors it isn't so bad because, with text, you are basically just putting words in the right order. But with pictures or music you really start seeing the limitations. MacPaint, for example, won't let you turn images; the ability just isn't there. In addition, it's not so much that the specific ability isn't there, but that the ways the program presents ideas doesn't match the way you think. Some people may not think in terms of the specific lines or line quality and other terms of form and tone as they are presented. Instead of there being just *one* right word processor or graphics program, people will soon be looking for a program that suits the way they work. Does this program match the way I think? Does it flow with me when I want to do something with it? That's one kind of aesthetics.

> *"What I am doing is building very visual, concrete models of what goes on inside the computer."*

Another kind of aesthetics can be found in the way a program expresses something to you. For instance, take the solar-system simulation I mentioned earlier. With educational software like that, the issues are different. How well does the program explain the subject? How eloquent is it? Does it let you interact with it in such a way that you really get insights that are different than you would get from just watching a movie of the same thing? There will be more kinds of aesthetics in the future. It so hard to predict. When movies started, people didn't have any idea what they would be like. Computers are just starting now and we don't have the slightest idea about their future.

INTERVIEWER: As you develop a new programming language, do you plan the whole thing out beforehand or figure it out as you go along?

LANIER: I know a little bit about it before I really start. I've been doing partial language versions on smaller machines and working my way up to the complete version.

INTERVIEWER: *You have quite a collection of musical instruments. Which is your favorite?*

LANIER: I don't know. It changes every week. I belong to the instrument-of-the-week club. They mail me this funny instrument from some different part of the world every week. Actually, musical instruments have a lot to do with computers. They're one of the best examples of user interfaces in the world. They're very inspiring to study.

INTERVIEWER: *How can the computer be used in music?*

LANIER: As an example, I have a program that makes an editor for canons. A canon is like a round, where people sing or play the same melody, but the melodies start at different times and then mingle together. With this program, you enter one note at one place and the program automatically enters all the voices. You can immediately hear how the canon comes together. Usually, canons are very hard to write, but with this program, they can be much easier to write.

INTERVIEWER: *Do you think more and more people are going to be composing music with the help of computers?*

LANIER: Maybe. I hope so. Music is already pretty easy to make when you come right down to it. It's really a question of motivation. For the serious composer, the computer is just great. Now, the composers have to copy all the different parts of the music for all the different musicians, so the computer's wonderful for them. With popular music now, you basically just listen to it, but I think more and more music will become interactive. You will actually interact with the music, with other people, and with dance. I think we'll see a lot of that soon.

INTERVIEWER: *Do you ever apply your background in composing music to developing your programming language?*

LANIER: A lot of people who are into computers and math are also into music. Music is similar to programming languages in that it has a fairly elaborate kind of notation, music notation. But even more, it's the musical instruments themselves that are a lot like what I am trying to do. Because, with my language, you interact with a program while it's running instead of specifying in advance what it should do and then hoping it will run right. It's more like playing a musical instrument rather than looking at a piece of music.

INTERVIEWER: *Do you consider programming an art, or a science, or a skill, or a trade, or...?*

LANIER: Well, computers don't have any quality in themselves. They're absolutely empty things, tabula rasa. Since they are such empty minds, it depends entirely on the person involved, more so than in any other field of human endeavor. That's why I'm designing my language to be able to take on so many different forms; it will have to do that to meet the needs of different people. I treat programming more as an art than anything else. I was talking with Peter Deutsch on a television program last weekend. He said programming was a craft. Then there are some people who think of it as mathematics. It just depends on the person.

INTERVIEWER: *Do you ever get tired of working with computers and programs all the time?*

LANIER: Oh, sure, especially the way they are today. Computers are very frustrating machines to work with, and programming can drive you crazy. Yes, definitely.

INTERVIEWER: *Do you work regular hours?*

LANIER: You know the answer to that one; they're very irregular. Especially these days with the company. I tend to work in the middle of the night just so I can get things done.

INTERVIEWER: *Are you working on other things besides your language?*

LANIER: Well, it's all just the language. There are specific parts of the language that have applications in different areas. For instance, there's one subset of what we're doing that applies to medicine; we're doing some projects for the local hospital.

Developing my language is frustrating in a way. I'd like to spend twenty-four hours a day working with the language instead of having to share my time with running a company. But the programming work itself is great. It's really fun. Any time there's an improvement, it's very tangible; it's right there on the screen. That kind of progress is very gratifying.

INTERVIEWER: *When you were involved with games, what kind of games did you do?*

LANIER: I did music for various people's games. There are some Electronic Arts programs out with my music. My most successful game is called Moon Dust. It made the Omni top ten in 1983 and supported me for a year. It's a very abstract and experimental game, which made its success all the more delightful. It has music and little spaceships that fly around leaving fading trails that sparkle. You fly the spaceships and influence the music, trying to play it but not hit any wrong notes. There was a scoring system that nobody paid any attention to. I think people just liked playing with the pretty music and the pretty visuals.

INTERVIEWER: *What do you think about the future of computers?*

LANIER: Computers right now are ridiculous. They hardly do anything for people. In the near future, it's going to be a boring struggle for the marketplace. Everybody will be concentrating on these big companies that still have not computerized. But there are software and hardware developments that, in the next few years, will totally turn the computer world around. They'll catch everyone by surprise. So it will become very interesting.

> "People should be able to speak and breathe programs just like they talk now."

The whole structure of the computer world is based on the assumption that computers and programs are difficult to make. And that's the reason program vendors like Lotus can become so monolithic; finally, there's a decent program and there's an avalanche of popularity. In the future, there will be a multitude of very good programs and anybody will be able to make them.

INTERVIEWER: *Are you saying that an individual will write his own programs in the future?*

LANIER: Well, of course most people won't, but a lot of people will. It will be just like books today. Everyone's basically literate, and the difference between a person who writes a book and the person who doesn't is a question of drive, enthusiasm, and business sense, not a question of being able to write or not. Creating programs will be the same way.

Also, if somebody wants to come out with a new computer that isn't MS-DOS standard, they won't be scared to do so because it will be so much easier to have a software base for it. Today, people are building whole computers just to run certain software. In the future, it will be totally the opposite. Compatibility won't be as important when it's easy to make software. It will be like transcribing a piece of music from clarinet to violin: You have to change little things here and there, but it won't be that big a deal.

INTERVIEWER: *Do you see the computer becoming more of a creative tool and less business oriented?*

LANIER: Actually, the business world is, like computers, entirely created by people. God didn't come down and say there will be a corporation and it will have a board of directors. We made that up. Business is a very ritualistic thing. It changes very slowly, so it's hard to say what will happen in business in the future. It won't necessarily be rational. You know that legions of business people still use Cobol programs on big machines, even though it doesn't make any sense at all? What can one say about that?

In general, I think computers will be used for creative purposes more, and for business more. Right now, computers don't do that much for people. Word processing is somewhat better than typing, and databases occasionally work pretty well, especially for large companies. The problem is that software is so hard to write. Instead of a constantly evolving body of software getting better and better, we have a situation in which evolution just freezes when a certain software reaches a certain adequate level. Everyone's so glad just to have something that works.

INTERVIEWER: Do you think that eventually programming languages will replace spoken and written languages like English?

LANIER: Not at all. English will never be replaced by a programming language, because there's so much built up around it. There's Shakespeare, there's all our expressions. . . .

INTERVIEWER: Well, what about hieroglyphics? They disappeared.

LANIER: That's because all the people who used them were killed. But even if they were still around, they probably would be using a descendant of hieroglyphics. I think computers will provide a new form of expression, and people will recognize that both English and computers are good for expressing different things. In some areas today, English is being stretched. When you talk about ideas, in philosophy, economics, politics, people almost never understand what they are saying to each other. With computers, you can actually build models of whole interactive systems of ideas, or concepts, or even styles of thinking. These will be better expressed by models built on a computer. English is very good at describing, and computers are good at modeling. In the future, the two will become mixed and each will be just a part of the way we communicate with each other. Together they will improve the way we communicate. And whenever people communicate, they stand a better chance at having empathy for one another.

INTERVIEWER: Do you think the concept of the Dynabook will ever become a reality?

LANIER: Only as a passing phase. The Dynabook is one thing that will move through pretty quickly, probably within the space of a decade.

INTERVIEWER: *Move through into what?*

LANIER: Well, I'll tell you, but you might not believe me. Let's see, right now your interaction with a computer is confined to a screen. What if the computer affected the way you perceive things? Not changing the real physical world, but creating essentially 3-D objects around you. They aren't really there, but people can see them and share the experience. People's daily lives will include images that are computer generated. That's the technology we are working on. And, unfortunately, I can't really describe it in any more detail now. I know it sounds totally loony, but it's really going to happen.

INTERVIEWER: *The computer will generate objects that aren't really there? Perceptual models?*

LANIER: I know that sounds very confusing. Let's just say they are well-controlled hallucinations. Actually, it's nothing that weird. It will all be very straightforward. One thing I can say is, you'll probably wear special glasses that will help create the images. And people will be able to share these images and talk by radio.

INTERVIEWER: *So, instead of having a printer next to our computers, we'll have some kind of image generator?*

LANIER: Yes, right. There was a cartoon in the Sunday paper last week that showed a hacker turning into different forms. Did you see that? It was amazingly on track. I think that, ultimately, computers will generate additional realities for us. And they will do this in ways that won't detract from the physical world, but will in fact help us appreciate the real world.

INTERVIEWER: *Do you see genetics merging with computers?*

LANIER: Maybe. There may be optical computers, there may be chemical computers. There are obviously biological ones because parts, if not all, of our brains are computers. It's a hardware question. How do you get the actual technology of the computer to work? But there's an entirely different question that is the important one to me: What culture do you make up so you can actually use this technology? The technological question is basically engineering, you know. If we want to make a Dynabook, someone will figure out how to make one. If you want to make a very, very dense memory that's based on enzymes or some ridiculous thing, who knows, somebody can figure out how to do it. But when it comes to culture, you really have to invent it—invent a whole new world out of nothing. When you have a Dynabook, what do you do with it? How does it operate with the rest of the world? And how does it fit in with regular books? With lunch boxes? With video games?

INTERVIEWER: *Don't cultures just evolve?*

LANIER: No, they're invented. They're made up, either by people who are conscious of making them up or by people who aren't conscious that they're making them up. The twentieth century is full of examples because we've made up so much stuff. TV didn't exist before, and now a lot of people in America spend more time watching TV than anything else except sleeping.

INTERVIEWER: *But when TV was invented, they didn't know they were creating a culture.*

LANIER: No. The people who invented the actual TV tube and stuff didn't do it. The people who created the culture were the people in Hollywood who made up the programs, and the people who figured out how to sell TV. There's a whole bunch of people who did it, not just one person. Photography was made up from scratch by people who had to figure out what the hell a photograph was and what it meant. The same with movies. What's happened to computers so far has been made up by people. I think it's good to be conscious of the process. I'm glad that, from the beginning of computers, people have been thinking about the political and ethical implications. The computer world itself has really benefited from that. I think so far it's been a somewhat more self-conscious endeavor than TV or photography.

> *"Programming will soon be judged... more on its quality and aesthetic content, and less on... whether it works or not."*

INTERVIEWER: *What about the power of information? Is that the most important aspect of computers? So many people say that's what makes the computer so important to our society.*

LANIER: Well, all the computer can really do is manipulate information. And information is a rather broad term. It basically covers all human experience. But when people talk about the power of information, I think what they mean is something more specific, that our society is organizing itself more and more around things that don't physically exist. Information, concepts of living, computer memories, the true existence of a corporation, one's wealth, or power, or status, or one's job—all these can be defined by information held in a computer. We are in a transition period. Until now, what we have wanted from life had to be got by manipulating physical matter. Now, we are just starting to organize our lives according to information. Eventually, our very experiences will be generated by information instead of the other way around. That will be the true information age.

INTERVIEWER: *Won't the physical world's importance be diminished?*

LANIER: No, not one bit. Not any more than having computer music threatens acoustic instruments, or having photography threatens the existence of painting. I believe it will help us get a much more objective view, a more appreciative view, of the physical world. And of nature. I think it will spawn a stronger ecology movement, for instance. Just on a practical level, people will be able to have experiences without having to change the physical world, without screwing it up. This is a very large topic. I'm writing a book on it, by the way. It's called *New Natures*, about what it will be like to have arbitrary worlds.

INTERVIEWER: *Do you think some young people who are interested in computers today are thinking along the same lines?*

LANIER: Yes, I think so. It's very hard to generalize, in spite of the stereotypes. Like the one that programmers all dress terribly, stay up all night, and all that. There's a current generation that is pretty much oriented toward the Macintosh type of thing. I think we are at a very fundamental level right now. People are still trying to come up with a decent piece of software for somebody to use. In the next few years, life is really going to change. It's very exciting to think that it's the young kids, the generation being born right now, who are going to grow up with this new technology. They are going to be the ones to really benefit from what we've been talking about.

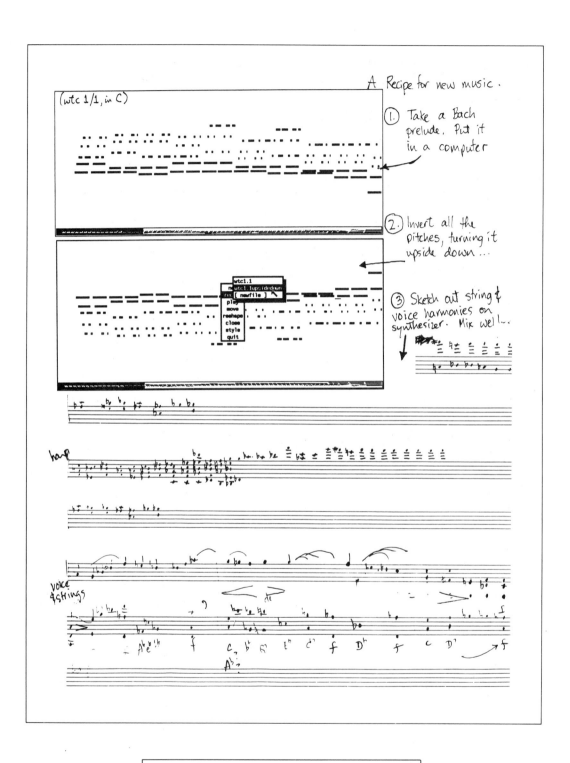

A new way to compose music from the mind of Michael Hawley. The Appendix (pages 357-360) describes Hawley's ideas for a musical computer.

Michael Hawley

CURRENTLY working as a digital audio programmer for The Droid Works, an affiliate of Lucasfilm Ltd. charged with the monumental task of computerizing the filmmaking process, Michael Hawley has been involved in the development of the software for the SoundDroid, which is the all-digital sound studio in a box. It is capable of storing, recording, editing, and mixing sound, as well as reproducing it for immediate playback.

Hawley, who is twenty-four, got involved with computers and programming as a youth growing up in New Providence, a suburb of New York City. Throughout high school and college, he worked at the neighboring Bell Labs offices in Murray Hill. While cultivating his interest in computers at Bell Labs, Hawley pursued serious studies in music and the piano at Yale University, where, in 1983, he earned his bachelor's degree in music and computer science. Shortly after graduation, he went to IRCAM (Institut de Recherche et Coordination Acoustique Musique) in Paris as a visiting researcher from Bell Labs. While in Paris, he prototyped user interfaces for computer-music applications, and also performed in the world premiere of a sonata for two pianos and electronic tape in the IRCAM concert series. After IRCAM, Hawley moved west and joined The Droid Works in Marin County, California.

A film crew with lights, cameras, and sound equipment milled about the grounds as I approached the building where the offices of The Droid Works were located. This was my first indication that The Droid Works was actually more a part of the movie-entertainment industry than of the traditional software and computer industry.

Michael Hawley led me into the office he shares with another programmer. He had blondish-brown, tousled hair and a dark moustache, and he was wearing a bicycle racing outfit and wire-rimmed, blue-tinted sunglasses. In Hawley's half of the room, he had arranged his synthesizer, amplifier, and speakers adjacent to his computer terminal and keyboard. In this somewhat overcrowded and cluttered environment, Hawley goes about his work and his passion, composing music and creating computer programs that manipulate and edit music, sound tracks, and film. At several points during the interview, Hawley turned to his keyboard to play a piece he had composed or to demonstrate how the software he has developed can be used to manipulate sounds and create music. His mission, I gathered, is to master the tools of computers and software so that he can apply them to music, the arts, and other media. In an enthusiastic, articulate, and playful manner, Hawley related his experiences as a programmer and as a musician.

HAWLEY: I understand you're just off the plane from Seattle. I was recently up in the Northwest on a fantastic trip. There was an international computer-music conference in Vancouver.

INTERVIEWER: Yes, I read about it, but I didn't go.

HAWLEY: Maybe you were at Digicon? No, that was the week before. There are so many computer conferences. Well, here's the story and, I promise, it does relate to programming.

David Salisen, who works here in the graphics group, flies small planes, so we decided that it would be real neat to fly up to Vancouver in a small plane. Margaret Minsky was here, and so she and Mark Leather, who is a hardware designer and also in the graphics group here, and David and I all piled into the plane and flew up. It was fantastic. We circled around the top of Mt. Shasta, went right over Crater Lake, and buzzed through the steam inside the crater of Mount St. Helens. In your own small plane, you can just go wherever you feel like going, so we popped over to the Olympic Peninsula and went backpacking for three days, and then flew into Vancouver. Mark and Margaret couldn't go to the conference, so we dropped them in Seattle, and David and I went on to Vancouver.

The conference was kind of a drag. Computer-music conferences can be stuffy, but the people were wonderful, some papers were interesting, and the salmon sushi was great. Right after the conference, a woman I sold some MusicDroid T-shirts to suggested that since we had a plane, we should go over to the west shore of Vancouver Island to some hot springs out in the middle of nowhere. That was probably the prettiest flying of the entire trip. I never knew there were so many mountains on Vancouver Island. They're really jagged, waves and waves of them. They look something like Loren Carpenter's fractal mountains.

> *"As a new experimental tool, the computer is highly valued."*

We set the plane down on a weedy little runway near a tiny town called Tofino. From there we took a cab into the middle of the town—a very picturesque coastal fishing village, with fishing boats in the harbor going buga-buga-buga, and mountains tumbling into the sea, and little fingers of fog lacing the hillsides. In Tofino we arranged to take a seaplane up to the hot springs. They packed the three of us and a small native Indian family into a DeHavilland Beaver, and we flew up and right down again, and got out in the middle of nowhere. The Indians had a reservation farther on, so they kept going.

We hiked through dense coastal rain forest over rotting boardwalk trails for about two miles. It was just like the first scene from *Raiders of the Lost Ark*, with the moss hanging down and the sunlight filtering through. Finally we arrived at the hot springs, which were simply beautiful. Hot water bubbled up out of the ground and trickled down about two hundred yards, where it went into the ocean. Along the way, the water flowed over a waterfall about ten feet high. If you stood underneath, you got a really nice hot shower. From there, it flowed through a succession of little pools between the rocks, each one big enough to hold three or four people comfortably. The rocks were covered with soft, slimy moss. Each pool was a little bit cooler than the previous one, so you could find any temperature you wanted, from the coolness of the ocean to as hot as you could stand it. Down at the bottom of this area you could sit in the pool and have hot water "jacuzziing" all over your back, and every once in a while a big ocean wave would come rolling in and freeze you, then some more hot water would flow down to warm you up again.

We set up camp and ate dinner. I had brought a bottle of sake along, so we put it in the water and warmed it up, and sat there with not a soul around, drinking sake and watching the stars come out. It was perfect. The next day we hiked out and flew back.

INTERVIEWER: *How does this relate to computers and programming?*

HAWLEY: The point was not just to go to the computer-music conference and suck up the technology; how you get there can be just as interesting and just as important. You shouldn't waste opportunities when they arrive. It's the same thing in programming. You uncover lots of stones along the way. New doors and unexpected passageways open up as you develop a program. Workstations and personal computers are kind of like small planes: There are discoveries just waiting to be made if people steer them in the right direction (and get lucky).

INTERVIEWER: *What are you working on at Lucasfilm?*

HAWLEY: How much do you know about Lucasfilm and what happens in the computer division? Shall I give you the spiel?

INTERVIEWER: *Yes.*

HAWLEY: Okay. It goes something like this: Around 1979, George Lucas offered a contract to anyone to come in and computerize the most interesting aspects of filmmaking. The people who impressed him most were from the New York Institute of Technology—Ed Catmull, Alvy Ray Smith, and some others. So they packed up, moved to Marin County, and began the Lucasfilm computer-research division. Catmull identified three primary areas of application. One was graphics and image processing, or image research. Another was audio and sound, and the third was what you could call "word processing" for filmmakers. In the film business, they needed a "word processor" program for the people who cut pictures, because it takes a long time to snip celluloid with razor blades and paste it together, just like it does to type and retype and edit text on an old-fashioned typewriter.

The graphics group has done basic research in computer imagery, just as they set out to do, and they've been relatively unfettered in that regard. Only a couple times have they had to go off and do productions. For instance, they created the genesis sequence from the second *Star Trek* movie, some segments in the *Star Wars films*, and a beautiful little computer-generated animation last year. Most recently, they created a fantastic sequence for a Spielberg

306

film called *The Adventures of Young Sherlock Holmes*. There's another group within the graphics division that's doing laser scanning and printing of color film. They use three color lasers—red, green, and blue—to read and write color film at very high resolution. This is something like the laser printing you know—you can turn the little pixels on and off—but this one is in color, and can both read and write. The lasers are supposed to be an input/output device for the Pixar. The idea is, if you want to, say, create a scene in which Princess Leia flies through Muir Woods on a speeder bike, you take pictures of Leia sitting in front of a blue screen matte, and pictures of Muir Woods, and scan it all in using the lasers. Once you have the data, you can use the Pixar to composite the images together. Since it's a digital process, the compositing is perfect, without the ugly "matte lines" you can get with the optical process. It's also very fast.

The graphics group built a machine that is pretty interesting, called the Pixar Image Computer, which you may have heard of, since the group is spinning off to form a new company called Pixar. The Pixar is a specialized computer for processing digital images. The architecture of the machine came out of some very nice algorithms for picture compositing, so it's efficient and very elegant. I think it was Lucas who said, "Not only is the Pixar like a custom hot rod for picture compositing, but everyone else wants to use it to drive to work in." It has profound and far-reaching potential for applications in medical imagery, modeling of seismic data, and more. Just about any kind of graphical data that you can splat up on a screen, you can manipulate with this machine in dazzling ways. The graphics group has focused on research, and their general goal all along has been to bring the richest possible kinds of computer imagery to the world of filmmaking. Computer creations have to be rich to stand in the same scene with natural images.

INTERVIEWER: *What about the audio group within Lucasfilm?*

HAWLEY: I'm in the audio group, and our charter was also quite general—to computerize anything and everything that had to do with sound in the filmmaking process. That's turned out to be a very interesting problem. If you look at the post-production phase of filmmaking, two or three people can edit the pictures, but it takes a large staff of people to deal with all the sound. There's so much sound in the background and foreground that people don't consciously notice, but they'd miss if it weren't there. Reels and reels of dialogue, music, special effects like spaceship noises, laser blasts, a special track for Darth Vader's heavy breathing, all in different versions and renditions, to give mixers the best ingredients to blend. It's a monumental job. A lot of information has to be tracked.

Andy Moorer was brought in to head our group. He's a pioneer in computer music and digital audio, with degrees from MIT and Stanford. He used to work at IRCAM in Paris. That's Pierre Boulez's Institut de Recherche et Coordination Acoustique Musique, an institute for research in acoustics and new music. Andy formed this group and set about building a computer called

> "Lucasfilm seemed the ideal place for computer-science research."

the ASP, Audio Signal Processor. What the Pixar does for graphics, the ASP does for audio. Once the sounds are turned into numbers, you can do all sorts of arbitrary and wonderful things with them. For instance, you can take the functionality in a big multitrack Hollywood mixing desk—the equalizers, level meters, and various kinds of processors—and squash it all down into a program inside this machine. With the ASP, machines like equalizers are no longer pieces of hardware; they are just little chunks of microcode that buzz around inside the machine. They can do whatever you want them to do.

We've used the ASP in a system called SoundDroid, which is like a word-processing system for sound people. You look at a screen and see images that represent different sound tracks, and you can cut and paste bits of sound simply by pressing on a touch screen. You don't have to wait for film to rewind, or for audio tapes to be cut and copied. You can very freely sprinkle bits of sound all around without having to directly manipulate the film. It's a big leap up, and will have some profound implications in the compositional process, just as word processing does for people who compose text.

The third group built a machine called the EditDroid. The idea behind this machine is word processing for picture cutters. The film is transferred to a video media, like video disc or video tape, and that gives a computer random access down to an individual frame. With the help of this computer, you only have to cut the actual film once. Using the EditDroid, you can very freely cut and splice bits of film and experiment and play with your composition, and then press a button to instantly preview what you've assembled. When you've achieved a good performance, you press a button and the EditDroid spits out a list that tells where you're supposed to cut the real film.

So the Pixar, the SoundDroid, and the EditDroid are the three most tangible "products" of the computer division.

INTERVIEWER: *How did you get involved in all of this?*

HAWLEY: Before I explain that, I should quickly tell you where things are now and where they're going at Lucasfilm. George Lucas is trying to keep his focus on making films. He is a filmmaker, not a computer scientist, and he doesn't want to diversify and diffuse his funds, especially not now, because he's pouring lots of money into the construction of Skywalker Ranch. Skywalker will be a moviemaking enclave. It's splendiferously beautiful; it has a grand scale, like a good French chateau, and it's secluded in the woods of northern Marin. It promises to be a filmmaker's paradise.

Building the ranch is a costly undertaking, and it's one reason why there haven't been any big Lucasfilm productions for a while, as you may have noticed. Lucasfilm seems content to spin off the computer division to form new companies. The graphics group will become Pixar, and will market the Pixar processor and other high-quality image technology. And there's our company, which is called The Droid Works, which will sell EditDroid, SoundDroid, and other computerized assistants for filmmakers. So bits and pieces of the computer division are spinning off now, and people are kind of dizzy as we move out of the research stage and into development, to get these systems out into the hands of real filmmakers. That's where we are right now.

How did I get into all this? Well, let's see. I was born on a Marine Corps base in southern California, moved to New Jersey before I was one, and was seduced into computing at an early age. Bell Labs at Murray Hill was right up the hill from my house.

INTERVIEWER: *That's where you grew up?*

HAWLEY: Yes, I grew up in New Providence, a little suburb of New York, with no movie theater, no bars. But Bell Labs was up there on the hill, and I got a job working in the linguistics department there doing some computer stuff when I was fifteen or sixteen, just old enough to get working papers. I picked up on the computer projects—there was some pretty neat research going on there. One fellow had built a digital synthesizer, which was particularly fun to play with.

From high school through college, various other people at Bell Labs picked me up, saying, "Here, why don't you try this for a while," and I would. For a couple years (off and on) I worked in a cognitive psychology group doing really interesting, basic research into problems of communication, especially between people and computers. Psychologists are particularly excited about computers, because it's like having a big lens you can use to zoom in and see what's going on in people's minds.

INTERVIEWER: In what way does a computer help psychologists look into people's minds?

HAWLEY: As soon as you put a computer in the middle of a communications process, the information gets squeezed through a tight little channel, and you can use the computer to count, massage, and simply observe the information in new ways. Computers constrain users, and force designers to think deeply about what people really want to do with an application, and about how tasks are best presented. They help us focus on communications problems and force us to appreciate the psychological boundaries in ways we couldn't before. As a new experimental tool, the computer is highly valued. New discoveries require new tools.

After high school and my experience at Bell Labs, I went to Yale and did a double major in music and computer science. I spent most of my time playing piano, which at the time was more fun than computing. But it's a painful way to make a living compared to computer science....

INTERVIEWER: So many people are involved in both music and computers. Do you see a lot of parallels between the two?

HAWLEY: Absolutely. On general principles, I think mixing up computers with artistic media is a refreshing way to approach and think about both art and technology.

Through Yale and during summers, I continued working at Bell Labs. After school, I bought a 1966 Ford station wagon for $150, drove to Alaska and went canoeing for a while. Then I came back and worked at Bell Labs some more, and then spent a month at Barry Vercoe's experimental music studio at MIT. It's now part of the Arts and Media Technology Center there. And then I went to IRCAM in Paris.

INTERVIEWER: What did you do at IRCAM?

HAWLEY: I played the worst piece ever written for piano. Actually, I went over to IRCAM to be a visiting researcher from Bell Labs, and to prototype user interfaces for computer-music applications. This was the fall of 1983, and people were just beginning to use bit-mapped graphics displays in the real world. Before then, graphics displays were relegated to research places, like

Xerox PARC. So I carried a big, bit-mapped graphics terminal from Bell Labs with me on the plane to Paris. I got it over there, and I thought I had all the right papers. At least, I had everything IRCAM told me to get, but Customs thought otherwise. I tried to walk through the gate, saying, "Oh no, no, nothing to declare, not me," but they snagged me. That was the beginning of a succession of interrogations and fines. The upshot of it was, they took my terminal away, and owing to normal French bureaucratic red tape, it was not released for about five weeks. About a third of my time in Paris was burned from the start.

I found myself with five weeks of nothing to do. I spent my time learning about the computer research that was going on at IRCAM, and boning up on my knowledge of French language, French food, and French wine.

INTERVIEWER: *Paris is not a bad place to be with nothing specific to do.*

HAWLEY: Right! And I could hardly resist getting roped into playing a piano concert. A crazy Romanian pianist came by my office one night and said, "Hey, want to play a concert?" The concert was on my birthday in November, the concert fee was enticing, and besides, there was nothing for me to program in the meantime, since my terminal was still stuck in customs. The concert was in the Grande Salle of the Centre Georges Pompidou, and it was the world premiere, the Creation Mondiale of a massive work, and the composer was flying in. It sounded great, so I said, "Sure, what the heck."

INTERVIEWER: *What piece did you play?*

HAWLEY: It was a sonata for two pianos and electronic tape: a huge and curious work, about 30,000 rather random notes, often harshly banged out on two beautiful, Hamburg "D" concert grands.

We played the concert, which failed in the public eye, I believe, but I had a blast. Half the audience left, and many others booed. A small crowd of my IRCAM friends were there, and applauded loudly, and gave me flowers. The piece was an hour long—and that was after we'd cut about half of the slow parts. To a non-musician the score must have looked like the aftermath of an accident involving manuscript paper and a coal miner with a bad cold. But

> *"What I like about programming is that it really helps you think about how we communicate, how we think, how logic works, how creative arts work."*

311

IRCAM was a real experience, a beautiful and very interesting place to be.

INTERVIEWER: How did you get from IRCAM to Lucasfilm?

HAWLEY: At IRCAM I met a consultant who was working at Lucasfilm, among other places. He connected me with Andy Moorer. At the time, AT&T was divesting itself of Bell Laboratories, so Lucasfilm looked even more promising to me.

I moved west. The work looked fun; they wanted me to work on graphic interfaces for the audio and signal processor, and to think about music things. Of course I said yes. The job interview alone was entertaining enough....

INTERVIEWER: How was the job interview at Lucasfilm entertaining?

HAWLEY: After we talked for a while, Andy said, "Well, let me walk you around and show you some of the stuff that's happening." At the time, they were working on *Indiana Jones and the Temple of Doom*, which I didn't really know anything about. Everyone kept mumbling about "Indy II," and for a minute I thought, "Great, another car-chase movie, right." We walked up to the mixing theater, and Andy was explaining all the problems of mixing, how you mix for weeks and then the director says, "Well, we're cutting fifteen frames here," and you've got to go back and do it all over. It's like telling an undergraduate to retype his term paper on an old-fashioned typewriter. So we walked into the mixing theater, and I was still kind of dizzy because I'd never really been to California before, and there on a big screen was a poor guy in a turban.... Have you seen the movie?

INTERVIEWER: No.

HAWLEY: Well, this will sort of spoil it for you. There was a guy in a turban and loincloth, chained to something, screaming his head off, and a bad guy reaches right into his chest and rips his heart right out with his bare hands. Heck, I'd just gotten off the plane and stepped into a strange theater, just in time to see some poor slob get his heart ripped out. As if that weren't bad enough, I watched while the mixers ran the scene backwards and forwards, ten or fifteen times, trying to get the slurping noises to sound right. So, yes, that's sort of how I lost my heart to the film business. I've been working here now for about a year and a half.

I'm planning to go back to graduate school in the fall of 1986, because I've always felt that I've been in the middle of a long year off after Yale. There are some more general things I need to study that I don't have the time to attend to, especially now that we're getting heavily into development.

INTERVIEWER: *What are you going to go back to school to study?*

HAWLEY: Computer science and music, mostly. I want to keep doing the sort of things I'd be doing here for the computer division if it were still whole and intact; for example, assembling computerized scores and sound tracks in conjunction with computer-generated films. But that won't be possible here soon. For one thing, the graphics and audio groups will be separate companies, which is a shame. Pictures and sound have worked so well together in the past that it seems they belong together. Financially, I suppose it's efficacious to split up the computer division, at least for the next few years.

INTERVIEWER: *Aren't there communication channels in place? Can't the two groups work together even though the groups will be separate and independent companies?*

HAWLEY: Sure, in the best of all possible worlds, but it'll never be like sharing the same building where we trip over each other's machinery all the time. The research-oriented powers-that-be are in touch, and they talk about their dreams and what they'd like to do, but it's just not going to be so easy to pull it off, not in the short term, anyway.

INTERVIEWER: *What do you especially like about working at Lucasfilm as a programmer?*

HAWLEY: Lucasfilm seemed the ideal place to do computer-science research. Here we've got this incredibly rich communications medium—film—which has pictures and sounds and dialogue and story lines and music and effects. When you bump that up against an information technology, like computer programming, all sorts of new discoveries are bound to fall out. The colors on the screen are so rich, and the scenes have to be so captivating and intriguing to look at. That places a huge burden on the computers. The idea is not to duplicate things that you could go out and film or record, but to use computers to synthesize images and sounds with enough complexity to make them interesting and beautiful to people who are watching the films. With our current bronze-age computers, it takes quite a long time to compute these things, but it can be worth it.

INTERVIEWER: *What do you like about computers and programming?*

HAWLEY: I'm still trying to figure that out. I wrote forty thousand lines of code last year. After many frustrating years, one does get weary of writing grungy computer programs. What I like about programming, though, is that it really helps you think about how we communicate, how we think, how logic works, how creative arts work. Computers are communication and information tools, and communication is a beautiful thing. It's why telephones and personal computers were such an instant hit. The computer is probably the ultimate tool for looking at the problem of communication.

I like the idea of combining music and computers, because music seems an especially rich medium. Music also seems close to emotions and feelings. I think you can compute a lot less and produce more emotional response with music than with pictures. There still aren't any decent word processors for composers, but then, musical data structures are demanding. Musical scores are complex, and time, real time, is a critical component. Persuading a computer to perform music in real time is a difficult job. Think of everything you have to know to accompany a performer, for instance: You have to understand from top to bottom how an accompanist follows a performer through a score. You have to know the score, and you have to be able to turn vibrations in the air into pitches, recognize notes, and do all the pattern matching to track the performance. It's a very hard problem, but someday soon the technology will exist to build very interesting computer accompanists, a far cry from the "samba" switch on an electronic organ. It can almost be done with the equipment we have now.

> *"If there's one thing a computer's good at, it's helping you combine diverse elements."*

INTERVIEWER: *How do you think computers are going to affect the arts?*

HAWLEY: Profoundly. Computers will have the same sweeping effect that they have had on aspects of everyday life.

So many new things can be done with computers. I think often great new ideas come from recombining old ideas in new ways, and if there's one thing a computer's really good at, it's taking huge piles of information, mixing it together, and letting you play with the results. That helps foster new ideas.

Difficult, philosophical kinds of problems remain to be sorted out. For example, composing prose on a word processor is not like composing prose on a typewriter, because when you use a typewriter you have to get your ideas down coherently, produce a statement with direction, and see that the message gets across. You're constrained, because you don't want to retype the damn thing. Speaking is similar: When you're speaking, you can't go back easily and fix little grammatical mistakes. With typing and telephones, you spend more time planning out what you're going to say and making sure the message gets across clearly so you don't have to retype or repeat it. With a word processor, it's so easy to make changes: You can bounce around, back and forth, cut and paste and copy and snip and grab from anywhere. That makes it gratuitously easy to accidentally break little threads of thought that might otherwise have run through your writing. Nowadays, English teachers are all complaining about how they can distinguish whether a student did his work on a word-processor or on a typewriter, because word-processor prose looks like a collage. It's a valid point. This is a new technology and it affects how people create. You can do different things with it, and you have to be aware that you're creating in a different way.

As I said before, if there's one thing a computer's good at, it's helping you combine diverse elements, like a cook mixing the same old ingredients up into something new. People are going to have to get used to taking the time to put things together in different ways than they have before.

INTERVIEWER: In terms of sound and filmmaking, what kinds of things do you see happening as a result of computer programs manipulating them?

HAWLEY: The word-processing analogy carries right over into filmmaking. Today, when you mix the sound effects into a movie, you sit in a mixing theater at a big desk, and the film rolls by on the screen. You adjust knobs and watch the peak meters. When you stop, a sequence has been mixed. You've made a pass at a mix, and then the film has to rewind so you can listen to it again. Usually, there's five minutes of dead time while you wait for the film to rewind. In the past, the dead time has been used to plan the gestures and refinements for the next pass through the mix. But when computers arrive, the dead time won't be there.

I was sitting at a mix for a film called "Latino" and they were short one sound effect. A soldier was crawling through the grass, and you heard the rustling of his arm as he reached for a detonator. Before he could set off the bomb, though, he got shot, and flopped over. The body-flop noise was missing. All the mixer wanted to do was just copy the arm-rustling noise down a little farther in time, maybe adjust it a little, boost up the level equalizer differently, and have it serve as the body flop. But to do that took at least five minutes, because he had to press a button, talk into a microphone and say, "Hey, Joe, can you take the reel of Foley effects on track three out of sync and slip it forward a hundred and seventy-five frames?" Two minutes later a voice said, "Ok, done." So the mixer tried the tape, and of course the tape was not at quite the right place, so they had to search around until they found it, and then they made the copy and put the tape back in sync where it belonged, and five minutes passed. With the technology we have now, you just touch the glass of a computer screen once or twice, and not only has the copy been made, but you're auditioning it. It takes a few seconds. You don't have to wait for rewind time. It's a very different situation; the computer's always saying, "Okay, I'm ready, sure, go ahead, any time you're ready, I'm ready!"

One day I was talking with Francis Ford Coppola's mixer, who came through to see our droid. He was a sly and crafty guy and was duly dazzled and blown away by the technology. So many new tools, so many new things to think about. But he said, "Don't forget that the five minutes of rewind time is never dead time. If you are a good mixer you are always planning out the gestures and effects you're going to be making, you're mentally going through the process to help put down a coherent five minutes of performance. With your machine, you have lost that thinking time." You've gained something else, but you've lost something. With every new feature, it seems a desirable old feature goes away, or gets left by the wayside. There's room for both to co-exist. People have to realize that they still need to take the time to produce good art, good films, good music.

Music is seeing the same kind of problem. There's a proliferation of synthesizers and drum machines, and now it's possible to control them cheaply with computers. The trend is often to run blindly towards new technology. You have to be aware of what you're giving up in the process.

INTERVIEWER: Tell me about the work you have done at Lucasfilm with music programs.

HAWLEY: This past summer I brought in a friend who's at Cornell, a Ph.D. student in computer science. I thought we'd work on a MusicDroid, which is supposed to be a musician's tool, the ultimate computer musician's tool. We'd like to have a system that John Williams could use to prototype orchestral scores, trying them on a symphony of synthesizers without having to rent the London Philharmonic, producing legibly printed parts with relative ease. Or, we might want to give him the option of composing specifically for electronic instruments in new ways that people haven't thought of before. That's our vision.

This program I'll demonstrate to you is a very small first step in that direction. Here we have a cheap, off-the-shelf synthesizer that costs a thousand dollars, and it has lots of different sounds...the organ sounds we have created are pretty good. [Hawley plays on the synthesizer.]

Actually, if I turn it up...I have a hundred-dollar, super cheap Hammond organ reverb that does the trick. Instant Cathedral of St. John the Divine? These synthesizers are really cheap, and now you can control these things from your computer. For instance, I think this will still work. It'll probably sound horrible but you never know what you'll discover....

INTERVIEWER: *So you wrote this?*

HAWLEY: Yes. [Hawley keeps playing with the program and the synthesizer.] It can play the score really fast [he demonstrates] or it can play the score upside down, which turns out to be quite interesting. Upside down, the low notes fall at the top and the high notes come at the bottom; major turns into minor, minor turns into major, and you get something very different and strangely beautiful. That's accomplished very simply. A five-line computer program can turn music upside down, producing something very new.

Here we're looking at the music I just played on the keyboard, using a score editor. You can slide this little scroll bar around to look at the end of the piece, or, you remember I played a couple of clunky chords down at the end? You can zoom in or out on that section of the piece. If you want, you can zoom to the lowest-level view and play around with it, which can be very rewarding.

"With every new feature, it seems a desirable old feature goes away, or gets left by the wayside. There's room for both to coexist."

You see, it doesn't matter so much where the music comes from; what matters is how it got here. We're combining an old idea—a beautiful Bach prelude here—with new ones—a computer-controlled synthesizer, and a simple program to implement full harmonic inversion.

In a way, Bach did the same sort of thing when he was around, except he did it by knowing everything there was to know about the music of his time. He was a virtuoso on every instrument of his day, a master of all the important instrumental idioms and compositional genres. He was able to blend a variety of styles—French gallant court style, north German baroque, Italian—synthesizing them to create something new.

INTERVIEWER: *Did you help design the programs as well as write them?*

HAWLEY: Yes. My role here is to work on some of the lower-level interface software—graphics libraries, device drivers for touch screens and synthesizers, things like that. But I also have a big say about design.

I've done research and design work on some interesting projects. Here's a word-processing program I developed that's kind of neat. I have a directory called Books that contains some great literary works. *Alice in Wonderland, Moby Dick, War and Peace.* . . .

INTERVIEWER: *Did you type them in?*

HAWLEY: No, no. You send a check for thirty-five pounds to the Oxford Text Archive, and they'll send you a computer tape full of stuff. I was interested in it for use in databases.

I hashed up all these texts into a big concordance, something like a thesaurus. I can type along in this word-processor program, and when I want to find out how a partiular word has been used in a book or by an author, I just click on it with the mouse, and, blammo, I get a little window that contains half a dozen examples of how great authors have used this word in the various books in the database. Our verbal patterns tend to move in the same channel every time, but now all of a sudden, click, I can see how Tolstoy and other authors used the particular word I just typed.

Another program takes text and, using the same database, scribbles down random semi-grammatical English to complete your sentence. If you are typing along and get writer's block, you press a button and the program starts walking on from the last word that you wrote, going off into random directions. Every once in a while you get hit with a little bit of serendipity, and you find a new idea that you might not have found otherwise. This program is actually a research project for the SoundDroid group here; this is research related to the management of big databases.

INTERVIEWER: *Has anyone in particular influenced you in the areas you are pursuing?*

HAWLEY: Of course. All the people here, Andy Moorer, Alvy Smith, Ed Catmull; and Tom Landauer and Max Matthews at Bell Labs. The ideas of Marvin Minsky and Alan Kay are sometimes inspiring. I don't think there's a single most influential person, because I am generally more interested in synthesizing (combining) technologies than exploring narrow areas.

INTERVIEWER: *Do you see any problems with computers?*

HAWLEY: Well, mainly just the "generic" problem, the same problem that plagues all new technology, which is that people think they're getting something for nothing. Marketers tout computers as being timesavers, claiming life is going to be so much easier after you have your computer. A seductive line, but it's not really to the point. I wouldn't begin to suggest that having *Alice in Wonderland* whiz by on my screen here is any replacement for sitting in front of a fireplace with a nicely bound copy of the book and looking out over a flowery cloister in England somewhere. That's not what computers are for, and hurts me to see highly evolved older technologies cast off as people jump to get on this bandwagon. That's a big problem.

INTERVIEWER: You don't see that happening with music? Take, for example, classical instruments. Do you think they will eventually be replaced by sounds created by synthesizers?

HAWLEY: Yes and no. The point of having computers around is not to replace or imitate or fool people into thinking that they're hearing these old wonderful technologies. You shouldn't use a computer to, as I said earlier, generate a picture of something that you'd go out and photograph, or to produce a sound like an organ. What we want is to be able to achieve and understand the kind of complexity that makes images or sounds beautiful. Simulation is a good way to understand the problem, but simulation is not the goal. I'm more interested in doing new things that I couldn't do before. For instance, one thing I couldn't do before was play a pipe organ in a cathedral and a marimba at the same time and juggle the sounds around right here in my office. Today, for about what a piano used to cost, consumers can buy synthesizers that can be controlled by computers, and they can produce sounds of beautiful complexity. There's going to be a day when you can press a button and have your computer crank out Muzak, if that's what you want it to do. There's a dark side to every powerful technology.

I went back to Yale a month ago and I visited my old piano teacher who is in his seventies now, a very grand old man, and he said that he went to an Old Fellows' dinner in one of the colleges, and one of the old codgers got up and gave a talk about how...what was the recurring line...whenever you embrace something new, something old is lost. At the time, hurricane Gloria had just come through and people were complaining that they didn't have lights. When my teacher was a Yalie, they didn't have electric light, they had candles. He said that wasn't so bad, because not only did hurricanes not knock them out, but candles didn't buzz like fluorescent lamps, and they illuminated books in a different way.

People who allow themselves to stay in the dark and remain ignorant will never know what it's like to read a book by candlelight, or to play on an old lute in a nice concert hall. But if they're adventurous about their learning, they'll go out and explore old technologies as well as the new, so they can appreciate both and understand how everything fits into the big picture. There's a big risk of making shallow use of computer technology without fully appreciating what's behind it and where it came from, but I have a fair amount of faith that people will do more or less the right thing. Sometimes it's scary.

"There's a dark side to every powerful technology."

The world is always changing. Bach was around three hundred years ago. Three hundred years is not all that long; there aren't that many grandparents separating Bach and me. But his daily life was so different. He wrote all his music by hand on a piece of paper using a quill pen. He couldn't get into a plane and fly across the country to talk to half a dozen people at MIT, like I can. He stayed in the same handful of towns in the same country with many of the same people. And look what he produced. Well, that's unfair, of course, people like Bach don't happen along every century. But the technologies of communication and transportation change how we deal with people in ways that we probably don't appreciate. Take relationships in our society; they are so different than they were years ago. Better in some ways, worse in others. People take it for granted today that if you don't like your job or your love life in Manhattan, you can just move to California and make a fresh start. Or hop in a plane and go to a South Pacific island and clear your brain. Changing paths is a relatively easy option, and that de-emphasizes the need to work through problems. You just push a button and the music changes, flip a switch and the lights are out, hop on a plane and go to Norway. It's a different world. Some things are better and some are worse. When the excitement of the new technology subsides, we can begin to view both sides in balance.

GLOSSARY

8080: A microprocessor chip produced by Intel Corporation. Many early microcomputers incorporated this chip.

ALGOL: ALGOrithmic Language. An international programming language designed for the expression and control of arithmetic and logical processes.

ALGORITHM: A prescribed set of rules or processes for the solution of a problem in a finite number of steps.

ALTAIR: An early microcomputer produced by MITS and sold as a kit.

ALTO: A workstation computer developed at Xerox PARC. The Alto featured an advanced language called SmallTalk, an input device called a mouse, and a networking technique to interconnect individual Altos.

APL: A Programming Language. A high-level, algorithmic/procedure-oriented language. An interactive language usually requiring the use of special terminals, having high value in mathematical and scientific work.

APPLICATION: A program written to accomplish a specific user task (such as payroll) as opposed to general-purpose or utility programs.

ARTIFICIAL INTELLIGENCE: Refers to the development of machines that can perform functions normally concerned with human intelligence, such as learning, adapting, reasoning, and automatic self-correction.

ASSEMBLER: A program that converts low-level computer source code into executable machine code. Also frequently used as a synonym for assembly language.

ASSEMBLY LANGUAGE: A low-level computer language that produces source code based on symbolic machine-language statements in which there is a one-to-one correspondence between each statement and an actual machine instruction.

BACKGROUND PROCESSING: Lower priority work done when high-priority or quick-response programs are inactive.

BASIC: Beginner's All-purpose Symbolic Instruction Code. A common high-level computer programming language that was developed by Dartmouth College.

BETA TEST: A test of hardware or software done outside the producer's environment by persons other than the producer.

BIT: The smallest quantity a computer can measure or detect; corresponds to a binary digit (either 0 or 1). Eight bits make up a **byte.**

BIT-MAPPED: Refers to a computer's display system in which each pixel on the screen corresponds to one (in black and white) or more (in color) bits in the computer's memory.

BOOLEAN ALGEBRA: A system of logic functions named after George Boole that uses operators such as AND, OR, NOT, EXCEPT, IF, and THEN to derive the solution of logical problems in which each element can be in one of two states, usually true or false.

BYTE: A unit of measure for computer memory and disk storage. One byte contains eight bits and can store one character (a letter, number, or punctuation symbol).

C: A programming language designed to optimize run time, size, and efficiency, developed by Dennis Ritchie at Bell Laboratories. C language is not machine-dependent, so programs can be freely transferred from machine to machine with a reasonable expectation that they will run correctly without modification.

CAD: Computer-Aided Design. An automated design and drafting system.

CD ROM: Compact Disc, Read-Only Memory. An optical storage system that uses a laser to detect pits on the surface of a rotating disk, which can store up to 540 megabytes of information.

CEO: Chief Executive Officer.

COBOL: COmmon Business Oriented Language. A programming language that uses English-language statements.

CODE: A system of character syntax and rules for a specific programming language. When programmers "code," they are writing a computer program using a specific programming language. "Looking at code" generally means reading program listings.

COMDEX: An annual exposition of computer hardware, software, and related products.

COMPILE: To "crunch" a program written in a high-level language into a program more easily interpreted by the machine, which means that the program will execute more quickly.

COMPILER: A computer program that generates and assembles executable machine code from a program written by a programmer in a high-level language.

COMPUTER GRAPHICS: Video displays and printed representations of computer-generated charts, graphs, and associated artwork.

CONDOR: A database-management system produced by Condor Computer Corporation.

CPU: Central Processing Unit. A section of a microcomputer that includes the circuits controlling the interpretations and executions of instructions.

CP/M: Control Program for Microprocessors. An operating system for 8-bit microcomputers, produced by Digital Research.

CROSS-COMPILE: To use a special type of compiler called a cross-compiler to compile a program on one type of a computer to produce executable code for a computer of another type.

CURSOR: An indicator used on a video terminal to highlight a character to be corrected or a position in which data is to be entered.

DATABASE: An electronic file consisting of related entries, references, or abstracts on a subject.

DATABASE MANAGEMENT SYSTEM: A software system whose primary function is to allow the user to create, manipulate, and retrieve database records for processing and display.

DATA STRUCTURE: A principle used to organize a collection of data or information for access purposes, such as a file, string, or matrix.

DEBUG: To search for, correct, and/or eliminate errors in a computer program.

DIGITIZE: To convert an analog measurement into a number expressed in binary, or base 2, digits.

DYNABOOK: Imaginary powerful computer small enough to fit into a bookbag. The Dynabook concept originated with Alan Kay.

EDITOR: A general-purpose text-editing program used to program source code.

ELECTRONIC MAIL: A system that allows the user to create, send, and receive messages electronically.

EXPERT SYSTEM: A computer system that can simulate decision-making processes generally associated with human thought.

EXTENSIBLE: An extensible language is one that allows the user to define new elements or modify existing ones.

FIFTH GENERATION: A term to describe the type of computer systems currently under development that rely heavily on processing speed and artificial intelligence.

FILE SERVER: The machine and software in a network where the network files are stored and manipulated.

FIRMWARE: Programs stored in a computer's permanent memory or ROM.

FONT: A complete assortment of letters, numbers, punctuation marks, etc. of a given size and design.

FORTH: An extensible language used on microcomputers to solve a range of problems.

FORTRAN: FORmula TRANslation. A high-level programming language developed for numeric computations.

FUNCTIONAL SPECIFICATION: A description of a language's or system's operating characteristics and limitations.

GEM: A graphics-based user interface developed by Digital Research that uses icons to represent files, windows to represent directories and sub-directories, and menus for user control.

GIGABYTE: A unit of measure roughly equal to 1 billion bytes.

HACK: A slang term meaning to write a computer program.

HACKER: A slang term for a programmer.

HERCULES CARD: A display adapter card that allows for high-resolution texts produced by Hercules Computer Technology.

HIGH-LEVEL LANGUAGE: A problem-oriented or procedure-oriented language as distinguished from a machine-oriented and/or mnemonic-oriented language.

INTERACTIVE: Refers to two-way communication between a computer and its user involving a user's orders and responses.

INTERFACE: A common boundary between two units of different characteristics, or the interconnection of two different types of components, circuits, equipment, or system elements.

INTERPRETER/INTERPRETIVE LANGUAGE: A program used to translate source code into machine language each time it is run.

LISA: Microcomputer produced by Apple Computer, Inc.

LISP: LISt Processing. An interpretive language developed to manipulate symbolic strings and recursive data.

LIST PROCESSING: The processing of data stored in an ordered sequence (list).

LOCAL AREA NETWORK: A system that allows a large number of computers, peripherals, or terminals to share resources within a small area.

LSI: Large Scale Integration. A technology that allows the construction of a computer chip containing many hundreds of thousands of logic gates.

MAILMERGE: A feature of many word-processing programs that allows personalized form letters to be created.

MAINFRAME: A large-size central computer system. Mainframe computers most commonly have a word length of 32 bits and a memory capacity ranging from approximately 512K to 16 megabytes.

MEGABYTE: 1,048,576 bytes.

MICROCOMPUTER: An inexpensive computing system usually consisting of a single microprocessor chip and support components (including semiconductor memory), which is usually housed in a small enclosure that includes a keyboard.

MICROPROCESSOR: A complete processor on a single chip, which functions as the CPU of a microcomputer.

MICROSOFT WORD: A word-processing program produced by the Microsoft Corporation.

MINICOMPUTER: A midsize computer system that generally incorporates semiconductor or magnetic core memory, and offers from 4K words to 64K words of storage and a cycle time of 0.2 to 8 microseconds or less.

MIS: Management Information System. A system in which data are recorded and processed for operational purposes.

MODULA-2: A programming language produced by Volition Systems. Features include: modules, separate compilation, program libraries, concurrent processes and low-level machine access.

MODULE: In hardware, an interchangeable "plug-in" item, which may be combined with other interchangeable items to form a complete unit. In software, a sequence of instructions for performing a given task.

MS-DOS: MicroSoft Disk Operating System. An operating system developed by Microsoft Corporation for 16-bit microcomputers.

MULTIMATE: A word-processing program produced by SoftWord Systems Incorporated.

MULTIPLE-PROCESS OPERATING SYSTEM: An operating system that allows the user to have more than one context established at a time.

OCTAL ABSOLUTE: A numbering system using eight as a base instead of two, as in binary, or ten, as in decimal.

OEM: Original Equipment Manufacturer. A manufacturer that provides equipment or pieces for other manufacturers.

OPERATING SYSTEM: A program that manages and controls processing within a computer system.

PARSE: To separate a programming statement into basic units that can be translated into machine instructions.

PASCAL: A high-level language named for Blaise Pascal.

PC-DOS: A version of the MS-DOS operating system used on the IBM PC.

PDP SERIES: A series of minicomputers produced by Digital Equipment Corporation. For example, PDP-8, PDP-9, etc.

PL-1: Programming Language 1. A compiler invented for IBM computers. Digital Research Corporation developed a version for microprocessors.

PRIMITIVE: A basic or fundamental unit. Often refers to the lowest level of machine instruction.

PROGRAMMING LANGUAGE: A language with specific syntax, rules, words, and terms used to write a computer program, e.g., BASIC and PASCAL.

PUBLIC DOMAIN: A designation for uncopyrighted software usually available at no charge to the general public.

R:BASE SERIES: A single-user relational database program produced by Microrim, Inc.

REAL TIME: A speed sufficient to give an answer within the time the problem must be solved.

RECURSION: Repetition of the same operation or group of operations.

RETRIEVE: The operation of locating and obtaining a particular item or group of items from a storage system containing a number of items.

ROM: Read-Only Memory. A computer's permanent memory.

SCANNER: An instrument that examines or samples the state of various processes, files, or physical states.

SCREEN INTERFACE: The portion of a computer program that controls what appears on a video screen.

SEMICONDUCTOR: Material (usually impurified silicon) with an electrical conductivity between that of a metal and an insulator, which has characteristics that allow the current passing through it to be controlled and used.

SNOBOL: StriNg-Oriented symBOlic Language. A programming language that manipulates character strings.

SPREADSHEET: A software package that electronically simulates a business or scientific worksheet.

SWITCHER (program): A utility program written by Andy Hertzfeld for the Apple Macintosh that allows the user to have more than one application in memory at one time and to switch between them quickly.

SYSTEMS DESIGN: Specifications of the working relations between all the parts of a system.

TIME-SHARING SYSTEM: A system in which a central computer's time is shared among several users.

TOP-DOWN PROGRAMMING: A method of structured programming in which the total system is designed and then broken down into separate modules.

TRS-80: Microcomputer produced by Radio Shack, Inc.

UNIX: A real-time operating system developed by Bell Labs for mini- and microcomputers.

USER-FRIENDLY: A computer program that is easily used and understood by a wide variety of people.

USER INTERFACE: The portion of a computer program that interacts with the user. Generally refers to what the user sees on the video screen.

VAX: A type of computer manufactured by Digital Research.

VENTURE CAPITAL: Capital available for investment in a new enterprise.

VISICALC: A business-oriented electronic-spreadsheet program produced by Software Arts, Inc.

VISION: Integrated operating environment package that allows users to work with any number of applications on the screen at the same time. Produced by VisiCorp.

VMS: Virtual Memory Storage. A system in which memory is organized into two sections, primary and secondary, with the latter being divided into "pages" of 4096 bytes or more. This system allows the use of programs that are larger than the amount of available primary storage, in that modules of the program can be brought into primary storage from the secondary storage (usually a disk drive or other mass storage device) as needed.

WINDOW: A defined portion of a CRT screen where information can appear independent of the main display.

WORDPERFECT: Word-processing program, produced by Satellite Software International.

WORD PROCESSOR: A program and/or machine dedicated to formatting and editing text.

WORDSTAR: Word-processing program produced by Micropro International Corporation.

WORDWRAP: A feature of word processing where words that extend beyond the margins of one line are automatically shifted to the next line.

WORKSTATION: A computer that combines word-processing, data-processing, and data-communication equipment. Also refers to a terminal connected to a larger computer dedicated to performing a certain task or tasks, such as business, engineering, or scientific applications.

XEROX PARC: Xerox Palo Alto Research Center. A technological research center opened in 1970 by Xerox Corporation.

Z80: 8-bit microprocessor produced by Zilog Corporation.

Using CL is similar to placing your pencil on a piece of paper, and then
writing something down. The main ~~difference~~ advantage is that CL provides you with
a "magic" piece of paper that has the ability to do computations like a
calculator. Before we actually use CL, you ~~must~~ should learn the definition
of a few terms that are used to refer to parts of the computer screen.
Here is an example of a simple application using CL, as it would appear
on the screen, with those parts labelled:

   The screen is divided into two sections: the top three lines (the
menu/status area) and the data area below. The data area is where data
actually appears. The data area is divided up into rows and columns.
The rows are numbered and the columns are named by letters. The intersection
of a row and a column is called an entry. Each entry can be referred to
by indicating its column and row, e.g. *B7*. You can place either numbers
(called values) or text   (called labels) at an entry.
   The highlight on entry B5 above is called the cursor. You can move
the cursor from entry to entry using the arrow keys on the right of the
keyboard. This is the first thing that you should learn to do in order
to use CL. The character in the upper right corner of the screen (called
the direction indicator) will tell you which way the arrow keys will make
the cursor move. If the direction indicator is a minus sign (-) then the
cursor will move left and right. If it is an exclamation point (!), then
the cursor will move up and down. The right arrow always moves you forward
(from A to B, or 1 to 2) while the left arrow always moves you backward
(from B to A, or 2 to 1). You can switch the direction indicator between
! and - by pressing the space bar. Try moving the cursor around on the
screen to get used to how it works. You might notice that the beginning

Two pages from the first VisiCalc manual. The program was called CalcuLedger (CL) at that time. Note
Bricklin's handwritten editorial changes.

Replicate

The replicate command is used to copy the contents of an entry
into other entries. It is useful when a group of entries (such as a
row) are all similar expressions. For example, you could set an entry to
be the sum of the two entries above it. You could then use the replicate
command to make the other entries in that row also be the sum of the
two entries above them. Entries whose contents have been set using the
replicate command are no different than entries that have been set
by hand, and can be displayed by pointing to them with the cursor and
modified individually just like any other entry.

Any type of entry may be replicated -- expressions in value entries,
label entries, blank entries, ~~and the other special entry types~~. If the
entry is a value entry, then the replicate command can make ~~a few~~ changes
to the expression as it copies it into each new entry. ~~For example,~~
when a reference ~~to another entry~~ appears in an expression, the replicate
command gives you ~~the~~ options ~~of having~~ the copy refer to the exact same
entry (by not modifying the reference), ~~or having~~ it refer to the entry that
is in the same relative position to the entry with the copy as the originally
referenced entry was to the entry being copied. ~~You can also make~~
~~modifications to numeric values that appear in an expression.~~ You can
~~have the value incremented by a constant amount~~ each time that ~~it is copied~~.
The examples at the end of this section should help you understand how
these expression modifications works.

To use the replicate command you first type /R. It will then ask you
what you want to replicate. It will have the current entry already filled
in on the input line (line 3 of the menu/status area). You ~~then posit~~ion
~~the cursor on the entry that you want to copy (if its the current entry~~
~~then you don't have to do anything), and then~~ press RETURN. CL will then

FRAME MANAGER

3-15-82

(1)

Good morning Robert. Your task is to figure out

1) frame organization in the db. How are they organized, accessed, threaded.

2) proc (frame) accessing & threading

- all frames have a universal 32-bit address

→ - on 8088 this yields 16-b seg addr & 16-b logical addr

- all pointers to other frames consist of a 32-bit name. Passing this frame name through a translation table gives a 32-bit po frame pointer (above mentioned)

At runtime we have the frame space — a heap or string space like memory area. All frame refs are via the frame name. As this passes through the translation/lookup code, if the frame isn't in mem, the space, it's brought from disk. If it's not on disk, an error occurs.

At one end of frame space is the frame stack. The frame mngr also includes the core interpreter for the frame language. The interpreter & language use the stack. When a cell is evaluated it's first put on the stack and all its referenced cells & frames are evaluated.

These eight pages of notes written by Robert Carr and addressed to himself reveal the early thought processes in the development of Framework, a word-processing/spreadsheet program.

② 2-15-82

[will the Frame Language be Reverse Polish Notation? (Prefix)]

This is how values are kept up to date. Simple grind it through EVAL of whole reference tree.
—or do we want a clever scheme of knowing what's been changed & what hasn't?

now, where do _values_ live? and what does it mean for a frame to be sent to the execute port?

- each cell has at least 2 corresponding cells (a 3rd for format?). 1 for the ~~the~~ "frame language instance" or text; 1 for the "value" of that f.l. instance. ~~&~~ If all the cell has is text, as in a paper, then it doesn't make sense for it to have a value. If it does have a f.l.i. then the value is empty until the first time the user sends the f.l.i. to the execute port.

  No. the "value cell" corresponding to the formula cell will be in a totally different frame, a temporary twin frame cloned from the first only for the life of the value port.

  Also, probably any kind of formatting info, if we have it, should go to a separate frame.

  The execute port keeps the source & value frames associated.

  Fn.

③

Frames then are a collection of variable length cells.
Cells can have at least 3 _types_ of data:
- text
- text that is a frame language instance
- number

Q: cell typing? What will we have? if cell types support sequences and records & arrays then it'll be a cinch to implement all indices and info about frames ontop of the frames

Frames have some kind of frame map, to tell where cells are, & what they are too.

I want frame cells to be easily changeable in size, deletable, insertable.

If a frame cell of plain text is a sequence, then the editor obviously has an easy time of it.

Since the frame space will be in a different part of memory than Pascal, there'll have to be read & write word procs, then most all the frame mngr can be written in Pascal. Then, later, what needs to be faster can be written into assembler & deal with that memory directly. Then the pascal code will be additional documentation for the key assembler routines.

(y)

initially in assembler we'll need

Read Byte (32 - bit)
Write Byte (32-bit addr into frame space)
Move Bytes (from: 32b, to: 32b; count:)
↳ also used to move data between Pascal
data space and frame space, as well as
in frame space.

but can
be in
Pascal too

{ frame name to pointer routines, simple translation

sequence implementation

frame space

Disk:

} in frame space the
frames could be all
contiguous. Then resplit
onto blocks at write out.

} on disk frames
must live on
fixed length
blocks of some
kind.

Ok, for now we'll have the plan:

- frames are (potentially) split across blocks on disk.
- but when a frame is read in (possibly forcing other
frames out!) it is read into a contiguous chunk.
- finally the frame is split across blks again at
write out time.

> chose this design ↑ because) envision memory being
big enough for a frame space large enuf to hold.
most all frames. Hence at system starting
we read all frames in, at system turn off we
write them all out.
But what about a frame changing it's size, it'll
force all the others to shift in memory?
(↳ No, the current frame, or any frame that's about to

337

Ⓢ

be changed in size, will first be brought to the top of
the frame pile, next to free space.   Since all editing
is confined to one frame at a time (except multiple
windows? and couldn't value frames also change size
at execute time if we allow string types for cells & values?)
only the current frame to change will be changing in
size.   And we've just moved him to the top of the
frame pile (and shifted over his old spot).

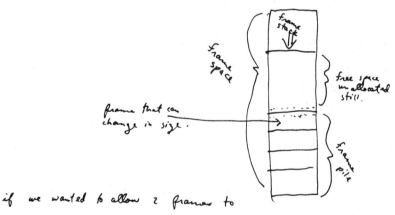

frame
space

frame
start

free space
unallocated
still.

frame that can
change in size.

frame
pile

if we wanted to allow 2 frames to
concurrently change, we'd have frame space
like so :

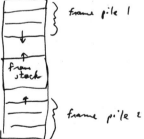

frame pile 1

frame
stack

frame pile 2

or some such monstrosity.

⑥

But I like the first picture of frame space. It'll
work well: 1) Frames that are often changing in
     multiple
size ~~will~~ "concurrently" will be small
ones, easily copied to & from the
top of the pile. The changing ones
will collect in a working set at the
top of the pile so not much shifting has
to be ~~done~~ done

2) when the user's editor 2 or more large
frames, almost always only one will be
edited and the others only read or copied.
— is this really true? I hope so. I
envision the frames most always being small,
anyways.

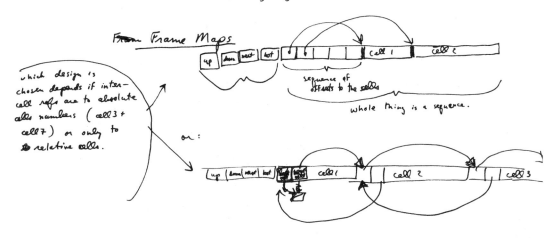

~~From~~ Frame Maps

which design is
chosen depends if inter-
cell refs are to absolute
cell numbers (cell 3 +
cell 7) or only to
relative cells.

or:

sequence of
offsets to the cells

whole thing is a sequence.

up | down | next | last   cell 1   cell 2

up | down | next | last   cell 1   cell 2   cell 3

the typing
bootstrapping

⑦

Frame Linking

these procs
in
assembler. {

translation
Frame name to pointer table   (a table of which frames
are in mem and where) ~~assembler time~~

a sequence of 2 32-bit entries.

Then otherwise, whatever kinds of   linking   I decide for.

e.g.:

new Frame name := Up , Down, Next, Last (frame name);

⑧

Frame Cells

how to give frame cells meaningful names for
reference ?

have absolute or relative (or both) inter-cell refs ?

⑨

Current Position = Current Cursor Loc

one for every port

globally there is one current pos.   this consists of:

- cur Port ?
- cur Frame
- cur Cell
- cur byte in Cell.

Now how is a cell displayed ?   sent to it's
bitmap which is then sent to the graphics buffer?

So what happens when one character is inserted into
a cell ?

1) the char is inserted into the cell itself, adjusting
pointers, after 1st move the cells frame to the top
of the frame pile if necessary

2 redisplays of whole cell
sounds like alot for every
character change to my
mind, but it gives up the
whole dynamicness of the display
etc: dynamically changing justification
in cells etc, as you type into a cell it gets
bigger & bigger, other cells get pushed down, etc. etc.
and all with relatively simple code.   as soon as I try to only
redisplay the current line only, then the code gets much worse.

2) that cell is then redisplayed to the bit mag

3) which bitmap is then redisplayed to the graf buffer

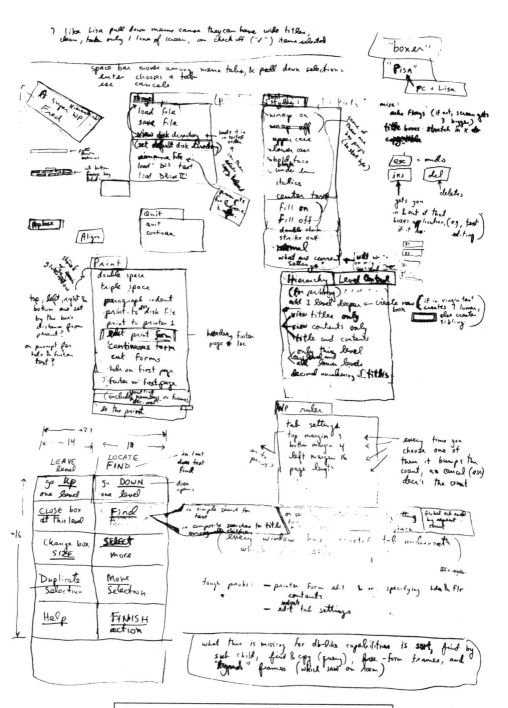

Robert Carr, principal developer of Framework, calls these sketches "Spreadsheet Wanderings."

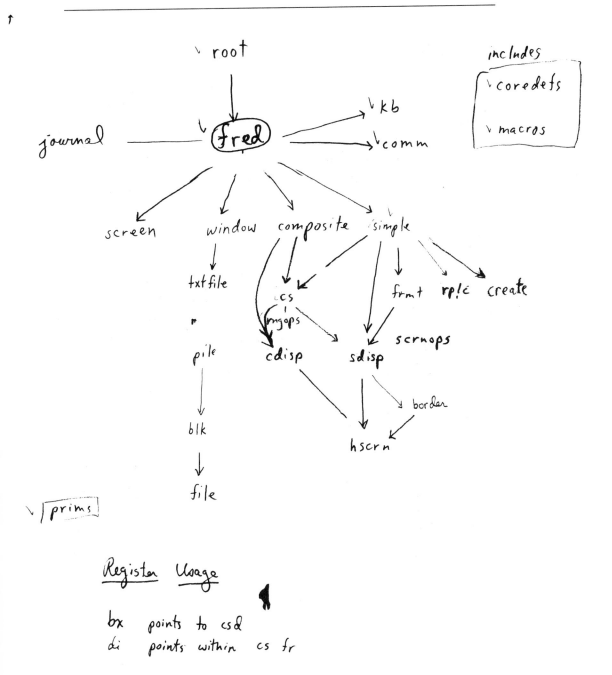

↑

\ root

includes

\ coredefs

\ macros

\ kb

journal ——— (fred) ———→ \ comm

screen   window   composite   \ simple

txtfile   \ cs   frmt   rplc create

r   rngops

pile   cdisp   sdisp   scrnops

blk   border

file   hscrn

\ [prims]

Register Usage

bx   points to csd
di   points within cs fr

This sketch from Robert Carr shows how "the internal code organization falls into place." "Fred" was the code name for Framework.

343

Menus :

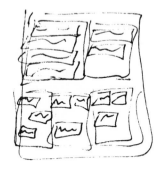

Hierarchical Tre

at lowest

User

Properties :

fn

used to —: formatting

rt, flt, cntr justify   } position props

fill, justify, no-fill   } text props

normal (rounded to integer) dollars
full detail (scientific)   } number props

[there are no units, user can easily edit
   numbers to put those in)

italic, bold, under line, blink
     inverse
uppercase, lowercase   } character props

protected   } ca

ea

al

Sketch from Robert Carr of the hierarchical tree of
menus for Framework.

 to menus

el are single frames:
    each button is a choice
    some choices may be on at same time
    each choice specifies the other sibling
        choices which must be off, & those which must
        be on (e.g. hitting [Justify] turns [Fill] button on also).
    each choice has an associated action routine

moves through menu w/ normal commands

nd does a [doit] on selection

hoice has a msg which is displayed when it's selected

voked choices redisplay immediately their action

(the simple code for insert frame pops the
  sel & calls composite code for insert frame

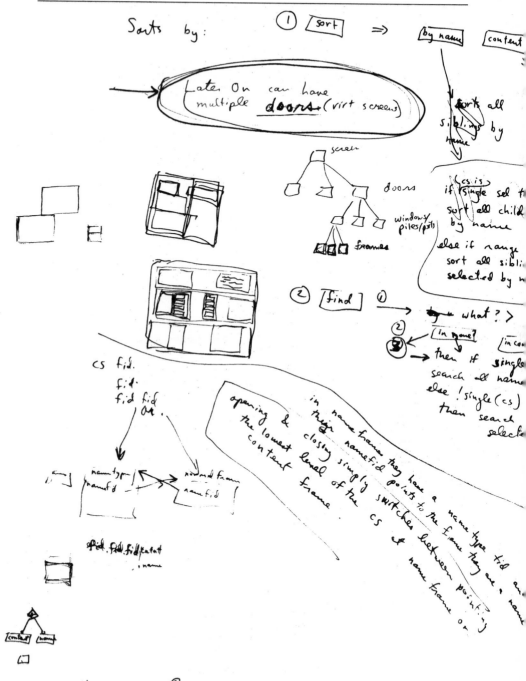

Sorts by: ① [sort] ⇒ [by name] [content]

Later On can have
multiple **doors** (virt screens)

sort all
siblings by
name

screen

doors

windows
piles/pats

frames

if (cs is
single) sel
sort all child
by name

else if range
sort all sibli
selected by n

② [find] ①
→ what? >

② [in name?] [in co]

then if single
search all name
else ! single (cs)
then search
selecte

cs fid.
fid
fid fid
at.

nametype
namefd

normal frame
namefid !

in name frame they have a name type tid
their namefid points to the frame they are
opening & closing simply switches between points
the lowest level of the cs at name frame o
content frame

fid fid fidfcatat
name

content namef

- No name tabs, @ same time as frame box, not even for window
- But do echo path
- name tab should probably be 0th elt of map (even in simples, they completely ignore 0th elt), then a closed frame is simply a sel

346

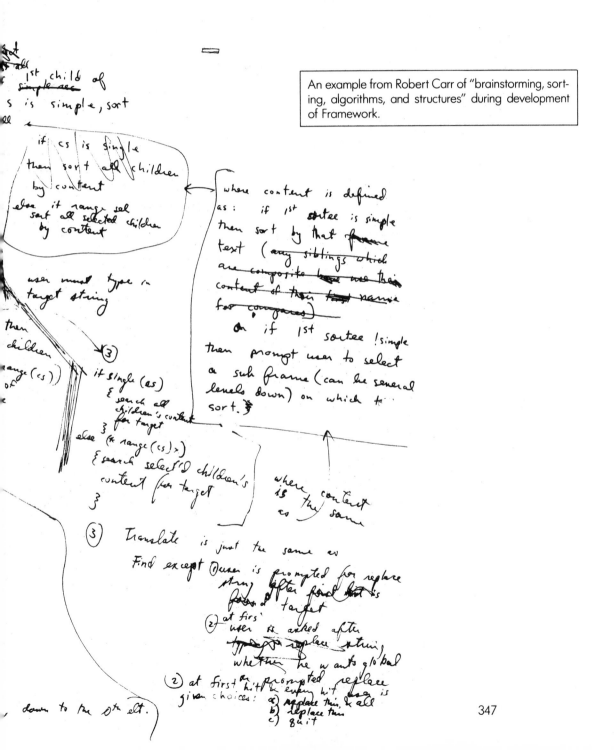

An example from Robert Carr of "brainstorming, sorting, algorithms, and structures" during development of Framework.

BASIC MPU 8080/Z80   GATES/ALLEN/DAVIDOFF   MACRO %50(272)=1 21:12 21-FEB-78 PAGE 1-4
F3   MAC   17-FEB-78 19:18   SOME EXPLANATION

```
363    02380    SUBTTL  SOME EXPLANATION
364    02390    COMMENT *
365    02400
367    02410
368    02420    ALTAIR BASIC CONFIGURES MEMORY AS FOLLOWS:
369    02430
370    02440    LOW LOCATIONS    (NON-TIMESHARING VERSION)
371    02450
372    02460        RST        SUBROUTINES
373    02470
374    02480                   0        STARTUP
375    02490                            INITIALLY A JMP TO THE INITIALIZATION CODE
376    02500                            BUT CHANGED TO A JMP TO READY.
377    02510                            RESTARTING THE MACHINE AT 0 DURING PROGRAM
378    02520                            EXECUTION CAN LEAVE THINGS MESSED UP.
379    02530
380    02540                   1        SYNCHK
381    02550                            A CHECK IS MADE TO MAKE SURE THE
383    02560                            CHARACTER POINTER POINTS AT A SPECIFIC
384    02570                            CHARACTER. IF NOT THE "SYNTAX ERROR"
383    02580                            ROUTINE IS CALLED. IF SO
384    02590                            THE CHRGET RST IS DROPPED INTO SO
385    02600                            THE CHARACTER AFTER THE MATCHED
386    02610                            ONE WILL BE PUT IN [A] AND
387    02620                            THE CONDITION CODES WILL REFLECT THIS
388    02630                            EXAMPLE: SYNCHK THENTK (THE MATCH CHARACTER IS
389    02640                            GIVEN IN THE LOCATION AFTER THE RST)
390    02650                            WOULD CHECK TO MAKE SURE [H,L] POINTED TO A THENTK
391    02660                            AND IF SO FETCH THE NEXT CHARACTER INTO [A].
392    02670                            IF NOT, A "SYNTAX ERROR" WOULD BE GIVEN.
393    02680
394    02690                   2        CHRGET
395    02700                            USING [H,L] AS THE TEXT POINTER
396    02710                            THE TEXT POINTER IS INCREMENTED
397    02720                            AND THE NEXT CHARACTER IS FETCHED INTO [A]
398    02730                            IF THE CHARACTER IS A " " IT IS SKIPPED
399    02740                            OVER AND THE NEXT CHARACTER IS FETCHED.
400    02750                            THE STATEMENT TERMINATORS ":" AND 0
401    02760                            LEAVE THE ZERO FLAG SET.
402    02770                            THE NUMERICS "0" THROUGH "9" LEAVE THE CARRY
403    02780                            FLAG SET. THE CURRENT CHARACTER CAN BE
404    02790                            REFETCHED INTO [A] BY DOING A MOV A,M
405    02800                            IF THE CONDITION CODES MUST BE SET UP AGAIN
406    02810                            DCX M,CHRGET WILL WORK. IT IS VERY DIFFICULT
407    02820                            TO REEXAMINE THE CHARACTER BEFORE THE CURRENT
408    02830                            ONE SINCE SPACES MAY BE IN-BETWEEN.
409    02840                            DCX H,DCX M,CHRGET WILL NOT ALWAYS WORK.
410    02850
411    02860                   3        OUTCHR
412    02870                            THE CHARACTER IN [A] IS PRINTED ON
413    02880                            THE USER'S TERMINAL. [A] AND THE
414    02890                            CONDITION CODES ARE PRESERVED.
415    02900
416    02910                   4        COMPAR
417    02920                            [D,E] AND [H,L] ARE COMPARED AS UNSIGNED
```

BASIC MPU 8080/Z80   GATES/ALLEN/DAVIDOFF   MACRO %50(272)=1 21:12 21-FEB-78 PAGE 1-5
F3   MAC   17-FEB-78 19:18   SOME EXPLANATION

```
418    02930                            DOUBLE-BYTE INTEGERS. CARRY IS SET IF
419    02940                            [H,L] IS LESS THAN [D,E] ZERO IS SET IF THEY
420    02950                            ARE EQUAL. [A] IS SMASHED. THE ONLY DEFINITE
421    02960                            THING THAT CAN BE SAID ABOUT [A] ON RETURN
422    02970                            IS THAT IF THE ZERO FLAG IS SET, [A] WILL
423    02980                            EQUAL 0.
424    02990
425    03000                   5        FSIGN
426    03010                            THE FAC (FLOATING ACCUMULATOR)
427    03020                            WHICH IS USED TO STORE NUMERIC RESULTS
428    03030                            IS CHECKED TO SEE WHAT SIGN ITS
429    03040                            VALUE HAS.
430    03050
431    03060                   6        PUSHM
432    03070                            A DOUBLE BYTE QUANTITY POINTED
433    03080                            TO BY [H,L] IS PUSHED ONTO THE
434    03090                            STACK. [B,C] IS SET EQUAL TO THE
435    03100                            VALUE PUSHED. [H,L] IS INCREMENTED BY TWO.
436    03110
437    03120                   7        IN THE 4K VERSION RST 7 IS UNUSED AND THE LOCATIONS
438    03130                            ASSOCIATED WITH IT ARE USED TO CONTINUE
439    03140                            THE CODE FOR RST 6. IN THE 8K A JMP IS MADE
440    03150                            AROUND THE FIRST THREE RST 7 LOCATIONS
441    03160                            DURING RST 6 EXECUTION. RST 7 INITIALLY
442    03170                            CONTAINS A RET. BUT THE USER CAN CHANGE IT TO
443    03180                            A JMP TO AN INTERRUPT SERVICE ROUTINE.
444    03190
445    03200                   (IN THE TIMESHARING VERSION, THE MONITOR GOES
446    03210                    INTO THE LOW AREA, AND THE BASIC INTERPRETER
447    03220                    FOLLOWS IT. THE RESTART ROUTINES DOCUMENTED
448    03230                    ABOVE ARE CALLS TO SUBROUTINES INSTEAD.)
449    03240
450    03250    FUNCTION DISPATCH ADDRESSES
451    03260                    FUNDSP CONTAINS THE ADDRESSES OF THE
452    03270                    FUNCTION ROUTINES IN THE ORDER OF THE
453    03280                    FUNCTION NAMES IN THE CRUNCH LIST.
454    03290                    THE FUNCTIONS THAT TAKE MORE THAN ONE ARGUMENT
455    03300                    ARE AT THE END. SEE THE EXPLANATION AT ISFUN.
456    03310
457    03320    THE OPERATOR TABLE
458    03330                    THE OPTAB TABLE CONTAINS AN OPERATORS PRECEDENCE
459    03340                    FOLLOWED BY THE ADDRESS OF THE ROUTINE TO PERFORM
460    03350                    THE OPERATION. THE INDEX INTO THE
461    03360                    OPERATOR TABLE IS MADE BY SUBTRACTING OFF THE CRUNCH VALUE
462    03370                    OF THE LOWEST NUMBERED OPERATOR. THE ORDER
463    03380                    OF OPERATORS IN THE CRUNCH LIST, AND IN OPTAB IS IDENTICAL.
464    03390                    THE PRECEDENCES ARE ARBITRARY EXCEPT FOR THEIR
465    03400                    COMPARATIVE SIZES. NOTE THAT THE PRECEDENCE FOR
466    03410                    UNARY OPERATORS SUCH AS NOT AND NEGATION ARE
467    03420                    SETUP SPECIALLY WITHOUT USING A TABLE.
468    03430
469    03440    THE RESERVED WORD OR CRUNCH LIST
470    03450                    WHEN A COMMAND OR PROGRAM LINE IS TYPED IN
471    03460                    IT IS STORED IN BUF. AS SOON AS THE WHOLE LINE
472    03470                    HAS BEEN TYPED IN (INLIN RETURNS) CRUNCH IS
```

A portion of the original source code for 8080 BASIC written by Bill Gates and Paul Allen in 1975. This historic program is the first high-level language written for a microcomputer (the MITS Altair). The notes shown here appear at the beginning of the program and describe how memory is configured.

348

```
BASIC MPU 8080/Z80    GATES/ALLEN/DAVIDOFF    MACRO X50(272)=1 21112 21-FEB-78 PAGE 1-6
F3       MAC    17-FEB-78 19118         SOME EXPLANATION
```

```
473                      03480          CALLED TO CONVERT ALL RESERVED WORDS TO THEIR
474                      03490          CRUNCH VALUES. THIS REDUCES THE SIZE OF THE
475                      03500          PROGRAM AND SPEEDS UP EXECUTION BY ALLOWING
476                      03510          TABLE DISPATCHES TO PERFORM FUNCTIONS,STATEMENTS,
477                      03520          AND OPERATIONS. THIS IS BECAUSE ALL THE STATEMENT
478                      03530          NAMES ARE STORED CONSECUTIVELY IN THE CRUNCH LIST.
479                      03540          WHEN A MATCH IS FOUND BETWEEN A STRING
480                      03550          OF CHARACTERS AND A WORD IN THE CRUNCH LIST
481                      03560          THE ENTIRE TEXT OF THE MATCHED WORD IS TAKEN OUT OF
482                      03570          THE INPUT LINE AND A RESERVED WORD TOKEN IS PUT
483                      03580          IN ITS PLACE. A RESERVED WORD TOKEN IS ALWAYS EQUAL
484                      03590          TO OCTAL 200 PLUS THE POSITION OF THE MATCHED WORD
485                      03600          IN THE CRUNCH LIST.
486                      03610
487                      03620  STATEMENT DISPATCH ADDRESSES
488                      03630          WHEN A STATEMENT IS TO BE EXECUTED, THE FIRST
489                      03640          CHARACTER OF THE STATEMENT IS EXAMINED
490                      03650          TO SEE IF IT IS LESS THAN THE RESERVED
491                      03660          WORD TOKEN FOR THE LOWEST NUMBERED STATEMENT NAME.
492                      03670          IF SO, THE "LET" CODE IS CALLED TO
493                      03680          TREAT THE STATEMENT AS AN ASSIGNMENT STATEMENT.
494                      03690          OTHERWISE A CHECK IS MADE TO MAKE SURE THE
495                      03700          RESERVED WORD NUMBER IS NOT TOO LARGE TO BE A
496                      03710          STATEMENT TYPE NUMBER.  IF NOT THE ADDRESS
497                      03720          TO DISPATCH TO IS FETCHED FROM STMDSP (THE STATEMENT
498                      03730          DISPATCH TABLE) USING THE RESERVED WORD
499                      03740          NUMBER FOR THE STATEMENT TO CALCULATE AN INDEX INTO
500                      03750          THE TABLE.
501                      03760
502                      03770  ERROR MESSAGES
503                      03780          WHEN AN ERROR CONDITION IS DETECTED
504                      03790          (E) MUST BE SET UP TO INDICATE WHICH ERROR
505                      03800          MESSAGE IS APPROPRIATE AND A BRANCH MUST BE MADE
506                      03810          TO ERROR. THE STACK WILL BE RESET AND ALL
507                      03820          PROGRAM CONTEXT WILL BE LOST. VARIABLES
508                      03830          VALUES AND THE ACTUAL PROGRAM REMAIN INTACT.
509                      03840          ONLY THE VALUE OF (E) IS IMPORTANT WHEN
510                      03850          THE BRANCH IS MADE TO ERROR, (E) IS USED AS AN
511                      03860          INDEX INTO ERRTAB WHICH GIVES THE TWO
512                      03870          CHARACTER ERROR MESSAGE THAT WILL BE PRINTED ON THE
513                      03880          USER'S TERMINAL.
514                      03890
515                      03900  IMPURE STORAGE
516                      03910          ALL TEMPORARIES,FLAGS,POINTERS, THE BUFFER AREA,
517                      03920          THE FLOATING ACCUMULATOR,AND ANYTHING ELSE THAT
518                      03930          IS USED TO STORE A CHANGING VALUE SHOULD BE LOCATED
519                      03940          IN THIS AREA. CARE MUST BE MADE IN MOVING LOCATIONS
520                      03950          IN THIS AREA SINCE THE JUXTAPOSITION OF TWO LOCATIONS
521                      03960          IS OFTEN DEPENDED UPON.
522                      03970
523                      03980  TEXTUAL MESSAGES
524                      03990          CONSTANT MESSAGES ARE STORED HERE, UNLESS
525                      04000          THE CODE TO CHECK IF A STRING MUST BE COPIED
526                      04010          IS CHANGED THESE STRINGS MUST BE STORED ABOVE
527                      04020          OSCTMP, OR ELSE THEY WILL BE COPIED BEFORE
```

```
BASIC MPU 8080/Z80    GATES/ALLEN/DAVIDOFF    MACRO X50(272)=1 21112 21-FEB-78 PAGE 1-7
F3       MAC    17-FEB-78 19118         SOME EXPLANATION
```

```
528                      04030          THEY ARE PRINTED.
529                      04040
530                      04050  FNDFOR
531                      04060          MOST SMALL ROUTINES ARE FAIRLY SIMPLE
532                      04070          AND ARE DOCUMENTED IN PLACE. FNDFOR IS
533                      04080          USED FOR FINDING "FOR" ENTRIES ON
534                      04090          THE STACK. WHENEVER A "FOR" IS EXECUTED AN
535                      04100          16 BYTE ENTRY IS PUSHED ONTO THE STACK.
536                      04110          BEFORE THIS IS DONE, HOWEVER, A CHECK
537                      04120          MUST BE MADE TO SEE IF THERE
538                      04130          ARE ANY "FOR" ENTRIES ALREADY ON THE STACK
539                      04140          FOR THE SAME LOOP VARIABLE. IF SO, THAT "FOR" ENTRY
540                      04150          AND ALL OTHER "FOR" ENTRIES THAT WERE MADE AFTER IT
541                      04160          ARE ELIMINATED FROM THE STACK. THIS IS SO A
542                      04170          PROGRAM THAT JUMPS OUT OF THE MIDDLE
543                      04180          OF A "FOR" LOOP AND THEN RESTARTS THE LOOP AGAIN
544                      04190          AND AGAIN WON'T USE UP 16 BYTES OF STACK
545                      04200          SPACE EVERY TIME THE "NEXT" CODE ALSO
546                      04210          CALLS FNDFOR TO SEARCH FOR A "FOR" ENTRY WITH
547                      04220          THE LOOP VARIABLE IN
548                      04230          THE "NEXT" AT WHATEVER POINT A MATCH IS FOUND
549                      04240          THE STACK IS RESET. IF NO MATCH IS FOUND A
550                      04250          "NEXT WITHOUT FOR" ERROR OCCURS. GOSUB EXECUTION
551                      04260          ALSO PUTS A 5 BYTE ENTRY ON STACK
552                      04270          WHEN A RETURN IS EXECUTED FNDFOR IS
553                      04280          CALLED WITH A VARIABLE POINTER THAT CAN'T
554                      04290          BE MATCHED. WHEN "FNDFOR" HAS RUN
555                      04300          THROUGH ALL THE "FOR" ENTRIES ON THE STACK
556                      04310          IT RETURNS AND THE RETURN CODE MAKES
557                      04320          SURE THE ENTRY THAT WAS STOPPED
558                      04330          ON IS A GOSUB ENTRY. THIS ASSURES THAT
559                      04340          IF YOU GOSUB TO A SECTION OF CODE
560                      04350          IN WHICH A FOR LOOP IS ENTERED BUT NEVER
561                      04360          EXITED THE RETURN WILL STILL BE
562                      04370          ABLE TO FIND THE MOST RECENT
563                      04380          GOSUB ENTRY. THE "RETURN" CODE ELIMINATES THE
564                      04390          "GOSUB" ENTRY AND ALL "FOR" ENTRIES MADE AFTER
565                      04400          THE GOSUB ENTRY.
566                      04410
567                      04420  NON-RUNTIME STUFF
568                      04430          THE CODE TO INPUT A LINE,CHUNCH IT,GIVE ERRORS,
569                      04440          FIND A SPECIFIC LINE IN THE PROGRAM,
570                      04450          PERFORM A "NEW", "CLEAR", AND "LIST" ARE
571                      04460          ALL IN THIS AREA. GIVEN THE EXPLANATION OF
572                      04470          PROGRAM STORAGE GIVEN BELOW THESE ARE
573                      04480          ALL STRAIGHTFORWARD.
574                      04490
575                      04500  NEWSTT
576                      04510          WHENEVER A STATEMENT FINISHES EXECUTION IT
577                      04520          DOES A "RET" WHICH TAKES
578                      04530          EXECUTION BACK TO NEWSTT. STATEMENTS THAT
579                      04540          CREATE OR LOOK AT SEMI-PERMANENT STACK ENTRIES
580                      04550          MUST GET RID OF THE RETURN ADDRESS OF NEWSTT AND
581                      04560          JMP TO NEWSTT WHEN DONE. NEWSTT ALWAYS
582                      04570          CHRGETS THE FIRST CHARACTER AFTER THE STATEMENT
```

```
583   04580         NAME BEFORE DISPATCHING. WHEN RETURNING
584   04590         BACK TO NEWSTT THE ONLY THING THAT
585   04600         MUST BE SET UP IS THE TEXT POINTER IN
586   04610         (H,L). NEWSTT WILL CHECK TO MAKE SURE
587   04620         (H,L) IS POINTING TO A STATEMENT TERMINATOR
588   04630         IF A STATEMENT SHOULDN'T BE PERFORMED UNLESS
589   04640         IT IS PROPERLY FORMATTED (I.E. "NEW") IT CAN
590   04650         SIMPLY DO A MNNZ AFTER READING ALL OF
591   04660         ITS ARGUMENTS, SINCE THE ZERO FLAG
592   04670         BEING OFF INDICATES THERE IS NOT
593   04680         A STATEMENT TERMINATOR NEWSTT WILL
594   04690         DO THE JMP TO THE "SYNTAX ERROR"
595   04700         ROUTINE. IF A STATEMENT SHOULD BE STARTED
596   04710         OVER IT CAN DO LHLD TEMP.KEY SINCE THE (H,L)
597   04720         AT NEWSTT IS ALWAYS STORED IN TEMP. OF COURSE
598   04730         CARE MUST BE TAKEN THAT NO ROUTINE
599   04740         THAT SMASHES TEMP HAS BEEN CALLED.
600   04750         THE "C" CODE STORES TEMP IN OLDTXT. AND CURLIN (THE
601   04760         CURRENT LINE NUMBER) IN OLDLIN SINCE THE ^C CHECK
602   04770         IS MADE BEFORE THE STATEMENT POINTED TO IS
603   04780         EXECUTED. "STOP" AND "END" STORE THE TEXT POINTER
604   04790         IN (H,L) WHICH POINTS AT THEIR TERMINATING
605   04800         CHARACTER IN OLDTXT.
606   04810
607   04820   STATEMENT CODE
608   04830         THE INDIVIDUAL STATEMENT CODE COMES
609   04840         NEXT. THE APPROACH USED IN EXECUTING EACH
610   04850         STATEMENT IS DOCUMENTED IN THE STATEMENT CODE
611   04860         ITSELF.
612   04870
613   04880   FRMEVL, THE FORMULA EVALUATOR
614   04890         GIVEN AN (H,L) POINTING TO THE STARTING
615   04900         CHARACTER OF A FORMULA FRMEVL
616   04910         EVALUATES THE FORMULA AND LEAVES
617   04920         THE VALUE IN THE FLOATING ACCUMULATOR (FAC).
618   04930         (H,L) IS RETURNED POINTING TO THE FIRST CHARACTER
619   04940         THAT COULD NOT BE INTERPRETED AS PART OF THE
620   04950         FORMULA THE ALGORITHM USES THE STACK
621   04960         TO STORE TEMPORARY RESULTS:
622   04970
623   04980         0. PUT A DUMMY PRECEDENCE OF ZERO ON
624   04990            THE STACK
625   05000         1. READ LEXEME (CONSTANT,FUNCTION,
626   05010            VARIABLE,FORMULA IN PARENS)
627   05020            AND TAKE THE LAST PRECEDENCE VALUE
628   05030            OFF THE STACK.
629   05040         2. SEE IF THE NEXT CHARACTER IS AN OPERATOR
630   05050            IF NOT RETURN. THIS MAY CAUSE
631   05060            OPERATOR APPLICATION OR AN ACTUAL
632   05070            RETURN FROM FRMEVL.
633   05080         3. IF IT IS, SEE WHAT PRECEDENCE IT HAS
634   05090            AND COMPARE IT TO THE PRECEDENCE
635   05100            OF THE LAST OPERATOR ON THE STACK
636   05110         4. IF # OR LESS REMEMBER THE TEXT
637   05120            POINTER AT THE START OF THIS OPERATOR
```

```
638   05130            AND DO A RETURN TO CAUSE
639   05140            APPLICATION OF THE LAST OPERATOR.
640   05150            EVENTUALLY RETURN TO STEP 2
641   05160            BY RETURNING TO RETAOP
642   05170         5. IF GREATER PUT THE LAST PRECEDENCE
643   05180            BACK ON, SAVE THE CURRENT
644   05190            TEMPORARY RESULT, OPERATOR ADDRESS
645   05200            AND PRECEDENCE AND RETURN TO STEP 1.
646   05210
647   05220         RELATIONAL OPERATORS ARE ALL HANDLED THROUGH
648   05230         A COMMON ROUTINE. SPECIAL
649   05240         CARE IS TAKEN TO DETECT TYPE MISMATCHES SUCH AS 3+"F"
650   05250
651   05260   EVAL -- THE ROUTINE TO READ A LEXEME
652   05270         EVAL CHECKS FOR THE DIFFERENT TYPES OF
653   05280         ENTITIES IT IS SUPPOSED TO DETECT.
654   05290         LEAVING PLUSES ARE IGNORED.
655   05300         DIGITS AND "." CAUSE FIN (FLOATING INPUT)
656   05310         TO BE CALLED. FUNCTION NAMES CAUSE
657   05320         FORMULA INSIDE THE PARENTHESES TO BE EVALUATED
658   05330         AND THE FUNCTION ROUTINE TO BE CALLED. VARIABLE
659   05340         NAMES CAUSE PTRGET TO BE CALLED TO GET A POINTER
660   05350         TO THE VALUE, AND THEN THE VALUE IS PUT INTO
661   05360         THE FAC. AN OPEN PARENTHESIS CAUSES FRMEVL
662   05370         TO BE CALLED RECURSIVELY, AND THE "1" TO
663   05380         BE CHECKED FOR. UNARY OPERATORS (NOT AND
664   05390         NEGATION) PUT THEIR PRECEDENCE ON THE STACK
665   05400         AND ENTER FORMULA EVALUATION AT STEP 1, SO
666   05410         THAT EVERYTHING UP TO AN OPERATOR GREATER THAN
667   05420         THEIR PRECEDENCE OR THE END OF THE FORMULA
668   05430         WILL BE EVALUATED. WHEN FRMEVL DOES A RETURN
669   05440         BECAUSE IT SEES AN OPERATOR OF HIGHER PRECEDENCE
670   05450         IT DOES NOT PASS THE TEXT POINTER IN (H,L) SO
671   05460         AFTER THE UNARY OPERATION HAS BEEN PERFORMED
672   05470         ON THE FAC THE TEXT POINTER MUST BE FETCHED FROM
673   05480         A TEMPORARY LOCATION THAT FRMEVL USES AND
674   05490         A RETURN BACK TO FRMEVL DONE.
675   05500
676   05510   DIMENSION AND VARIABLE SEARCHING
677   05520         SPACE IS ALLOCATED FOR VARIABLES AS THEY ARE
678   05530         ENCOUNTERED. THUS "DIM" STATEMENTS MUST BE
679   05540         EXECUTED TO HAVE EFFECT. 6 BYTES ARE ALLOCATED
680   05550         FOR EACH SIMPLE VARIABLE, WHETHER IT IS A STRING,
681   05560         NUMBER OR USER DEFINED FUNCTION. THE FIRST TWO
682   05570         BYTES GIVE THE NAME OF THE VARIABLE AND THE LAST FOUR
683   05580         GIVE ITS VALUE. (VARTAB) GIVES THE FIRST LOCATION
684   05590         WHERE A SIMPLE VARIABLE NAME IS FOUND AND (ARYTAB)
685   05600         GIVES THE LOCATION TO STOP SEARCHING FOR SIMPLE
686   05610         VARIABLES. A "FOR" ENTRY HAS A TEXT POINTER
687   05620         AND POINTER TO A VARIABLE VALUE SO NEITHER
688   05630         THE PROGRAM OR THE SIMPLE VARIABLES CAN BE
689   05640         MOVED WHILE THERE ARE ACTIVE "FOR" ENTRIES ON THE STACK.
690   05650         USER DEFINED FUNCTION VALUES ALSO CONTAIN
691   05660         POINTERS INTO SIMPLE VARIABLE SPACE SO NO USER-DEFINED
692   05670         FUNCTION VALUES CAN BE RETAINED IF SIMPLE VARIABLES
```

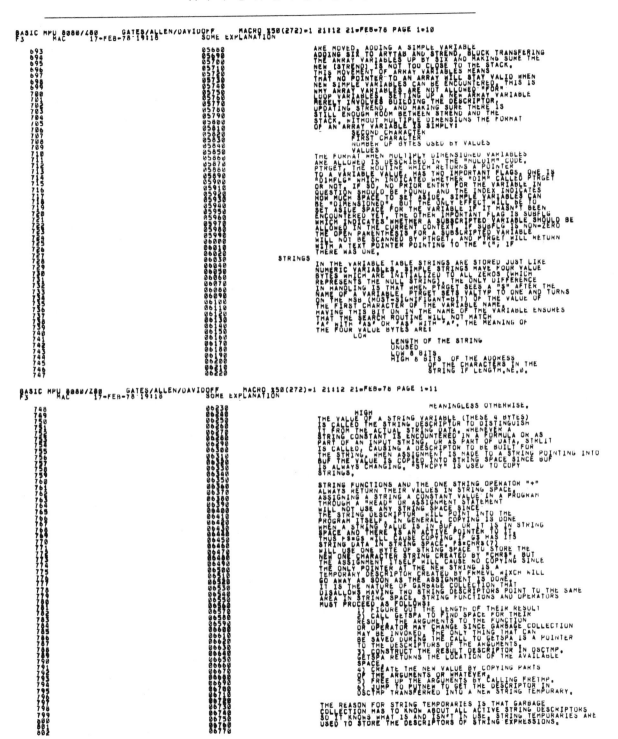

```
693    05680    ARE MOVED, ADDING A SIMPLE VARIABLE
694    05690    ADDING SIX TO ARYTAB AND STREND, BLOCK TRANSFERING
695    05700    THE ARRAY VARIABLES UP BY SIX AND MAKING SURE THE
696    05710    NEW (STREND) IS NOT TOO CLOSE TO THE STACK.
697    05720    THIS MOVEMENT OF ARRAY VARIABLES MEANS
698    05730    THAT A POINTER TO AN ARRAY WILL STAY VALID WHEN
699    05740    NEW SIMPLE VARIABLES CAN BE ENCOUNTERED. THIS IS
700    05750    WHY ARRAY VARIABLES ARE NOT ALLOWED "FOR"
701    05760    LOOP VARIABLES. SETTING UP A NEW ARRAY VARIABLE
702    05770    MERELY INVOLVES BUILDING THE DESCRIPTOR,
703    05780    UPDATING STREND, AND MAKING SURE THERE IS
704    05790    STILL ENOUGH ROOM BETWEEN STREND AND THE
705    05800    STACK. WITHOUT MULTIPLE DIMENSIONS THE FORMAT
706    05810    OF AN ARRAY VARIABLE IS SIMPLY:
707    05820        SECOND CHARACTER
708    05830        FIRST CHARACTER
709    05840        NUMBER OF BYTES USED BY VALUES
710    05850        VALUES
711    05860    THE FORMAT WHEN MULTIPLY DIMENSIONED VARIABLES
712    05870    ARE ALLOWED IS DESCRIBED IN THE "MULDIM" CODE.
713    05880    PTRGET, THE ROUTINE WHICH RETURNS A POINTER
714    05890    TO A VARIABLE VALUE, HAS TWO IMPORTANT FLAGS. ONE IS
715    05900    "DIMFLG" WHICH INDICATED WHETHER "DIM" CALLED PTRGET
716    05910    OR NOT. IF SO, NO PRIOR ENTRY FOR THE VARIABLE IN
717    05920    QUESTION SHOULD BE FOUND, AND THE INDEX INDICATES
718    05930    HOW MUCH SPACE TO SET ASIDE. SIMPLE VARIABLES CAN
719    05940    BE "DIMENSIONED" BUT THE ONLY EFFECT WILL BE TO
720    05950    SET ASIDE SPACE FOR THE VARIABLE IF IT HASN'T BEEN
721    05960    ENCOUNTERED YET. THE OTHER IMPORTANT FLAG IS SUBFLG
722    05970    WHICH INDICATES WHETHER A SUBSCRIPTED VARIABLE SHOULD BE
723    05980    ALLOWED IN THE CURRENT CONTEXT. IF SUBFLG IS NON-ZERO
724    05990    THE OPEN PARENTHESIS FOR A SUBSCRIPTED VARIABLE
725    06000    WILL NOT BE SCANNED BY PTRGET, AND PTRGET WILL RETURN
726    06010    WITH A TEXT POINTER POINTING TO THE "(", IF
727    06020    THERE WAS ONE.
728    06030
729    06040    STRINGS
730    06050        IN THE VARIABLE TABLE STRINGS ARE STORED JUST LIKE
731    06060    NUMERIC VARIABLES. SIMPLE STRINGS HAVE FOUR VALUE
732    06070    BYTES WHICH ARE INITIALIZED TO ALL ZEROS (WHICH
733    06080    REPRESENTS THE NULL STRING). THE ONLY DIFFERENCE
734    06090    IN HANDLING IS THAT WHEN PTRGET SEES A "$" AFTER THE
735    06100    NAME OF A VARIABLE, PTRGET SETS VALTYP TO ONE AND TURNS
736    06110    ON THE MSB (MOST-SIGNIFICANT-BIT) OF THE VALUE OF
737    06120    THE FIRST CHARACTER OF THE VARIABLE NAME.
738    06130    HAVING THIS BIT ON IN THE NAME OF THE VARIABLE ENSURES
739    06140    THAT THE SEARCH ROUTINE WILL NOT MATCH
740    06150    "A" WITH "A$" OR "A$" WITH "A". THE MEANING OF
741    06160    THE FOUR VALUE BYTES ARE:
742    06170        LOW
743    06180            LENGTH OF THE STRING
744    06190            UNUSED
745    06200            LOW 8 BITS
746    06210            HIGH 8 BITS  OF THE ADDRESS IN THE
747    06220                         OF THE CHARACTERS IN THE
                                     STRING IF LENGTH.NE.0.
```

```
748    06230                         MEANINGLESS OTHERWISE.
749    06240        HIGH
750    06250    THE VALUE OF A STRING VARIABLE (THESE 4 BYTES)
751    06260    IS CALLED THE STRING DESCRIPTOR TO DISTINGUISH
752    06270    IT FROM THE ACTUAL STRING DATA. WHENEVER A
753    06280    STRING CONSTANT IS ENCOUNTERED IN A FORMULA OR AS
754    06290    PART OF AN INPUT STRING, OR AS PART OF DATA, STRLIT
755    06300    IS CALLED, CAUSING A DESCRIPTOR TO BE BUILT FOR
756    06310    THE STRING. WHEN ASSIGNMENT IS MADE TO A STRING POINTING INTO
757    06320    BUF THE VALUE IS COPIED INTO STRING SPACE SINCE BUF
758    06330    IS ALWAYS CHANGING. "STRCPY" IS USED TO COPY
759    06340    STRINGS.
760    06350
761    06360    STRING FUNCTIONS AND THE ONE STRING OPERATION "+"
762    06370    ALWAYS RETURN THEIR VALUES IN STRING SPACE.
763    06380    ASSIGNING A STRING A CONSTANT VALUE IN A PROGRAM
764    06390    THROUGH A "READ" OR ASSIGNMENT STATEMENT
765    06400    WILL NOT USE ANY STRING SPACE SINCE
766    06410    THE STRING DESCRIPTOR WILL POINT INTO THE
767    06420    PROGRAM ITSELF. IN GENERAL, COPYING IS DONE
768    06430    WHEN A STRING VALUE IS IN BUF OR IT IS IN STRING
769    06440    SPACE AND THERE IS AN ACTIVE POINTER TO IT.
770    06450    THUS F$=G$ WILL CAUSE COPYING IF G$ HAS ITS
771    06460    STRING DATA IN STRING SPACE. F$=CHR$(7)
772    06470    WILL USE ONE CHARACTER OF STRING SPACE TO STORE THE
773    06480    NEW ONE CHARACTER STRING CREATED BY "CHR$", BUT
774    06490    ASSIGNMENT ITSELF WILL CAUSE NO COPYING SINCE
775    06500    THE ONLY POINTER TO THE NEW STRING IS A
776    06510    TEMPORARY DESCRIPTOR CREATED BY FRMEVL WHICH WILL
777    06520    GO AWAY AS SOON AS THE ASSIGNMENT IS DONE.
778    06530    IT IS THE NATURE OF GARBAGE COLLECTION THAT
779    06540    DISALLOWS HAVING TWO STRING DESCRIPTORS POINT TO THE SAME
780    06550    AREA IN STRING SPACE. STRING FUNCTIONS AND OPERATORS
781    06560    MUST PROCEED AS FOLLOWS:
782    06570        1) FIGURE OUT THE LENGTH OF THEIR RESULT
783    06580        2) CALL GETSPA TO FIND SPACE FOR THEIR
784    06590           RESULT. THE ARGUMENTS TO THE FUNCTION
785    06600           OR OPERATOR MAY CHANGE SINCE GARBAGE COLLECTION
786    06610           MAY BE INVOKED. THE ONLY THING THAT CAN
787    06620           BE SAVED DURING THE CALL TO GETSPA IS A POINTER
788    06630           TO THE DESCRIPTORS OF THE ARGUMENTS.
789    06640        3) CONSTRUCT THE RESULT DESCRIPTOR IN DSCTMP.
790    06650           GETSPA RETURNS THE LOCATION OF THE AVAILABLE
791    06660           SPACE.
792    06670        4) CREATE THE NEW VALUE BY COPYING PARTS
793    06680           OF THE ARGUMENTS OR WHATEVER.
794    06690        5) FREE UP THE ARGUMENTS BY CALLING FRETMP.
795    06700        6) JUMP TO PUTNEW TO GET THE DESCRIPTOR IN
796    06710           DSCTMP TRANSFERRED INTO A NEW STRING TEMPORARY.
797    06720
798    06730    THE REASON FOR STRING TEMPORARIES IS THAT GARBAGE
799    06740    COLLECTION HAS TO KNOW ABOUT ALL ACTIVE STRING DESCRIPTORS
800    06750    SO IT KNOWS WHAT IS AND ISN'T IN USE. STRING TEMPORARIES ARE
801    06760    USED TO STORE THE DESCRIPTORS OF STRING EXPRESSIONS.
802    06770
```

BASIC MPU 8080/Z80   GATES/ALLEN/DAVIDOFF   MACRO %50(272)=1 21112 21-FEB-78 PAGE 1-12
F3   MAC   17-FEB-78 19:18   SOME EXPLANATION

```
803    06760    INSTEAD OF HAVING AN ACTUAL VALUE STORED IN THE
804    06770    FAC, AND HAVING THE VALUE OF A TEMPORARY RESULT
805    06780    BEING SAVED ON THE STACK, AS HAPPENS WITH NUMERIC
806    06810    VARIABLES, STRINGS HAVE THE POINTER TO A STRING DESCRIPTOR
807    06820    STORED IN THE FAC, AND IT IS THIS POINTER
808    06830    THAT GETS SAVED ON THE STACK BY FORMULA EVALUATION.
809    06840    STRING FUNCTIONS CANNOT FREE THEIR ARGUMENTS UP RIGHT
810    06850    AWAY SINCE GETSPA MAY FORCE
811    06860    GARBAGE COLLECTION AND THE ARGUMENT STRINGS
812    06870    MAY BE OVER-WRITTEN SINCE GARBAGE COLLECTION
813    06880    WILL NOT BE ABLE TO FIND AN ACTIVE POINTER TO
814    06890    THEM. FUNCTION AND OPERATOR RESULTS ARE BUILT IN
815    06900    DSCTAP SINCE STRING TEMPORARIES ARE ALLOCATED
816    06910    (PUTNEW) AND DEALLOCATED (FRETMP) IN A FIFO ORDERING
817    06920    (I.E. A STACK) SO THE NEW TEMPORARY CANNOT
818    06930    BE SET UP UNTIL THE OLD ONE(S) ARE FREED. TRYING
819    06940    TO BUILD A RESULT IN A TEMPORARY AFTER
820    06950    FREEING UP THE ARGUMENT TEMPORARIES COULD RESULT
821    06960    IN ONE OF THE ARGUMENT TEMPORARIES BEING OVERWRITTEN
822    06980    TOO SOON BY THE NEW RESULT.
823
824    06990    STRING SPACE IS ALLOCATED AT THE VERY TOP
825    07000    OF MEMORY. MEMSIZ POINTS BEYOND THE LAST LOCATION OF
826    07010    STRING SPACE. STRINGS ARE STORED IN HIGH LOCATIONS
827    07020    FIRST. WHENEVER STRING SPACE IS ALLOCATED (GETSPA)
828    07030    FRETOP, WHICH IS INITIALIZED TO [MEMSIZ], IS UPDATED
829    07040    TO GIVE THE HIGHEST LOCATION IN STRING SPACE
830    07050    THAT IS NOT IN USE. THE RESULT IS THAT
831    07060    FRETOP GETS SMALLER AND SMALLER, UNTIL SOME
832    07070    ALLOCATION WOULD MAKE [FRETOP] LESS THAN OR EQUAL TO
833    07080    [STKTOP]. THIS MEANS STRING SPACE HAS RUN INTO THE
834    07090    STACK AND THAT GARBAGE COLLECTION MUST BE CALLED.
835    07100
836    07110    GARBAGE COLLECTION:
837    07120      0. MINPTR=[STKTOP]  [FRETOP]=[MEMSIZ]
838    07130      1. REMMIN=0
839    07140      2. FOR EACH STRING DESCRIPTOR
840    07150         (TEMPORARIES, SIMPLE STRINGS, STRING ARRAYS)
841    07160         IF THE STRING IS NOT NULL AND ITS POINTER IS
842    07170         GT MINPTR AND LT FRETOP
843    07180         MINPTR=THIS STRING DESCRIPTORS POINTER
844    07190         REMMIN=POINTER AT THIS STRING DESCRIPTOR
845    07200      END
846    07210      3. IF REMMIN.NE.0 (WE FOUND AN UNCOLLECTED STRING)
847    07220         BLOCK TRANSFER THE STRING DATA POINTED
848    07230         TO IN THE STRING DESCRIPTOR POINTED TO BY REMMIN
849    07240         SO THAT THE LAST BYTE OF STRING DATA IS AT
850    07250         [FRETOP]. UPDATE FRETOP SO THAT IT
851    07260         POINTS TO THE LOCATION JUST BELOW THE ONE
852    07270         THE STRING DATA WAS MOVED INTO. UPDATE
853    07280         THE POINTER IN THE DESCRIPTOR SO IT POINTS
854    07290         TO THE NEW LOCATION OF THE STRING DATA.
855    07300         GO TO STEP 1.
856    07310
857    07320    AFTER CALLING GARBAGE COLLECTION GETSPA AGAIN CHECKS
```

BASIC MPU 8080/Z80   GATES/ALLEN/DAVIDOFF   MACRO %50(272)=1 21112 21-FEB-78 PAGE 1-13
F3   MAC   17-FEB-78 19:18   SOME EXPLANATION

```
858    07330    TO SEE IF [A] CHARACTERS ARE AVAILABLE BETWEEN
859    07340    [STKTOP] AND [FRETOP] , IF NOT AN "OUT OF STRING"
860    07350    ERROR IS INVOKED.
861    07360
862    07370    MATH PACKAGE
863    07380      THE MATH PACKAGE CONTAINS FLOATING INPUT (FIN),
864    07390      FLOATING OUTPUT (FOUT) FLOATING COMPARE (FCOMP),
865    07400      AND ALL THE NUMERIC OPERATORS AND FUNCTIONS.
866    07410      THE FORMATS,CONVENTIONS AND ENTRY POINTS ARE ALL
867    07420      DESCRIBED IN THE MATH PACKAGE ITSELF.
868    07430
869    07440    INIT --  THE INITIALIZATION ROUTINE (FOR NON-T/S VERSION)
870    07450      INITIALIZATION FIRST LOOKS AT THE SWITCH REGISTER
871    07460      TO SEE WHAT TYPE OF I/O SHOULD BE DONE.
872    07470      ANY NON-STANDARD I/O CAUSES LOCATIONS IN BASIC
873    07480      TO BE CHANGED. THEN THE AMOUNT OF MEMORY,
874    07490      TERMINAL WIDTH,AND WHICH FUNCTIONS TO BE RETAINED
875    07500      ARE ASCERTAINED FROM THE USER. A ZERO IS PUT DOWN
876    07510      AT THE FIRST LOCATION NOT USED BY THE MATH-PACKAGE
877    07520      AND TXTTAB IS SET UP TO POINT AT THE NEXT LOCATION.
878    07530      THIS DETERMINES WHERE PROGRAM STORAGE WILL START. THE
879    07540      HIGHEST MEMORY LOCATION MINUS THE AMOUNT OF DEFAULTED
880    07550      STRING SPACE (50) GIVES THE FIRST LOCATION USED BY THE
881    07560      STACK. SPECIAL CHECKS ARE MADE TO MAKE SURE
882    07570      ALL QUESTIONS BY INIT ARE ANSWERED REASONABLY, SINCE
883    07580      ONCE INIT FINISHES THE LOCATIONS IT USES ARE
884    07590      USED FOR PROGRAM STORAGE.  THE LAST THING INIT DOES IS
885    07600      CHANGE LOCATION ONE TO BE A JUMP TO READY INSTEAD
886    07610      OF INIT, ONCE THIS IS DONE THERE IS NO WAY TO RESTART
887    07620      INIT.
888    07630
889    07640    (IN THE TIMESHARING VERSION, THE INITIALIZATION
       07650    PROCESS IS COMPLETELY DIFFERENT, SEE TSINIT.MAC)
890    07660
891    07670    STORAGE
892    07680              A ZERO
893    07690    [TXTTAB]  POINTER TO NEXT LINE'S POINTER
894    07700              LINE # OF THIS LINE (2 BYTES)
895    07710              CHARACTERS ON THIS LINE
896    07720              ZERO
897    07730              POINTER AT NEXT LINE'S POINTER
898    07740                  (POINTED TO BY THE ABOVE POINTER)
899    07750              REPEATS
900    07760    LAST LINE: POINTER AT ZERO POINTER
901    07770              LINE # OF THIS LINE
902    07780              CHARACTERS ON THIS LINE
903    07790              ZERO
904    07800              DOUBLE ZERO (POINTED TO BY THE ABOVE POINTER)
905    07810    [VARTAB]  SIMPLE VARIABLES, 6 BYTES PER VALUE,
906    07820              2 BYTES GIVE THE NAME, 4 BYTES THE VALUE
907    07830              REPEATS
908    07840    [ARYTAB]  ARRAY VARIABLES, 2 BYTES NAME, 2 BYTE
909    07850              LENGTH, VALUE (EXTRA IF LENGTH ON)
910    07860              REPEATS
911    07860    [STREND]  FREE SPACE  ...
912    07870              ... REPEATS ...
```

Storage layout for BASIC

(low memory)

[—TXTTAB]

zero	(1 byte)
pointer to next line	(2 bytes)
binary line #	(2 bytes)
character on line	(see note 11)
zero	(1 byte)

<Repeat above for each line>

zero   (2 bytes)

[VARTAB] Simple variables. 6 bytes per variable
2 bytes give the name
4 bytes give the value.
<Repeat for each variable>

[ARYTAB] Array variables
2 byte name.
2 byte length.
values —

Repeats for each array

[STREND] lowest location for stack

[STKTOP] Free space   (SP can be in here)
most recent stack entry
stack

[FRETOP] bottom of stack / lowest location for strings

[FRETOP] free space
current string usage
STRINGS

[MEMSIZ] highest machine location.

This scheme allows for simple
table management. Only collector
is for strings which aren't in 4K BASIC.

COMPUTER NOTES/SEPTEMBER,1975

Software Notes

by Bill Gates

Though the most difficult and enjoyable part of writing a program is the design of data structures and program flow, it is also important to use the least number of instructions possible to perform each function in a program. For instance:

```
CALL SUB1      should be replaced by
RET

JMP SUB1       unless something fairly
               tricky is being done
```

with return addresses. The JMP is faster, takes one less byte, and uses no stack space. An instruction book on programming the 8008 ignores this simple fact!

JMPs should be avoided wherever possible. By rearranging code you can often avoid having an unconditional JMP by falling into the routine you were JMPing to.

The beginning programmer will use lots of SHLDs, LHLDs, STAs and LDAs when they are not necessary. The stack can be used to save temporary values in most cases. SHLDs, LHLDs, LDAs and STAs should only be used for values referenced in many different contexts within a program, i.e. an I/O parameter or the current line number.

A good technique for familiarizing yourself with the instruction set is to go out of your way to use every instruction at least once (except perhaps DAA). Go through the instruction set from time to time and look closely at the instructions you seem to use very rarely. With few exceptions (DAA, SPHL) all the instructions can be used to advantage, even in small programs. One of the most overlooked instructions is XTHL. When all the accumulators have values that must be saved and a value needs to be taken off the stack, XTHL is the only instruction that can be used.

```
Example:   ;Exchange [B,C] with [H,L]

PUSH B     ;put [B,C] on the stack

XTHL       ;[H,L] = top stack entry =
           [B,C]

           ;[H,L] goes on the stack

POP B      ;[B,C] = original [H,L]
```

Sometimes the simple way of doing things is the best. PUSH B/POP D may seem like a tricky way of setting [D,E] = [B,C], but the obvious sequence MOV D,B/MOV E,C is much faster.

Some tricks involve instruction sequences which at first sight seem meaningless. For instance: SUB A or XRA A. Subtracting A from itself or exclusive-oring A with itself are the only one-byte ways of setting A=0. MVI A,0 must still be used if the condition codes need to be preserved, but this is rare.

ADC A is equivalent to RAL, except it affects all the condition codes. SBB A sets A=0 if carry is off and A=377 if carry is on. The routine below uses this fact to convert A as a signed integer to a double byte signed integer in [H,L]:

```
MOV L,A   ;setup the low order
          ;now the sign must be
          ;"extended" by setting H=0
          ;if A=>0 and H=377 otherwise
RAL       ;Carry = 1 if A<0
          ;Carry = 0 if A=>0
SBB A     ;A=0 if old A was =>0
          ;A=377 if old A was <0
MOV H,A   ;setup the high order
```

```
The sequence:  INR E
               DCR E
```

doesn't modify any values, but it does set the condition codes (except carry) depending on what is in E. If E is being used as a flag to indicate, say, whether or not a decimal point has been seen, the zero flag is set up to do a conditional JMP.

The subject of good decimal print routines has been discussed extensively in the Altair Software Department this week. This routine is one of the four or five I wrote this week -- each with its own advantages and disadvantages. This one is fairly tricky, in that it takes a little bit of looking at to understand.

```
#1 ;
   ;Print the binary unsigned number
   ;in [H,L] in decimal, suppressing
   ;leading zeros
   ;
   ;24 bytes (25 if saves D,E)
   ;ON RETURN:
   ;A = last digit in ASCII
   ;B,D = 255 (all constants in
   ;decimal)
   ;C,E = last digit -10
   ;H,L = 0
   ;
   ;Uses up to 18 bytes of stack
   ;Total compute time up to 85
   ;milliseconds
   ;
   ;IDEA: calculate a digit, save it
   ;          on the stack, and call the
   ;          digit calculator to calcu-
   ;          late and print higher order
   ;          digits, pop the digit off
   ;          and print it.
   ;
```

The following articles appeared in *Computer Notes*, a newsletter published by David Bunnell for users of the MITS Altair computer. Portions of Gates' handwritten manuscript are shown adjacent to corresponding sections of the newsletter.

Gates explains, "These [routines] show some pretty incredible tricks—really squeezing things to the utmost. The print routine is the shortest routine any of us ever came up with for taking a binary number and printing digits."

A bootstrap program to read paper tape had to be keyed into the Altair using the switches on the front of the computer. Gates wrote the bootstrap program shown in column three of the third page. He explains, "This is the shortest bootstrap program and is very, very tricky. People can look at the program for 15 minutes before they figure out how it works."

Print the binary un signed number in [H,L] in decimal. suppress leading zeros!

Idea for digit printer:
calculate a digit - save it on the stack and call the digit calculator to calculate and print higher order digits, pop the digit off the stack and print it.

Uses up to 18 bytes of stack. up to 85 milleseconds of compute.

-continued

Software Notes

```
DECOUT:   LXI B, -10      ;CALL here
GETDIG:   MOV D,B         ;[D,E] = -1
          MOV E,B         ;since B = 255
LOOPSB:   DAD B           ;Subtract 10 from [H,L] until [H,L] < 10. Carry
                          ;won't be set by the last DAD when [H,L] < 10.
          INX D           ;increment the count
          JC LOOPSB       ;loop subtracting
          PUSH H          ;[L] = current digit -10
                          ;Save the current digit on the stack.  Change to
                          ;XTHL and add PUSH D at GETDIG to save [D,E].
          XCHG            ;[H,L] = old [H,L]/10
          MOV A,H         ;Set zero flag if [H,L] = 0
          ORA L
          CNZ GETDIG      ;If not zero, print the higher order digits and
                          ;then return here to print this digit.
          MVI A, "0" + 10 ;A = constant to add to digit
          POP B           ;pop the digit into C
          ADD C           ;A = ASCII of digit
          JMP OUTCHR      ;Jump to the routine to print A and return.  If
                          ;OUTCHR is located next, the JMP can be eliminated.
```

Parity is used as a check to detect errors in data transmission. Each data word is given an additional bit which is set to 1 if there are an odd number of 1's in the data and 0 otherwise. When the data is received the parity bit is checked to make sure it is set properly. Thus, if you are reading a 7-bit ASCII paper tape with the 8th bit used for parity, the parity of the entire 8 bits should be even.

The reason I first thought about a parity routine for the 8080 is that the parity condition code and all the instructions related to it (JPO, JPE, RPE, RPO, CPO, CPE) are seldom used. I wondered how difficult it would be to calculate parity if the parity flag were removed. A user-settable flag would be much more useful than the parity flag. BASIC uses the parity flag in only about eight places, and all of these are special tricks. Here is the smallest parity routine I've been able to write:

```
;Enter with number in A.  10 bytes.
;On exit, A=0 and all the other reg-
;isters are preserved.
;Carry is set depending on A's
;parity.
;Enter at ODDPAR for carry on to
;mean odd parity.

ODDPAR:   ADD A           ;Move a bit of A into carry.

          RZ              ;If all bits added into carry, return.

          JNC ODDPAR      ;If no bit moved into carry, rotate more.

;enter at EVNPAR for carry on to
;mean even parity

EVNPAR:   ADI 200         ;Complement the parity of the remaining bits

          JMP ODDPAR      ;Rotate more.
```

(Right side — handwritten notes)

Best digit printer
Short digit print out 24 bytes
; enter at Decout with number in [H,L]
```
DECOUT:   LXI  B,-10      ; base count
GETDIG:   MOV  D,B        ; set [D,E] = -1
          MOV  E,B        ; since [B] = 255

LOOPSB:   DAD  B          ; subtract 10 from [H,L]
          INX  D          ; until [H,L]<0.
                          ; increment the count.
          JC   LOOPSB     ; no carry if [H,L]>10.
          PUSH H          ; [L] = current digit-10
          XCHG            ; get [H,L]= old [H,L]/10
          MOV  A,H        ; see if it's done [H,L]=0
          ORA  L          ;
          CNZ  GETDIG     ; if not recursively
                          ; print the higher order
                          ; digits before printing this one

          MVI  A,"0"+10   ; constant to get char code
          POP  B          ; get the digit -10
          ADD  C          ; compute char code
          JMP  OUTCHR     ; print [A] and return.
```

Lets say the 8080 had no parity bit — minimal routine to do it. They didn't need parity! Is there a smaller routine?
```
; Compute parity.
; Enter with number in [A]
; on exit [A]=0 and all others preserved.
; Carry is set depending on [A]'s parity
; enter at opppar for carry on to mean
; odd parity

ODDPAR:   ADD  A          ; moves bit into carry
          RZ              ; if all bits added, return
          JNC  ODDPAR     ; if no bit in carry, rotate more
; enter at EVNPAR for carry on to mean even parity
EVNPAR:   ADI  200        ; complement parity of remaining
          JMP  ODDPAR     ; rotate more.
```

Software

By bill Gates

COMPUTER NOTES/JULY, 1975

Condition Codes

There seems to be some confusion about the condition codes. These are the Boolean (true/false) flags that are set/reset depending on the results of certain instructions. They are:

Z = zero - result was 0
S = sign - the most significant bit (MSB) of the result
P = parity - the result has an even number of ones in it
C = carry - an arithmetic operation generated a carry out of the most significant bit (i.e. adding 200 to 212)
CY_1 = first digit carry - this is used only for BCD arithmetic and will be elaborated on next month.

It is the condition codes that determine whether conditional JMP's, CALL's and RET's will be executed (i.e. RZ, CPE, JP). JM, CM, and RM (minus) are executed if the sign flag is on. JP, CP, and RP (positive) are executed if the sign flag is off. JZ, JNZ, CNZ, RZ, RNZ (zero/no zero) depend on the zero flag just as JC, JNC, CC, CNC, RC, RNC (carry/no carry) depend on the carry flag. CPE, JPE, RPE (parity even) are executed if the parity flag is on and CPO, JPO, RPO are executed when it is off.

The condition codes do not always reflect the value in A since IN, LDA, LDAX, MOV and MVI can change A but do not affect the condition codes. Instructions like INR C, DCR L, CMP B, CPI 3, STC, CMC and DAD B affect the condition codes, but not A.

Affect carry only: STC, CMC, RAL, RAR, RLC, RRC and DAD.

Affect all but carry: INR, DCR.

Affect all: ADD, ADC, SUB, SBB, CMP, ANA, ORA, XRA, DAA and their immediate counterparts (i.e. ADI,CPI).

Use carry to affect result: CMC, RAP, RAL, ADC, SBB, ACI, SBI, DAA.

The instructions XRA, ORA, ANA, XRI ORI and ANI always reset carry.

If the condition codes do not reflect A's value (i.e. you just did a LDA or MOV into A) and you want to see if A=0, use ORA A or ANA A. CPI 0, ADI 0 and ORI 0 also work but they are 2-bytes.

The only other instructions besides the ones in the list above that use the condition codes are PUSH PSW and POP PSW. Respectively, they SAVE/RESTORE the condition codes and A on the stack.

For tricky programmers a sequence like PUSH B / POP PSW may be used to set the condition codes. This has the effect of moving B into A (MOV A, B) and moving C into the condition codes. The PSW (condition code) format is

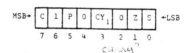

MSB→ | C | 1 | P | 0 | CY_1 | 0 | Z | S | ←LSB
7 6 5 4 3 2 1 0

Therefore if C was 201_8 before the POP PSW, zero and sign would be set and parity and zero would be unset. The bits marked '0' and '1' are constant and cannot be changed.

HINT #1

If you have a counter that can be bigger than 255 but is always less than 65535, it is convenient to use the following:

```
LXI B, count   ;set up counter
LOOP: code to be executed 'count'
               times
DCX B          ;decrement count
               ;does not affect
               ;condition codes

MOV A,B
ORA C          ;see if any bits set
JNZ LOOP       ;go back if so
```

HINT #2

For those who like to save bytes, and especially for those with 256-byte machines, (a byte is always 8 bits, which is a word on the 8800) RST's that are not used for interrupts, debug calls, monitor calls, etc. can be used to call subroutines that get called in many places (i.e. a character input subroutine). An RST is only 1 byte and a CALL is 3 bytes. Even if you have to put in a JMP so you don't overrun another RST location (0,10,20,30,40,50,60,70) you will probably save bytes.

Loading Software

Software from MITS will be provided in a checksummed format. There will be a bootstrap loader that you key in manually (less than 25 bytes). This will read a checksum loader (the 'bin' loader) which will be about 120 bytes.

For audio cassette loading the bootstrap and checksum loaders will be longer. All of this will be explained in detail in a cover package that will go out with all software.

For loading non-checksummed paper tapes here is a short program:

```
STKLOC: DW GETNEW
              (2 bytes-#1 low byte of
                   GETNEW address
              #2 high byte of
                   GETNEW address)

START:  LXI H,0
GETNEW: LXI SP, STKLOC
        IN <flag-input channel>
        RAL  ;get input ready bit
        RNZ  ;ready?
        IN <data-input channel>
CHGLOC: CPI <043 = INX B>
        RNZ
        INR A
        STA CHGLOC
        RET
                   (22 bytes)
```

Punch a paper tape with leader, a 043 start byte, the byte to be stored at loc 0, the byte to be stored at 1, - - - etc. Start at START, making sure the memory the loader is in is unprotected. Make sure you don't wipe out the loader by loading on top of it.

To run this again change CHGLOC back to CPI - 376.

Hypertext for C programmers.
This one turns music upside down.
E-Z!

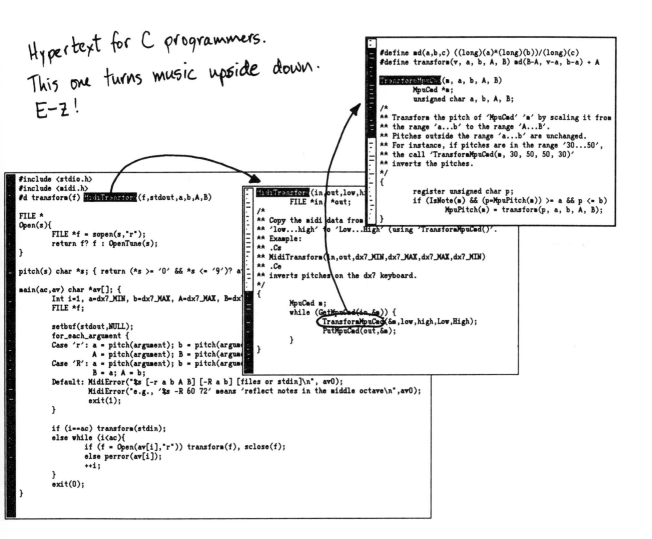

A program from Michael Hawley that inverts all pitches to turn music upside down. See page 302 for the results of this technique.

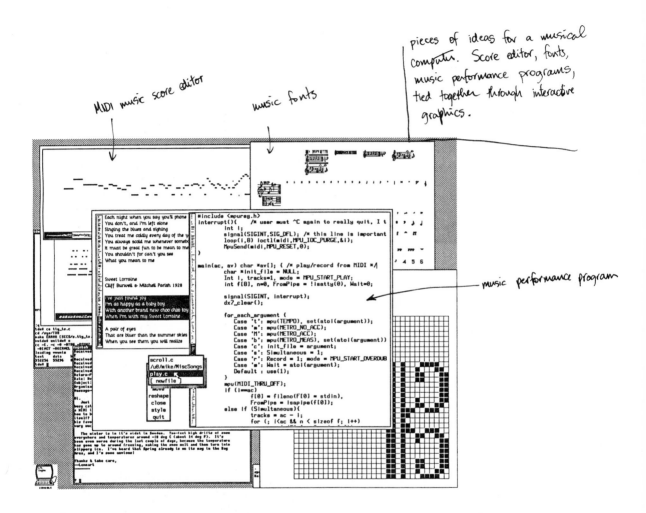

pieces of ideas for a musical computer. Score editor, fonts, music performance programs, tied together through interactive graphics.

MIDI music score editor

music fonts

music performance program

Michael Hawley from Lucasfilm Ltd. provides his ideas for a musical computer. His handwritten notes describe different components of the screen and supporting language.

graphical patching of microcodes
- starts as a picture; then ② becomes a language
       ~~~~~ implementation follows.

Delete: left button to delete item, mi...
              delete region.

.Mail mis
Subject:
another faction just suggested spicy thai here in s.r.,
followed by the first meeting of the skywalker astronomy club (a...
up at the ranch. maybe you want to come up and stargaze.
and cheer me up.
Cc:
.From mis Thu Nov 7 17:21:10 1985
Received: from dagobah by do; 07 NOV 85 17:21:10 PST
From: mis (Mark Seiden, Lucasfilm System Group, 415-485-5011)
To: mike
Received: by dagobah; 07 NOV 85 17:22:27 PST
Subject: cheer up

I have too much to do tonight — finishing my '84 taxes and 85 estimates.
I need to be cheered up too.

c   xab1
c.c   xadc1
cmd.c   xadd
font   xdac1
list.h   xeq1
md   xeq2
slice.bits   xfader1
slice.pic   xrevsend1
symbols   xslice.bits
tax   xslider
x.c   xxfade1
x2pan2   xxfade2
x3pan1

jem's box

.spr
Wait!   uh...█

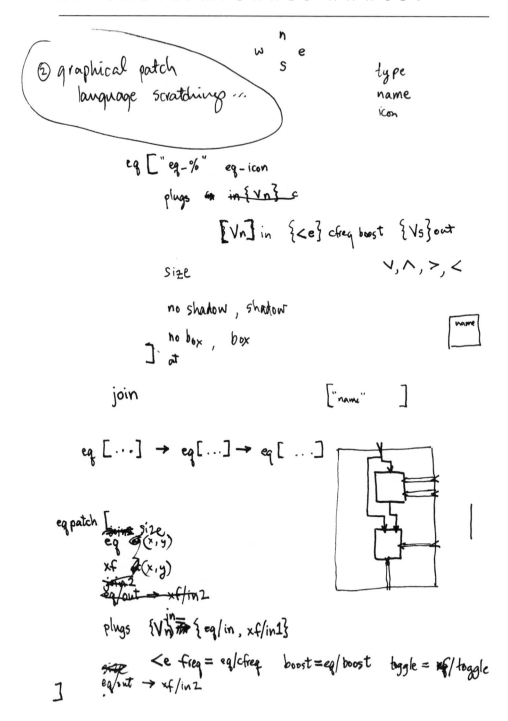

② graphical patch
   language scratchings ...

$$\begin{array}{c} n \\ w \quad\quad e \\ s \end{array}$$

type
name
icon

eq ["eq-%"   eq-icon

   plugs ~~in~~ ~~in~~ {Vn} c

      [Vn] in {<e} cfreq boost {Vs} out

             ∨,∧,>,<

   size

   no shadow , shadow

     no box , box

  ] at

  join   ["name"   ]

eq [...] → eq[...] → eq[...]

eq patch [~~join~~ size,
    eq @(x,y)
    xf @(x,y)
    ~~join 2~~
    ~~eq/out → xf/in2~~
   plugs {Vn in = {eq/in, xf/in1}

    ~~size~~ <e freq = eq/cfreq   boost = eq/boost   toggle = xf/toggle
  ]   eq/out → xf/in2

360

```
; File IconBounce.TXT
;-----------------------------------------------------------------------
;
;    IconBounce uses custom plotting routines to bounce a lot of icons
;    around on the deskTop.
;
;       written by Andy Hertzfeld, Nov 17 1985
;
;-----------------------------------------------------------------------

INCLUDE MacSys:MacTraps.D

; System definitions, etc.

IOCompletion    EQU     12              ;offset to completion routine address
IOFileName      EQU     18              ;offset to fileName
IOVRefNum       EQU     22              ;offset to volume refNum
IOFileType      EQU     26              ;offset to type byte, permissions
IOMisc          EQU     28              ;offset to misc param
IOBuffer        EQU     32              ;offset to buffer pointer
IOByteCount     EQU     36              ;offset to count
IONumDone       EQU     40              ;offset to number done
IOPosMode       EQU     44              ;offset to positioning mode
IOPosOffset     EQU     46              ;offset to position value

EvtMsg          EQU     2               ;offset to message field
EvtMeta         EQU     14              ;offset to metaKey field
Where           EQU     10              ;mouse offset in event record
portRect        EQU     16              ;offset to portRect

ScreenRow       EQU     $106            ;rowBytes of screen [word]
Ticks           EQU     $16A
KeyMap          EQU     $174
Time            EQU     $20C
ScrnBase        EQU     $824
CurApRefNum     EQU     $900
WmgrPort        EQU     $9DE

MaxX            EQU     512
MaxY            EQU     342

; Icon Data Structure

NextIcon        EQU     0               ;handle of next structure
IconData        EQU     4               ;128 byte 32 by 32 bitmap
IconMask        EQU     132             ;128 byte mask
IconPosition    EQU     260             ;longword position
IconVelocity    EQU     264             ;velocity

IconDSSize      EQU     268             ;total data structure size

; Global Variable Definitions

QuickBase       EQU     -4              ;quickDraw globals
MyEvent         EQU     QuickBase-200   ;my event record
QuitFlag        EQU     myEvent-2       ;boolean for exiting
WhichWindow     EQU     QuitFlag-4      ;whichWindow result

NumIcons        EQU     WhichWindow-2   ;# of icons allocates
FirstIcon       EQU     numIcons-4      ;handle of 1st one
LastIcon        EQU     FirstIcon-4     ;handle of last one

BigBuffer       EQU     LastIcon-4      ;pointer to big buffer

XDEF            START

START:

; first allocate some zeroed space by clearing it off the stack

                MOVE    #511,D0         ;need about 2K bytes
ClearLoop
```

> Andy Hertzfeld, principal developer of the Macintosh operating system and more recently the Switcher program and ThunderScan digitizer, provides this original program for the Macintosh. Hertzfeld says, "The program ... rapidly animates icons on the screen."

```
                    CLR.L    -(SP)
                    DBRA     D0,ClearLoop

; now grow the heapZone as large as we can make it

                    MOVEQ    #64,D0
                    SWAP     D0                  ;get huge number
                    _NewHandle                   ;grow out the heap
                    BNE.S    InitWorld           ;we expect the error
                    _DisposHandle                ;if it not, dispose it

; initialize QuickDraw and the toolBox

InitWorld
                    PEA      QuickBase(A5)       ;push address of QuickDraw vars
                    _InitGraf                    ;initialize QuickDraw
                    _InitFonts                   ;initialize the font manager
                    _InitCursor                  ;get the arrow cursor
                    _InitWindows                 ;initialize the window manager
                    _InitMenus                   ;ditto for menus

                    CLR.L    -(SP)               ;our recovery proc is  NIL
                    _InitDialogs                 ;initialize dialogs
                    _TEInit                      ;and text edit, too

                    BSR      SetHourGlass

; initialize our globals

                    CLR.B    QuitFlag(A5)
                    CLR.W    numIcons(A5)

                    CLR.L    FirstIcon(A5)
                    CLR.L    LastIcon(A5)

; allocate the big buffer

                    MOVE.L   #24000,D0
                    _NewPtr
                    BNE      ErrorExit
                    MOVE.L   A0,BigBuffer(A5)

; display title message

                    MOVE.L   WmgrPort,-(SP)
                    _SetPort
                    PEA      BigRect
                    _ClipRect

                    MOVE.L   #$000E0038,-(SP)
                    _MoveTo

                    PEA      TitleString
                    _DrawString

; allocate the icons

                    BSR      AllocIcons

                    _HideCursor

                    MOVEQ    #31,D0
                    _FlushEvents

; start the main event loop

MainLoop
                    _SystemTask

                    BSR      HandleEvent     ;check for events and handle them
                    BSR      AnimateIcons

                    TST.B    QuitFlag(A5)
```

```
                BEQ.S   MainLoop

                _ExitToShell            ;back to finderLand

; HandleEvent checks for events and handles them as necessary.  It handles
; the menu commands and all interaction with the user.

HandleEvent
                SUBQ    #2,SP           ;make room for result
                MOVE.W  #-1,-(SP)       ;we want every event
                PEA     myEvent(A5)     ;stick it in our global
                _GetNextEvent           ;get the event

                TST.B   (SP)+           ;did we get one?
                BEQ.S   NoEvent         ;if not, we're done

                MOVE.W  myEvent(A5),D0  ;get the event number
                BEQ.S   NoEvent         ;ignore the Null event
                CMP     #9,D0           ;only care about 1st 9 events
                BGE.S   NoEvent

                ADD     D0,D0           ;double for word index
                LEA     EvtDispatch,A0  ;get the address of the table
                ADD.W   0(A0,D0),A0     ;get routine address
                JMP     (A0)            ;go to it!

; here is the event dispatch table

EvtDispatch
                DC.W    NoEvent-EvtDispatch
                DC.W    MyMouseDown-EvtDispatch
                DC.W    MyMouseUp-EvtDispatch
                DC.W    MyKeyDown-EvtDispatch
                DC.W    NoEvent-EvtDispatch
                DC.W    MyKeyDown-EvtDispatch
                DC.W    MyUpdateEvt-EvtDispatch
                DC.W    MyDiskInsert-EvtDispatch
                DC.W    MyActivate-EvtDispatch
MyDiskInsert
MyMouseUp
MyActivate
NoEvent
                RTS


; Handle keyboard events

MyKeyDown
                ;ST     QuitFlag(A5)
                RTS

; handle update events

MyUpdateEvt
                RTS

; the following routine handles mouseDowns.  First call FindWindow
; to classify where the mouse went down

MyMouseDown

                ST      QuitFlag(A5)
                RTS

; AllocIcons opens the desktop, and allocates an icon data structure for
; each ICN# in the file.

AllocIcons
                SUBQ    #2,SP
                PEA     DeskTopName
                _OpenResFile
                TST     (SP)
                BMI     ErrorExit
```

```
                    SUBQ     #2,SP
                    MOVE.L   ICNRType,-(SP)        ;push ICN# type
                    _CountResources               ;get # of resources
                    MOVE.W   (SP)+,D3              ;keep in D3
                    BLE      ErrorExit

; limit the # of icons to 64, unless the option key is down

                    BTST     #2,KeyMap+7
                    BNE.S    NoILimit

                    CMP      #64,D3
                    BLE.S    NoILimit

                    MOVEQ    #64,D3

; OK, now loop for each icon

NoILimit
                    MOVEQ    #1,D4                 ;init index
AllocIcLoop
                    SUBQ     #4,SP                 ;make room for result
                    MOVE.L   ICNRType,-(SP)        ;push ICN#
                    MOVE.W   D4,-(SP)              ;push index
                    _GetIndResource               ;get it
                    MOVE.L   (SP)+,D5              ;got it?
                    BLE      DoneAllocIcon

; we have the icon handle, so allocate the structure

                    MOVE.L   #IconDSSize,D0
                    _NewHandle
                    BNE      ErrorExit

                    MOVE.L   A0,A3                 ;get new handle
                    MOVE.L   (A3),A2               ;handle->ptr

                    CLR.L    (A2)+                 ;link is zero
                    MOVE.L   A2,A1                 ;set up dest

                    MOVE.L   D5,A0
                    MOVE.L   (A0),A0               ;set up source
                    MOVE.L   #256,D0               ;256 bytes to move
                    _BlockMove

                    ADD.L    #256,A2               ;skip over save area

; generate positions 0 < x < 512,   0 < y < 302

                    SUBQ     #2,SP
                    _Random
                    MOVEQ    #0,D0
                    MOVE.W   (SP)+,D0
                    DIVU     #302,D0
                    SWAP     D0
                    ADDQ     #1,D0
                    MOVE     D0,(A2)+

                    SUBQ     #2,SP
                    _Random
                    MOVE.W   (SP)+,D0
                    AND.W    #511,D0
                    ADDQ     #1,D0
                    MOVE     D0,(A2)+

; generate velocitys from 1 to 8

                    SUBQ     #2,SP
                    _Random
                    MOVE.W   (SP)+,D0
                    AND      #7,D0
                    ADDQ     #1,D0
```

```
                MOVE.W  D0,(A2)+

                SUBQ    #2,SP
                _Random
                MOVE.W  (SP)+,D0
                AND     #7,D0
                ADDQ    #1,D0
@2
                MOVE.W  D0,(A2)+

; link it in the list

                MOVE.L  LastIcon(A5),D0
                BNE.S   LinkItIn

                MOVE.L  A3,FirstIcon(A5)
                MOVE.L  A3,LastIcon(A5)
                BRA.S   BumpICount
LinkItIn
                MOVE.L  A3,LastIcon(A5)
                MOVE.L  D0,A0
                MOVE.L  (A0),A0
                MOVE.L  A3,(A0)                 ;link it in
BumpICount
                ADDQ    #1,numIcons(A5)

DoNextIcon
                ADDQ    #1,D4                   ;bump index
                CMP     D3,D4                   ;done?
                BLT     AllocIcLoop
DoneAllocIcon
                _CloseResFile

                RTS

; ShowIcon is the routine that plots an icon.  It is adopted from the
; BigCursor routines.  The handle of the icon data structure is passed
; in A3.

ShowIcon
        MOVEM.L D0-D7/A0-A4,-(SP)       ; save registers
        MOVE.L  (A3),A3                 ; de-reference icon data structure

        MOVEQ   #32,D5                  ; size of icon
        MOVEQ   #16,D6                  ; half size

        LEA     IconData(A3),A2         ; cursor data bitmap address
        LEA     IconMask(A3),A4         ; cursor mask bitmap address

; first handle the x coordinate

        MOVE    IconPosition+2(A3),D0   ; get left
        MOVEQ   #15,D2                  ; upper left X-coordinate
        AND.W   D0,D2                   ; bit offset within word

        AND     #$FFF0,D0               ; truncate to nearest word
        BGE.S   @0                      ; if positive, skip

        MOVEQ   #0,D0                   ; minimum upper left X-coord of 0
        ADD.W   D6,D2                   ; adjust right shift count

; if shift count > 15, just move over a word

@0
        CMP     D6,D2                   ;is it?
        BLT.S   @7                      ;if not, skip

        SUB     D6,D2                   ; reduce bit index
        ADD.W   D6,D0                   ; bump base point
@7

; establish "last word" boolean
```

```
        CLR.W    -(SP)

        MOVE     D0,D1                ; copy coordinate
        SUB.W    #MaxX-32,D1          ; upper left X-coord <= 512-32
        BLT.S    @2                   ; branch if <= 512-32

        MOVE.W   #MaxX-32,D0          ; maximum X-coord of 512-32
        ADD.W    D1,D2                ; adjust left shift count
        ST       (SP)                 ; set the boolean
; handle the y coordinate

@2      MOVE.W   D5,D4                ; 32 rows

        MOVE.W   IconPosition(A3),D1  ; get Y-coordinate

;   Display the icon on the screen.

        MOVE.L   BigBuffer(A5),A1     ; offscreen memory address
        LSR.W    #3,D0                ; convert X-coord to bytes
        ADD.W    D0,A1                ;  and add to screen address
        MOVE.W   ScreenRow,D5         ; bytes per row on screen
        MULU     D5,D1                ;  * Y-coord
        ADD.L    D1,A1                ;  added to screen address

        SUBQ     #4,D5                ; bias D5 for loop

        TST      D2                   ; is shiftcount = 0?
        BEQ.S    BotFastLoop          ; if so, go ultra fast

; OK, for added speed, two different loops, depending on the
; if we need the 3rd word (as specified by the top of stack boolean)

        TST.B    (SP)+
        BNE      BotCur1Loop
        BRA.S    BotCurLoop           ; test for rows=0

; here is the icon plotting loop. First do the leftmost 32 bits

ShowCurLoop
        MOVE.L   (A2)+,D0             ; get the data
        MOVE.L   D0,D6                ; copy for later
        LSR.L    D2,D0                ; shift into place

        MOVE.L   (A4)+,D1             ; get the mask
        MOVE.L   D1,D7                ; copy for later
        LSR.L    D2,D1                ; shift into place
        NOT.L    D1                   ; complement mask

        AND.L    D1,(A1)              ; bit-clear with the mask
        OR.L     D0,(A1)+             ; plot the data

; now handle the rightmost 16 bits

        MOVEQ    #16,D1
        SUB.W    D2,D1                ; compute left shift count

        ASL.W    D1,D6                ; shift the data
        ASL.W    D1,D7                ; shift the mask
        NOT.W    D7                   ; complement the mask

        AND.W    D7,(A1)              ; bit clear the mask
        OR.W     D6,(A1)              ; plot the data
@0
        ADD      D5,A1                ; bump to next row
BotCurLoop
        DBRA     D4,ShowCurLoop       ; loop till done

DoneShowLoop
        MOVEM.L  (SP)+,D0-D7/A0-A4    ; restore registers
DoneShow
        RTS
```

```
; this loop is used when we're near the right edge and don't have to
; plot the third word

ShowCurlLoop
        MOVE.L  (A2)+,D0                ; get the data
        LSR.L   D2,D0                   ; shift into place

        MOVE.L  (A4)+,D1                ; get the mask
        LSR.L   D2,D1                   ; shift into place
        NOT.L   D1                      ; complement mask

        AND.L   D1,(A1)                 ; bit-clear with the mask
        OR.L    D0,(A1)+                ; plot the data

        ADD     D5,A1                   ; bump to next row
BotCurlLoop
        DBRA    D4,ShowCurlLoop         ; loop till done

        BRA     DoneShowLoop

; special fast loop for the 6% case where we don't have to shift

FastLoop
        MOVE.L  (A2)+,D0                ;fetch the data
        MOVE.L  (A4)+,D1                ;fetch the mask
        NOT.L   D1                      ;complement mask

        AND.L   D1,(A1)                 ;plot the mask
        OR.L    D0,(A1)+                ;plot the data

        ADD     D5,A1
BotFastLoop
        DBRA    D4,FastLoop

        ADDQ    #2,SP                   ;discard boolean
        BRA     DoneShowLoop

; Error handling routines

ErrorExit
        DC.W    $F123

        RTS


; AnimateIcons is the mainline routine that bounces the icons

AnimateIcons
        BSR     GrayBuffer              ;fill big buffer with gray

        BSR     UpdateIconPositions
        BSR     DrawIntoBuffer

; now move the buffer onto the screen with blockMove

        MOVE.W  ScreenRow,D0
        MULU    #20,D0
        ADD.L   ScrnBase,D0
        MOVE.L  D0,A1                   ;screen is destination
        MOVE.L  BigBuffer(A5),A0        ;big buffer is source

        MOVE.L  #20608,D0
        _BlockMove

        RTS

; DrawIntoBuffer goes through the icon data structure, drawing each icon

DrawIntoBuffer
        MOVE.L  A3,-(SP)                ;save work reg

        MOVE.L  FirstIcon(A5),D0        ;get first one
        BEQ.S   DoneDIB                 ;if empty, skip
```

367

```
DIBLoop
        MOVE.L  D0,A3

        BSR     ShowIcon

        MOVE.L  (A3),A0
        MOVE.L  (A0),D0
        BNE.S   DIBLoop
DoneDIB
        MOVE.L  (SP)+,A3
        RTS

; UpdateIconPositions animates the icon positions

UpdateIconPositions

        MOVE.L  FirstIcon(A5),D0        ;get first one
        BEQ     DoneUIP                 ;if empty, skip

UIPLoop
        MOVE.L  D0,A0
        MOVE.L  (A0),A0

        MOVE.L  IconPosition(A0),D0
        MOVE.L  IconVelocity(A0),D1

; OK, bounce in the x position

        ADD.W   D1,D0                   ;compute new position
        BGE.S   @0                      ;if > 0, skip

        SUB.W   D1,D0                   ;undo it
        NEG.W   D1                      ;toggle velocity
@0
        CMP.W   #510,D0
        BLT.S   BounceY

        SUB.W   D1,D0
        NEG.W   D1

BounceY
        SWAP    D0
        SWAP    D1

        ADD.W   D1,D0
        BGE.S   @0

        SUB.W   D1,D0
        NEG.W   D1
@0
        CMP     #302,D0
        BLT.S   NextBounce

        SUB.W   D1,D0
        NEG.W   D1

NextBounce
        SWAP    D0
        SWAP    D1
        MOVE.L  D0,IconPosition(A0)
        MOVE.L  D1,IconVelocity(A0)

        MOVE.L  (A0),D0
        BNE     UIPLoop
DoneUIP
        RTS


; GrayBuffer fills the 322 scan lines at GrayBuffer with gray

GrayBuffer
```

```
        MOVE     #160,D2                  ;# of scan line pairs - 1
        MOVE.L   BigBuffer(A5),A0         ;point to the buffer
FillGLoop
        MOVE.L   #$55555555,D0            ;get gray
FillGLoop2
        MOVE.L   D0,(A0)+                 ;fill a long
        MOVE.L   D0,(A0)+                 ;fill a long
        MOVE.L   D0,(A0)+                 ;fill a long
        MOVE.L   D0,(A0)+                 ;fill a long
        MOVE.L   D0,(A0)+                 ;fill a long
        MOVE.L   D0,(A0)+                 ;fill a long
        MOVE.L   D0,(A0)+                 ;fill a long
        MOVE.L   D0,(A0)+                 ;fill a long
        MOVE.L   D0,(A0)+                 ;fill a long
        MOVE.L   D0,(A0)+                 ;fill a long
        MOVE.L   D0,(A0)+                 ;fill a long
        MOVE.L   D0,(A0)+                 ;fill a long
        MOVE.L   D0,(A0)+                 ;fill a long
        MOVE.L   D0,(A0)+                 ;fill a long
        MOVE.L   D0,(A0)+                 ;fill a long

; OK, now a scan line is done, so flip the gray

        NOT.L    D0
        BMI.S    FillGLoop2

        DBRA     D2,FillGLoop2

        RTS

; SetHourGlass installs the hourGlass (watch) cursor

SetHourGlass

        SUBQ     #4,SP
        MOVE     #4,-(SP)
        _GetCursor

        MOVE.L   (SP)+,A0
        MOVE.L   (A0),-(SP)
        _SetCursor

        RTS


; Constants, etc.

ICNRType
        DC.B     'ICN#'
DeskTopName
        DC.B     7,'DeskTop'
BigRect
        DC.W     0,0,1000,1000
TitleString
        DC.B     60,'IconBounce by Andy Hertzfeld...  Press mouse button '
        DC.B     'to exit. '
```

369

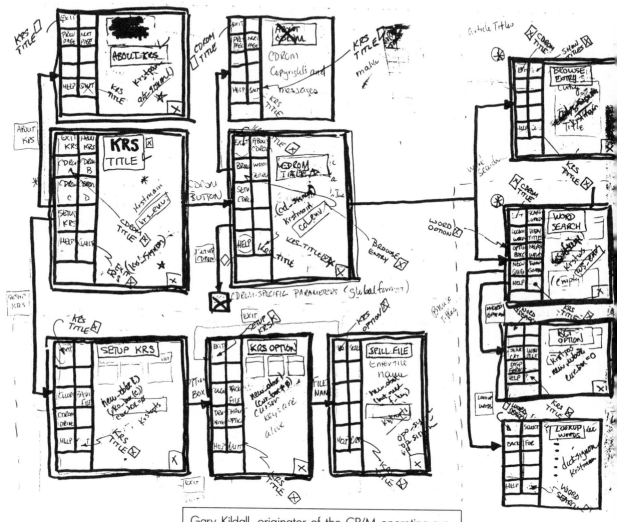

Gary Kildall, originator of the CP/M operating system, provides the following explanation of a sketch pertaining to his more recent project, a retrieval system for a CD ROM encyclopedia. "This diagram shows the interrelationship between the menu panels of the character-based Knowledge Retrieval System. The squares on the left of each screen show original (and changed) function-key assignment. The arrows show transitions from one panel to another. New menus were added during the implementation cycle, and annotations show C language subroutine names for painting the panels. This diagram provided a graphic picture of the KRS structure during development of the product."

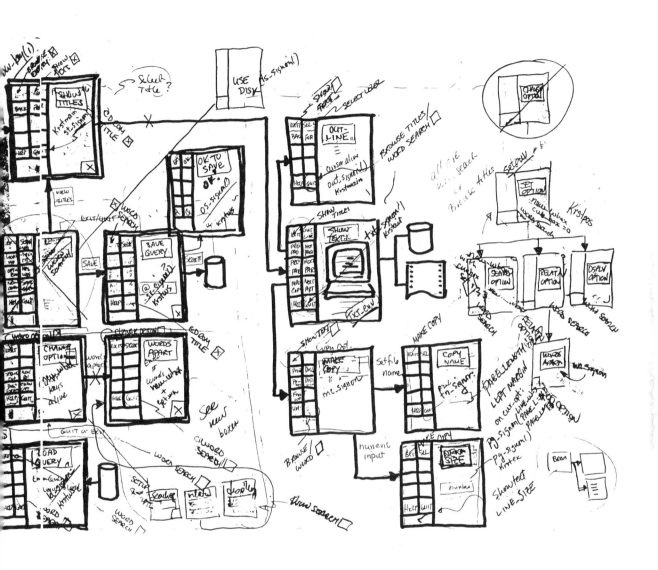

371

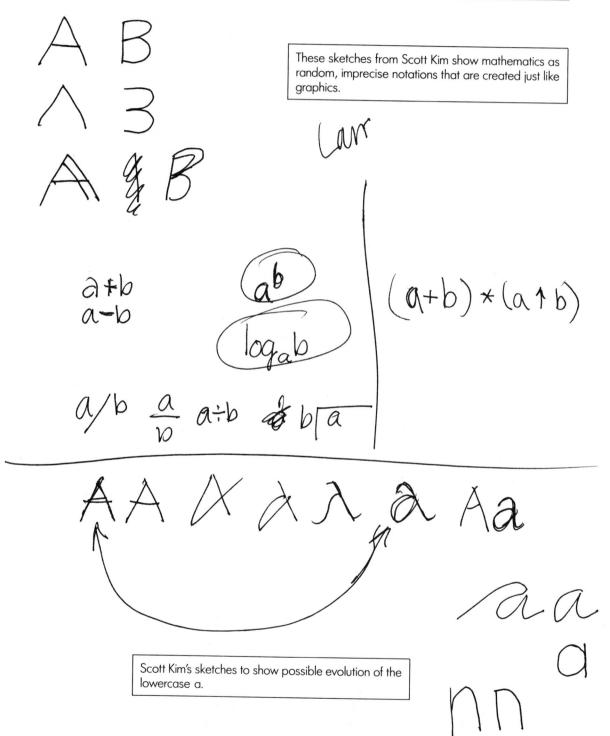

These sketches from Scott Kim show mathematics as random, imprecise notations that are created just like graphics.

Scott Kim's sketches to show possible evolution of the lowercase a.

©1981 Scott Kim

1/24/86

Actually it's $e \cdot t1 \lozenge f2 \to t1 \lozenge f2'$, succeeds if $f2$ fit $e = f2'$ fit e

We only need t in apply, so we could put it in as a convenience faster the (but different from) coerce.

$$\{ F :: t_1 \to t_2 \text{ or } F :: t_1 \lozenge f_2, f_2 \# t_1 \Rightarrow \text{type } E_0 \Rightarrow t_2 \},$$

$$'E_0 :> t_0' ,\} \quad \overset{E_0 \Rightarrow e_0}{t_0 = t_1} \quad \overset{E_0 \Rightarrow \ell_0}{\text{or}} \quad t_0 = t_{11} \lozenge f_{02}, t_1 = t_{11} \lozenge f_{12}, f_{02} \# t_{11} \Rightarrow \text{type fit } E_0 = F_{12} \# t_{11} \text{ fit}$$

$$\text{or coerce } F! (t_0, t_1) \leadsto f_{01}, f_{01} \# t_0 = t_1, 'E_0' :> e, \},$$

$$\{ f! e_1 \leadsto e \text{ else } f! e_1 = e_2 \}$$

is this too strong?

yes — we might need to do it again

$(t_1) H :: , \text{ and } E :: f_{12}$

_____

$$F \; E_1 :> t_2 \Rightarrow \ell_2$$

$((\lambda N' : t_{11} \text{ in } \lambda N'' : f_{12} N' \text{ in } F(N', N'')) \text{ fit } E_1) \text{ and } E_1$

$$\{ E_1 :> t_1 \Rightarrow e_1$$
$$\text{or } E_1 :> t_{11} \lozenge f_{12} \Rightarrow e_0, t_1 = t_{11} \lozenge f_{12}', f_{12} \# t_{11} \Rightarrow \text{type fit } E_1 = f_{12} \# t_{11} \Rightarrow \text{type fit } E_1$$
$$\text{or } E_1 :> t_1', \text{coerce } F! (t_1', t_1) \leadsto f_1, f_1 \# t_1' = t_1, E_1 \Rightarrow e_1 \}$$

This formulation also forces coerce F to evaluate successfully

This should be viewed as an alternative to keeping the :: rule for $\lozenge$

The :: rule also has a $\oplus$ clause. This is currently needed so that LET will work on formals defined with $\oplus$. This is not just a convenience, since the LET is supplied not by the programmer, but by the rule for λ or !. And coerce can't do it, because LET doesn't have a target type.

Furthermore, we are going to add a clause

$$E :: \text{type } \alpha \; t \quad \Rightarrow \quad E :: t$$

The currently proposed alternative is the in function. The :: clause, however, would allow us to have keyword parameters for far to any function whose parameter type is dod.

• A related question is dropping of named in ** and =>>. The current rule is this this. Or far doesn't drop names, but λ does far =>, but not far =>>. If we make a coercion far $t_1 \lozenge f \subseteq t_2 \lozenge f$ if type of t_1 = type of t_2, we wouldn't need this. Of course, this could be a :: rule. Or it could be far type of $t_1 = t_2$.

Butler Lampson, senior engineer at the Systems Research Center of Digital Equipment Corporation, contributes these notes that reveal the mathematical detail and thought processes that go into designing programs.

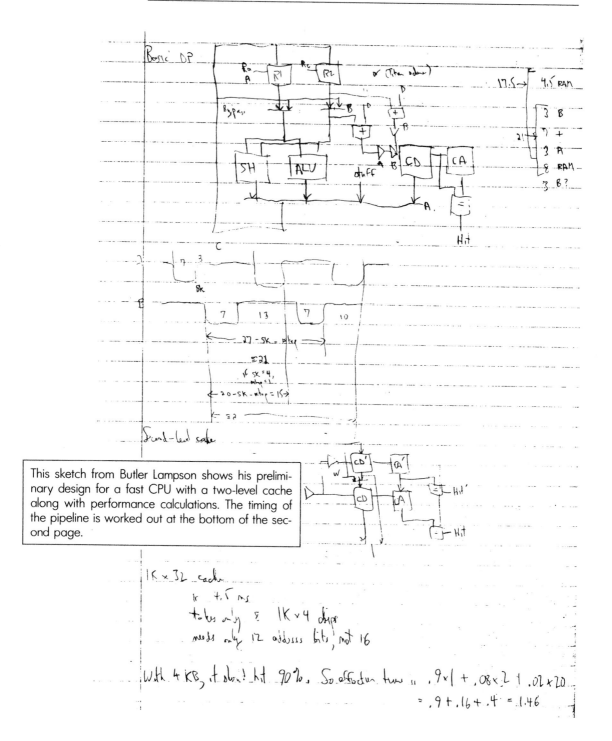

This sketch from Butler Lampson shows his preliminary design for a fast CPU with a two-level cache along with performance calculations. The timing of the pipeline is worked out at the bottom of the second page.

Conclusion — 20 is much too much. We need another level.

Try $.9 \times 1 + .095 \times 4 + .005 \times 20$
   $= .9 + .38 + .1 = 1.38$
Not much better

$.9 \times 1 + .08 \times 2 + .015 \times 5 + .005 \times 20$
$= .9 + .16 + .08 + .1 = 1.24$

Maybe the first scheme isn't so bad. Compare

$.8 \times 1 + .18 \times 2 + .02 \times 20$
$= .8 + .36 + .4 = 1.56$

Not much worse. The .8 is conservative from DC's '90 measurements (4 KB DM).

So ~.5 cycles/cache ref will go into miss stalls.
One VAX inst does 2/3 read ref, 1/3 write, roughly. So there are also per instruction

By secondary cache. $1 \ MByte = 64K \times 32 \times 4.$ So 4 banks of 64K. If a 4ns cycle is feasible, we can get a word every 12ns from 128 chips. Stuffing out the 4 words to 100 MB/s would be a perfect match for a 128-bit word. Humble

The pipeling is   R inst   A   8 to ns
                       R inst   B
                       R reg   A   4.5 RAM, 3 bypass + latch   7.5/8
                       ALU / cache B   4 add/subtract 4.5 RAM }   12.5/16 to etc. C does as ns
                       ALU / cache A   4 = latch   There's lots more time for data
                       W reg   B   this is where we can stop it easily

On a stall, the B clock gets stopped, so the cache address (latched by E after addressing) holds its stalled value. The instruction register holds at the next instruction. The write from the stalled instruction is stopped. This all seems fine. I'm not clear on what would happen if we tried to delay the write another cycle, which we bypass, in order to give more time for the stall.

If trees are not too big this must work. It may work inefficiently if the tree is unbalanced.

Tentative conclusion — see FOS:.

14 Dec 84   Name server

TYPE

$D = UID \times SV^*$ directory

$S = UID \to DC \times \#bind:N \times up:(SN \times parent:UID)^*$ server

$N = CHAR^*$ name

$UN = N^*$ universal name

$SN = UU$ server name

$DC = f: U \to V \times \lambda: (N^* | \perp) \times \omega f: UID \times clock, lastSplit: TS$ directory contents

$V = D | A | D \times N | ...$

PROC

Contact: $A \to S$

FindServer: $\cdot \to S$

Lookup: $N \times DC \to V = dc(n)$

Lookup*: $N^* \times D \to V = Lookup^*(tail\ n^*, Lookup(head\ n^*, GetDC(d)))$

GetDC: $D \to DC = IF\ x \neq \perp\ THEN\ x\ ELSE\ GetDC(d.vid, tail\ d.sv^*)\ END$
       $WHERE\ x = head\ d\ s^*(d.vid)$

GetDCHere: $S \times D \to DC = IF\ x \neq \perp\ THEN\ x\ ELSE\ GetDCHere(s, (d.vid, tail\ d.sv^*))\ END$
       $WHERE\ x = IF\ s' = s\ THEN\ s'(d.vid)\ ELSE\ \perp$
         $WHERE\ s' = head\ d.s^*$

ULookup: $UN \times S \to V = IF\ v \neq \perp\ THEN\ Lookup^*(n^*, s)$
         $ELSE\ ULookup(un, s')\ WHERE\ s' \in s.up$
         END
           $WHERE\ v, n^* = ULHere(un, s)$

ULHere: $UN \times S \to V \times N^* =$
       $IF\ un = \perp\ THEN\ (\perp, \perp)$
       $ELSIF\ \exists dc, vid:\ s(vid) = dc\ AND\ dc.h = un\ THEN\ ((vid, s), \perp)$
       $ELSE\ (v, (n^*, n))\ WHERE\ v, n^* = ULHere(un', s)\ WHERE\ un = (un', n)$
       END

> These two pages are Lampson's initial notes for data structures and invariants for a large-scale distributed name server. The polished, typed version of the same material appears on the next two pages.

INVARIANT

$d = (uid, s^d) \Rightarrow \exists s \in s^d : s(uid) \neq \bot$ Some listed server stores the directory
     $? \vee \forall s : S : s(uid) = \bot$?

$\forall s$ $(\forall s' \in s.up \quad s'.lvl < s.lvl) \vee s(root) \neq \bot$ Up defines a spanning tree of all servers rooted in a, servers that stores the root

$\forall uid$ $\exists s : s(uid) \neq \bot \Rightarrow$ reachable $(uid, root)$ Any directory can be reached from the root
   reachable : UID × DC → BOOL $\equiv \exists m : dc(m).uid = uid \vee$ reachable $(uid, dc(m))$
$\forall d : dc.h \neq \bot \Rightarrow d.uid = ULookup(dc.h).uid$ h is correct; this can be weakened
    WHERE $dc = GoodDC(d)$

$\exists (sn, uid) \in s.up : (x \neq \bot \text{ AND } Contact(x).lvl < s.lvl) \text{ OR } s(root) \neq \bot$
       WHERE $x = s(uid)(last\ sn)$

?? $\forall dc \quad dc("replicas") = (d, m) \text{ AND } Lookup(m, d) = sn^x \text{ AND }$
       $\forall s \exists uid : s(uid) = dc.self \Rightarrow \exists sn \in sn^* :$
                 $Contact(ULookup(sn)) = s$

Dont :   Changes to h
        &
        Replication
        Changes to s^d and d

$\forall s_1, s_2, uid : s_1(uid) \neq \bot \text{ AND } s_2(uid) \neq \bot \Rightarrow s_1(uid) \equiv s_2(uid)$
             All copies of D are the same, modulo distribution

17 Dec 84   Update abstraction

TYPE   U : (DC → DC) × UID   , Pool = (SU ∪ × U)*

Properties : $\forall dc : u(dc) \neq \bot$ total
        $u_1 \circ u_2 = u_2 \circ u_1$ commute
   ?? $u \circ u = u$ idempotent

PROC

   CreateUpdate : DC × Uarg → U
   StartUpdate : S × UID × Uarg → .
     st. $s(uid) = u(s_0(uid)) \wedge pool' = pool_0 \cup pool_{-1} \wedge ad(uid) = ad_0(uid) \cup_?$ {u}
AddToda. decl $(s(uid) \neq \bot \Rightarrow \exists' (sn, u) \in pool_{-1} : sn \in S.self) \wedge$
otoff $(sn, u') \in pool_{-1} \Rightarrow u' = u$
      WHERE $u = CreateUpdate(s_0(uid), arg)$

   DoUpdate : · → .
     st. $\exists (sn, u) \in pool_0 \wedge (sn, u) \notin pool' \wedge s(u.uid) = u(s_0(u.uid))$
      WHERE $sn \in s_0.self$

```
TYPE
  NAT = ****                              NATural number
  UID = NAT                               Universal IDentifier
  T = NAT                                 Time; e.g., GMT (not site-dependent)
  TS = T X UID                            TimeStamp
  TX = T X extend: T                      Timeout eXpiration
  OK = yes | no

  DI = UID                                Directory Identifier
  SI = DI                                 Server Identifier
  N = CHAR*                               Name
  DN = N X di: (DI | NIL)                 Directory Name wrt d; invalid
                                            if di#NIL AND d(dn.n).di#dn.di
  FN = DI X DN*                           Full Name of a D from root di
  SN = FN X DN X TX                       Server Name; C.GetV(sn.fn, sn.dn.n):SA
  Link = FN X TX                          tx times out Link, as in DR
  LD = linked | direct                    kind of FN, or follow final link
  Lim = TX X LD                           MIN TX used in name lookup, used Link

  DR = DI                                 D Reference; REP is DL.
(* A FN through dr is guaranteed valid only until dr^.br.tx *)
  BR = DI X N X TX | NIL                  Back Reference; REP is TS->BL
  D = V                                   Directory; REP=REP V abstractly,
(* DC** concretely.  The other components of DC
   are really the values of names in d.v; e.g., d.di=d("&di"). *)
    X DI                                  self
    X w: (DI->FN)                         well-known DIs (for old roots)
    X h: (FN X Lim)**                     help: FNs of d; may be invalid
(* protection and authentication data *)
    X RL
    X AA
    X K                                   Key for this dir viewed as a principal
(* time-stamps *)
    X lastTS: TS                          largest TS of any U to d
    X allUpTo: TS                         u IN REP d AND u.ts<d.allUpTo=>
                                            u IN FollowDR(d.di)
    X BR                                  ds(d.br.di)(d.br.n).di=d.di

  V = L->(VV X TS)                        Value: tree with L arcs, TS nodes, Mk
  VV = Mk | V                               leaves. REP V=U** X TS, REP U**=W
  Mk = absent | present                   what to MaKe L* into in an update
  L = N | Tag | AV                        Label
  Tag = CHAR*                             labels fields of a d(n) value.
(* The value of the tag "&type" is the type of d(n). *)
  AV = BYTE*                              Atomic Value
  LTree = (L X LTree)**                   stripped V: tree, L arcs, empty leaves
  LT = L X TS
  LTL = LT* X L*                          designate V reached by the path
(* (Labels(lt*), l*), with TS matching lt*.ts. *)
  VD = FN X LTL X LD                      V Designator;
(* fn short for (fn, nullLTL, direct) and (fn, ltl) for (fn, ltl, direct). *)

  Vr = U** X TS                           REP V: set of updates (with REP W) X TS
  U = f: (V->V) X TS                      Update; REP=Y.
  W = Y**                                 REP REP V: updatable with a Y
  Y = LT* X Mk                            REP U: set lt* component to mk
(* =============== Types below this point are for DC/S/SU/E =============== *)
  DL = DI X SN**                          Directory Locator, REP DR
  BL = DI X N X TX X Link                 Back Locator. REP BR=TS->BL.
(* Normally br(ts)#% for 1 TS (0 for root), bl.link.fn^.di=bl.di. *)
  DC = D                                  Directory Copy.
    X copies: SN**                        updated like a D component
(* A server s updates only sn's in copies with sn.dn.di=s.si. *)
    X inSN: BOOL                          updated like a D component
    X On
```

```
D: (* DIRECTORY *) MODULE
   EXPORTS [Snapshot .. Resolve],
           FirstRoot, NewRoot, NewD, RemoveD, ChangeN,
           $FollowFN, $FollowDR
   IMPORTS R.GetRights, Env, V.(GetV, FrozenLink)
   ▪
INVARIANT
1 ds(di)#% <=> BRPath(di) WHERE BRPath: DI->BOOL =
   LET dr=di,br=dr^.br,dr'=br.di; di=root OR dr'^(br.n).di=di AND BRPath(br.di))
         I.e., the D's in ds form a tree rooted in root whose arcs are DRs that
         are the reverse of the BR backpointers. D3 means that the tree you see
         can shift around if BRs are changing faster than allUpTo. REP is DC1.
2 dr'^(n):DR=dr => EXISTS tx: (dr'.di, n, tx)=dr^.br AND tx>=dr.tx
         I.e., each DR is pointed to by a BR with a longer timeout. REP is DC2.
3 d=dr^ => {u IN u** | u.ts<d.allUpTo} <= REP d <= u** WHERE u**=REP ds(dr.di)
         I.e., FollowDR gives an answer that includes all the updates to D
         before allUpTo, and any selection of those later. REP is SU1-2.
4 (fn, lim) IN d.h AND lim.tx>now => dr^ IS d AND dr.tx>now WHERE dr=fn^
         I.e., h entries are valid unless timed-out.
5 d.w(di)=fn => fn:FN AND fn.di=d.di AND fn^.di=di
         I.e., a d.w entry for a DI is a FN for it from d. Not enforced.
6 (fn.di=root OR FollowDR(root).w(fn.di)#%) AND
  ( (fn', n)<=fn => FollowDR(fn'^.di)(n):DR ) =>
  Get((fn, ltl, direct), {})#%
         I.e., Get looks up an FN to yield a D if its DI is root or is defined
         in root's w, and each N in its DN* can be looked up to yield a DR.

PROCEDURE
(* These implementations are not real. I.e., they describe what the procedures
   do, but aren't identical to any code in the system. These operations are
   actually implemented in NS and DC in the server, called remotely from the
   clerk. *)
```

Pebble summary   26 January 1986

Syntax

Binary operators: ', (2) ~ (3)—› (4) * (5)
Everything associates to the right

E = N
  | N : T   (6)
  | £ T IN E   (1)
  | LET B IN E   (1)
  | IMPORT B IN E   (1)
  | F ° E   (7)

  | N:~E | '(N$_1$, ...)':~E | N'(T')':~E
  | REC D$_1$~E$_1$, ... | REC N$_1$'(T$_1$:~E$_1$'), ...
  | B$_1$; B$_2$ (2) ??
  | B\$N   (6)
  | E WHERE B   (1)
  | D—»T | D ** E   (4, 5)
  | E$_1$. N | E$_1$ .N'(E$_2$')   (6)
  | E: N: (6)

  | '(')
  | { E } | T{ E }
  | *prefix?p* E | E$_1$ *infix?p* E$_2$ | E *postfix?p*
  | E$_1$ AND E$_2$ | E$_1$ OR E$_2$ (5, 4)
  | IF (E$_0$ => E$_1$) '| ... '|=› E$_2$ | IF (E$_0$ => E$_1$) '| ... FI
  | CASE E$_0$ OF (E$_1$ '(D ') => E$_2$) '| ... |=› E$_3$ END
  | E$_0$ BUT (E$_1$ '(D ') => E$_2$) '| ... END
  | LOOP E END
  | FOR N IN E$_1$ DO E$_2$ THEN E$_3$ END
  | FOR N IN E$_1$ WITH E$_4$ COLLECT E$_2$ THEN E$_3$ END

Lampson provides these samples of syntax and semantics for a programming language with data types
as first-class values. The semantics are given partly by
rewriting into a simpler form of the language (the
"sugar") on the second page, and partly by logical
inference rules on the last two pages.

Pebble summary   26 January 1986

Sugar

Write	*For*	*Provided*
N:~E	N: t~E	E:> t
'(N_1, N_2, ...')~E	N 1:~fst E, '(N_2, ...')~snd E	
N'(?T')~E	N:~£ ?T IN E	
£ D IN E	£ D→t IN E	LET newc#d IN E:>t
		and newc not in t
£ IN E	£ void IN E	
REC D_1~E_1, ...	'(fix '(D_1 * ...') '(£ B': '(D_1 * ...')	
	IN LET B' IN '(E_1, ...')')	
REC N_1'(T_1')~E_1, ...	REC N_1: t_1~*£ T_1 IN E_1, ...	
B_1; B_2	B_1, LET B_1 IN B_2	??
B\$N	IMPORT B IN N	
E WHERE B	LET B IN E	
D→»T	D%'(£ D→type IN T')	
D ** T	D◊'(£ D→type IN T')	
E_1. N	'(snd xt⁻¹ t')`\$N'(E_1')	E_1:> t
E_1. N'(E_2')	'(snd xt⁻¹ t')`\$N'(E_1, E_2')	E_1:> t
E: T:	T: type ** E: T@'(£ T: type IN T')	
()	nil	
{ E }	'(MkSet t') E	fst E:> t
or		
T{ E, ...}	SingleSet'(T, E') u ...	
T{}	EmptySet T	
{ E, ...}	SingleSet'(t, E') u ...	E:> t
prefix?p E	E . op'("*prefix?p*"')	
E_1 *infix?p* E_2	E_1 . op'("*infix?p*"') '(E_2')	
E *postfix?p*	E . op'("*postfix?p*"')	
E_1 AND E_2	IF E_1 => E_2 |=> false	
E_1 OR E_2	IF E_1 => true |=> E_2	

Pebble 86 Summary

Rules

Introduction   £   :

$$\{ t == d_1 \to t_2 \text{ or } t == d_1 \mathcal{X} f_2, f_2 ! \text{ newc}(n) \leadsto t_2 \},$$
$$\text{rho(depth)} + 1 = n, \text{rho[depth} = n] \mid - \text{LET newc}(n)_{\#d1} \text{ IN } \mathbf{t_2}\text{-}E :: t_2 \Rightarrow e$$

$$\overline{}$$

$$(£ \ T \text{ IN } E) :> t \Rightarrow c \mid ([], e, n)$$

$$\frac{T :: \text{type}}{N: T :: \text{type} \Rightarrow N : t}$$

Elimination   N   apply LET   IMPORT

$$\frac{\text{rho}(N) == t \leadsto e', \ e' \leadsto\!\!\gg e}{N :> t \Rightarrow e}$$

$$\{ F :: t_1 \to t_2 \text{ or } F :: t_1 \mathcal{X} f_2, f_2 \#_{t1 \to type} E_1 \Rightarrow t_2 \},$$
$$\{ E_1 :: t_1 \Rightarrow e_1 \text{ or } E_1 :> t_1', \text{coerceF}! (t_1', t_1) \leadsto f_1, f_{1\#t1' \to t1} E_1 \Rightarrow e_1 \},$$
$$\{ f ! e_1 \leadsto e_2 \textbf{ else } f ! e_1 = e_2 \}$$

$$\overline{}$$

$$F \circ E_1 :> t_2 \Rightarrow e_2$$

$$\begin{array}{ll}
B :: \text{void}, & E :: t \Rightarrow e \\
\textbf{or } B :: (N: t_0) \Rightarrow t_1 & \text{rho}[N = t_0 \leadsto b] \mid - E :: t \Rightarrow e \\
\textbf{or } B :: d_1 \Diamond f_2, \text{snd } B :> d_2 \Rightarrow b_2, \text{LET fst } B \text{ IN LET } b_{2\#d2} \text{ IN } E :: t \Rightarrow e
\end{array}$$

$$\overline{}$$

$$\text{LET } B \text{ IN } E :> t \Rightarrow e$$

$$\frac{B :> d \Rightarrow b, \text{rho}_0 \mid - \text{LET } b_{\#d} \text{ IN } E :: t \Rightarrow e}{\text{IMPORT } B \text{ IN } E :> t}$$

Auxiliary   ::   #   ~>   ~»

$$\begin{array}{ll}
E :> t & \\
\textbf{or } E :: t \ @ f_2 & \\
\textbf{or } E :: t', t \ u \ t' = t & \text{could be coercion} \\
\textbf{or } t == N: t', E :: t' & \text{could be coercion} \\
\textbf{or } t == t_1 \Diamond f_2, \text{fst } E :: t_1, \text{snd } E :: f_2 \text{ fst } E & \\
\textbf{or } t == t_1 \mathcal{X} f_2, E :: t_1 \mathcal{X} f_2', t_1 == t_1' / s_1, \text{ for all } e_1 \text{IN } s_1: (f_2 ! e_1 \leadsto t_2, f_2' ! e_1 \leadsto t_2', t_2 = t_2')
\end{array}$$

$$\overline{}$$

$$E :: t$$

382

```
FILE:   PES01   21-SEP-74 14:30:03      PAGE 30

1
2
3       ; PRPLC
4       ; PROPAGATE LOCAL CONNECTION:
5       ; PARAMS: A:LC, B:CN
6       ; IF CN=(DP,GN,APN), CALL DEFP(CN,DP,GN,APN)
7       ;   TO DEFINE THE PIN.
8       ; IF LC=(CP), SCAN BACKPANEL WIRELIST AND FOR EVERY
9       ; (CN,BWPN) FIND LC ON THAT CARD AND CALL PRPLC(LC,CN)
10      ;   RECURSIVELY.
11      ; IF LC=(ESCC,REL), SCAN LC'S AND CALL PRPLC(LC,CN) RECURSIVELY.
12      ;
13      PRPLC:  AOS     CLOCK           ; FOR DEBUGGING PURPOSES...
14              TRNN    A,777777        ; RETURN ON NULL LC
15              RET
16              TRNE    A,400000
17              JUMPA   PRPLC2 ; BRANCH IF ESCAPE BYTE
18              TRZN    A,200000        ; UNLESS CONNECTOR PIN
19              JUMPA   DEFP            ; CALL DEFP AND RETURN
20              SKIPGE  RGPRI(B)        ; RETURN IF CARD IS MASKED
21              RET
22              MOVEM   A,PRPLLC        ; SAVE IN CASE OF ERROR
23              MOVEM   B,PRPLCN        ; LIKEWISE
24      ; SCAN BACKPANEL WIRELIST:
25              IMULI   B,MXCP
26              ADD     B,A
27              MOVE    X,B
28              HX      X,RGGCH
29              TRZN    X,400000
30              JUMPA   [SKIPN  NOSLER
31                       ERR(PRP,<S-L BACKPANEL MISMATCH, LC: >)
32                       RET]
33      ; NEXT LOAD PIN IS IN X, FINISHED IF 0.
34      PRPLC1: JUMPE   X,[RET]
35              MOVE    B,X
36              IDIVI   B,MXCP  ; CN TO B, BWPN TO C.
37              MOVE    A,RGCT(B)       ; CARD TYPE TO A
38              MOVE    A,DNCTP(A)
39              PUSH    P,X             ; SAVE X FOR RECURSIVE CALL
40              MOVE    X,C             ; BWPN (CP) TO X
41              HXR     A,A,DNCPH
42      ; NOW LC AND CN ARE SET UP IN A AND B.
43              CALL    PRPLC
44              POP     P,X             ; RESTORE X
45              HX      X,RGGCH         ; FETCH CDR OF THE WIRE
46              TRNN    X,400000
47              JUMPA   PRPLC1
48              ERR(PRP,<GARBAGE WIRE, LC: >)
49
50      ; THESE VARIABLES CONTAIN THE LC AND CN PASSED TO PRPLC
51
52      LS(PRPLLC)
53      LS(PRPLCN)
54
55      ERRPRP: SAV(<A,B,C>)
56              MOVE    A,OJFN
57              MOVE    B,PRPLLC        ; GET LC
58              JNUM(4)
59              JTXT(< CN: >)
60              MOVE    B,PRPLCN        ; GET CN
61              JNUM(4)
62              REST(<C,B,A>)
63      ;
64      ; ESCAPE BYTE IS IN A
65      ; GET BASE FOR RELATIVE ADDRESS:
66      PRPLC2: MOVE    C,RGCT(B)
67              MOVE    C,DNCTP(C)      ; BASE
68              LDB     X,BPREL(A)      ; RELATIVE ADDRESS
69              LDB     D,BPESCC(A)     ; COUNT TO D
70      PRPLC3: JUMPLE  D,[RET]
71              PUSH    P,X
72              HXR     A,C,00
73              PUSH    P,B
74              PUSH    P,C
75              PUSH    P,D
76              CALL    PRPLC
77              POP     P,D
78              POP     P,C
79              POP     P,B
80              POP     P,X
81              ADDI    X,1             ; INCREMENT POINTER
```

This compiler of wirelists into a simulator for hardware is an example of "early Hungarian" code written by Charles Simonyi in 1972. Simonyi wrote the compiler for the PDP-10 computer in the then popular "Tenex" coding style and with the earliest use of the type-based naming conventions that are equally valid for native or high-level code.

The manuscript for this book was prepared and submitted to Microsoft Press in electronic form. Text files were processed and formatted using Microsoft Word.

Illustrations by Charles Solway

Cover design by Min Yee

Interior text design by Darcie Furlan

Text composition by Microsoft Press in Aster and Futura Light with display in Aster Italic, using the CCI-400 composition system and the Mergenthaler Linotron 202 digital phototypesetter.

Other Titles from Microsoft Press

CD ROM: The New Papyrus
The current and future state of the art
Edited by Steve Lambert and Suzanne Ropiequet
$34.95 hardcover, $21.95 softcover

Running MS-DOS 2nd edition
Microsoft's guide to getting the most out of its standard
operating system   *Van Wolverton* $21.95

The Peter Norton Programmer's Guide to the IBM PC
The ultimate reference guide to the *entire* family of
IBM personal computers   *Peter Norton* $19.95

Word Processing Power with Microsoft Word
Professional writing on your IBM PC
Peter Rinearson $16.95

Getting Started with Microsoft Word
A step-by-step guide to word processing
Janet Rampa $16.95

Managing Your Business with Multiplan
How to use Microsoft's award-winning electronic spreadsheet
on your IBM PC   *Ruth Witkin* $17.95

The Apple Macintosh Book 2nd edition
Cary Lu $19.95

Excel in Business
Number-crunching power on the Apple Macintosh
Douglas Cobb $22.95

The Printed Word
Professional word processing with Microsoft Word on the
Apple Macintosh   *David A. Kater, Richard L. Kater* $17.95

Microsoft Macinations
An introduction to Microsoft BASIC for the Apple Macintosh
The Waite Group: Mitchell Waite, Robert Lafore, Ira Lansing $19.95

AppleWorks
Boosting your business with integrated software
Charles Rubin $16.95

Command Performance: Lotus 1-2-3
The Microsoft desktop dictionary and cross-reference guide
Eddie Adamis $24.95

Available wherever fine books are sold.